A FABLED LAND

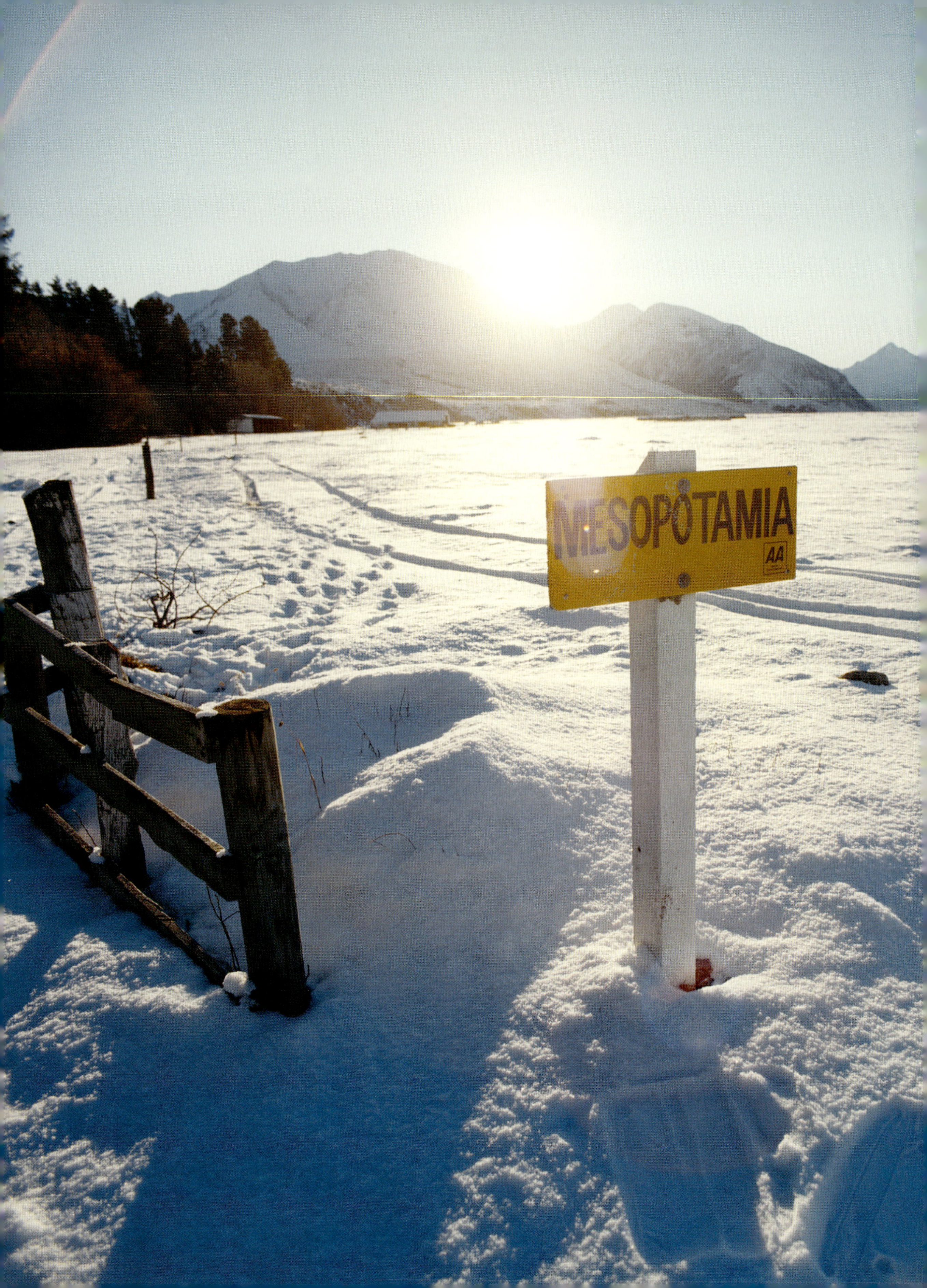
MESOPOTAMIA
AA

A FABLED LAND

THE STORY OF CANTERBURY'S FAMOUS **MESOPOTAMIA STATION**

BRUCE ANSLEY WITH PETER BUSH

RANDOM HOUSE
NEW ZEALAND

creative nz
ARTS COUNCIL OF NEW ZEALAND Toi Aotearoa

The assistance of Creative New Zealand is gratefully acknowledged by the author.

A RANDOM HOUSE BOOK published by Random House New Zealand
18 Poland Road, Glenfield, Auckland, New Zealand

For more information about our titles go to www.randomhouse.co.nz

A catalogue record for this book is available from the
National Library of New Zealand

Random House New Zealand is part of the Random House Group
New York London Sydney Auckland Delhi Johannesburg

First published 2012

© 2012 text by Bruce Ansley; photographs by Peter Bush unless otherwise
credited; maps Roger Smith at Geographx

The moral rights of the author have been asserted

ISBN 978 1 87746 063 0

This book is copyright. Except for the purposes of fair reviewing no part of this
publication may be reproduced or transmitted in any form or by any means,
electronic or mechanical, including photocopying, recording or any information
storage and retrieval system, without permission in writing from the publisher.

Design: Kate Barraclough
Cover photographs: Peter Bush
Printed in China by Everbest Printing Co. Ltd.

> This book is dedicated to the Prouting family, who made us welcome and never complained about us poking into their lives; and especially to Sue Prouting for looking after us so well.

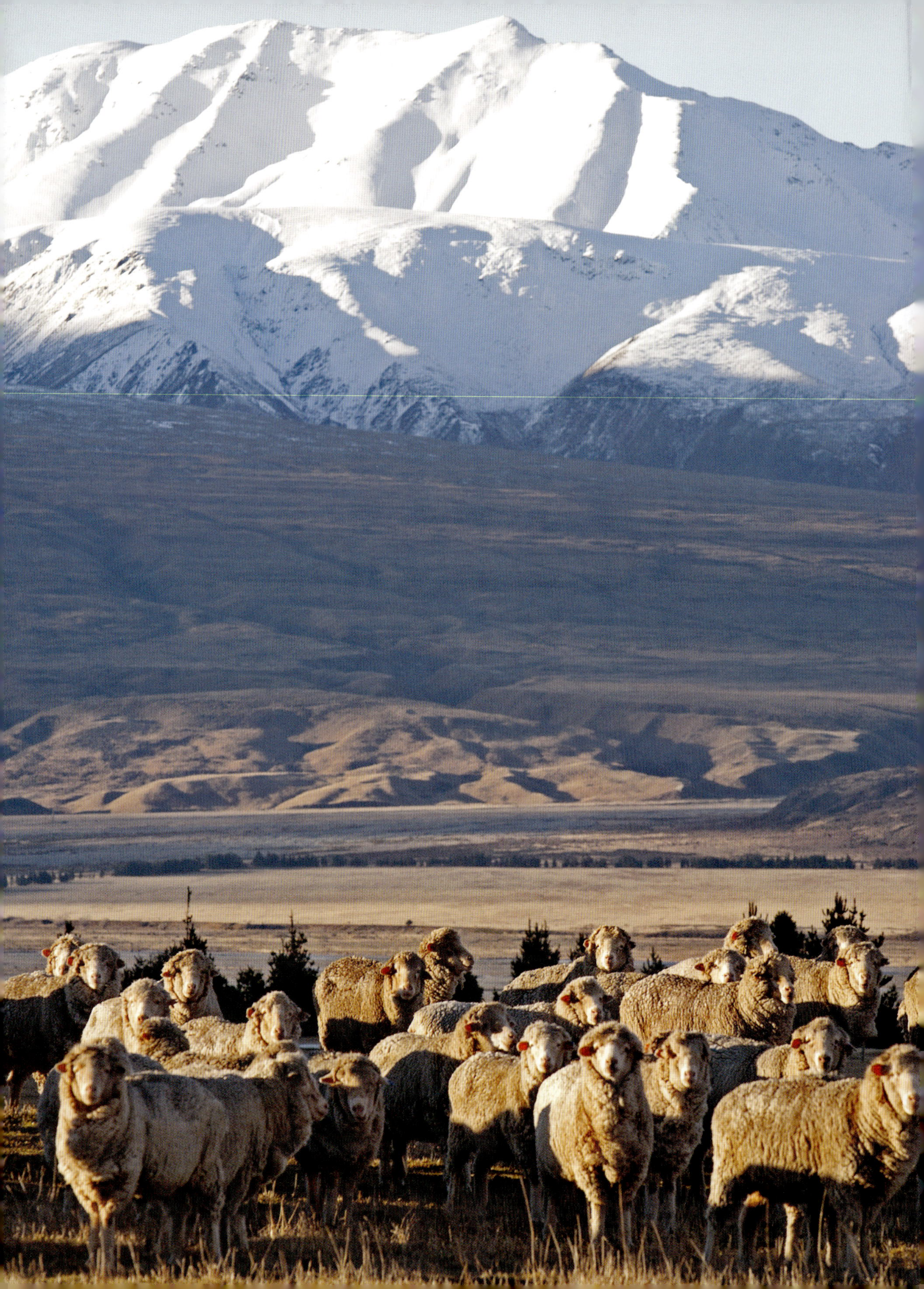

CONTENTS

MAPS _____ 8

ONE _____ 12

TWO _____ 22
PHOTO ESSAY: THE AUTUMN MUSTER _____ 48

THREE _____ 70
BUSHY COMES TO MESOPOTAMIA _____ 92
PHOTO ESSAY: DEER _____ 94

FOUR _____ 106
PHOTO ESSAY: TAILING _____ 124

FIVE _____ 142
PHOTO ESSAY: DIPPING _____ 160

SIX _____ 172

SEVEN _____ 188
BUSHY ON NEROLI'S WEDDING _____ 201
PHOTO ESSAY: SHEARING _____ 202

EIGHT _____ 220
PHOTO ESSAY: THE CATTLE MUSTER _____ 236

THE FOUR SEASONS AT MESOPOTAMIA
WINTER _____ 252
SPRING _____ 280
SUMMER _____ 296
AUTUMN _____ 314

THE PROUTING FAMILY TREE _____ 334

ACKNOWLEDGEMENTS _____ 336

Map labels

MAIN DIVIDE SOUTHERN ALPS
CLOUDY PEAK RANGE
JOLLIE RANGE
ARROWSMITH RANGE
Lake Stream
Cameron River
Mt D'Archiac
Clyde River
Lawrence River
POTTS RANGE
South Branch Ashburton River
TWO THUMB RANGE
Havelock River
SIBBALD RANGE
Potts River
Lake Clearwater
Macaulay River
Mesopotamia
Rangitata River
HARPER RANGE
Godley River
SINCLAIR RANGE
BEN McLEOD RANGE
TARA HAO
SHERWOOD RANGE
CLAYTONS
Lake Tekapo
TWO THUMB RANGE
FOUR PEAKS RANGE
Lake Tekapo
Opuha River
FAIRLIE
79

0 20km

PALMER RANGE
Rakaia River
BIG BEN RANGE
BLACK HILL RANGE
TAYLOR RANGE
MT HUTT RANGE
Lake Heron
77
WINTERSLOW RANGE
CLENT HILLS
North Branch Ashburton River
METHVEN
Mt Somers
South Branch Ashburton River
Mayfield
77
to
Christchurch
1
Peel
Forest
Hinds River
ASHBURTON
Arundel
Rangitata River
Hinds
ERALDINE
Orari River
Rangitata
1
to Timaru
N

MAIN DIVIDE OF THE SOUTHERN ALPS
ARMOURY RANGE
JOLLIE RANGE
CLOUDY PEAK RANGE
Lawrence River
POTTS RANGE
D'Archiac
Mt Coates
Forbes River
Clyde River
Mt Potts
Havelock River
Carneys Creek
Camp Creek
Erewhon Homestead
TWO THUMB RANGE
The Growler
Exeter
Alma
BLACK MOUNTAIN RANGE
Mt Potts Homestead
Potts River
Black Birch Creek
BRABAZON RANGE
North East Gorge Stream
Bush Stream
Mt Sinclair
Rangitata River
Mesopotamia Homestead
TWO THUMB RANGE
Bush Stream
SINCLAIR RANGE
Macaulay River
BUTLER DOWNS
Rangitata Gorge Rd to Arundel
Bullock Bow Saddle
Forest Creek
Butler's Hut
BEN McLEOD RANGE
TWO THUMB RANGE
SHERWOOD RANGE
N

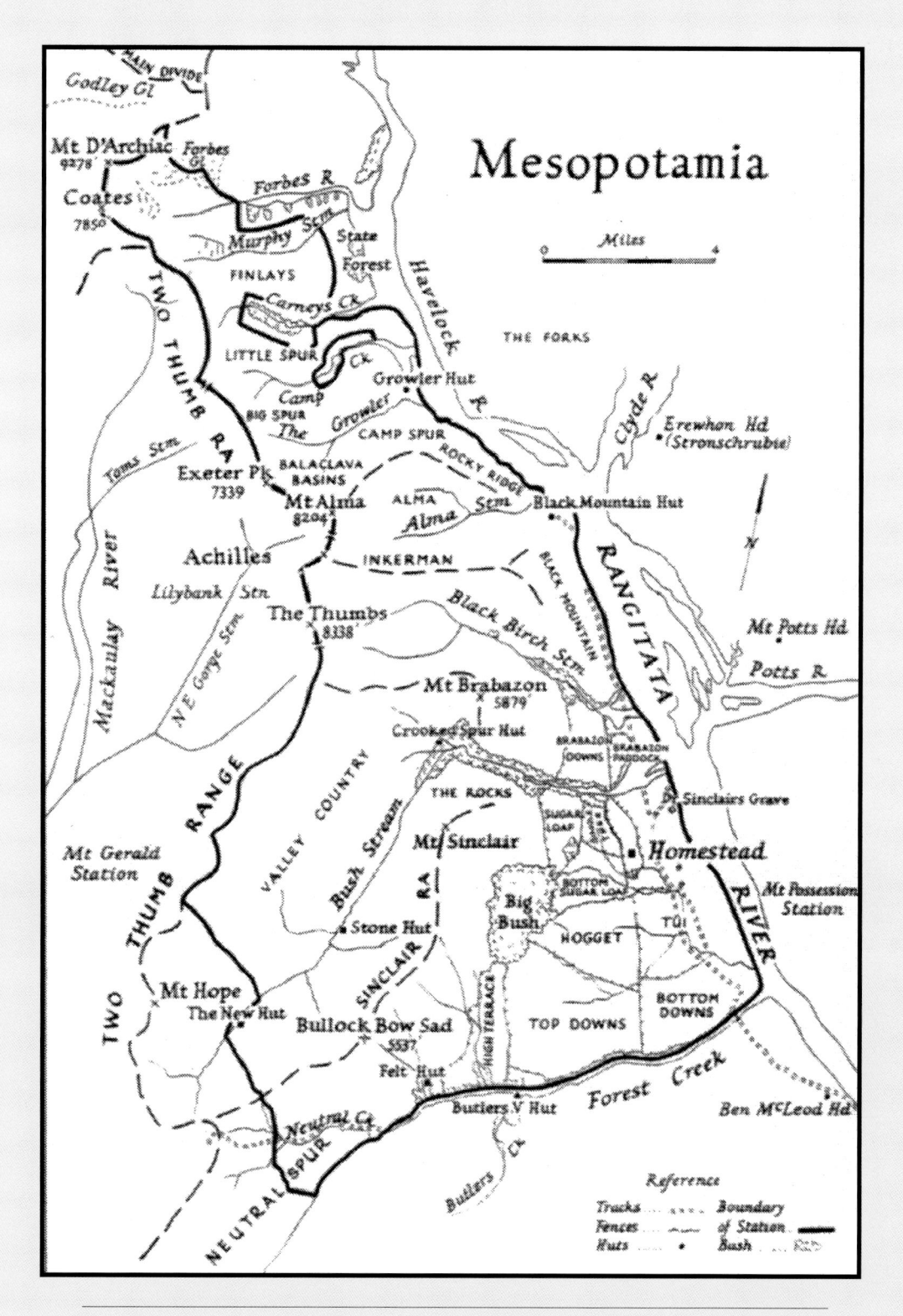

↑ **ABOVE**
Mesopotamia Station boundaries outlined as they were in 1960, from *Mesopotamia Station* by Peter Newton, published by Mesopotamia Station.

01

NTE

ACHILLES • THE TWO THUMB RANGE • D'ARCHIAC • CROOKED SPUR • HOGGET • THE GROWLER • BRABAZON • NEUTRAL SPUR • CLYDE RIVER • ROCKY RIDGE • BLACK MOUNTAINS • LITTLE SPUR • FINLAYS • FORBES RIVER • BIG BUSH • BLACK BIRCH STREAM • TOP DOWNS • BULLOCK BOW SADDLE • BALACLAVA BASINS • EXETER PEAK • SINCLAIR RANGE • FOREST CREEK • INKERMAN • THE ROCKS • MOUNT SINCLAIR • SUGARLOAF • MOUNT HOPE

WHEN NEROLI PROUTING was only eight years old she found herself in one of those extraordinary adventures that make city people tuck closer to the fire. Neroli was one of the family who owned Mesopotamia Station but she was then a child on Mount Arrowsmith Station, whose homestead huddled beside Lake Heron deep in mountains rising to the Southern Alps in ranks of bony peaks.

People of the high country are unusual, perhaps differing most in what they consider usual. Neroli was to become a high country legend herself much later when in her early twenties she took over Mount Arrowsmith Station and ran it on her own.

A stranger might stand on this land and wonder that anything could survive here, least of all human beings. But the Proutings were mountain people, spreading out from Mesopotamia in the upper Rangitata Valley. They were used to the heat and cold, the wind, the snow and ice and rain and the nor'wester that could blast-freeze a human body one moment and singe its body hair the next. The high country does everything in extremes.

Mount Arrowsmith Station was right on the edge, even by high country farming standards. It lay in a valley to the north of Mesopotamia, between the Rangitata and Rakaia rivers. Its homestead stood at an altitude of 760 metres, higher than all but a few farm homesteads in New Zealand.

One other feature set the station apart in the high country hierarchy: it had no land *below* that height. The farm started at the homestead and rose high above it. Even the Proutings thought it a cold place. Few of its slopes

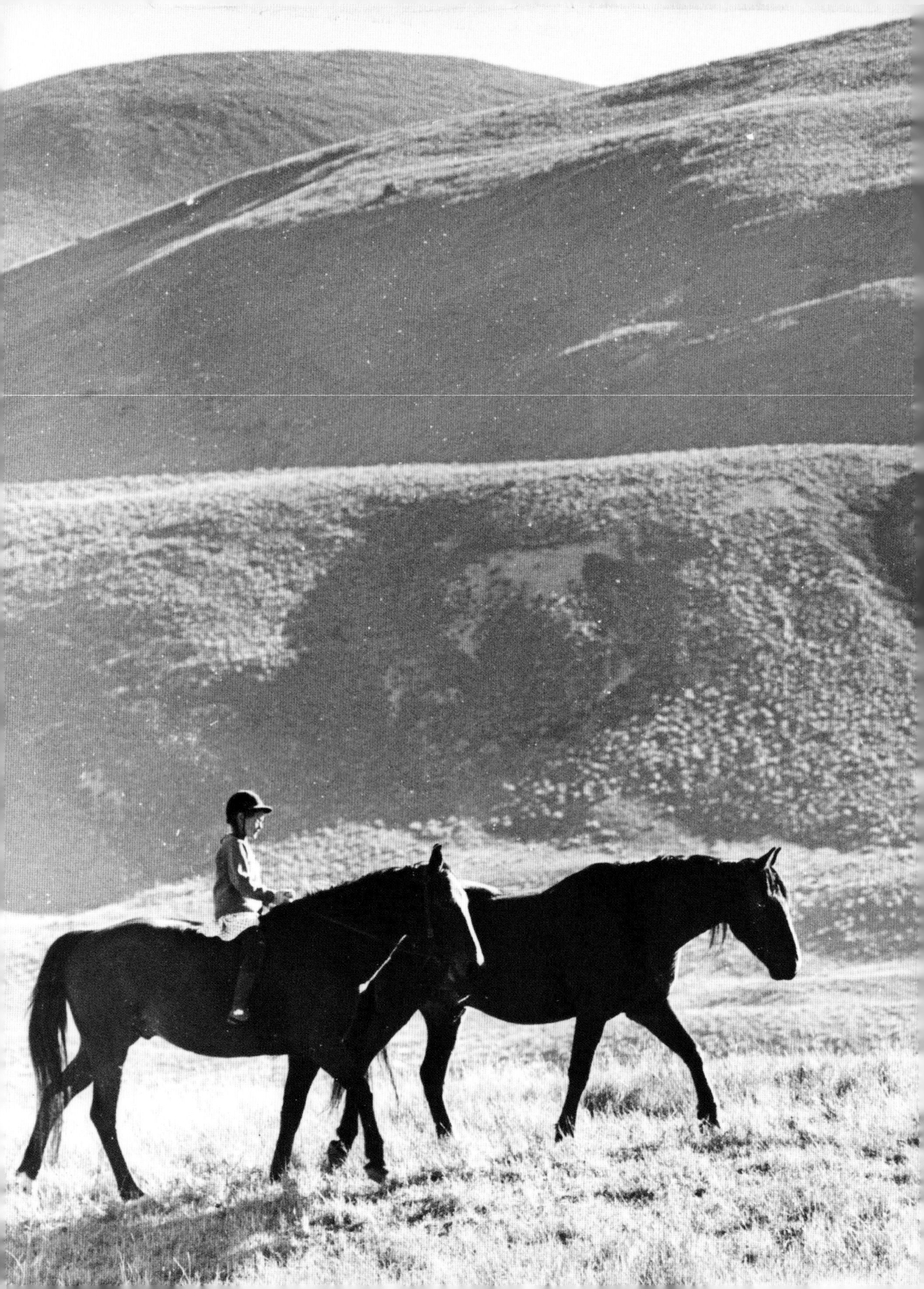

lay to the sun. The mountainscape transfixed visitors, but the Proutings had to work it every day of the year and even for people who seemed made of the same high-tensile wire as their fences this was hard country.

Laurie Prouting, Neroli's father, had left the family farm at Mesopotamia to take over Arrowsmith and sometimes he yearned for the fine balance of the home run with its high pastures, its downs and flats, its warmth. The job that day took him up the Ashburton River, separated from the homestead by a range of hills, mountains really, whose character was revealed by such names as the Pyramid, or Wild Man's Hill.

He'd borrowed a bulldozer from Mesopotamia, and he was working in a valley far from the homestead. Neroli and her younger brother Malcolm were too far from a school to travel each day along the narrow roads snaking from the Canterbury Plains in to Mount Arrowsmith. Instead, they took correspondence school lessons supervised by their mother Anne. They kept high country hours, starting around seven in the morning and finishing in the early afternoon.

This day Laurie had an after-school job for Neroli. He asked her whether, if she felt up to it when she'd finished her schoolwork, she would load the packhorse with diesel fuel for the bulldozer and bring it over to him where he was working.

It meant much of a day's travel by horseback, but he knew she *would* feel up to it. No matter how early Laurie got out of bed, Neroli was always up and dressed, asking if she could help with something, perhaps catching his horse for him and saddling it for the day's work.

She loved horses, she was good with them, and even as a child she was very able. So Laurie had no hesitation asking the child to do a job a grown man would have regarded as hard and, if he was not used to the mountains, dangerous too.

The track rose to over 1980 metres then dropped into the sharp-edged valley on the other side. Both of them knew it was an arduous ride. Telling the story many years later Laurie said, 'It was a long way with a pack team.'

Neroli agreed. 'A bloody long way.'

When she finished school the morning was already gone. She loaded the packhorse with cans of diesel, mounted her own horse and led the small procession through the gate. By then it was two in the afternoon, and the

← LEFT
Neroli Prouting, who more often than not rode bare back as a child, mustering horses.
Prouting Family Collection

shadows were already hinting at the night to come. All afternoon they plodded along, and into the growing dark. The mountains turned purple, then black.

Away up his valley Laurie worked until nightfall. Then he stopped the bulldozer, covered it up. No sign of Neroli. He let out a yell or two thinking perhaps she was near. No answer. '*Neroliiiii . . .*'

He decided she was not coming. 'So I off up the hill, taking the direct way over the hill and back down to the homestead.'

Again, to an outsider this seemed fraught. The hill was more a mountain. Most would not tackle it in the daylight, much less the dark, and the walk would take several hours.

He was well up the hill when he sensed movement in the valley he'd just left below. He peered into the gloom. Nothing but night. 'I don't have good hearing. But something I heard . . . was that something I heard? "*Neroliiiii . . . ?*" And finally this little voice called back in the dark. "*Daaaaaad.*"'

'I ran back down the hill. There was this little girl there with the horses, unloading. I got a lump in my throat. What would she have done if I hadn't come back? I thought, "What sort of a father am I?"'

'I rode the packhorse back, she rode the other one. She was as happy as. Not the least bit upset that I wasn't there when she arrived. She had everything planned out. But it shook me. Far more than it shook her.' I could feel the tear in his voice. It was a close thing, so close. In that colossal wilderness he'd almost lost his daughter.

Yet, Neroli laughed. She remembered the insouciance of childhood, safe in her wild life. The nor'wester was blowing, the hard wind of the high country, coming off the Tasman and shrieking over the Main Divide in great, freezing gouts. Neroli was used to it. 'It didn't really worry me. I wasn't panicked. There was nothing fearful, nothing that scared me or worried me.

'The only thing that *did* worry me was that Dad wasn't going to get the diesel into the bulldozer. That was my biggest fear, not being out alone in the dark with only two horses, because I would have survived. I trusted the horses. They would have taken me home, kept me warm, done everything. My plan was, just keep walking with the horses. Horses can see in the dark, incredibly.

'It would have been scary if you were the scary type. I probably would be now. I never thought about Mum worrying about me. And I did find Dad.

> **She remembered the insouciance of childhood, safe in her wild life. The nor'wester was blowing, the hard wind of the high country, coming off the Tasman and shrieking over the Main Divide in great, freezing gouts. Neroli was used to it.**

But he didn't show his concern or surprise or whatever.'

Laurie *was* concerned. Three decades later he said, 'What brought the lump to my throat was that I nearly left her. She was on the other side of a mountain range, but she wasn't the least bit put out. She said she would just have unloaded the diesel and gone home.'

Even now, the journey was far from routine. Neroli said, 'He took my horse and I hopped on the packhorse, and we went back upstream into the wind and the night and the dark and cold and my horse tripped up. I went over but the horse was stumbling around and I ended up being sideways in the saddle. The pack saddles have hooks on them and I got my jacket caught up so now I was like a fence staple on its side, hooked up, winded, couldn't breathe, couldn't speak, and the horse was just plodding along, bonk, bonk, *bonk*.

'He was massive, about 17.2 hands, a big black packhorse and I was gasping out "*Dad!*" whenever I could because I couldn't breathe and he couldn't hear me because he was miles away whistling along and it took him forever to notice. He finally saw me: "What the bloody hell are you doing over that side?"'

She laughed. She laughs easily. An aura of physical confidence envelopes her like a spell. Besides, from the living room of the relaxed farm homestead she now shares with her husband Harley, gentle downs running out to the Plains, a safe distance from both the mountains and her childhood, it all seemed so, well, *unlikely*, although some thirty years later she remembered every detail. She thought it a lot of fuss over what, in the end, was just another day on the farm, and the packhorse story was not even the most perilous she could remember.

A worse one was this: A snowstorm had swept Mount Arrowsmith Station and many of the merino sheep were trapped. They had to be led out of the snow to feed or they would simply die where they were. The Proutings had to stamp out paths in the snow and lead the sheep along the tracks to safety, a traditional method called snow-raking. Merinos were hard to spot in the snow because they were almost the same colour. But Laurie knew where the trapped sheep were and Neroli and her younger brother Malcolm were called into action.

Neroli, still only a child, was snow-raking on a feature called the Thumb, a thumb-shaped knob of rock about 1920 metres high. 'I thought, because I was cunning and I didn't have very good dogs then, I'd go up to the right of the Thumb then cut back along, so I'd come down on top of the sheep. So I went right up to the top, which is quite a feat and it had taken me most of the day to get there.

'By then it was maybe two in the afternoon, and the sheep were hard to see in the snow, so I came back down, sneaky sneaky sneaky, and I was leading the horse because I could stand on top of the snow but he couldn't. He was breaking through up to his chest, and I was scrunching along and next thing I felt a tug on my reins and I turned around and the horse had gone.

'I thought, "Oh my God." The snow along the top was level, but underneath it was a little snippy creek in a gully. All I could see of the horse was these two wee ears in the snow.

'So I spent the rest of the day digging my horse out. He stayed calm because I didn't want him buggered through losing all his energy, and I got him out. By now we were in the shadow. I was soaking wet. I had thin gumboots and oh my God was I cold.

'So I went smoking downhill and back to where I could see my own tracks and went straight back home. But home was bloody miles away, maybe fifteen kilometres, and it took me a long long time to get there. I was freezing. I was lying along the horse's back and I had my hands under the saddle to keep warm and I was so *cold*. I got home and the horse stopped at the stable. I was frozen onto its back. The stable was up behind and you couldn't see it from the house. So I was screaming, stuck on the horse. And Dad came running down, pulled me off the horse and took me up to the house and put me in a cold shower.

'Then I was really screaming, then I was scared I was never going to be warm again: "It's cold it's so *cold*." All he said was, "If I heat you up too quick your blood will go all funny." That's all he said. And I had to sit there. Oh my God it was cold.

'Dad knew that I would come on down. He left his hill pole on the gate to show me that he'd gone home, that he wasn't mucking around looking for me. Then he said, "Did you get my hill pole?"

'I was that frozen. I sobbed, "No, I didn't get your hill pole. Sorry."'

WHEN I BEGAN writing this book my neighbour, who had spent many of her holidays camping up the Rangitata Valley near Mesopotamia, said: 'It's another world.'

Peopled, I thought, by a race apart.

→ RIGHT
Neroli out riding for the day, leading a friend. *Prouting Family Collection*

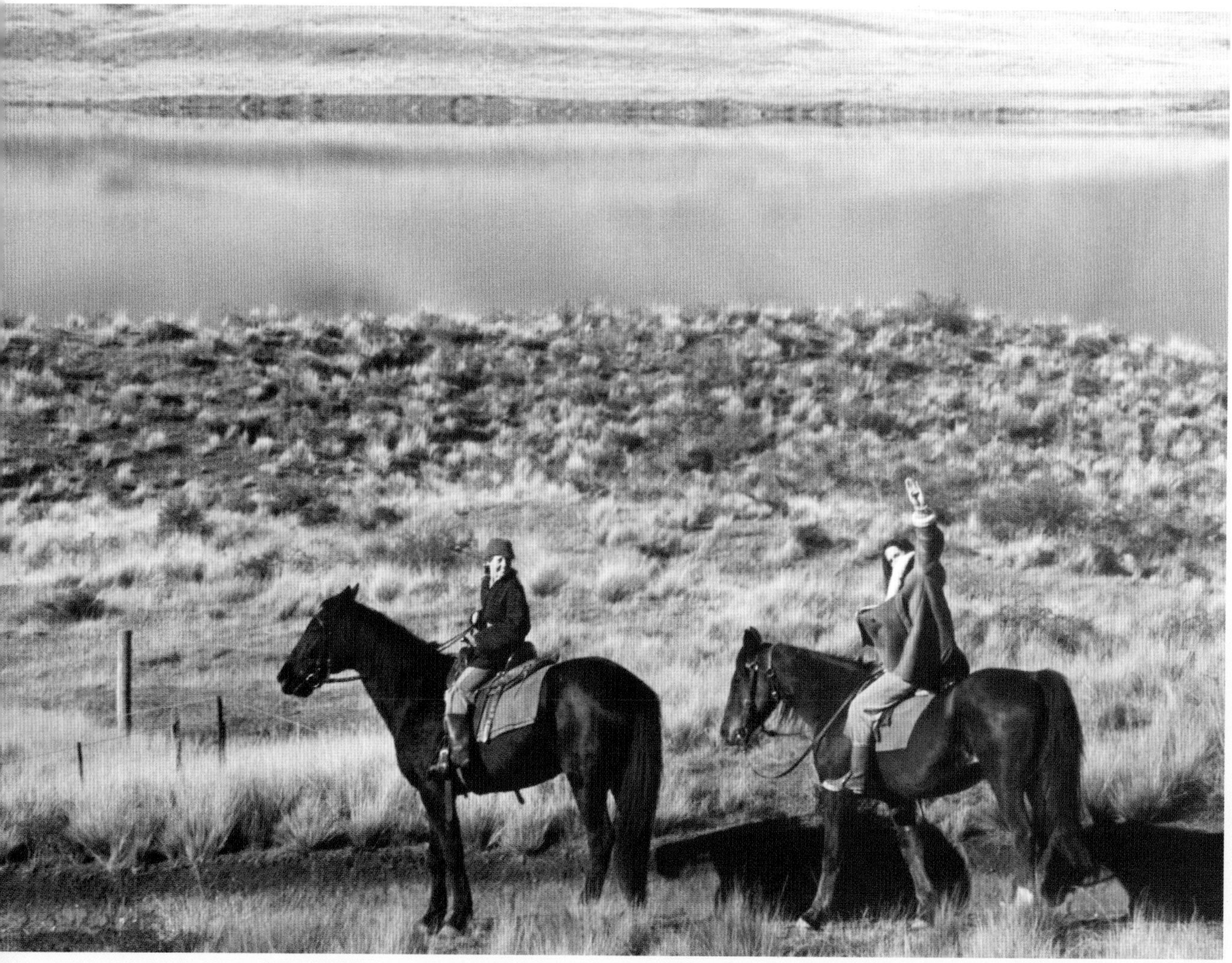

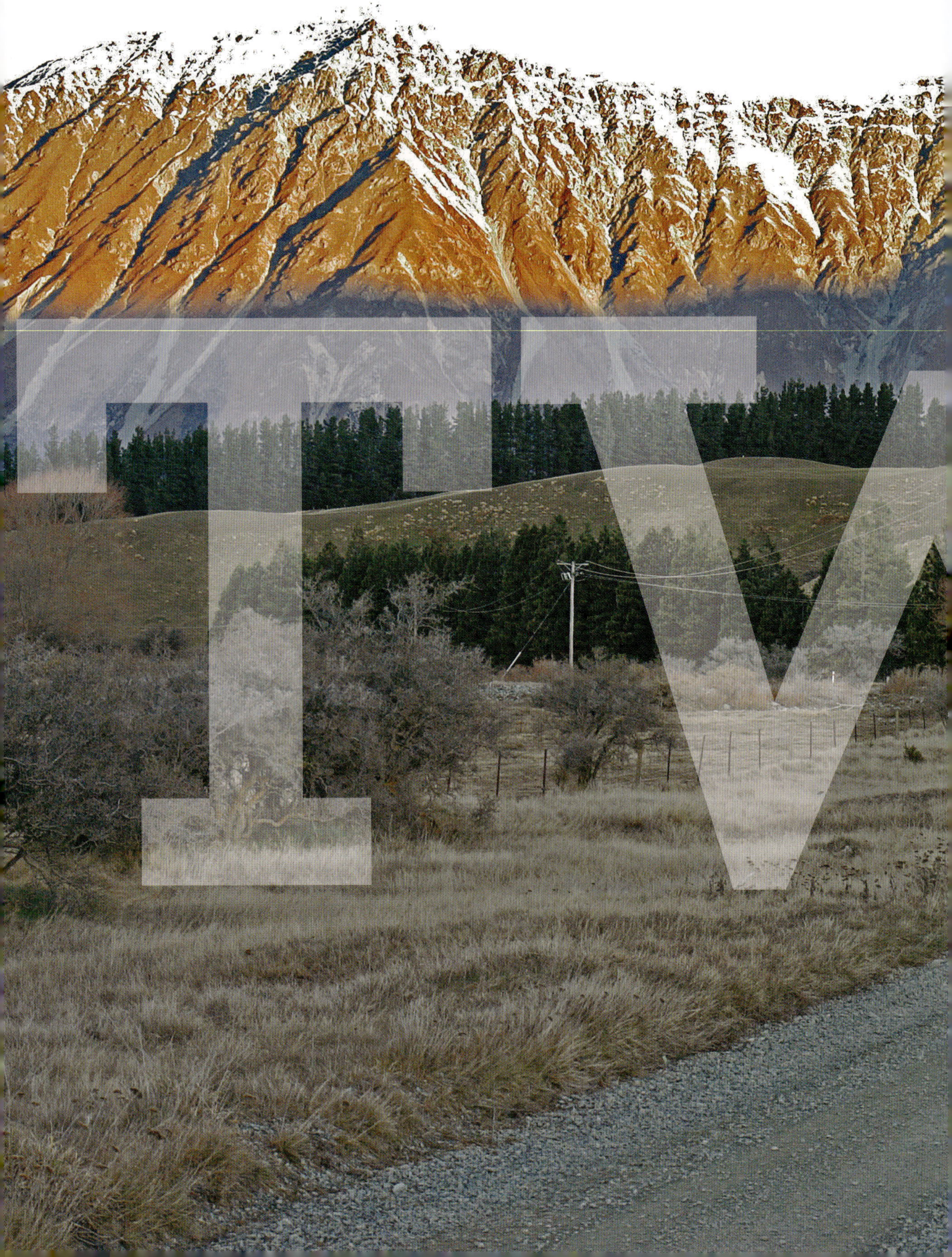

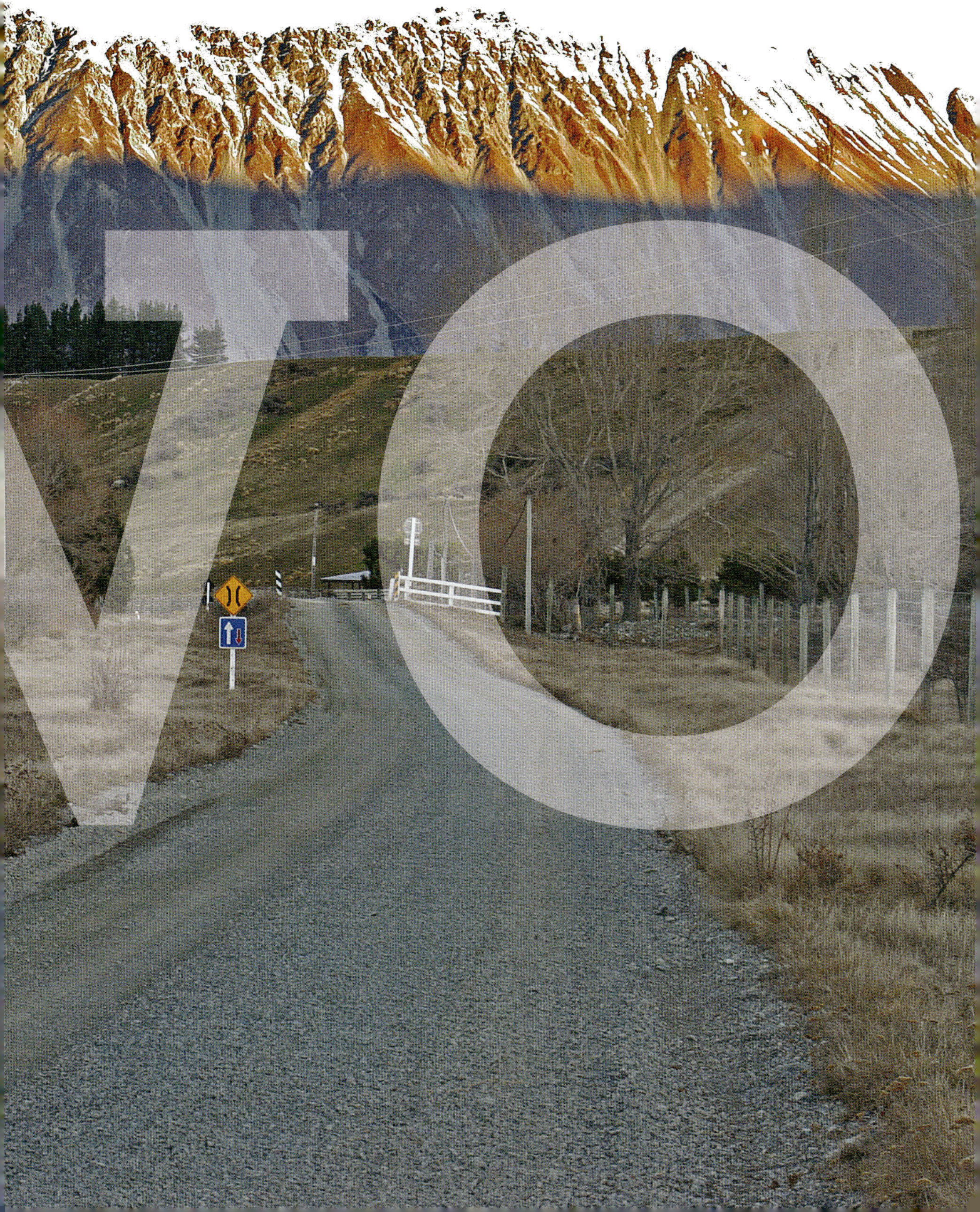
VO

ACHILLES • THE TWO THUMB RANGE • D'ARCHIAC • CROOKED SPUR • HOGGET • THE GROWLER • BRABAZON • NEUTRAL SPUR • CLYDE RIVER • ROCKY RIDGE • BLACK MOUNTAINS • LITTLE SPUR • FINLAYS • FORBES RIVER • BIG BUSH • BLACK BIRCH STREAM • TOP DOWNS • BULLOCK BOW SADDLE • BALACLAVA BASINS • EXETER PEAK • SINCLAIR RANGE • FOREST CREEK • INKERMAN • THE ROCKS • MOUNT SINCLAIR • SUGARLOAF • MOUNT HOPE

MESOPOTAMIA IS A FABLED LAND, the most famous high country station of them all. The station is unique even in a nation whose high country is as legendary as the Australian outback, for New Zealand has always celebrated its musterers and merinos. The hut sheltering in a gully, smoke curling from its corrugated-iron chimney, is as much a national emblem as the Southern Cross in the crystal skies above.

In this world Mesopotamia stood alone. It ran hard up against the black rock faces of the Southern Alps. It had a mountain as its corner-post and a torrent for its boundary. It was founded by a novelist and peopled by men and women whose lives are still largely unknown to folk in cities and towns.

Their isolation created its own mystique, for in this long thin nation people loved the notion of a land beyond reach. Its mystery added a fresh dimension to a small country, a space beyond the one most people knew.

Myths swirled the peaks ringing Mesopotamia. The station was founded by Samuel Butler, who set two of his three best-known novels, *Erewhon* and *Erewhon Revisited,* in this precipitous mountainscape. Anywhere on Mesopotamia it was easy to feel as his hero did, that the high pass at the head of the valley was the gateway to some enchanted land. Peter Jackson wove fairy tales through it in his *Lord of the Rings* trilogy.

The high country spoke its own language of terraces, spurs, bluffs and gullies, of camp ovens, kea, merinos, musters, matagouri, spaniard, tarns, huts and packhorses. The musterer lived on in television commercials, although his natural habitat did not do as well, shrinking year on year.

High country station names rang like verse: Stew Point, Erewhon, Bellamore, Black Forest, Blue Mountain, Cascade, Gem Lake, Irishman Creek, Leaning Rock, Minaret, Obelisk, Rainbow, Sunset, Temple Peak, Woodstock.

Mesopotamia Station had its own vernacular: Brabazon, the Black Mountain, the Bullock Bow and the Balaclava Basins, Mount D'Archiac and the quartet of mountain peaks named for the Battle of the River Plate: Exeter, Achilles, Ajax and Graf Spee. It had cols and glaciers and basins, hard flats and high terraces, tahr and chamois, enterprise, joy, disaster, tragedy.

Even now, when four-wheel drive vehicles and utes carry weekend adventurers all over the back country, Mesopotamia is still a long haul up the upper Rangitata Valley along the dusty road that runs from Peel Forest, a tiny village which has scarcely changed in a century and a half.

The Rangitata Gorge barricades the upper Rangitata, Mount Peel Station standing beside it as sentinel. Mount Peel has been owned by the Acland family since 1856. Its homestead stands amid oak woods looking as much like an English country house as it possibly can. A stone Anglican church settles elegantly beside it.

> **It is a mannered spot in an unruly landscape, manicured amid the tooth and nail, and it is hard to imagine that this country was once designated wasteland.**

It is a mannered spot in an unruly landscape, manicured amid the tooth and nail, and it is hard to imagine that this country was once designated 'waste land'. Yet it was, the Canterbury Association's land regulations ruling it unsuitable for, well, almost anything.

John Robert Godley, immortalised as the 'father of Canterbury', changed that. In 1851 Godley allowed the alleged wastelands to be occupied by farmers at peppercorn rentals, or as close to free as it was possible to get. All a budding runholder needed to do was put in a claim with a rough description, which might include a margin for error of hundreds of acres, then undertake to stock the land within nine months, later extended to a year.

Godley's change had two immediate consequences. First, it led to a new gold rush, the prize this time being vast tracts of land which were to prove

→ RIGHT
Looking upstream to Cloudy Peak, left, with the Main Divide at the end of the valley to the right. Mount Sunday, Edoras in *Lord of the Rings*, lies between the mountains to the right, and the river.

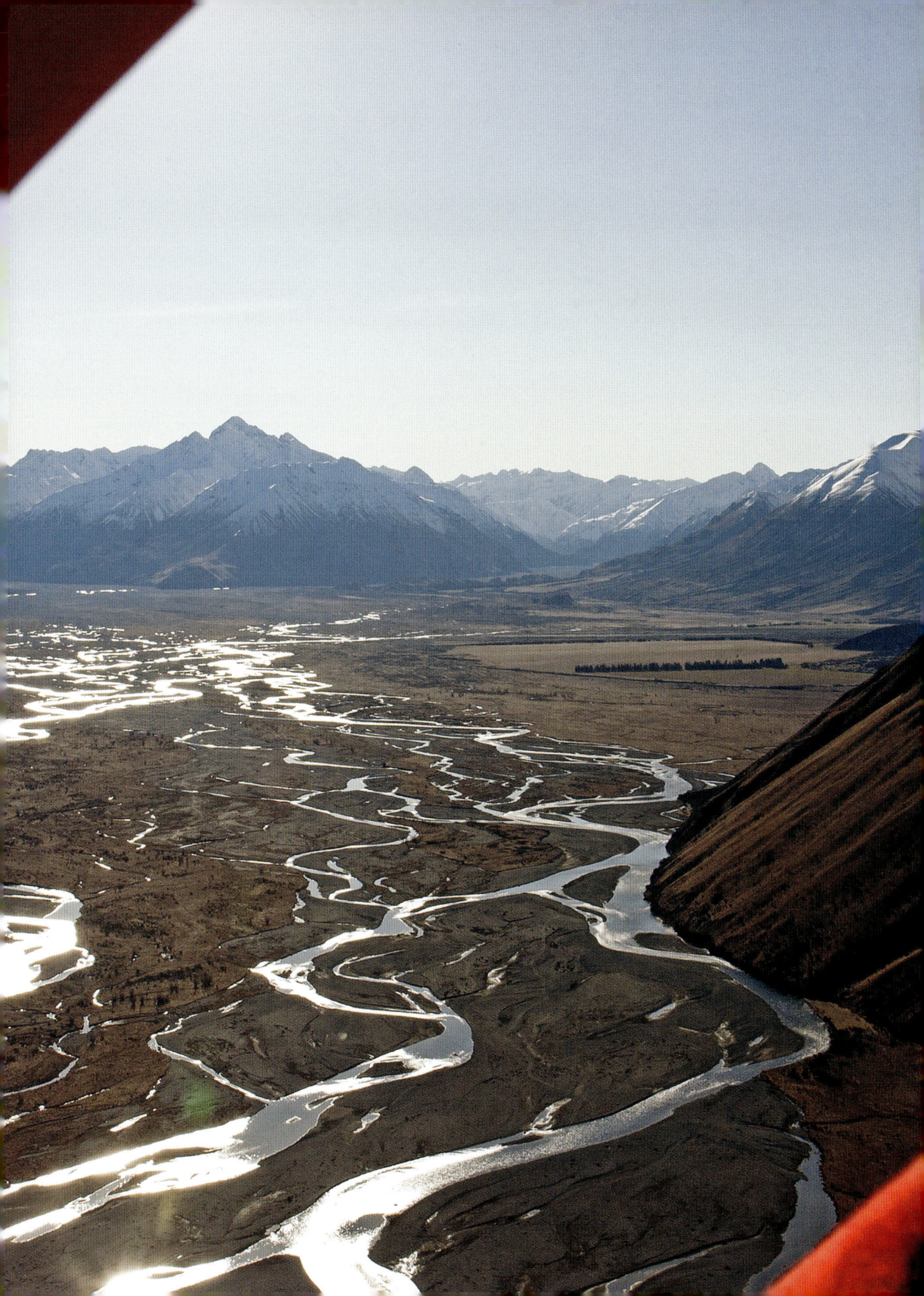

highly profitable. Secondly, everyone — farmers, adventurers, Australians, remittance men and rogues saddled up and raced into the high country to claim as much of it as they could. In 1850 the land was largely empty. Within five years very little was left unoccupied.

History labelled the runholders everything from landed gentry to squatters. A trickle of aristocratic blood ran through some veins and surviving runholders searched diligently for blue among their corpuscles. Oliver Duff, a former editor of the *NZ Listener*, once said of Canterbury: 'Its squatters were the best, and most foolish men New Zealand ever imported, for they had no sooner performed miracles of enterprise and endurance than they forgot that they were the creators of a brave new world and sent back to England for their top hats.' Yet they shared many qualities: mainly courage and resolve and an unbelievable capacity for hard work.

John Acland and his partner at the time, Charles Tripp (the two later split the run between them), took up a huge area of land between the Rangitata and Orari rivers on the high side of Peel Forest, running all the way back towards the Alps as far as Forest Creek, which was to become the lower boundary of Mesopotamia Station. They became the first to risk their capital on country regarded as too steep, too cold and too inhospitable for anything but mountain parrots and wild pigs.

OTHERS SOON FOLLOWED, probing towards the Main Divide in country strange enough for Samuel Butler to describe the Rangitata River in *Erewhon* as 'that desolate pathway of destruction'. He echoed the ancient Maori name, for Rangitata is said variously to mean 'close sky', 'day of lowering clouds', and 'the side of the sky'. All of those names together painted a picture of dark might. Even now, long settled, the landscape is overpowering.

The Rangitata Gorge is a choke between mountains and plains. Below the gorge the country spreads out into South Canterbury perfection, fine, ordered, peaceful. Above it, past the excellent gables of Mount Peel homestead, the country takes off its gloves.

The river has carved the land, shaped and sculpted it. The Rangitata is one of the great braided rivers found only in Alaska, Canada, the Himalayas and the South Island of New Zealand. In this country the river calls the shots. It has cut basins and terraces, bluffs, cliffs and spurs. Peter Jackson's orcs and goblins could live unseen behind the impenetrable spikes of ancient matagouri, hunting the peaks and passes, stalking their realm, known only to the tahr and chamois. Mountains rise on either side of the river, massive, but dwarfed by the granite slabs of the Southern Alps far ahead.

Samuel Butler wrote, 'Never shall I forget the utter loneliness of the prospect, the vastness of mountain and plain, of river and sky; the marvellous atmospheric effects, sometimes black mountains against a white sky, and then again, after cold weather, white mountains against a black sky.'

One and a half centuries later travellers can still see exactly what he meant. When they round the bend in the shingle road at White Rock which the locals call the *Wow!* Corner they need to be careful. The impact can make them swerve. Even people accustomed to this country do not so much look at the view as have it hit their senses like a blow. It bursts upon them in huge swathes of river flats and terraces, crags and ridges. Its colours — blues, greys, greens, yellows, black and white — sweep memory aside: the present is too vivid, dizzying.

Past Mount Peel Station the seal ends and today, far ahead on the long thread of grey shingle road, I see a stream of dust trailing something moving, a car perhaps, but invisible, insignificant in the huge landscape. The road is taking it through great river flats, the Rangitata blue beside iron-grey slate shingle, purple matagouri, the willows along the river blushing in autumn, ranks of pines angling down to the river and the two Thumbs on the far range giving the all-okay to the heavens with surrounding peaks as noble supporting cast. Nothing prepares strangers for this grand composition, no photographs, or paintings, nor anything seen before. It is experience on a new scale.

This country is peopled by a special breed of farmers and shepherds not much changed in their determination since Samuel Butler, who first saw the land in 1860. He wasn't the first, just the most eloquent. Nor did he round the *Wow!* Corner to be slammed in the modern way. In those days the route lay up the south branch of the Ashburton River and forked off into a valley running down to the upper Rangitata.

It was treacherous. Butler had to cross first the Rakaia River, then the Ashburton, then the Rangitata, a journey that soon claimed many lives. Butler himself, returning from Christchurch, almost drowned. He found the country he had been looking for at the end of the Rangitata Valley. He named it Mesopotamia, borrowing from the Greek for the land between two rivers.

His successors were more prosaic. Some, such as the musterer-historian Peter Newton, called it Meso. Others, notably the Prouting family who own it, call it Messie.

Butler arrived in New Zealand in January, on the run from his family at home. He was twenty-four years old. His father was the vicar in a small village near Nottingham. Butler grew up in a big, pleasant rectory in soft countryside among English graces and manners, but he was an unhappy boy. His parents believed that if they spared the rod, they would spoil the child. Samuel prayed, and learned, and if he did not he was whipped, or shut away somewhere, or punished by deprivation. His mother was as good at flogging him as was his father; he remained fond of his mother despite a sense of betrayal, but loathed his dad.

He was educated at Shrewsbury, a public school rescued and restored by his grandfather, and Cambridge University, where he achieved a First in Classics, a good degree but not a preferred qualification among high country farmers today. He spent six months in London as a curate's unpaid assistant in preparation for the clergy, and discovered he did not believe in his religion. Instead, he wanted to study art and music back at Cambridge.

His ambition provoked a long argument with his father, of course. Butler senior tried to shuffle his son back into line with a father's traditional weapon, money. He would finance only those options approved by himself. They reached, eventually, an odd compromise, the more peculiar because nothing in Samuel's life until then had suggested it.

→ RIGHT
Cottages at Mesopotamia, about 1868, from a William Packe watercolour. Butler's cottage is on the right. The cottage survived until 1927. *Canterbury Museum, 1993.103.20.*

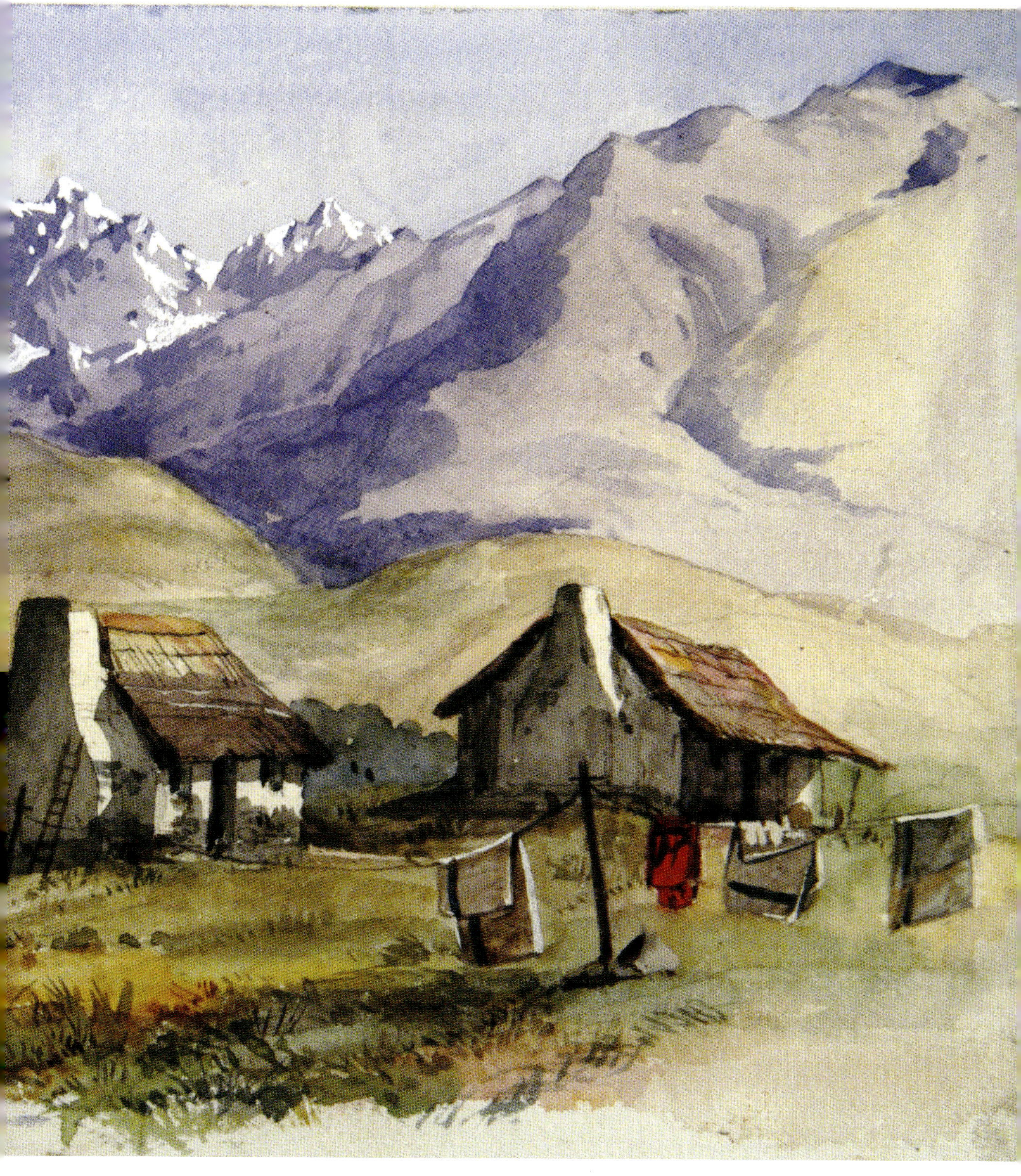

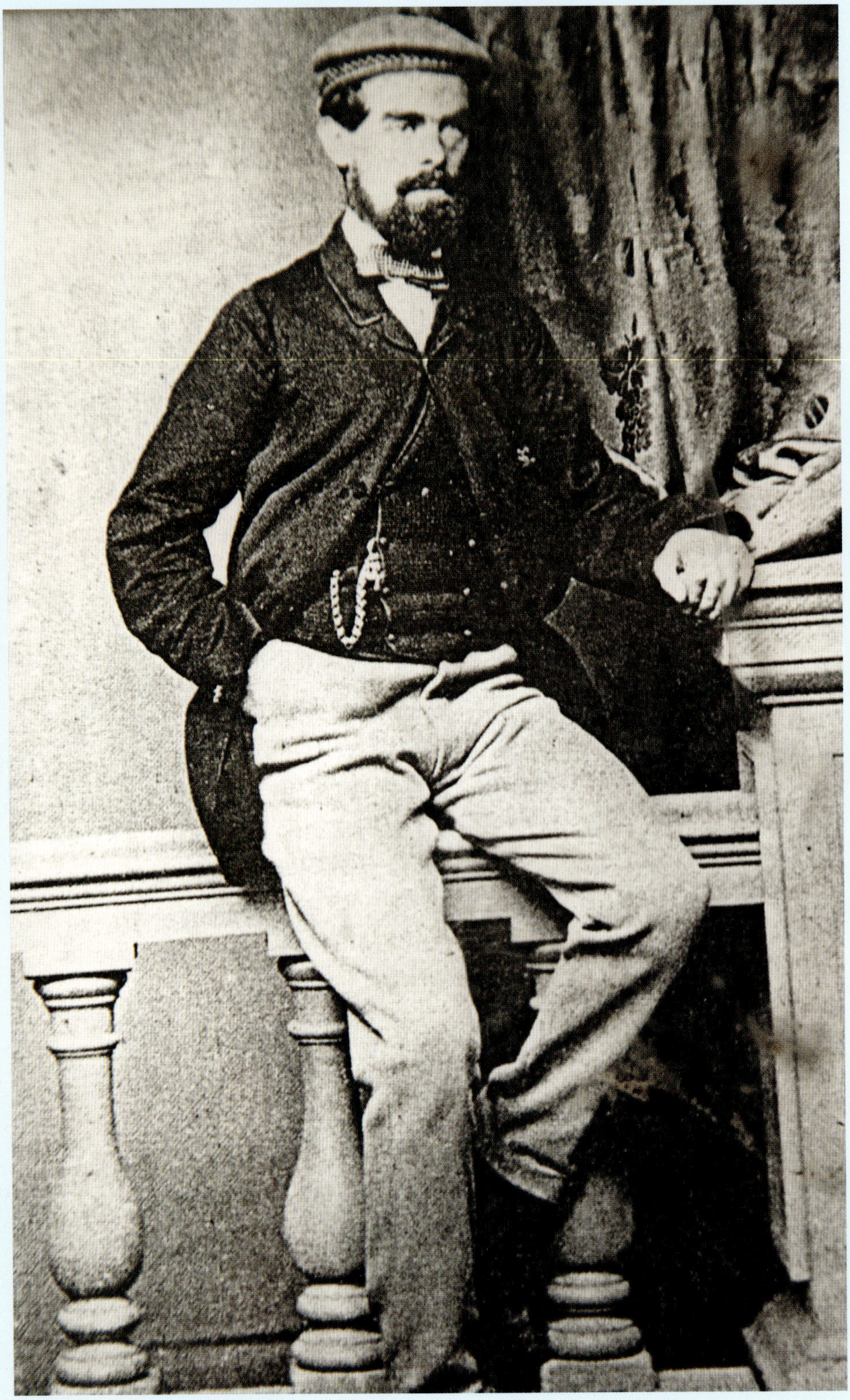

Butler would go to New Zealand and his father would continue paying his allowance for a year then advance the capital needed to set him up as a sheep farmer — in Canterbury, of course, because the Canterbury Association was dedicated to Church of England principles.

It might have been hard to say who was the more relieved when the young man set out for the colonies, Butler or his father. He sailed to Christchurch, growing happier as the distance between him and his family increased, arriving as a young man of privileged background, with no knowledge of farming, no qualifications as a pioneer, and landing in a town which was little more than a scattering of houses.

He bought a bay horse named Doctor, although he could scarcely ride, and started exploring, cheered by the arrival of £2000 from his father with the promise of more. Butler poked into the farthest corners of Canterbury, and during those journeys became the first European to see what later became Arthur's Pass, the main route between Canterbury and the West Coast. He did not investigate the pass, although he wrote: 'I firmly believe that this saddle will lead to the West Coast. I feel as though I had left a stone unturned.'

His courage and enterprise were remarkable, for nothing in his background fitted him for these adventures. The landscape before him rendered the English countryside he had come from so puny it was as if he had stumbled across another planet. In a letter home he wrote:

> *I despair of giving you an impression of the real thing. It is so hard for an Englishman to divest himself, not only of hedges and ditches, and cuttings and bridges, but of all signs of human habitation whatsoever, that unless you were to travel in similar country yourself you would never understand it.*

HIS SKETCHES OF Mesopotamia were annotated with descriptions such as 'ye horryble glaciers' and 'ye vexatious gullies'. He hated the unique, spiky matagouri, which he called wild Irishman: 'He does not appear to me to have a single redeeming feature being neither pleasant to the eye nor good for food.' He failed to recognise it as a legume-like plant which fixes nitrogen in the soil, and like other settlers burned it every chance he got.

← LEFT
Samuel Butler photographed in 1862, a bold figure perched atop a balustrade. *Prouting Family Collection*

He loathed spaniard, the orange speargrass of the high country which could run its spikes through almost anything: 'simply detestable'.

Butler found no good land left unclaimed until at last he made his way up the Rangitata River and turned into a tributary, Forest Creek. By now autumn had arrived in the high country. Undeterred by icy blankets, for even his tea-leaves were frozen, he climbed the hills rearing high above him and saw something overpowering:

Suddenly, as my eyes got on a level with the top, so that I could see over, I was struck almost breathless by the wonderful mountain that burst on my sight. The effect was startling. It rose towering in a massy parallelogram, disclosed from top to bottom in the cloudless sky, far above all the others.

HE HAD SEEN Mount Cook. He may also have been the first European to have seen the huge Bush Stream Valley, later simply known as the Valley, lying over the pass that later became known as the Bullock Bow. Much of the land lying between the Sinclair Range and the Rangitata River, which would later become part of his station, had already been claimed, but Butler's Mesopotamia began with claims on the western side of Forest Creek, and in the valley, and he added land as he bought it from neighbouring runholders.

At first Butler did not know whether sheep could live on this country, so high in the mountains amid the ice and snow, and so cold he later claimed that peoples' breath froze when it left their mouths and they had to break it off and put it in the frying pan to see what they were talking about. But he decided to spend a winter beside Forest Creek to answer the question.

He built what he called a V hut, but would now be called an A-frame, less than four metres long and around two wide, big enough for himself, an old Irishman and a cadet. He was some forty kilometres of rough country from the nearest house, probably scarcely better than his own, and a very long way from Christchurch. Even with modern roads and vehicles the trip from Christchurch to Mesopotamia takes around three hours. In Butler's day the journey was very different. Soon after he built his hut he had to return to Christchurch. On his way back to the Rangitata he was held up for two days at the Rakaia River, which was in flood and far too dangerous for the punt then used as a ferry.

On the third day he crossed, he and his companion swimming their horses behind the punt, with the clouds 'hung unceasingly on the mountain ranges'. The Ashburton River then confronted them. The river was high but passable, and they crossed wet to the saddleflaps. They camped in the open despite heavy snowfalls and set out the following morning in heavy rain, travelling towards the Rangitata, through country 'crumpled in an extraordinary manner'.

'Truly,' he wrote, 'it is a dismal place on a dark day, and somewhat like the world's end . . .' Finally they turned a corner and looked down upon the upper Rangitata Valley: 'Very grand, very gloomy, and very desolate.'

> 'Truly,' he wrote, 'it is a dismal place on a dark day, and somewhat like the world's end . . .'

The river was in flood, of course. They came across a party of men with a dray who had been forced to camp out for ten days then delayed for ten more by the flood. Butler had left the Irishman back at his hut; now he discovered that food he had arranged to send back to him had been delayed too. Would the Irishman have survived? Or had he simply starved to death?

Worried, they pushed on, going up one stream and down another, facing one difficulty then the next, once caught by quicksand. They got wet but just saved themselves from swimming, and finally reached the other side of the river, Butler carrying a cat in a sack to deal to rats so bold they stole food from the men's plates; she got wet when Butler's horse was struggling in the quicksand, but survived.

Even after crossing the river they had to cross more troublesome creeks: 'Sluggish and swampy, with bad places for getting in and out at; these, however, were as nothing in comparison with the river itself, which we all had feared more than we cared to say.' Until finally they turned up Forest Creek towards home, in the dark and heavy rain, and saw a light twinkling in the hut, and knew the Irishman was alive, to Butler's astonishment, 'for there was wonderfully little besides flour, tea and sugar for him to eat'.

The hut, however, had not done as well. It was soaked and soggy, with no fire. 'The place was as revolting-looking an affair as one would wish to see: coming wet and cold off a journey, we had hoped for better things.' They made tea and fried up some of the reeking beef which had been lying on the ground at least ten days on the other side of the Rangitata.

The 193-kilometre journey from Christchurch to Mesopotamia could take a week in a dray drawn by the six bullocks which Butler bought and hastily taught himself to drive. This was how he described crossing one of the fierce rivers on his first dray trip:

A dray going through a river is a pretty sight enough when you are utterly unconcerned in the contents thereof; the rushing water stemmed by the bullocks and the dray, the energetic appeals of the driver to Tommy or Nobbler to lift the dray over the large stones in the river, the creaking dray, the cracking whip, form a tout ensemble *rather agreeable than otherwise. But when the bullocks, having pulled the dray into the middle of the river, refuse entirely to pull it out again; when the leaders turn sharp around and look at you, or stick their heads under the bellies of the polars; when the gentle pats on the forehead with the stock of the whip prove unavailing, and you are obliged to have recourse to strong measures, it is less agreeable; especially if the animals turn just after having got your dray halfway up the bank, and twisting it round on a steeply-inclined surface, throw the centre of gravity far beyond the base: over goes the dray into the water.*

BUTLER SPENT A dismal winter in his Forest Creek Hut. He discovered his new sheep run was not a run at all. It needed more land to make it work, land that would be clear of snow most of the year. Men had been there before him, and the runs they had claimed dotted his map. But he found country that had not been allotted already, applied for it, and set about acquiring more from other settlers. Slowly, run by run, he built up his station.

By November of 1860, his applications to the Waste Lands Board began giving his address as Mesopotamia, Rangitata. One of those applications resulted in a Canterbury legend.

Butler had found a site for his new homestead, a section of land on a terrace above the Rangitata, looking over the panorama of rivers and mountains with Mount Sinclair rearing up behind and The Thumbs giving a jaunty V for victory in the background. It faced the sun, was sheltered from the wind, had plenty of water and sat near a patch of bush. It was as nearly perfect as anyone could expect in that inhospitable part of the world.

Unfortunately, the site was already occupied. A neighbour, Caton, had built a hut for his shepherd on what he regarded as *his* land. Butler set his men to work building his sod hut beside it, on what he had decided was *his* property. 'To allow him to remain where he was,' he wrote of Caton, 'was not to be thought of.'

The so-called 'waste lands' were free, but runholders were allowed to freehold their homestead sites. Neither man had yet done so; but both were certain the other would do it the moment he reached Christchurch. 'Not a moment to lose,' Butler wrote. An astonishing race followed. The two men, each determined to grab this tiny piece of land in its far-off valley while the grabbing was good, both of them prepared to fight tooth and nail, braved all the hell and high water the back country could throw at them: the cold, the dark, the swampy creeks and the crumpled country, the whole hard 193 horse-killing kilometres.

BUTLER CROSSED AND recrossed the flooded Ashburton River in the dark until he was too afraid to go on and waited for daylight. Dawn brought its own surprise. Turning around, he spotted Caton close behind.

A comedy followed, the two riding together, each aware of what the other was up to but politely not mentioning it. A long day in the saddle and another cold night followed, Butler driving his horse until it dropped, finding another and expecting to win when he sneaked past Caton asleep in an accommodation house, only to be rained on so heavily he had to seek shelter himself.

Next day he got to the Land Office early, fearing the worst: 'If it came to fists, I should get the worst of it — that was a moral certainty — and I really half-feared something of the kind.'

Caton got there before him. Butler's lawyer, though, had unbeknown to Butler entered his client's name in the book the previous day. Caton outsmarted himself. He promptly entered his name *above* Butler's, so transparent an act of dishonesty that the Commissioners of Waste Land threw out Caton's application and Butler had lost the race but won the battle. According to his biographer Peter Raby he went off to relieve his tensions by playing Bach fugues on his lawyer's piano. Then he went home to the place in the Rangitata Valley which was to remain the homestead site from then until now.

Abandoning the dark of Forest Creek, Butler moved into first the sod hut, then a new cob hut, constructing the second so well that it stood for almost seventy years. The hut might be there still had it not been neglected so badly that first the roof then the walls fell down and the ruin was finally demolished in 1927.

Butler set up the headquarters of his new station in that hut. His diet was basic, starting with mutton and bread for breakfast and scarcely improving. The weather was harsh; once a gale blew off part of his roof, so he could lie in bed and stare at the sky, and one bad winter more than a metre of snow lay on the ground, with a passage cut through it between the two huts.

Despite the hardships his hut became a little oasis of civilisation. He installed a piano which used up half the living room and in the evenings the mountains echoed to Bach. Books and easy chairs filled the place, and English watercolours hung on its rough walls.

Mesopotamia burgeoned. By the end of March 1861, it already extended over more than 16,200 hectares.

BUTLER CONSTANTLY SCOUTED for more land. He crossed the Rangitata River above Mesopotamia with John Holland Baker, a young surveyor. They travelled up the Clyde River and could see no way through. He rode back to the mouth of the Lawrence, a river heading towards the Main Divide at a tangent, and crossed there; a nonchalant description, for every crossing was dangerous in this precarious country with no help to be had.

The two climbed to the Lawrence's headwaters. On one side Mount Arrowsmith rose above the Arrowsmith Range. Butler chose the opposite side of the river valley, the side leading to the Alps. He crossed the Jollie Range over what is now the Butler Saddle, then headed down to the Rakaia River. Formidable, menacing, bleak, forbidding: a mountain of adjectives fitted this country perfectly.

Without hesitation, Butler and Baker climbed up what later became the Lauper Stream to what is now the Whitcombe Pass through the Southern Alps to the West Coast. They looked over to the other side, the west. Possibly no one had stood on that pass before. Maori preferred easier routes to carry pounamu or greenstone through this part of the mountains; hardly surprising, for while the route on the Canterbury side is easy enough as mountain passes go, it is terrifying on the other. Butler was single-minded. He peered over the top, saw that the bush and ravines to the west were unsuitable for sheep, and went home to Mesopotamia.

The mountainscape of Butler's novel *Erewhon* may have been fiction, but it accurately described the route, surrounded by 'a succession of rugged precipices and snowy mountainsides. The solitude was greater than I could bear; the mountain upon my master's sheep-run [which he called Mount Sinclair, the mountain standing behind the Mesopotamia homestead] was a

→ RIGHT
A photograph taken about 1870 by E.P. Sealy of Mesopotamia buildings. The house on the right was built by the Campbells, who owned the station from 1866 to 1885. The roof of Butler's cottage can be seen behind their house. *Prouting Family Collection*

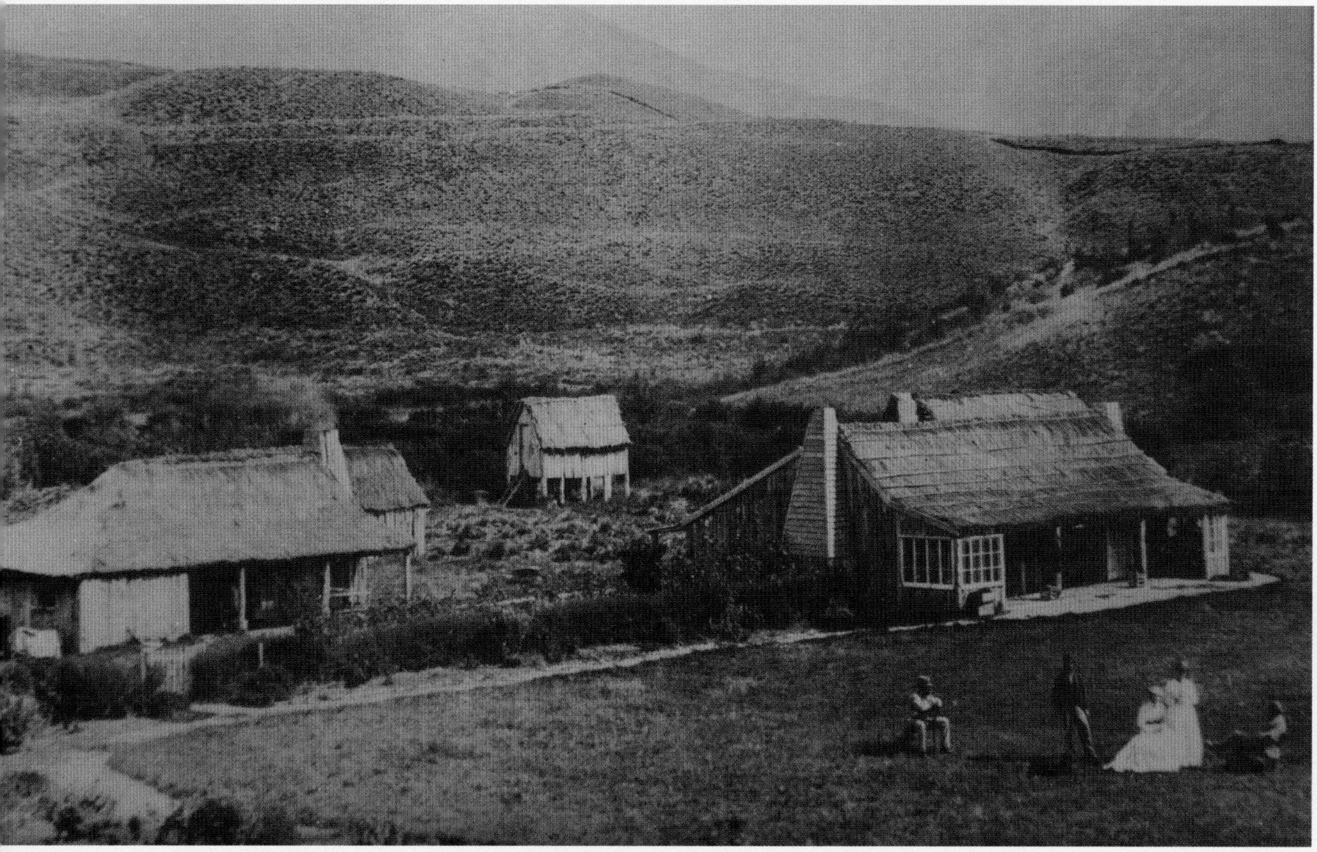

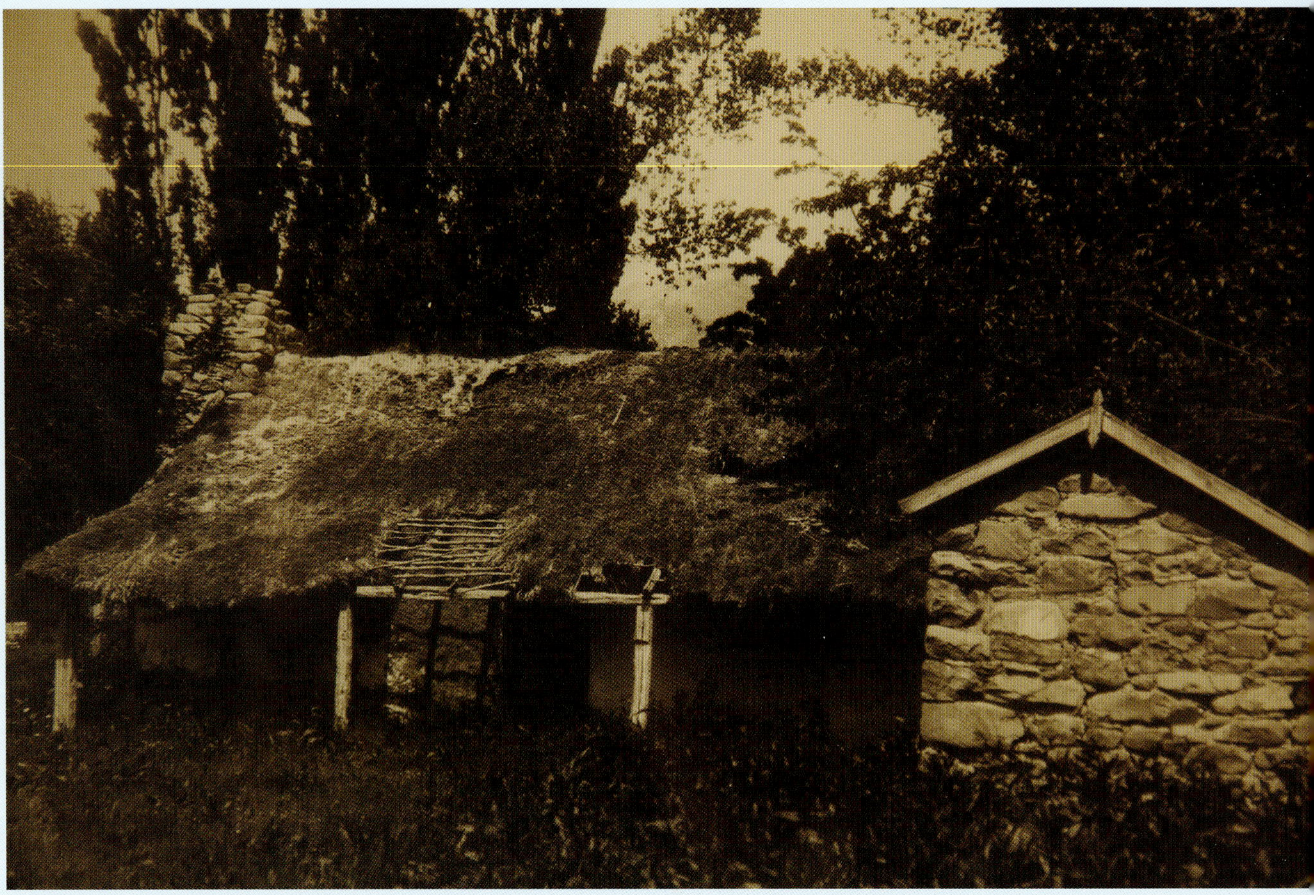

crowded thoroughfare in comparison with this sombre, sullen place. The air was dark and heavy which made the loneliness even more oppressive.'

At the top his hero found the way guarded by gigantic forms, barbarous stone fiends. Unlike his creator, the fictitious Butler hurried on, and found an easy path leading downhill to his utopia. Now it really *was* fiction, for Butler, of course, had never been down the other side.

Henry Whitcombe and Jakob Lauper travelled the route in 1863, as Butler was contemplating selling Mesopotamia and leaving New Zealand. Whitcombe was the Canterbury Surveyor, and his task was to find a route from Canterbury through the mountains to the rich West Coast goldfields. Lauper, a Swiss mountaineer, was his guide.

The two of them, Lauper laden down like a Sherpa, travelled over the pass then down into the West Coast, and almost immediately ran into trouble. Ravines, almost impassable bluffs and cliffs, torrents and waterfalls blocked their way. Lauper saved his leader with great courage and daring. Starving, freezing and near death the two finally arrived at the coast. Whitcombe made a raft of two decrepit Maori canoes and forced Lauper, a non-swimmer, to cross the river with him. The raft quickly broke up and the two were swept into the sea. Somehow Lauper survived; but the only trace of Whitcombe was his boots sticking out of the shingle. He had been drilled into the beach and was literally stone dead.

BUTLER PROSPERED ON Mesopotamia. He learned about sheep. He kept adding to his runs, spreading along the flanks of the Rangitata River over Mount Brabazon (named for his partner, John Brabazon) and as far towards the Alps as a merino could go without freezing solid. He rolled over the Sinclair Range behind his new homestead, into the vast empty space around the Bush Stream, which became known simply as the Valley. He presided over rivers, gullies, mountains, valleys, peaks and troughs, some of the most rugged country ever to run sheep in the South Island, until he had accumulated more than 24,000 hectares.

Poet, writer and musician he might have been, but Butler in New Zealand was a speculator. He seemed an indifferent farmer, spending more

← LEFT
Butler's cottage about 1920, in a bad state of repair. A little of the dairy on the right still stands. *Prouting Family Collection*

and more time in Christchurch and leaving the station to his manager. He wanted to double his capital, and he almost succeeded. In March 1864 he and his partner sold out. The man who bought Mesopotamia from Butler, William Parkerson, was also a speculator, although evidently he lacked Butler's resolution. He flicked on the station after a year or so and made £3500 on the deal.

Butler turned his original capital of £4800 into more than £8000 and, having created Mesopotamia's first success story, he went home to England, never to return. He and his novel left their mark on the land: Butler's Creek, Butler Range, Butler Saddle, Chowbok Col, Mount Butler, Erewhon Col. The title 'Erewhon' was taken to name a station directly across the river. Erewhon Station was originally named Stronschrubie until its owner, Frank Pawson, a Butler enthusiast who once managed Mesopotamia, renamed it.

A photograph taken in 1862 shows Samuel Butler as a bold figure perched atop a balustrade with drapes arranged artistically behind him and absolutely no trace of his rough hut in the mountains. A cap hides the thick dark hair, which formed a helmet, parted slightly to one side of his widow's peak.

He had a bushy goatee running into close-trimmed side-whiskers which stopped a couple of centimetres below his short sideburns, leaving a gap in the circuit.

> **His eyes were fierce and a slight scowl lurked around his bushy black eyebrows. He radiated resolution. A man would have been a fool to take him on. He seemed to be saying, 'I wrestled some of the most rugged land in the world, and I'm winning.'**

His eyes were fierce and a slight scowl lurked around his full black eyebrows. He radiated resolution. A man would have been a fool to take him on. He seemed to be saying, 'I wrestled some of the most rugged land in the world, and I'm winning.'

Samuel Butler's self-portrait hangs behind the curved curtain of glass enclosing the Christchurch Art Gallery Te Puna O Waiwhetu, the most comfortable and certainly the most stylish residence he ever had in New Zealand. Like his photograph the self-portrait avoided any sign of the prickly matagouri, or spaniard, or cabbage trees, or any trace of the New Zealand he lived in. He portrayed himself against a deep, bland brown.

There was a difference, however. He painted himself in 1873, the year *Erewhon* was published, when he was back in England. Although he had not long left New Zealand, he saw himself as a gentler, less weathered man. Same hair, same brows, but the later Butler wore a benign expression. He seemed pleased, perhaps with the profit he made on his New Zealand adventure, or to be wearing dry clothes, with no damper to eat, yards to fill or fences to mend.

Possibly he was relieved to be back in a civilisation that did not look at him askance, for he was known among his Rangitata neighbours as 'that strange man'. John Acland of Mount Peel tells the story of the first Mrs Acland who, after each visit by Butler (if not an atheist, at least a sceptic), would put lilac over hot coals and exorcise the homestead. The first Mrs Tripp worried over his attempts to convert the cook to atheism.

He *was* strange, in a society of sheep farmers, shepherds, hard men and strong women. He spent his spare time writing, often pieces for publication in the Christchurch *Press*, and painting, or playing the piano.

People might have frowned over the teacups. His penchant for prostitutes, however, must have soured their milk. He might have married Mary Brittan, a woman of social standing; instead, she married William Rolleston, the fourth and last superintendent of Canterbury, whose name is still attached to one of Christchurch's satellite towns and one of its Four Avenues.

Those things are still remembered in the Rangitata Valley, along with a few more technical items. For example, he thatched his hut the wrong way round. He started from the top, rather than from the bottom, so that the thatch overlapped upwards and was bound to leak. He was amazed when the ewes came back to their lambs after a day's tailing. 'As if that wasn't natural,' said Laurie Prouting many decades later. 'I'm thinking, what sort of a wally have we here?'

Certainly an adventurous one, an individualist prepared to chance his arm, work hard and endure. In those respects, not very different from high country farmers in the twenty-first century.

Even in 1918, on an occasion when a musterer received an urgent call to the bedside of his sick daughter in a nearby town, the ride out from Mesopotamia took two days. Crossing the Rangitata River to Mount Potts on the north side and dodging the mountains through swamps and valleys past Mount Somers was the favoured route, a four- or five-day round trip when there were no floods, snow or ice.

Charlie Dunstan, who drove an eight-horse wool-wagon to and from the station in the early twentieth century and set down some of his memories in 1957, wrote of 'a hazardous and lonely undertaking' — with compensations.

Coming home at the end of the five days journey I often used to stop at the top of the Potts cutting and gaze in wonder at those everlasting hills. What a sight it must have been to Butler. There is no hill in the whole of England bigger than the Surrey Hills, but to gaze on the headwaters of the Rangitata and the vast panorama of hills up to the great Divide with the Erewhon country in the centre, one was reminded of the inscription above the doors of the Canterbury Museum: 'Lo, these are parts of His ways but how little a portion is heard of Him.'

It must have been a great day in 1924 when the first wagon rolled from Peel Forest along the new route on the south side of the Rangitata, the opposite side to the old one, all the way to Mesopotamia. Then, in December 1926, the first lorry drove all the way to the station. The days of wagons and epic journeys were over.

NOW I CAN drive from Christchurch to Mesopotamia in three hours. I fly above the Rakaia River on a long, long concrete bridge with no sign of a punt, zoom over the Ashburton River scarcely knowing it is there, connect with the inland scenic route around the mountains' feet, slip over the Rangitata, turn off at Arundel's few houses, cruise through Peel Forest and past Mount Peel Station until the seal runs out and far ahead I see that dust trail streaking the valley. The road runs in and out of gullies, past cottages and farmhouses, around White Rock corner where the view strikes between the eyes, through three fords whose shingle slows the car only a moment, over Forest Creek on a bridge first built by Laurie Prouting's father Malcolm, past Scour Stream where a sign announces that I am now on Mesopotamia Station, and up to a junction in a maze of tracks.

One leads to the station's tractor shed, a second to the woolshed, another to the cookhouse and shearers' quarters. A driveway loops around a terrace, past several cottages and a school to the big two-storeyed homestead. One track goes to the airfield, another leads on to the conservation park at the end of the road.

There I find the cause of the dust. It is a tiny blue Toyota, driven by a woman dressed for a less remote neighbourhood.

→ RIGHT
Licence granted to Samuel Butler by the Commissioners of the Waste Lands Board in November 1860 to graze stock on one of the runs he acquired to form Mesopotamia. *Prouting Family Collection*

No. 331.

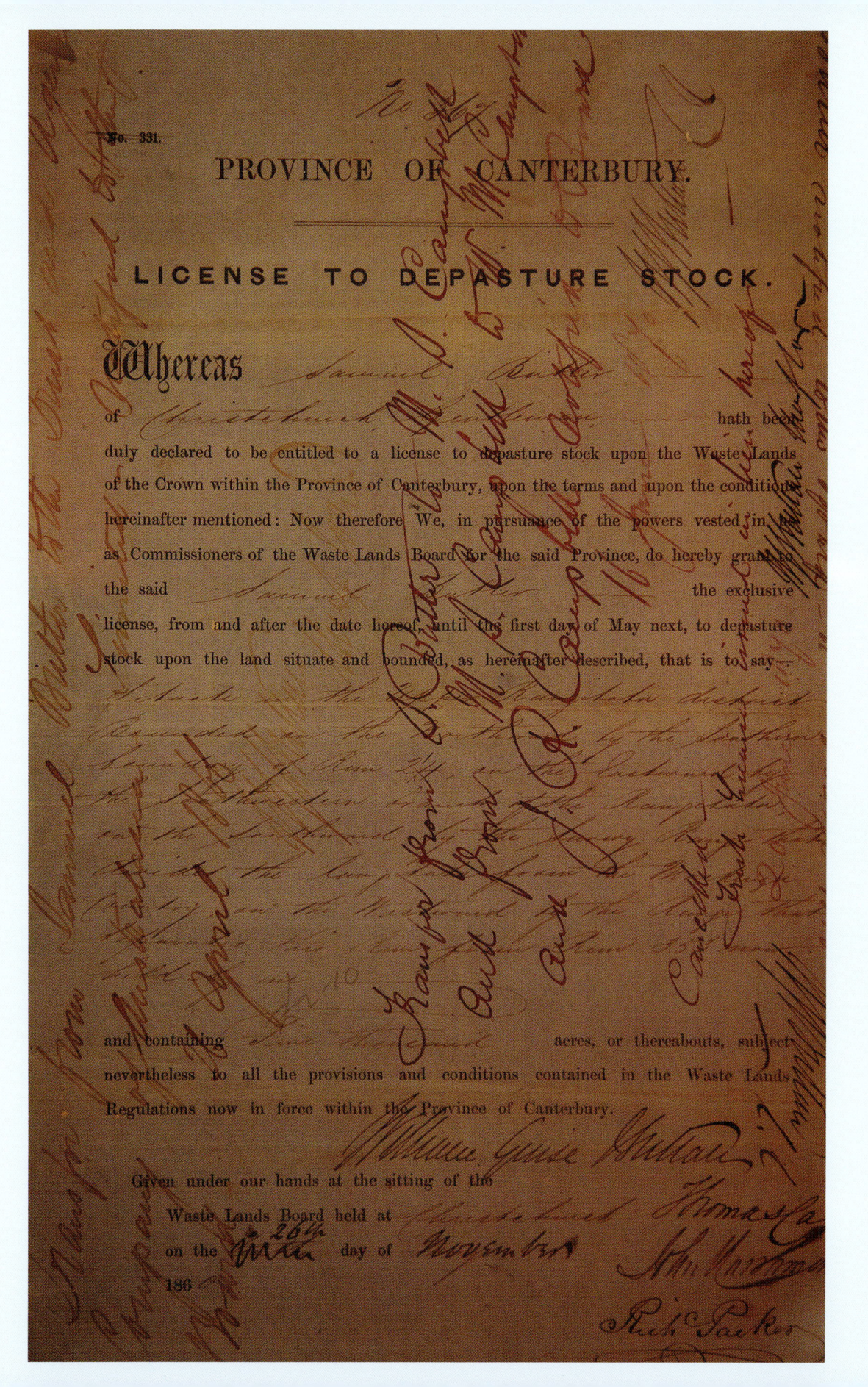

PROVINCE OF CANTERBURY.

LICENSE TO DEPASTURE STOCK.

Whereas Samuel Butler of Christchurch, _____ hath been duly declared to be entitled to a license to depasture stock upon the Waste Lands of the Crown within the Province of Canterbury, upon the terms and upon the conditions hereinafter mentioned: Now therefore We, in pursuance of the powers vested in us as Commissioners of the Waste Lands Board for the said Province, do hereby grant to the said Samuel Butler the exclusive license, from and after the date hereof, until the first day of May next, to depasture stock upon the land situate and bounded, as hereinafter described, that is to say—

_____

and containing _____ acres, or thereabouts, subject nevertheless to all the provisions and conditions contained in the Waste Lands Regulations now in force within the Province of Canterbury.

Given under our hands at the sitting of the Waste Lands Board held at Christchurch on the 26th day of November 186_

William Guise Brittan
Thomas ___
J. W. ___
Rich. Packer

'Excuse me,' she says. 'Could you tell me where I am?'

'Well, yes,' I say. 'You're on Mesopotamia Station.'

'Oh dear. Where does the road go?'

'Another few kilometres,' I say, remembering the way the road bounces over the rocky ground, crosses the steel bridge over Bush Stream, wrestles its way through ruts and bogs and finally judders into the Rangitata riverbed, 'then it stops.'

'Oh dear,' she says again, 'I think I've taken the wrong turning. I was driving to Christchurch, you see, and I wanted to take the inland route. Although,' she adds thoughtfully, looking at the mountains ahead, 'perhaps not *this* inland. Can I get through to the West Coast?'

I think about the last man who tried to find the nearest journey through the Southern Alps over the Whitcombe Pass, almost as badly equipped as she is now, enduring incredible hardship and drowning on the other side: 'No.'

She waves a map, one of those folding brochures picked up from a hotel lobby, or a tourist shop. It covers the entire Rangitata in a couple of strokes and has a single name: Erewhon Park, on the far side of the river.

'It's so close. I'll just drive across the river and go back down that road. Where's the bridge?'

Later I tell Malcolm Prouting the story. Malcolm is the latest Prouting to run Mesopotamia.

'They say tourists behave like sheep,' he says. 'But I've never seen sheep behave like tourists.'

↑ TOP LEFT
The title page of *Erewhon*, Samuel Butler, 3rd edition, London: Trubner & Co, 1872. Hocken Collections, Uare Taoka o Hākena, University of Otago, S12-602.

↗ TOP RIGHT
Samuel Butler's drawing of Mesopotamia Station. *Canterbury Museum, 1954.47.1.*

→ BOTTOM
It is believed that the person sitting on the wool bales is Charlie Dunstan, the teamster who for years used this wagon to take wool from Mesopotamia across the Rangitata River, up the Potts cutting and on to Mt Somers, where the wool was scoured. *Prouting Family Collection*

EREWHON

OR

OVER THE RANGE

"Τοῦ γὰρ εἶναι δοκοῦντος ἀγαθοῦ χάριν πάντα πράττουσι πάντες."
ARIST. Pol.

"There is no action save upon a balance of considerations."
(Paraphrase.)

Third Edition.

LONDON
TRÜBNER & CO., 60 PATERNOSTER ROW
1872
[All rights reserved]

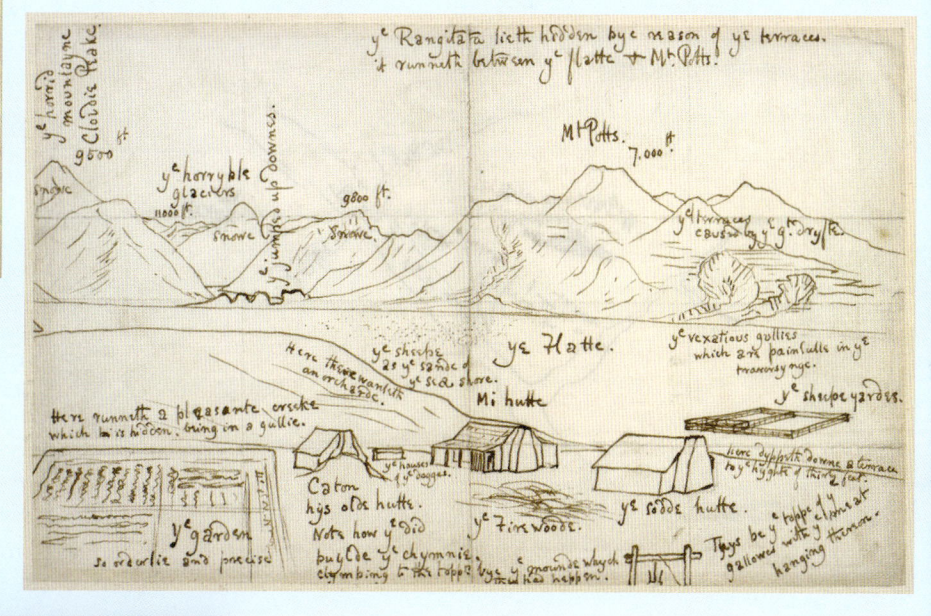

PHOTO ESSAY

THE
AUTUMN MUSTER

The great autumn musters on Mesopotamia Station were part of the New Zealand legend, vast rivers of sheep flowing up the Valley behind the Mount Sinclair Range and over the Bullock Bow Saddle to the downs and river flats of the Rangitata. Peter Bush was one of the musterers on this one, autumn in the early 1990s. After four days of leading packhorses, he reported, 'I could hardly lift my arms.'

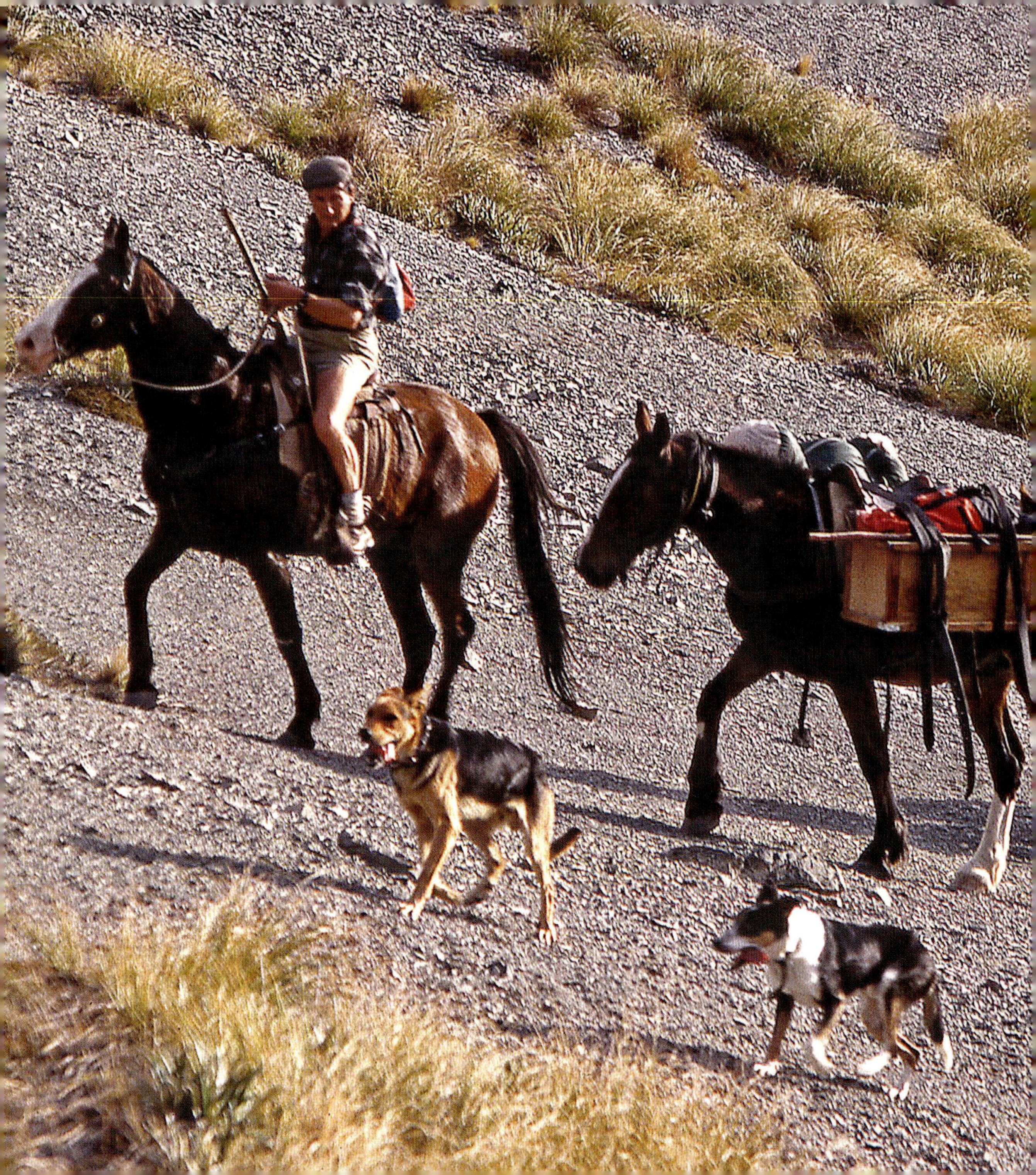

← LEFT
Mounted musterers with their packhorses and dogs heading for the Stone Hut. Laurie Prouting front, Chris O'Donnell rear.

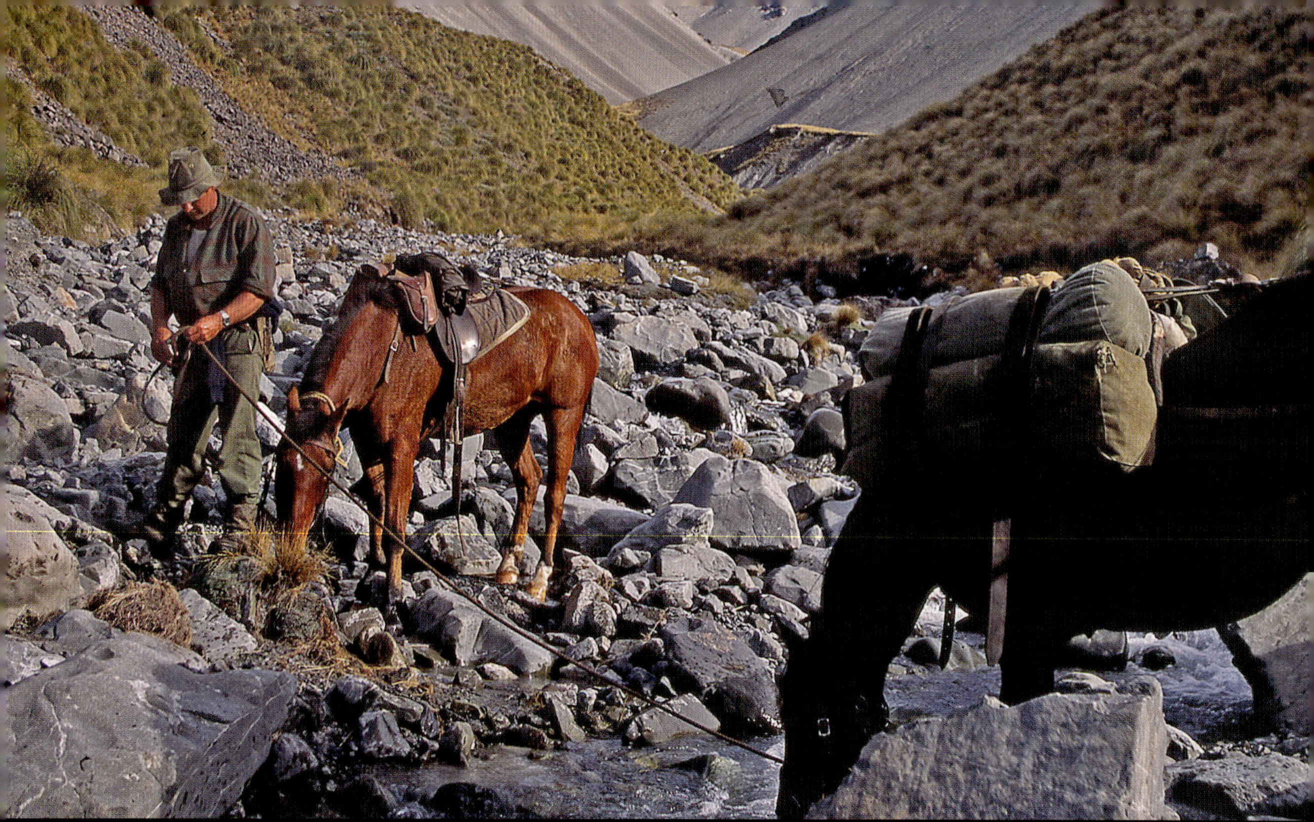

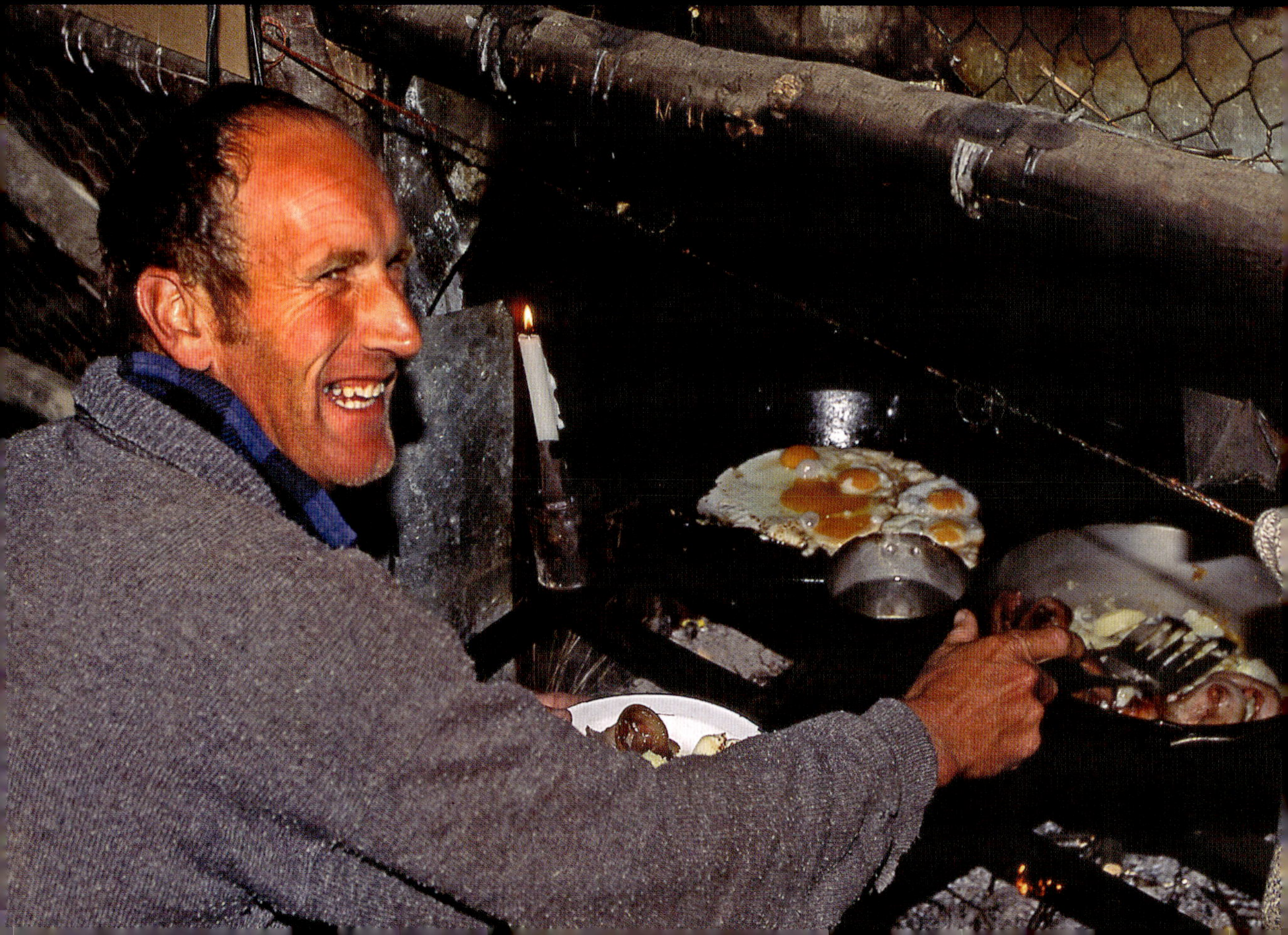

← **CLOCKWISE FROM FAR LEFT**
Horses slake their thirst in the freezing waters of a mountain stream, Chris O'Donnell keeping them company.

Guy Martin strides out with his ever-faithful dog in attendance.

Chris O'Donnell coaxes his horse and the following pack horse through the tussock.

Early morning breakfast at the Stone Hut, fried eggs being served up by Alf Wallis.

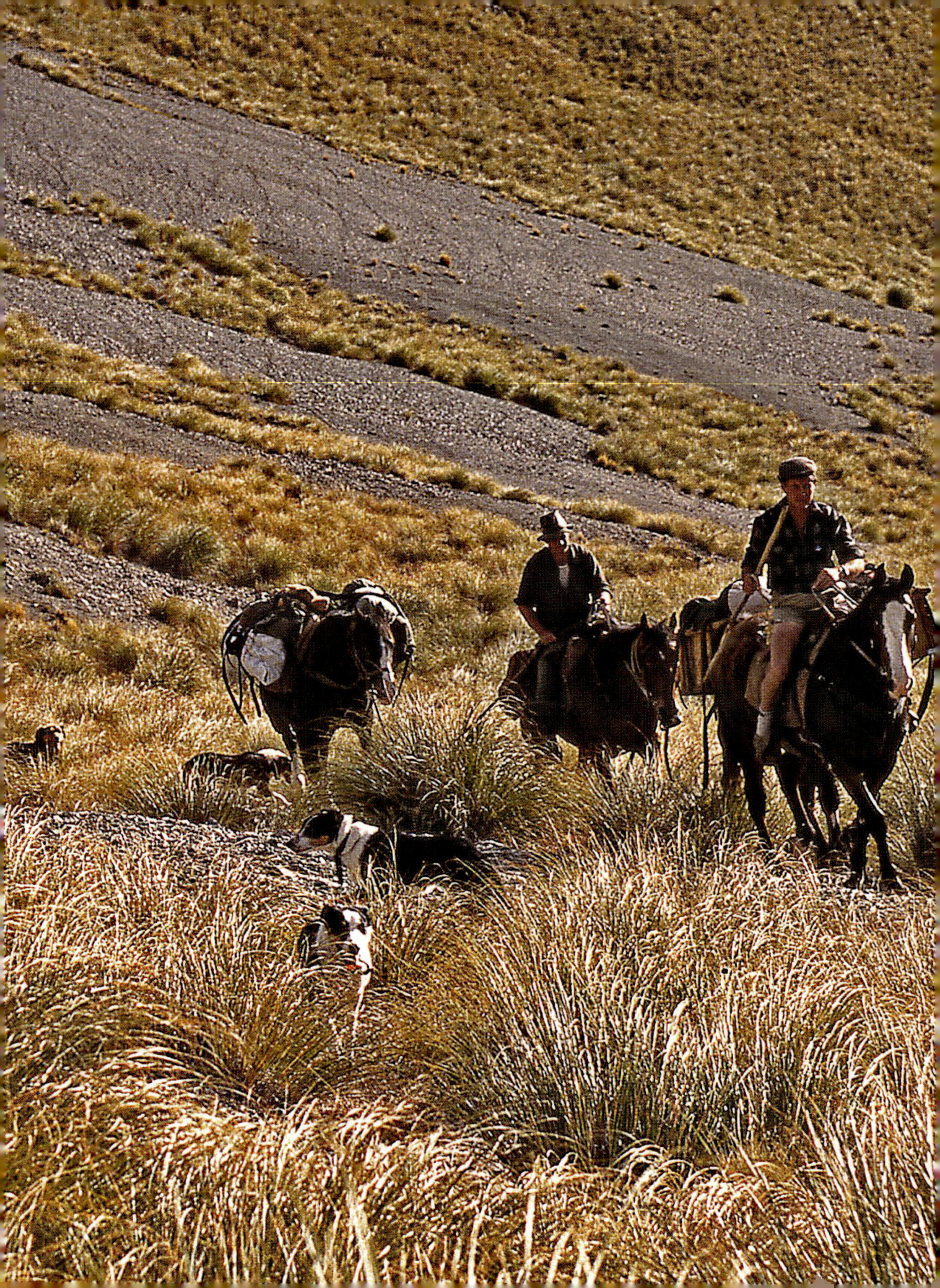

← LEFT
Heavily laden horses tackle the tussock track on their way to Stone Hut. Laurie Prouting front, Chris O'Donnell rear.

↑ INSET
Laurie Prouting on the top beat moves a mob of merinos.

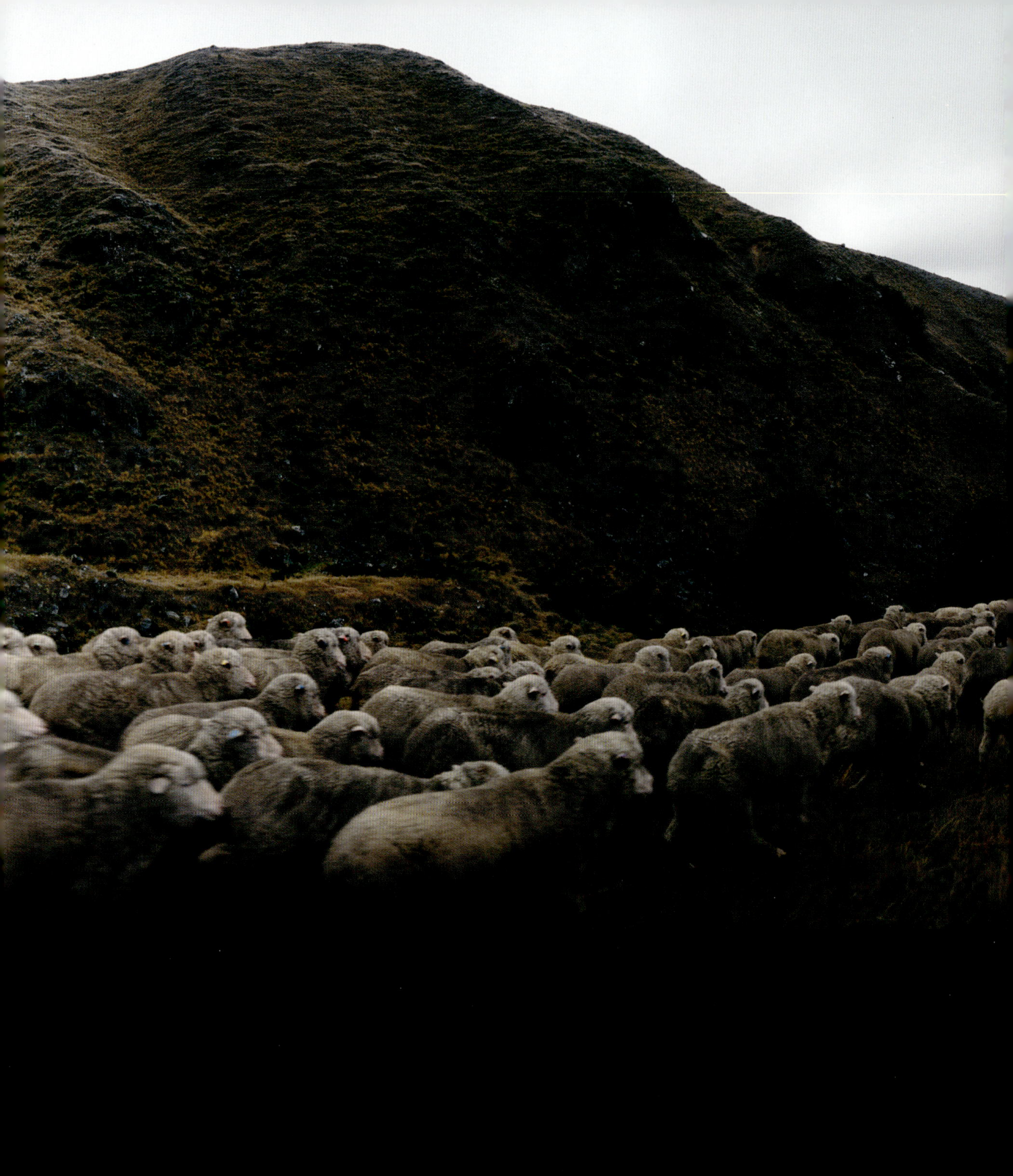

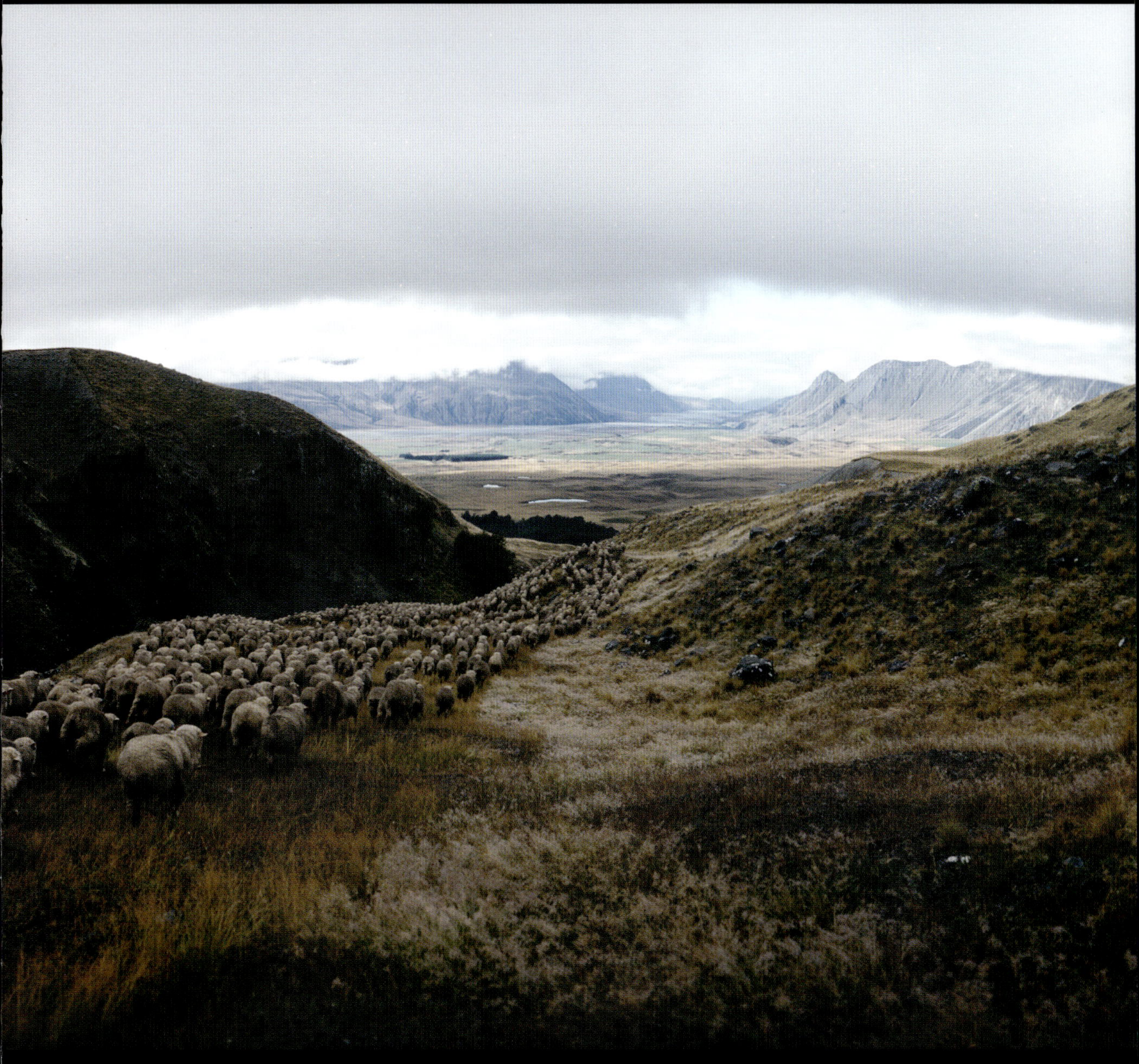

↑ INSET
Laurie and dogs.

→ RIGHT
A packhorse on the early-morning trail.

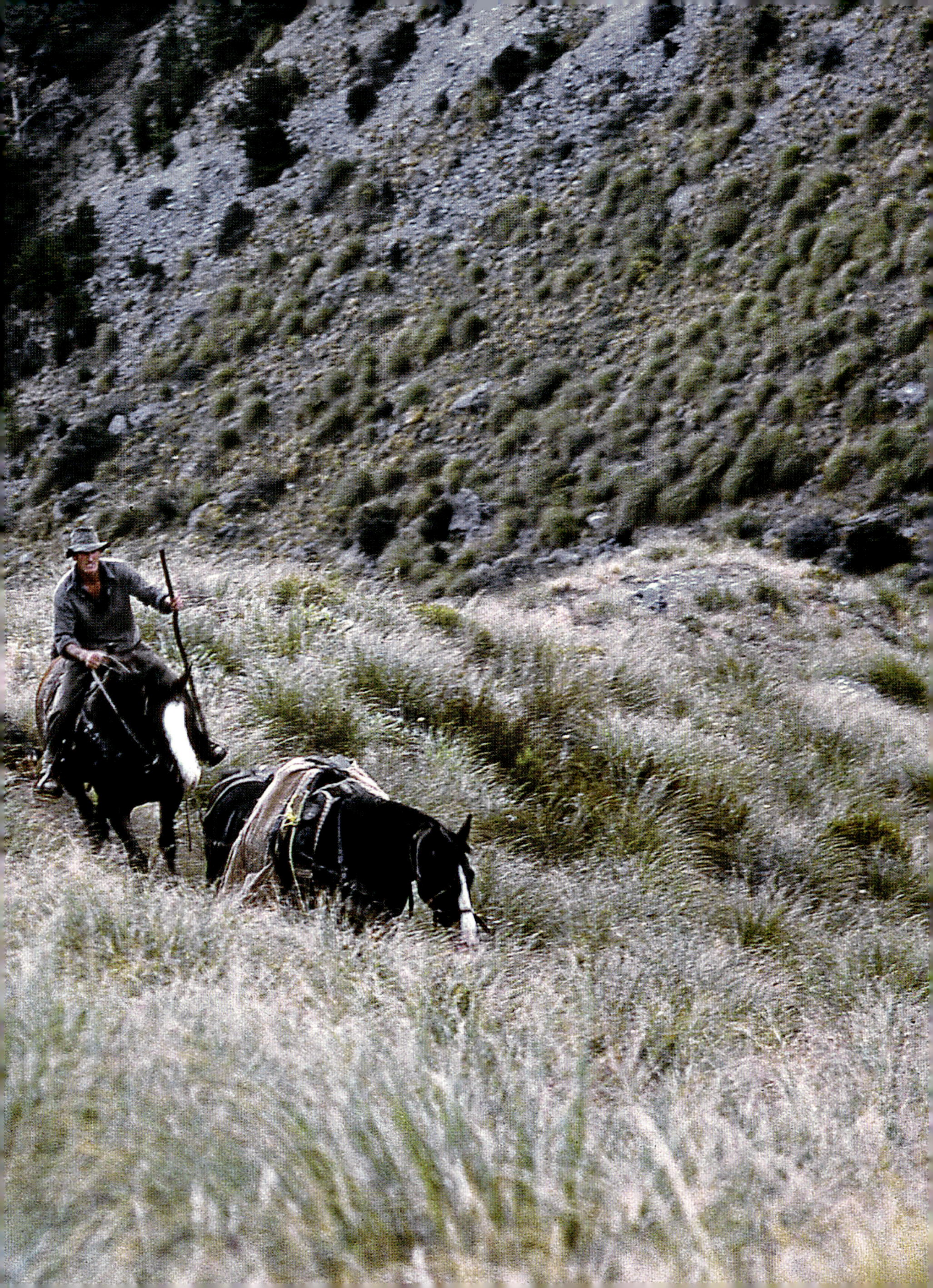

→ **CLOCKWISE FROM RIGHT**
Sure-footed horses and hardy musterers heading up a steep ridge towards the Crooked Spur Hut in the late afternoon sun.

Guy Martin checks a cut paw on one his dogs. Sharp gravel on the tops plays havoc with the paws of musterers' dogs.

Alf Wallis has a fast sluice-down in the freezing water of a snow-fed creek.

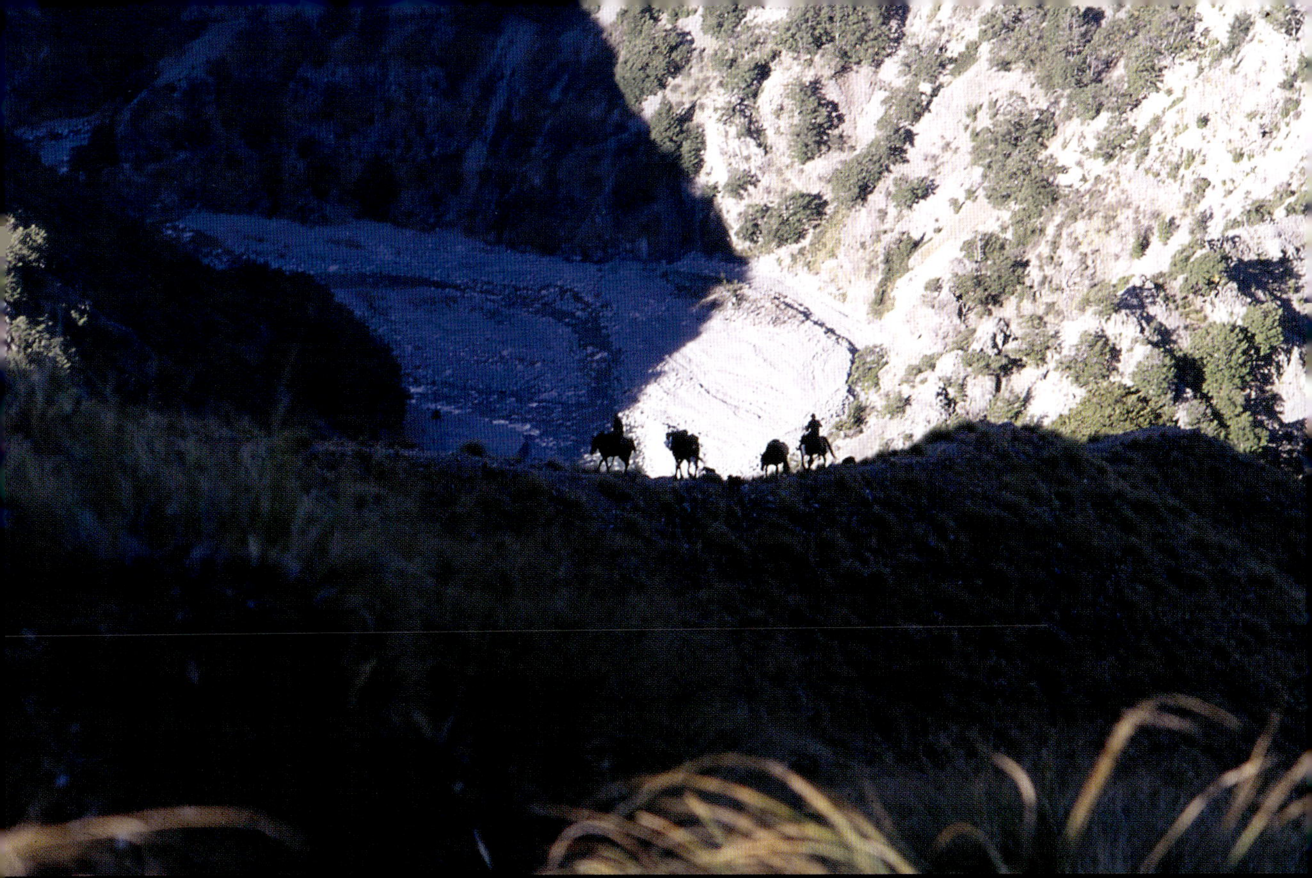

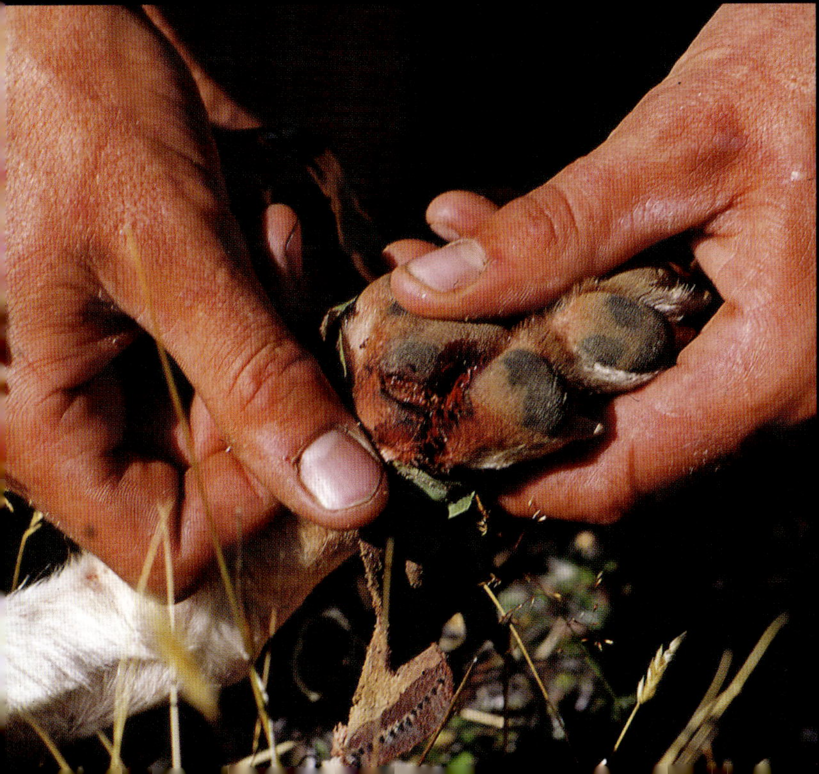

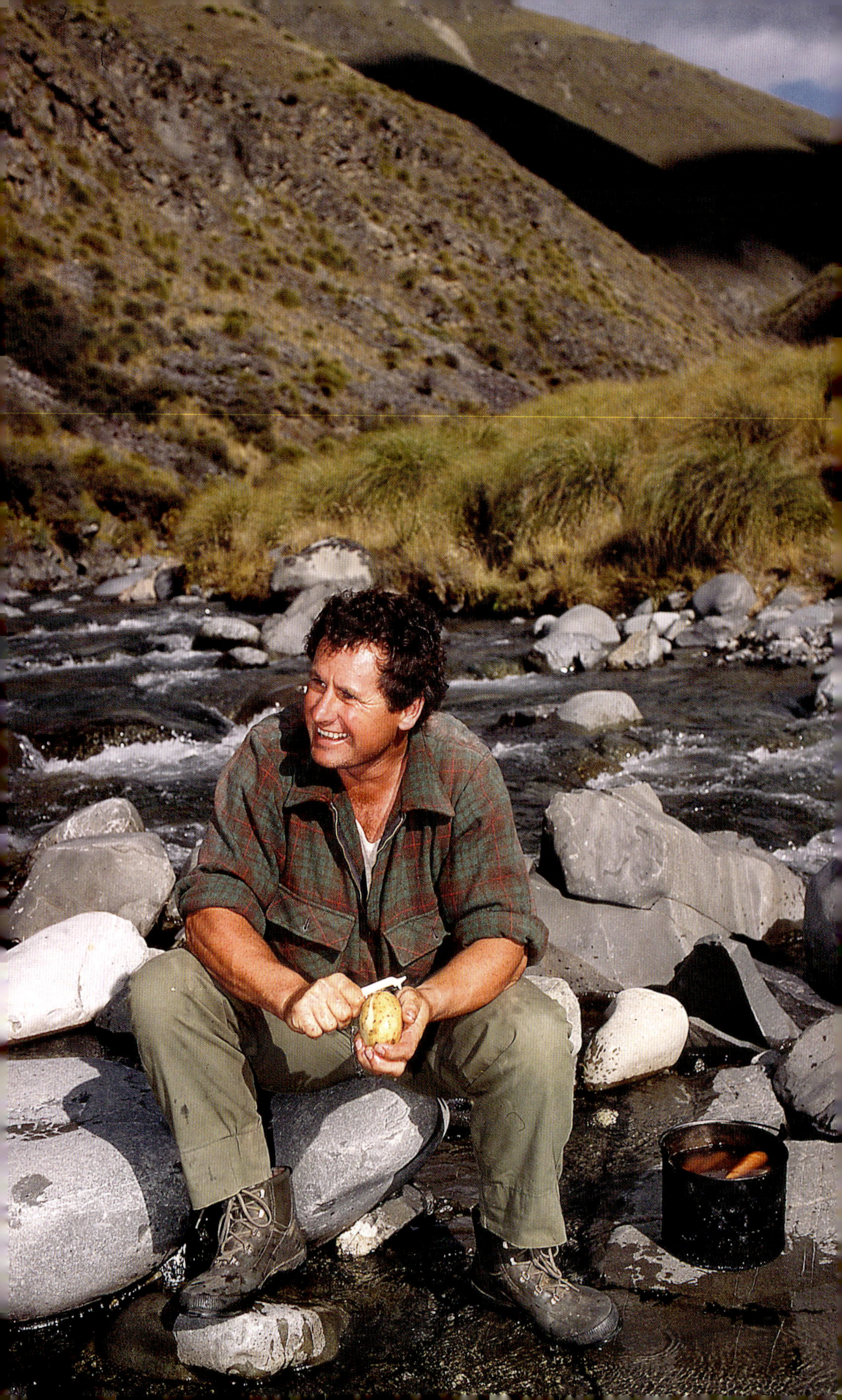

← LEFT
Chris O'Donnell on spud-peeling duty in the creek at the Stone Hut.

↑ ABOVE
Musterers relax over their evening meal in the cosy Stone Hut.

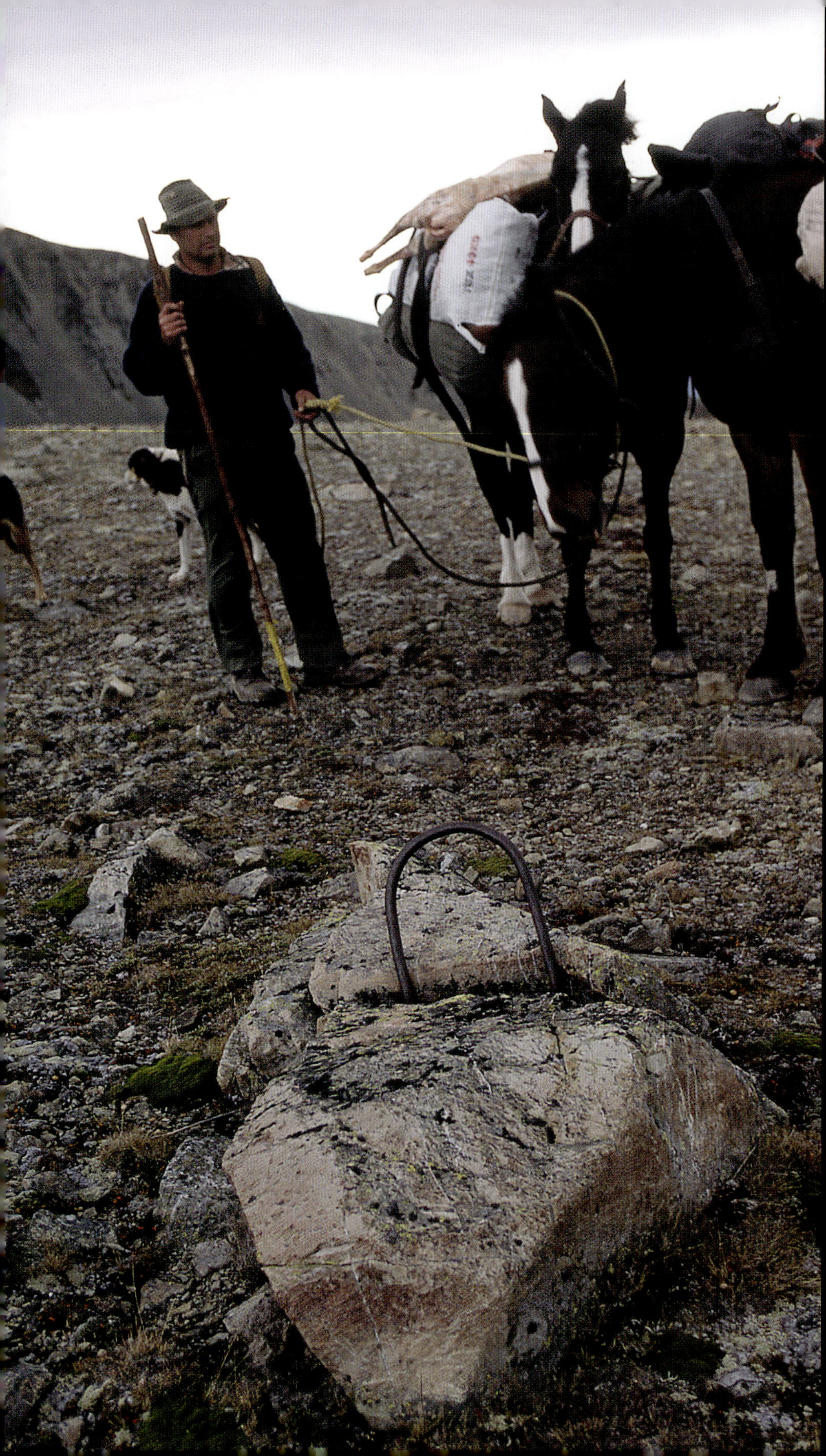

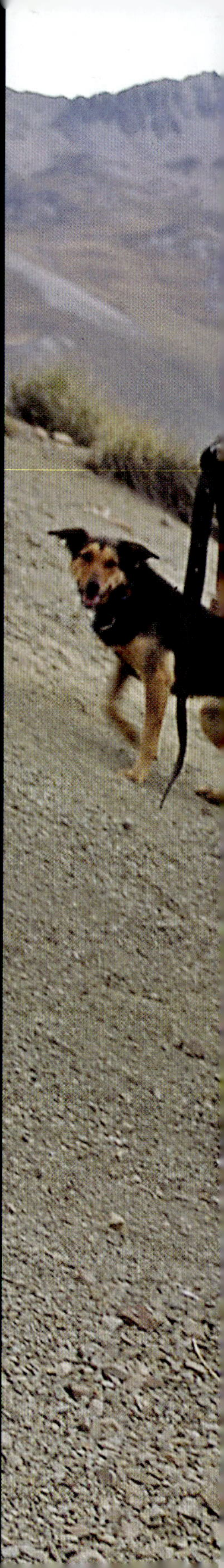

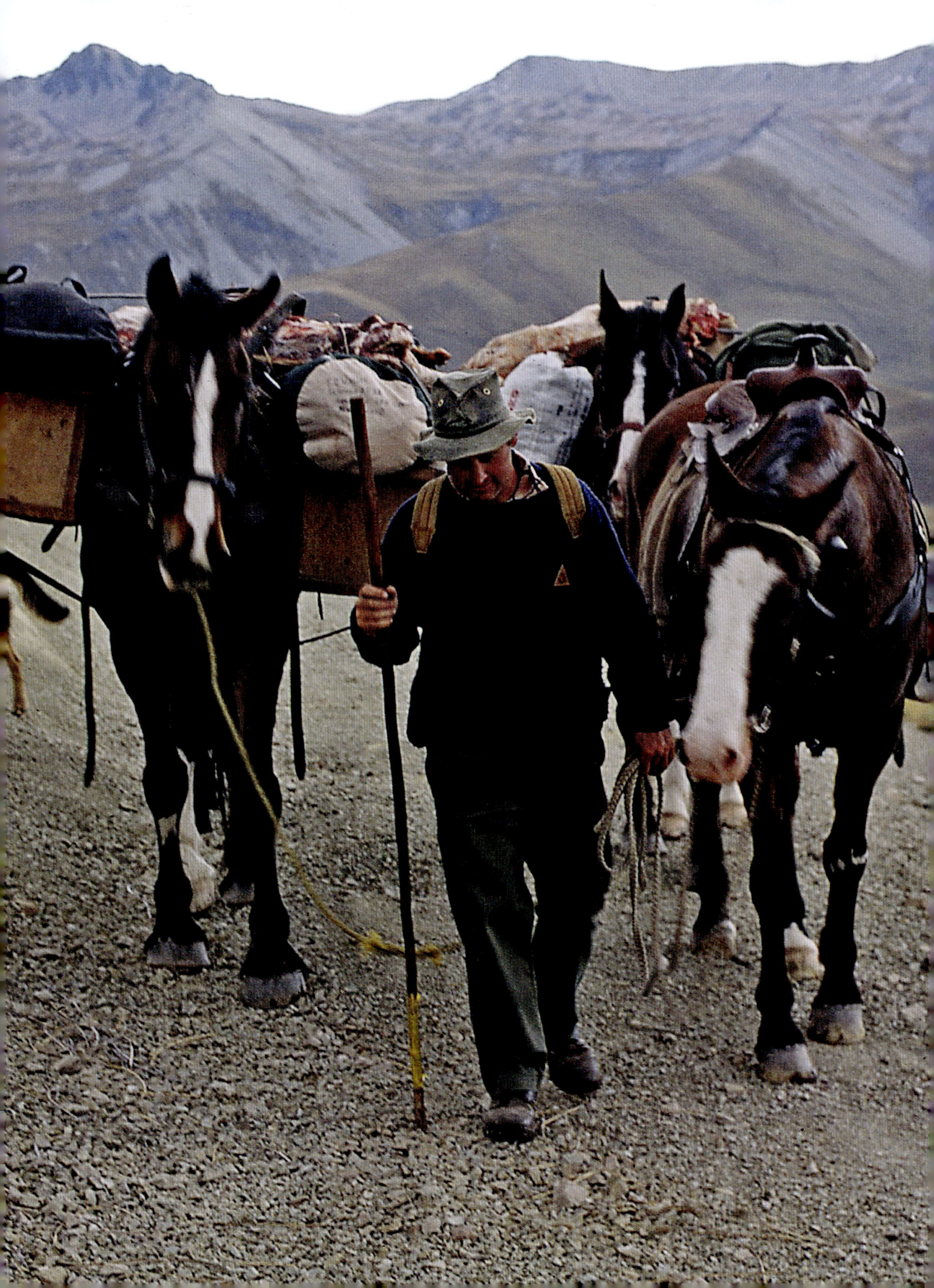

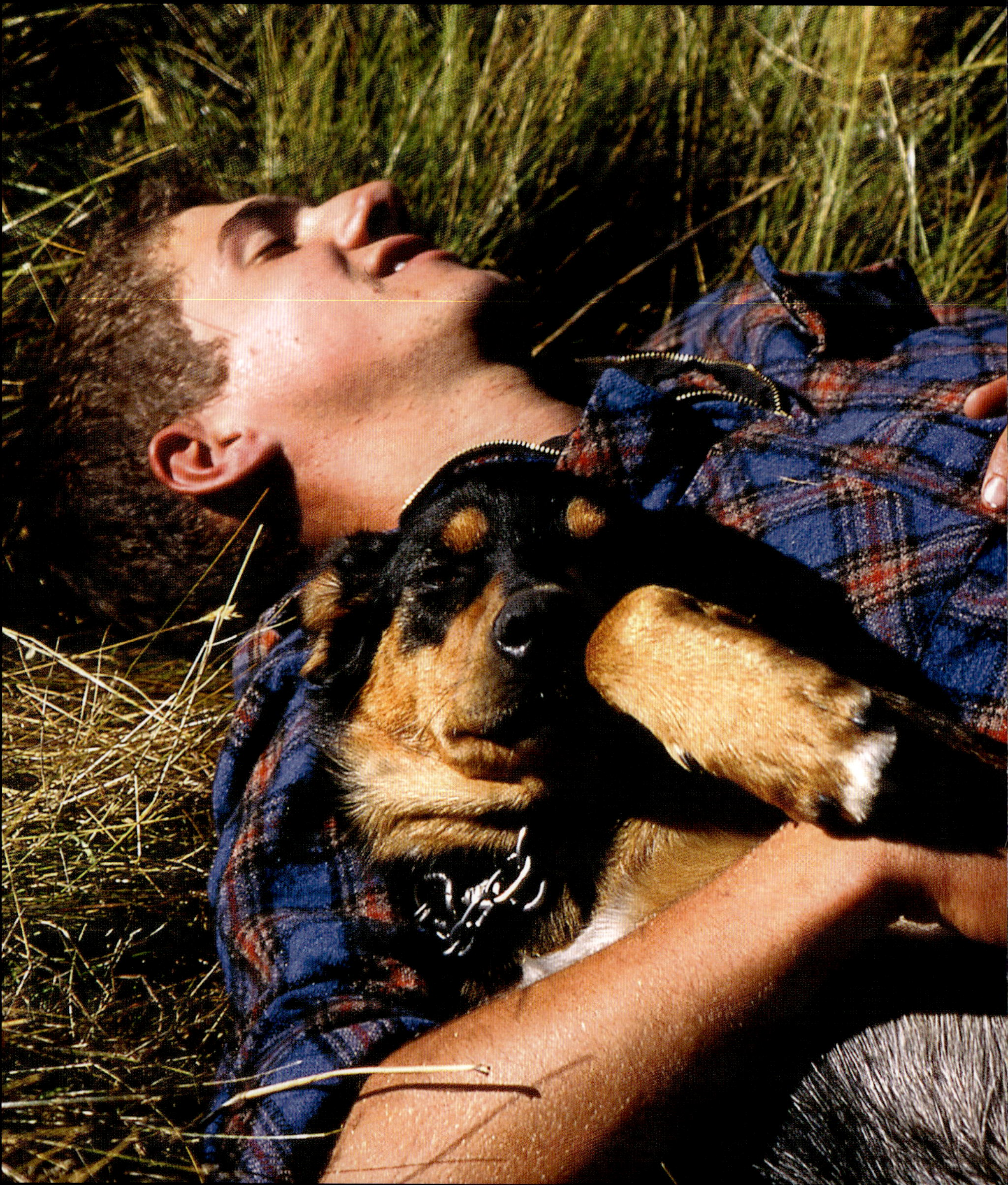

← ← **FAR LEFT**
Guy Martin rests up with his favourite dog.

← **LEFT**
Neroli Prouting, tough as anyone on the muster beat.

↑ **PREVIOUS SPREAD, LEFT TO RIGHT**
Chris O'Donnell gives the packhorses a spell at the Bullock Bow.

Chris O'Donnell leads his own mount and the two packhorses at the Bullock Bow and near the end of the three day muster.

→ **CLOCKWISE**

End the of muster; from left, Neroli with her Foxy, Laurie, Bruce Murcott, Alf Wallis and Guy Martin calling his dog.

Musterers and dogs head for the Rangitata Valley.

Welcome ride for the musterers and their dogs; Guy Martin fastening the tailgate of the ute, Neroli (second from right) standing on the tray.

Well-trained lone packhorse with two dogs for company heads for the Bullock Bow, on the last day of the muster.

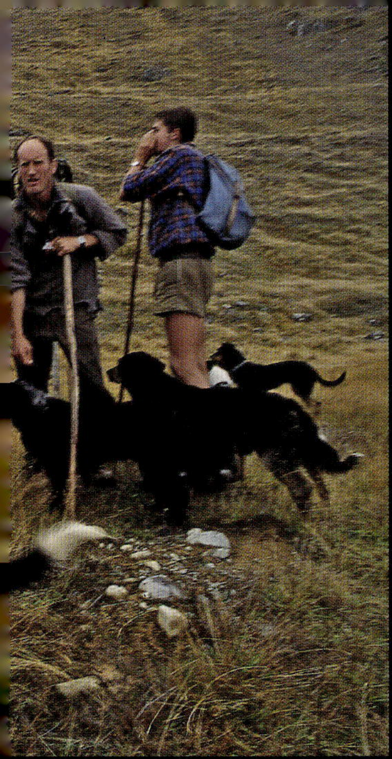

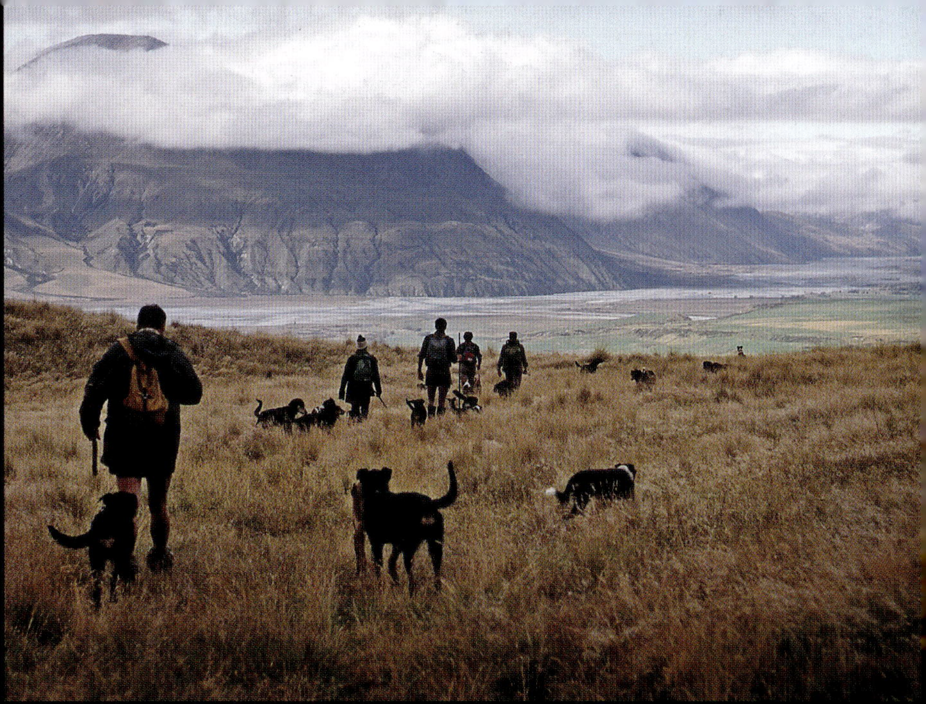

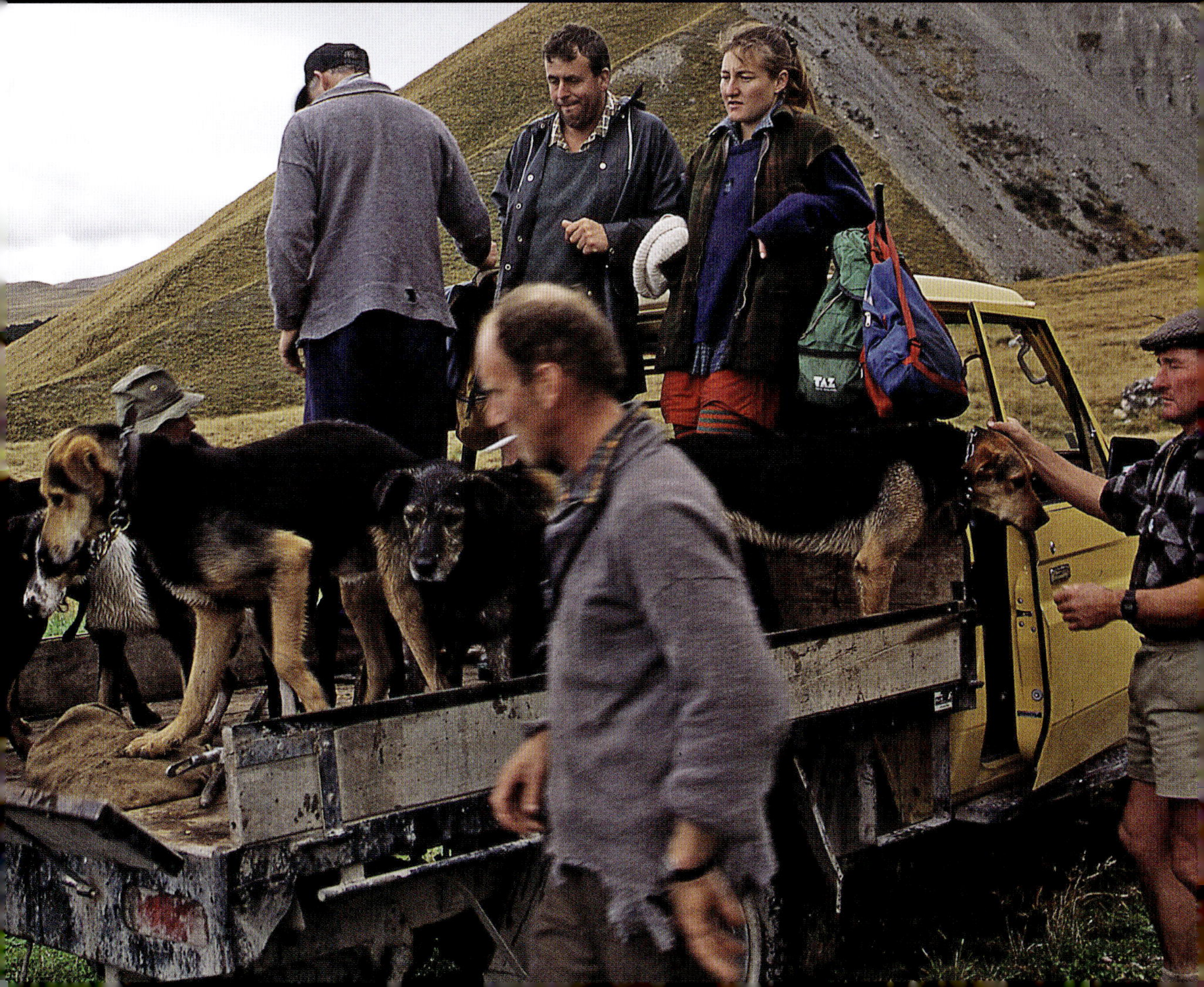
TAZ

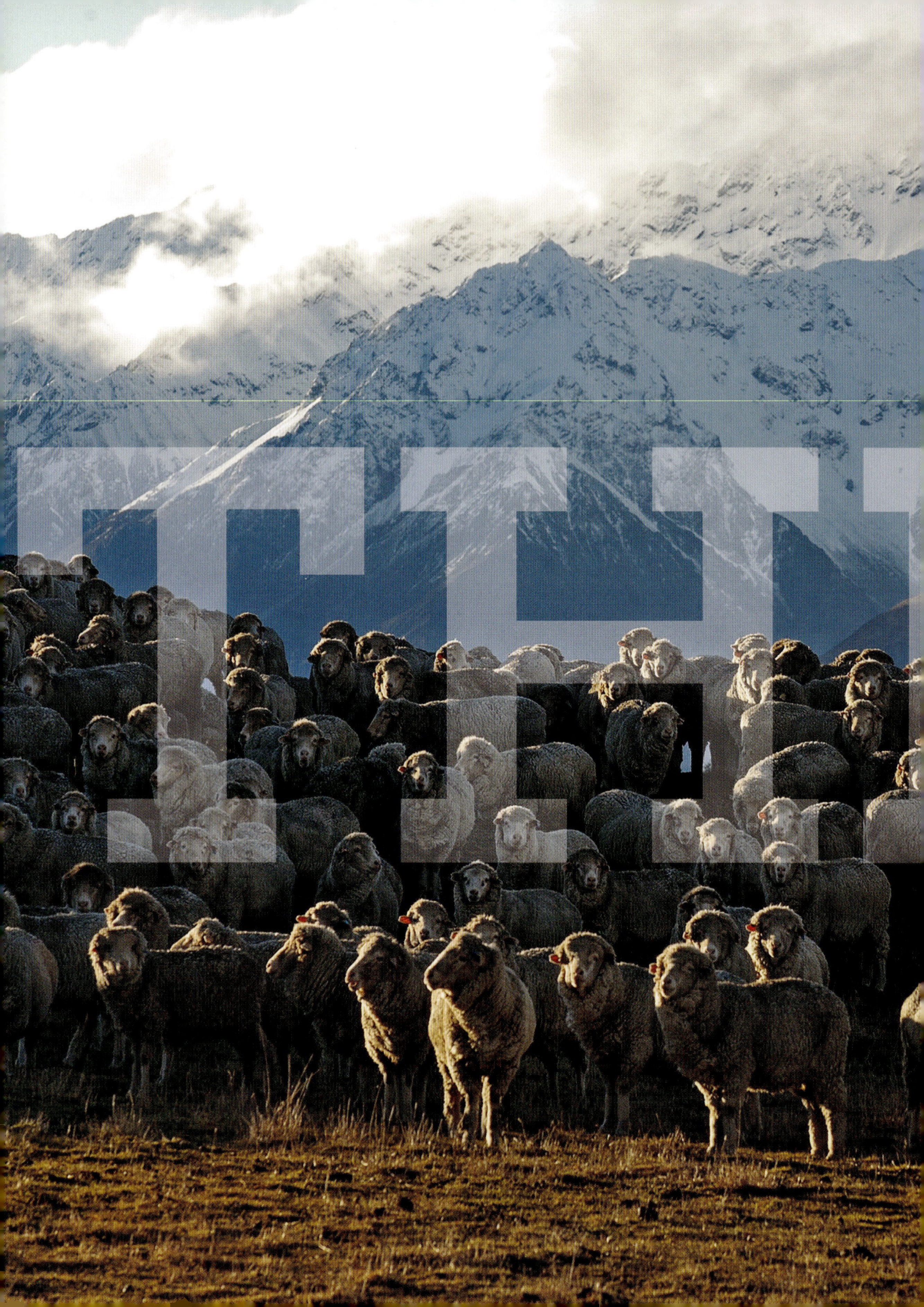

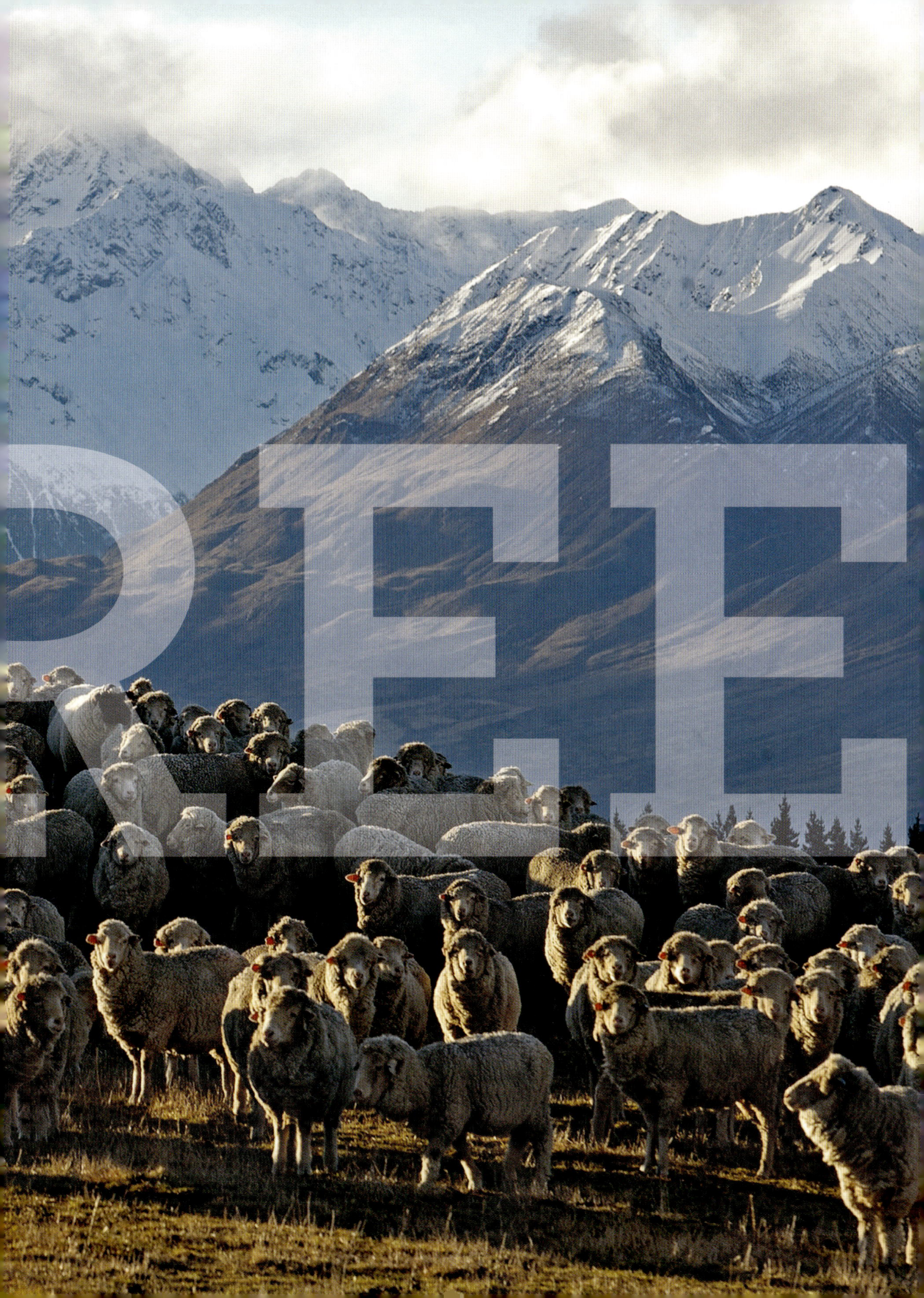

ACHILLES • THE TWO THUMB RANGE • D'ARCHIAC • CROOKED SPUR • HOGGET • THE GROWLER • BRABAZON • NEUTRAL SPUR • CLYDE RIVER • ROCKY RIDGE • BLACK MOUNTAINS • LITTLE SPUR • FINLAYS • FORBES RIVER • BIG BUSH • BLACK BIRCH STREAM • TOP DOWNS • BULLOCK BOW SADDLE • BALACLAVA BASINS • EXETER PEAK • SINCLAIR RANGE • FOREST CREEK • INKERMAN • THE ROCKS • MOUNT SINCLAIR • SUGARLOAF • MOUNT HOPE

SAMUEL BUTLER WAS the first man to make a profit from Mesopotamia. Some of his successors made money, and some did not. That has always been the way of things, not just at Mesopotamia but with all high country stations. But Mesopotamia was spectacularly broke when the first generation of Proutings came along.

Absentee owners had proliferated since Butler, and they did the station no good at all; and Butler, Laurie Prouting noted, was only on the place four years. 'So Mesopotamia never had a fair go.'

The last of those absentee owners were Sir William and Lady Nosworthy. Nowadays it is the fashion for wealthy people to buy into a high country station and build a house with a fine view. The Nosworthys were of a different generation. Sir William was the Member of Parliament for mid-Canterbury and Minister of Agriculture. When they stayed at Mesopotamia they lived in a little cottage, more of a hut really, on the terrace. It later became the first schoolroom on the station.

Sir William was nicknamed the Baron of Mesopotamia, although the title belied his nature: he was known on the station as a nice old bloke who would always invite callers in for a cup of tea. He could be droll, too. David McLeod was a musterer on the station then and later wrote of Sir William in his book *Many a Glorious Morning*. A big wether had escaped from a shearer and was jumping around the woolshed trying to get out when it met the Minister around a wool bale and made him jump too. 'He don't like these damn government men, does he?' said Sir William.

The MP fared no better than most of his predecessors. This was tough country in every sense, a rampant river, unforgiving land and harsh climate. None of them showed any respect for the Minister's standing. A year after he took over in 1917 the winter was bitter. He lost more than half his flock, some 11,000 sheep dying in the snow.

The disaster was followed by a plague of rabbits. Sheep rescued from the snow virtually starved to death because the rabbits had eaten everything to the roots. Stock losses were enormous. The surviving flock was halved, then dwindled to barely more than the 3000 Butler ran at the station's birth.

Mesopotamia eventually managed to control its rabbits and build up its stock numbers, only to be brought to its knees again by the Great Depression of the early 1930s. Plagued by storms, rabbits, absentee owners and the world economy, the property never recovered. By 1939 Mesopotamia was bankrupt. It went into receivership and the National Bank appointed Bob Buick, a one-legged World War I veteran, as supervisor.

Malcolm Prouting senior worked at Buick's Clent Hills Station on the other side of the Rangitata River. Malcolm went there when he was just fourteen years old. He had no money and little education. 'His parents never had the coin to keep him in school,' his son Laurie explained. 'That was the way things went in those days.'

Malcolm's determination was to overcome what most would see as a crippling start. He quickly became Buick's right-hand man. He married Thelma Gifkins whose parents, Frank and Maggie, owned a wool scour at Mount Somers down the valley. Thelma worked at Clent Hills too. Both of them were teenagers. They went on to have eight children, six boys and two girls. A portrait of Thelma painted some fifty years later depicted a slight smile and a level stare, the look of a woman who had faced a lifetime of hard work with grace and determination. Certainly she needed them, and courage too.

Buick had a great deal of faith in his young protégé. He made Malcolm Prouting manager of Mesopotamia in 1943 and the two of them set about improving the property: in essence, wiping out rabbits. Clearly, however, both Buick and the National Bank had a problem. Buick did not want the property. He had Clent Hills to run, and a young family to look after. The bank just wanted what all banks want, its money.

By now World War II was ending, and there were no takers for a down-at-heel high country station. Laurie: 'No one was interested in buying the place because most of those who would've been interested were still trying to get their feet on the ground after the war.'

Fate stepped in, lined up Malcolm as the right man, right place, right time. 'Bob Buick happened to be at the National Bank after yet another person had been to look at the place,' remembers Laurie. 'Bear in mind there was no homestead. There was a rough creek to cross, Forest Creek, which was more of a river than a creek, and no road from there on. So the property was semi-isolated, there wasn't a building on the place that was any good, it was derelict. Bob was a man of action. He said to the bank, "I know who's going to buy that place. Malcolm Prouting. The deal's done."

'Then he went home and told Malcolm. Malcolm was going to ask what he would do for money. Then he thought, "Bob knows how much money I've got." So he didn't. The end result was that the bank bankrolled him for the lot, £27,000. A lot of money then. Huge.

'The bank manager came up to the station. He had his wife with him and Bob had been talking about this Malcolm Prouting, a man who knew what he was doing. They met and the manager said, "But this is only a boy!"'

SAMUEL BUTLER WAS twenty-four when he founded Mesopotamia. Malcolm Prouting was twenty-two when he took it over in 1945. The two shared few attributes outside courage and determination. Eighty-five years separated them. Malcolm never played the piano, and he sired eight children. Butler never married, had no children. But Malcolm must have felt as Samuel Butler did when he stood on that wide landscape and imagined the job ahead of him.

He enjoyed some advantages over Butler. Even at a young age he was an experienced farmer. He knew the property, for he had managed Mesopotamia before he owned it.

By then Mesopotamia Station was most of a century old, no longer the raw country Butler had confronted. Yet Butler was better off in some ways. He owned his farm outright, paid for in cash. Malcolm had no equity in the station and owed a huge debt to the bank. Butler had to wrest a farm from the wild, but he did not have to deal with a pestilence of rabbits, nor one of bankers. Or, for that matter, a plague of absentee owners. Malcolm believed no one could get the best out of a place unless he owned it. When people asked him later in life his recipe for success, he'd say: 'Just take note, I was the first owner-manager of Mesopotamia since Samuel Butler.'

Prouting and Butler shared the one essential quality: neither baulked at hard work. By then Mesopotamia spread over more than 41,000 hectares of mountains, river flats, valleys, spurs and high terraces, a panoply of the huge, the vast and the truly astonishing.

The Proutings ruled this empire from a house called Rowans, originally a dingy four-room musterers' hut. They added a porch and a wash-house, piped clean fresh water down from the spring which was part of the reason Butler chose the site for his own homestead and which has never dried up. An outside toilet, no electricity, but the young family was thankful: they had running water. This modest affair became the Mesopotamia homestead.

Still standing in its small terrace off to one side of the new homestead, it is clad in vertical sheets of corrugated iron and is designed from the inside out, with a wide entranceway for boots and coats and farm paraphernalia leading to the big kitchen where Malcolm's burgeoning family could gather around the massive stove. Its iron walls and planked floors have endured. It has a solid feel about it, as if butting into the next half-century.

Laurie still remembers life there fondly. 'It was lovely being raised like that, walking around with candles. In mustering huts they shove a candle in an old beer bottle or something, but they could always fall out and set fire to everything, so we had the proper candlestick holders. We never ever used the Tilley lamp, we were more into those kerosene Aladdin lamps, which were quieter.

'We thought things were kind of modern when we got the four-gallon kerosene tin with a wee pump on it so we could fill the lamps and so on. Now we weren't spilling it everywhere, we had a hand pump. They were fun times and I think our parents enjoyed the fun as well. Quite often at night we couldn't do a hang of a lot and there was no such thing as my father reading the newspaper. It only arrived once a week and then the mail cart only came to within five miles of the homestead because there was no bridge over Forest Creek and that was considered the end of the road. We were kind of cut off. So we often played cards at night, Happy Families, and we didn't want anyone else to see our cards so we'd have barricades, chairs piled up and we were all in our own little dens.

'And the six-monthly haircutting business and Dad with the old squeezer clippers and we all had to line up and get shorn. And half the time the things were slow-moving and they'd get stuck in your hair. We never bothered how we looked because we were never on show, or very seldom. To go out was a big deal, it might have been once in two months before our parents were brave enough to throw us in the car and we were never too sure whether we could get home again or not because Forest Creek could carry a lot of water. But it was an hour's drive to the nearest village, Peel Forest, and we'd be bored to tears after the first half-mile and we'd start to play up. Don or Frank would sit on me and say "Look at that out the window," and I'd be struggling to get up and see and you can imagine the row.

'We hardly knew what Christmas was. If our parents didn't say anything it would almost sneak by. We never knew it was Christmas, we had no idea. Sometimes there might be a toy. But the toys we treasured were the ones our father made for us, an old nail box tipped over with wheels on it and that was a truck. Don't remember a lot of birthday parties. We went out for the odd picnic in the bush, harnessed up the horse and cart. Our grandmother was pretty good with a horse. Most boys love making fires and we could make a fire and boil the billy.'

> **He looked out of his window, high above the Rangitata River in its purple cradle of hills. Mesopotamia was hidden behind the bulk of Coal Hill yet he saw every detail of it. The station accounted for his entire life.**

He looked out of his window, high above the Rangitata River in its purple cradle of hills. Mesopotamia was hidden behind the bulk of Coal Hill yet he saw every detail of it. The station accounted for his entire life. 'The boys tended to do boy stuff and the girls, girls' stuff. We might have to dry the dishes, we had our chores to do, but we were normally out doing things, milking the cow, trapping rabbits, which was highly encouraged. We'd have loved to be able to shoot the rabbits but that wasn't allowed.

'Everything was done by hand, the washing on the washboard and the old tub, always the coal range. My mother baked bread in the coal range, we certainly never went hungry. Everything was purchased in bulk, there'd be a whole box of dates, for example, crated up from Iran or Iraq, a huge box of dried apricots, big boxes of sultanas and currants. We knew where they were kept. There was a shed that was meant to be vermin-proofed down by the cookhouse with a big bolt on the door although it was never padlocked, and if it was we certainly knew how to get into it, and we could lock ourselves in there and feast away.

'Our mother would have at least a couple of months' food on hand, with the family growing bit by bit. The older members of the family helped with the younger. Having someone else helping sounds easy but it was always another mouth to feed, someone else to look after. Everyone was living at close quarters. Quite often there was a cook in the cookhouse and there'd be somebody who wasn't getting on with the cook. If my father said it once he said it a hundred times, that he didn't mind the hard work of farming, it was the diplomacy thing he had to deal with. Mum was a very placid person. I never saw her get upset with anybody and I never saw her in an argument. She might voice a quiet opinion sometimes that someone wasn't pulling their weight. She was very stoic. She'd never get ratty with us. Our father would punish us but Mum never laid a hand on us. When my younger siblings were growing up, they'd be sitting at the table and ask Mum to get them a drink of water, and I'd think, how dare they, but Mum would get them a glass of water. She looked after us without any apparent fuss. We used to be trying, I know. Dad would have more control.

'We always milked the cow and we always had a big vegetable garden, so we were living off the land as much as we could. When there was a married couple in the cookhouse, generally the wife would be the cook and the husband the tractor driver, general handyman, gardener and the rest of it. There was never a tractor on the place in those early days but later when we had one and we were, say, drilling in a paddock, we'd run a few peas, and carrots, and those things that didn't need much attention.

'My mother must have been one of a kind to go out in that era, so remote, and I can't say I ever saw her troubled. I never saw her weeping. Even in later times when first Allan was killed and then Peter, Mum was terribly upset, distraught, but she never let us see her weeping.

'I don't think I ever saw a disagreement between our parents. Our father was kind of strict, we had to toe the line. The station ran with quite a few people at times. There'd always seem to be two married couples warring, or helpers in the house, and Mum would have to be the peacemaker. She would put up with everything.'

PHOTOGRAPHS OF MALCOLM show a dark-haired man with a resolute look about him, not tall but forceful. Something in the shape

↗ CLOCKWISE FROM TOP LEFT

Malcolm and Thelma's wedding photograph, 1939. *Prouting Family Collection*

Young Laurie Prouting with a four-legged friend. *Prouting Family Collection*

From left, Frank, Ray and Laurie Prouting sitting on the boundary gate at Forest Creek, 1949. *Prouting Family Collection*

MESOPOTAMIA
STATION

of his body, in the square way he faces the camera, speaks of strength and confidence, a man sure of himself and his ability to take crises head-on; just as well, for there were plenty of crises. His first winter in 1945 was the worst in Canterbury since 1918, its consequences including a plague of kea, or mountain parrots. The birds killed around a thousand sheep.

With nothing between them and ruin except their own enterprise Malcolm and Thelma went to work on their new property with the farmers' determination to do things well. They took on the rabbits, the scourge of the high country since they first spread through the valleys in the 1880s. When the Proutings moved onto the station the valley was alive with them.

Six decades later Laurie still marvels. 'My father was a very good strategist. Between Bob Buick and himself they figured out a way of killing the rabbits. It wasn't until they dealt the rabbits a mighty blow that they could turn the station around. He changed tactics. Until then, guys were paid for the skins and they were virtually farming the rabbits. They wouldn't shoot a doe, because she was their bread and butter. They were in clover as long as there were thousands of rabbits. Bob and Malcolm used phosphorus poison but the rabbits were dying an agonising death, squalling in pain, their stomachs almost literally burned out.'

The rabbits rapidly became bait-shy. Some farmers used arsenic to poison them, but it was dangerous. Arsenic came as a heavy powder and looked like flour, except that it weighed heavy as lead. Arsenic was cumulative, and enduring.

'A lot of guys smoked roll-your-owns in those days, rolling them with the same hands that handled arsenic. They got very careless.' Malcolm switched to strychnine. 'They'd smear a carrot with paste and cut it so there was only a bit left on the carrot but enough to bowl the rabbit. Both strychnine and arsenic were savage on secondary or collateral kills.

'These days everyone wants to ban 1080, but when you've messed around with those other poisons 1080 is just a wonder poison. It is biodegradable, it will break down. Arsenic won't. Even the old strychnine bottles were a pretty blue but very dangerous; a lot of bottle collectors have them but if they handle the bottle and lick their finger it's very dangerous still; it never breaks down. So they kept changing their poisons and got the rabbits down.'

He paused, looking up the valley, remembering when the orderly landscape once seemed to move under the sheer weight of their numbers.

'I started school at the age of four in 1943. Mum was never a scholar. She persevered with Frank and Don, teaching them by correspondence, but when I came along she wasn't going to teach three of us, so we all went to school at

Peel Forest. The first time I went to school I got a new school bag. We each got one. It seemed to be twice as big as I was. Our first job was to fill the bags with carrots. We each had our own carrot line to do before we went to school. We gave the rabbits three feeds of carrots before the carrots were poisoned with strychnine. We were never allowed to use the poison. As much as we wanted to.

'In places where the rabbits were thickest they built a pen. Everyone went through the scrub with tins making a noise and we actually mustered the rabbits into the pen, and clubbed them to death. Rabbits were four deep. By the time I got old enough to have a rifle they'd virtually broken the back of it and wiped out the rabbits. We used to take portable yards and put up a pen for tailing lambs, and the crucial part was when we had to get behind the ewes and lambs with lengths of scrim; everyone had to be on the mark, and right in the middle of it this a rabbit leapt up.

'My father bent down and picked up a stone and from ten metres away he hit the rabbit and killed it dead. And we stopped momentarily in awe. *Holy Nora!* Even in the middle of a crucial job he dealt to the rabbit. That's how passionate he was about holding his ground. By the end of 1948 the back of the rabbits was broken. The rabbiters still living were, to put it mildly, pissed off because he'd put them out of a job.'

Malcolm turned to other things. The old stable was exhausted. He built a new one in 1948. Corrugated iron, the New Zealand farming staple, was in short supply following World War II. Instead they used old 44-gallon drums, cutting them open, flattening the drums with a maul then nailing them to the framework as cladding.

When Malcolm's grandson, also named Malcolm, became the third generation of Proutings to run the station, he had to replace some of the stable's steel sheets. He found some drums and cut them open easily enough. But how did you flatten a piece of steel carefully rolled into a cylinder and designed to stay that way? The answer was, with great difficulty, bashing the curling steel with a maul for hours. His grandfather flattened dozens of them.

For the framework Malcolm senior used mountain beech, unmilled, the trees in the round hauled out of the station's beech forests. They went as hard as brick if kept out of the weather and stand today strong as ever, apparently impervious. They mended fences and built new ones and replaced buildings and tried to tame the river. Who knows what might have happened then?

Perhaps unending toil and sheer cussedness might have had the legendary happy ending and carried them through to their just reward. Possibly. But something else rolled into the countryside and made New Zealand farmers rich: The 1951 Korean wool boom. The Korean War created a huge demand for wool. American foreign policy led to one of the greatest economic booms in New Zealand's history. The price of wool shot up to a pound per pound, or about four dollars and 50 cents a kilogram; in today's figures, more than 60 dollars a kilogram. In 2011, the best year for wool in two decades, carpet wool prices rose to some seven dollars a kilogram.

Fine wool produced by high country merinos commands a premium; even so, rough arithmetic shows why, sixty years previously, the worried frowns on farmers' faces as they opened their bank statements changed to happy smiles. The whole of the country revelled in the countryside's new wealth. The wool boom spawned a new national saying: 'On the sheep's back.'

High country farmers were especially pleased. Accepted wisdom now says that, but for the boom, most stations in the country would have gone broke. Mesopotamia's 1947 accounts show that the station, and its young owners, were struggling. Then the good times rolled.

Malcolm found himself falling into the farming equivalent of a warm bath. In only a few years the Proutings went from penury to prosperity. By the early 1950s the unbelievable had happened: Malcolm had almost paid off the farm. Mesopotamia prospered, bloomed. Young Laurie, sent to school down the road at Peel Forest and living with his grandmother during the week, learned to expect something new when he went home each weekend: a new road to the station from Forest Creek, eight kilometres long, built by station staff at the station's expense, and a huge improvement on the old track.

Malcolm was a classic farmer. Before he built a new homestead, he reasoned, he must have a decent woolshed. By then Malcolm's father-in-law, Frank Gifkins, was broke. He came to work on the station. 'Frank was keen on his spot of Scotch. He lived in a wee hut above the cookhouse and he'd work away all day. He lived on the station until he died. Our mother looked after him. Our grandmother lived down in Peel Forest. They weren't apart, but he was bundled off up to Messie to get to work. He was a good worker, a good carpenter, and he was instrumental when they were building the woolshed.'

Malcolm bought what was left of Gifkins' wool scour, pulled the iron off it and used it to roof the woolshed. To mill the timber he shifted an entire sawmill up the valley from Arundel. It was quite a contraption, powered by

> **Malcolm found himself falling into the farming equivalent of a warm bath. In only a few years the Proutings went from penury to prosperity. By the early 1950s the unbelievable had happened: Malcolm had almost paid off the farm.**

pulleys and an old tractor with a hole in the radiator so that the millers had to keep a hose running into it all day.

They cut trees on the property, ran them through the sawmill and used the timber straight off the saw. The framework, however, was Malcolm's trusted unmilled mountain beech. The woolshed was huge for its time, designed with ingenuity and flair. The station provided not just the timber, but the labour too. At night the station hands finished work on the farm, tied up their dogs, picked up their hammers and went down to the woolshed.

Then came the prize: a new homestead. A grand two-storey place rose on the terrace, presiding over the collection of cottages that made Mesopotamia a village as much as a farm. The Arundel sawmiller brought his mill back up the valley. The station bought a traction engine. Malcolm hired a Geraldine builder. They did not go far for their raw materials.

'They hawked logs out of the bush for the homestead,' said Laurie, admiringly. He envied their freedom, their ability to charge ahead unobstructed. 'Those were the things you could do in those days. Hawked them out and down into the mill. So that timber never left the property either. They went way up the river with a tractor and trailer and cut totara trees down. On forest reserve. The Department of Conservation? What a laugh. Everything was from the station apart from the flooring which was rimu and bought from the West Coast. I was coming on ten years old. Away up there, up the river, was centuries away. Now I do it in a helicopter and it's a matter of minutes.'

The homestead was a grand place, and must have seemed all the more so to a family used to living in an old musterers' cottage. It stood as evenly balanced as a child's drawing; a big bay window in the front, looking over wide lawns and gardens towards the river and mountains, the main thoroughfare through the back door like any farm homestead.

This homestead, however, had unusual problems to overcome: its remoteness, the nearest shop hours away with the often-wild Forest Creek to cross. The Ashburton architect, said Anne Prouting, Laurie's wife, insisted on cupboards only to head height. 'Mum wanted cupboards to the ceiling but he wouldn't do it. He didn't want Mum to be standing on a stool. But he didn't realise that when you're living in the outback you're depending on things like preserves, which could have gone up the top.'

Yet the house had a wonderful innovation: electricity. Malcolm installed its own powerplant. The station had not long had a telephone line then; electricity lines to the far reaches of the Rangitata were still just a doodle on some power board engineer's pad.

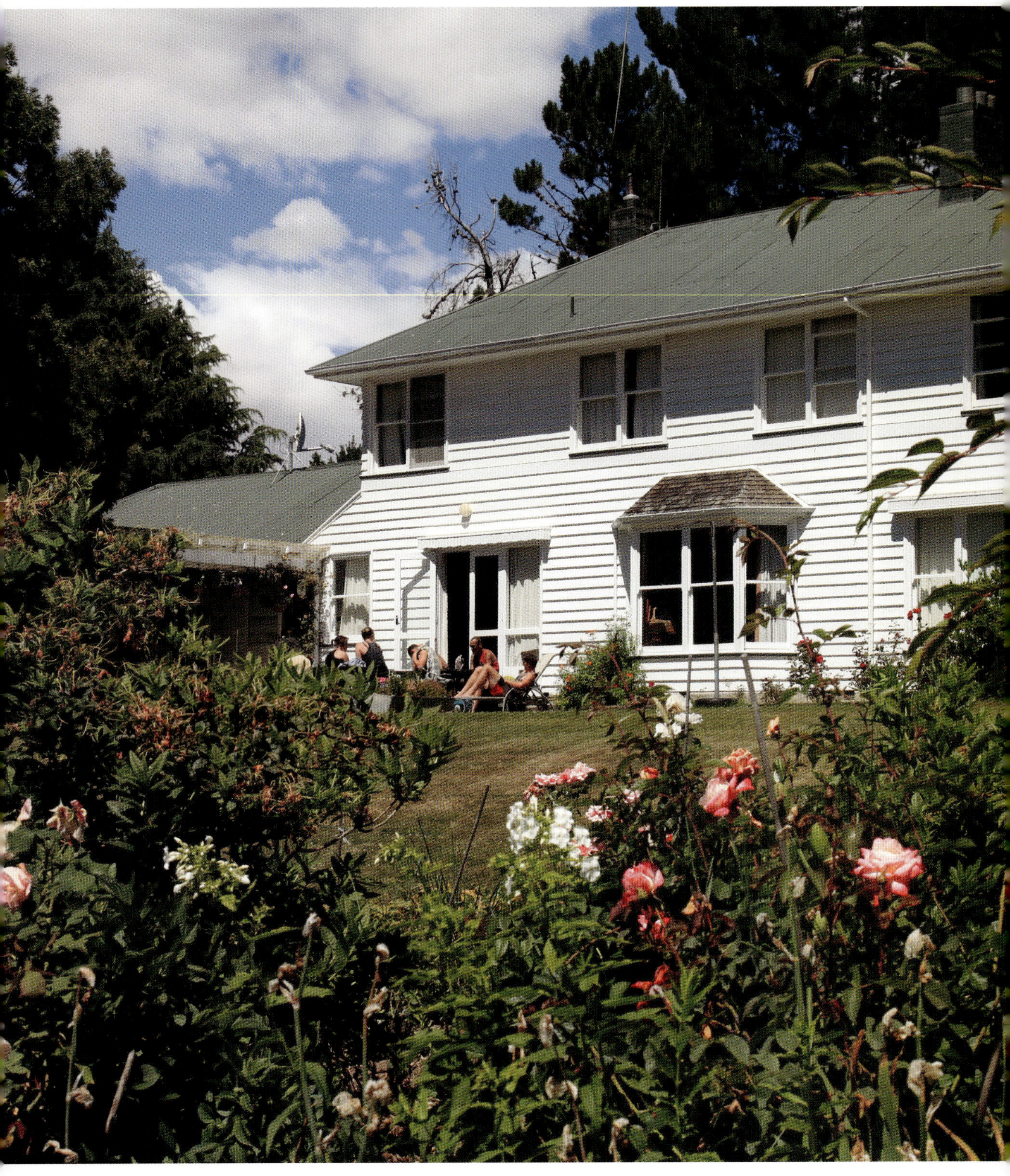

The young Thelma proudly moved into her new home with her burgeoning family. Laurie remembered the day life changed from the Rowans routine. 'When the big house was built in 1953 there were still the three youngest to come along. It was an entirely new experience. We had to smarten up and try to keep it as a new house. We weren't allowed to saunter in with our boots on, that's for sure.'

Malcolm turned to the next item on his list: Forest Creek. It could turn nasty in a moment and lock in everyone on the Mesopotamia side, especially in the spring thaw when, of course, the station was shearing its mighty flock and needed to get the bales out.

Carting wool was always a daunting job. At first the bales were loaded onto massive drays which were pulled through the Rangitata River by horse teams to Mount Potts and from there by the road on the north side of the river to the scour at Mount Somers. An old dray driver, Charlie Dunstan, wrote of the journey across the Rangitata River into the Ashburton Gorge on his eight-horse wagon as 'a hazardous and lonely occupation', and he remembered Ecclesiastes, chapter four, verse ten: ' . . . woe to him that is alone when he falls, for he has not another to help him up'.

Until the early 1950s, even in an advancing age of better roads and powerful engines, trucks loaded as many bales as they could get on their decks without breaking something and set off in convoy so they could tow each other through Forest Creek. For more everyday traffic, an old World War II Bren carrier sat beside the creek for the sole purpose of pulling vehicles through it. The machine had no battery, and to crank it up the marooned vehicle had to donate its own battery. And even in those days vandals went about their work: once they smashed every conceivable item on the old carrier, even the china spark plugs.

One year the road through the creek simply disappeared,

← LEFT
The Mesopotamia Station homestead built by Malcolm and Thelma Prouting in the early 1950s. It succeeded the old musterers' cottage they had lived in previously.

washed out in a flood. Malcolm hired contractors to repair it. But he needed a bridge, urgently. The local council refused to help, so he built one himself. No one thinks much about bridges. They cross rivers; drivers speed over them without so much as a glance at the way they are built or a thought for the unruly water below. Oh, it's a nuisance on the rare occasions when they are washed away, or being repaired, but heavy machinery rolls in and fixes everything up and soon they're back to normal.

Among roading engineers bridge-building is an art, and an arcane one. A bridge is a highly complicated affair. Yet Malcolm simply did what he always did, got on with the job. Christchurch city was then pulling up its tramlines, a decision it later regretted but which Malcolm found useful. The old tramlines were sunk into the creek bed as bridge piles. He hired machinery to put them in, but after that, as Laurie said, 'It was a station effort from go to woe. He bought a Caterpillar bulldozer and did all the

> **My father never walked around with his hands in his pockets. If he caught us with our hands in our pockets we'd get a rev-up. You didn't do that sort of thing. He never slouched, never leaned on a post, never was without something to do . . . He treated everybody with respect. I liked him very much. I loved him.**

work. My father was still unsure about spending money. He still considered himself pretty poor. So the stringers were all cut out of the bush, unmilled timber; they all had to be peeled; and the bridge was 100 metres long. Take all the bark off, dry them. We wouldn't refuse our father, that's for sure. He was fair. A hard taskmaster. He wouldn't expect us to work all the time but if we were playing and he or anyone else was working we weren't to interfere: "If you're not going to help, don't hinder. Get out of the road." We took that as a very clear message. We were usually helping.'

At last the bridge was finished. It was a great day in the station's history. Now a car or truck could drive all the way to the station without the drama of serious creeks or rivers to ford. People could set off from Peel Forest confident of getting through to Mesopotamia. As if on cue, the wool wave rolled, swelled, roared, broke. Prices plummeted. The boom days were over, yet the station still prospered.

Malcolm remained a towering figure in his sons' lives. More than 30 years after his death Laurie's regard for his father borders on reverence. 'My father never walked around with his hands in his pockets. If he caught us with our hands in our pockets we'd get a rev-up. You didn't do that sort of thing. He never slouched, never leaned on a post, never was without something to do. He was always busy. He was always very fair with visitors, hunters, trampers. He treated everybody with respect. I liked him very much. I loved him. All of us had the highest respect for our father. If Dad gave his word it would be done.

'And our mother. I wonder how she coped so well with all of us. She always seemed to be going into the home to have another child and we used to hate it when our bossy auntie came to look after us. My parents had very high moral standards. They weren't churchgoers. Dad said once, "If I ate an apple which didn't belong to me it would stick in my craw." Neither were teetotallers but they were the next step away from it. Mum would have a sherry at Christmas but that was it. Dad said, "You're a fool to drink whisky before you're fifty years old and you're a fool not to drink it after you're fifty."'

IN THE 1950s a new development changed the face of the country: aerial top-dressing. Aircraft fitted with hoppers could drop cheap fertiliser on even the hardest, most inaccessible land in the high country. The Proutings saw its potential immediately, not just for spreading fertiliser but for seeding and sowing too.

Early top-dressing pilots were often dashing characters. Certainly they impressed the young Laurie Prouting. They did more than that, for Laurie's life was to be shaped by flying. 'Those guys started in Tiger Moths and Austers and Piper Cubs; that really fascinated me. I remember a guy called Balfour, a stock agent. We heard that he flew down the main street of Oamaru upside down under the power wires. He'd never admit it. But I think he might have been right way up doing the same thing.'

Mesopotamia reacted to top-dressing like a thirsty creature to water. Its 1200–1600 hectares of river flats and nearly 8100 hectares of downs took wing. 'You could see virtually every run the aircraft made. We were just bowling along. And once we began using selenium, what a difference to our stock that made. Our stock health improved, we had feed to burn, we put on more cattle.'

Love of flying infected the family. Four sons, Laurie, Frank, Don and Peter, took to the air. The big family had started to transform itself into a farming dynasty. With his son Peter, Malcolm farmed the home property, Mesopotamia. He freeholded some of his leased land, and later carved off blocks big enough to be stations themselves, and gave them to two of his sons. Ray took Garondale Station, Don farmed Tui Station. Frank went north to Marlborough to farm in the Awatere Valley. The two girls, Valmai and Jennifer, married and left the farm for their own properties. Laurie moved into the mountains on the other side of the river and began farming Mount Arrowsmith Station.

Then, just as Mesopotamia seemed to have found a permanent spot on the crest of its wave, disaster struck. Young men, no matter what they do, take risks. Living on the edge is part of growing up. Six young men raised to meet life full-on, all of them used to taking risks, were a volatile mix. Allan, the second-youngest son, was killed in a car accident in 1974. He was eighteen.

Malcolm was devastated, but worse was to come. Peter, the youngest, had picked up the family passion for flying. He was sowing turnips on Mesopotamia, flying his Auster along the rising downs behind the homestead, when the aircraft's engine stopped. Dead.

Even some thirty years later Laurie's memory of that morning was vivid: 'Peter let the aircraft stall and it spun into the ground. He jettisoned the load, let the speed get back too far and tried to turn to get out of the rising ground where he was heading.'

The aeroplane spun out of the sky and buried itself in the stony ground virtually at his father Malcolm's feet. Peter was killed instantly. 'My father went down and got Peter out of the wreckage. He almost bust himself. Peter's crash helmet on impact had virtually decapitated him. Dad rang me and said, "I've got to tell you we lost Peter today." I can distinctly remember my next word. "Shit." I talked to Frank later. Funny, he said exactly the same. That happened on 6 February, Waitangi Day, 1980. A month and a half later, Dad got ill. Everybody was saying to him, "It's the shock."

'"No," he said, "I can understand shock. This is something different."

'Sure enough, he had leukaemia. They couldn't do anything about it. He was on the downhill run and he died in January the following year. He was sixty-three. A young sixty-three. Younger men had trouble keeping up with him.'

The cause of death was, officially, leukaemia. Laurie's own diagnosis went deeper: 'I'm certain the shock of Peter's death killed him.'

↗ TOP RIGHT
Malcolm Prouting Snr, 1964.

→ BOTTOM RIGHT
Malcolm and Thelma Proutings' gravestone in the tiny Upper Rangitata cemetery, surrounded by matagouri and not far from the river.

IN LOVING MEMORY OF
MALCOLM VELVIN PROUTING
LOVED HUSBAND OF THELMA
1917 – 1981
"GRIEVE NOT FOR HIS DEPARTURE,
BUT RATHER BE THANKFUL THAT HE EVER WAS"
THELMA MARJORIE PROUTING
1915 – 2004
"LIFE IS NOT MEASURED BY THE YEARS SHE LIVED
BUT THE LOVE SHE GAVE AND THE THINGS SHE DID"

→ RIGHT
Laurie Prouting in his Auster the day he rescued Peter Bush from the raging Rangitata River.
Prouting Family Collection

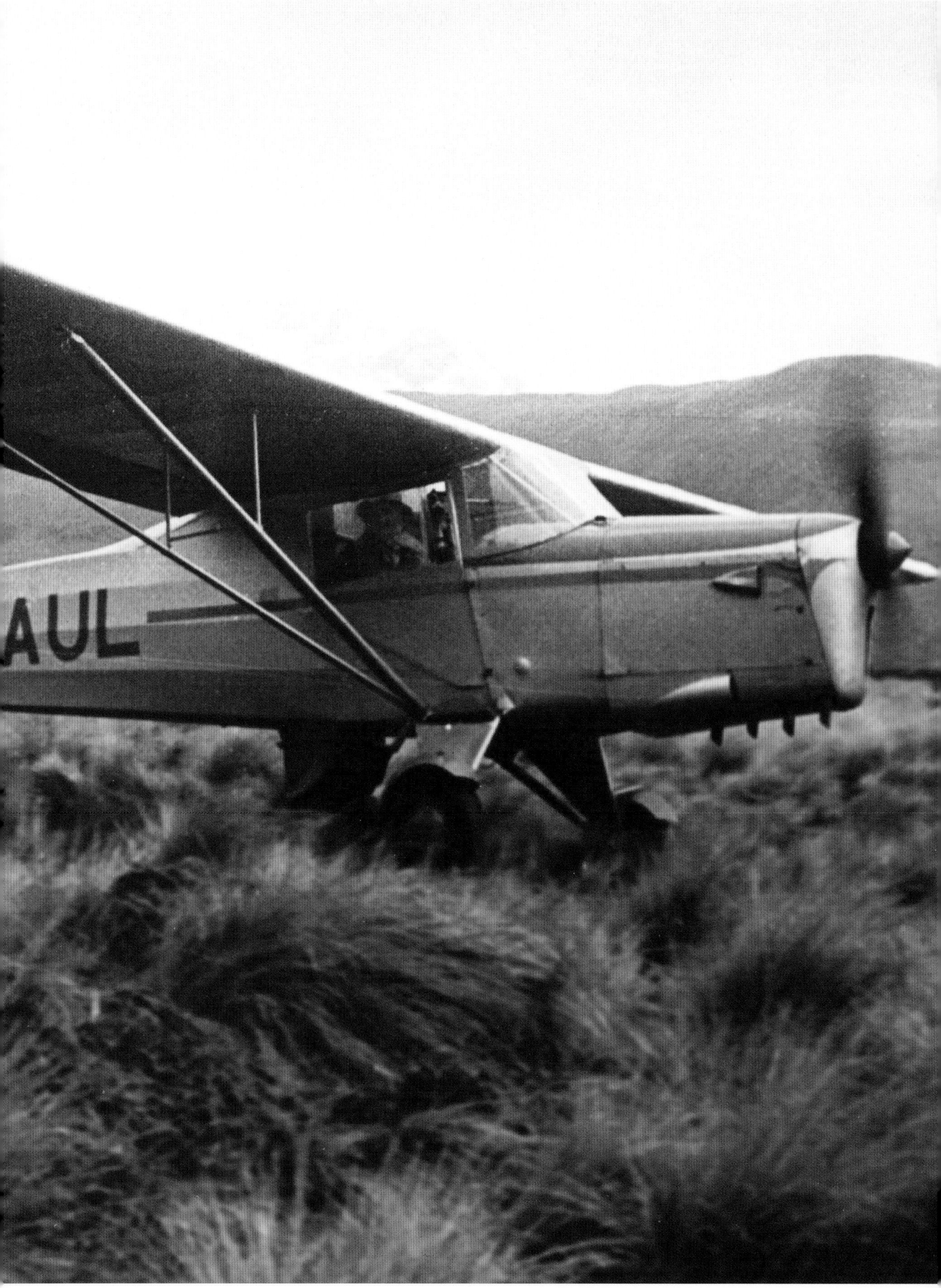
AUL

BUSHY COMES TO MESSIE

I knew Jack Acland from Mount Peel Station. He was chairman of the Wool Board and I did a lot of work for the board. It was 1970. The All Blacks were in South Africa. I was pretty keen on shooting and he said, 'Why don't you come down our way? One of the big stations down here is run by a good friend of mine, Malcolm Prouting.'

So Bob Hayman, Russell Stewart and I hired a Land Rover in Christchurch on a nor'west day in September. We called in to Mount Peel and Sir John and Lady Acland made us welcome. It was a bleak day but we bowled up the valley and asked Malcolm if we could go shooting; that Jack Acland suggested it. Malcolm kind of ran his eye over us. He said, 'One thing about it, Jack Acland does not run Mesopotamia. I do.' In a rather nice way.

Then he said, 'I think you've left your run too late. There's a nor'wester coming.'

But we wanted to do some shooting, so we set off, went through a number of gates into the riverbed and ended up on this vague track. Suddenly we could see the clouds and the first spots of rain. We came to the last tributary of the main river and I walked in but it was up to my waist, too deep for a Land Rover.

We picked out a dry spot where there were some stunted willows and we put up a rough tent. We'd spend the night out and hopefully cross in the morning. By then it was getting dark. The rain got heavier. Down came the tent and we got into the Land Rover.

It just kept raining harder. At midnight we felt a big bump and there was this huge log resting against the radiator. The car was just starting to float. Bob Hayman was an Aussie, a butcher, good driver, jack of all trades. But he couldn't swim a stroke. We decided to pack everything we could into our packs and if she tipped over we'd try to hang on, but if we couldn't we'd try to float. It was black. Heavy rain squalls. A greasy dawn came at last. A great sigh of relief. But the river was bank to bank. The island we'd camped on had disappeared.

Then up came an Auster. It flew over really low, waggled its wings and circled us a couple of times. The pilot waved. Laurie Prouting. So we sat it out. Two days later the river had dropped far enough. We took a lightweight pack with our sleeping bags and a rifle, and we crossed this last tributary. I hopped across with a rope and we pulled Bob over. We got to the Black Mountain Hut. But the hut was locked. Bob got a piece of fencing wire and picked this massive lock, which impressed me no end. We made ourselves comfortable.

The plane arrived up next day. Dogs in the hopper. I couldn't see where he was going to land but I didn't know Laurie. He landed. He said, 'Glad you guys made yourselves comfortable.' And he said, 'We must have forgotten to lock up but I'll show you where the key is.' He was being polite, of course. He knew it had been locked. He said the river had cut new channels. 'You've got to leave the Land Rover. When the river drops we'll see about towing it out.'

We had a couple of good days, shot a couple of tahr, then we walked out. It was totally miserable. Rain. When we got down to Messie Anne cooked this wonderful meal. I was starving. I ate the meal, climbed into the sack, and Russell and Bob staggered in about 11 o'clock, absolutely rooted.

We got a lift down to Mount Peel, spent the night there in manorial splendour and went through to Christchurch the next day. Rang the rental car guy and he said to leave the key on the front wheel and he'd send us the account.

I said, 'We haven't got the Land Rover.'

He blew up. 'You bastards from the North Island, you've got no idea.'

I said, 'Look mate, it was an act of God.'

He said, 'Don't give me that crap. Where are you?'

'Just leaving town now, mate.'

They got the Land Rover out. Laurie and someone cranked it up, used a horse to drag it back across the river, took it back to Christchurch and saved our bacon.

On the strength of that we became friends. I came back for musters and so on through the years. The big one was the huge muster in the eighties. It's part of history now.

To me it was magical. Once we were snow-raking; winter, blue sky, but tramping out these tracks with Blue, then head shepherd. We nursed some sheep along then about eight of them jumped out of the trench and got into a creek. Icicles. We got them back but a couple of them refused to move. We left them behind. Came down getting towards dark over these big boulders.

Blue made a cup of tea in a keening wind. Got down to the hut and someone had left the door open and the place was half full of snow and it was too late to go anywhere. About 10.30 at night Laurie came flying in really low. Dropped us some bundles. We thought, food! But no food, just sleeping bags. We got the fire going though.

I thought these people, they're hardy, they're tough and I'm a sort of city slicker. I have nothing but total admiration for them. None of them are clock-watchers. They respect each other, look after each other, and when you're there, they expect you to behave in the same way.

> "I thought these people, they're hardy, they're tough and I'm a sort of city slicker. I have nothing but total admiration for them."

PHOTO ESSAY
DEER

Deer now provide a substantial part of Mesopotamia's income. Deer velvet is sought-after internationally. It is the name given to the new, fleshy growth on stags which, if left, would harden into bony antlers. Instead, it is carefully removed under anaesthetics and frozen. Getting the deer from their paddocks into the shed takes skill and patience, for they take fright easily and unless they are carefully handled they can both injure themselves and damage their velvet.

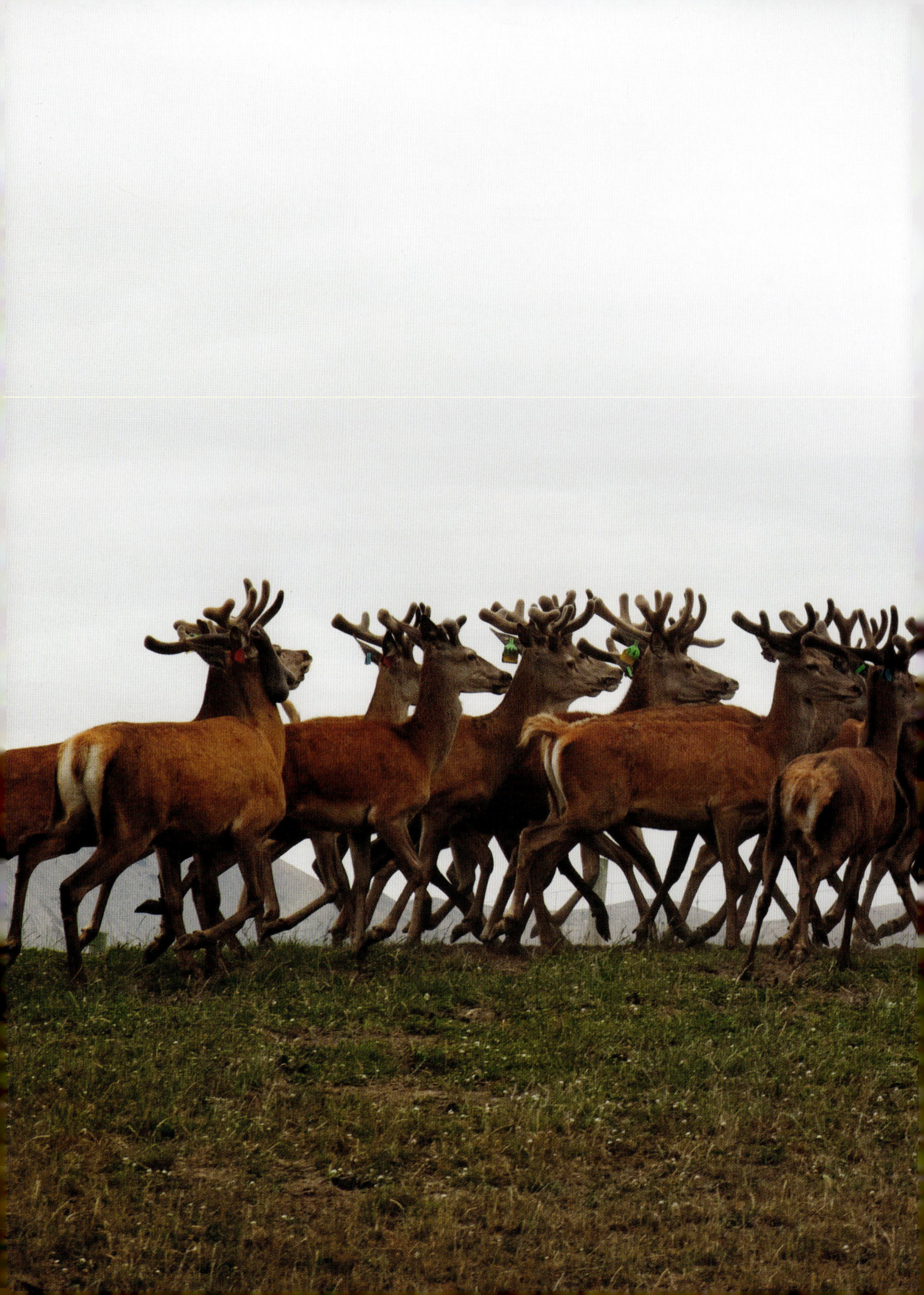

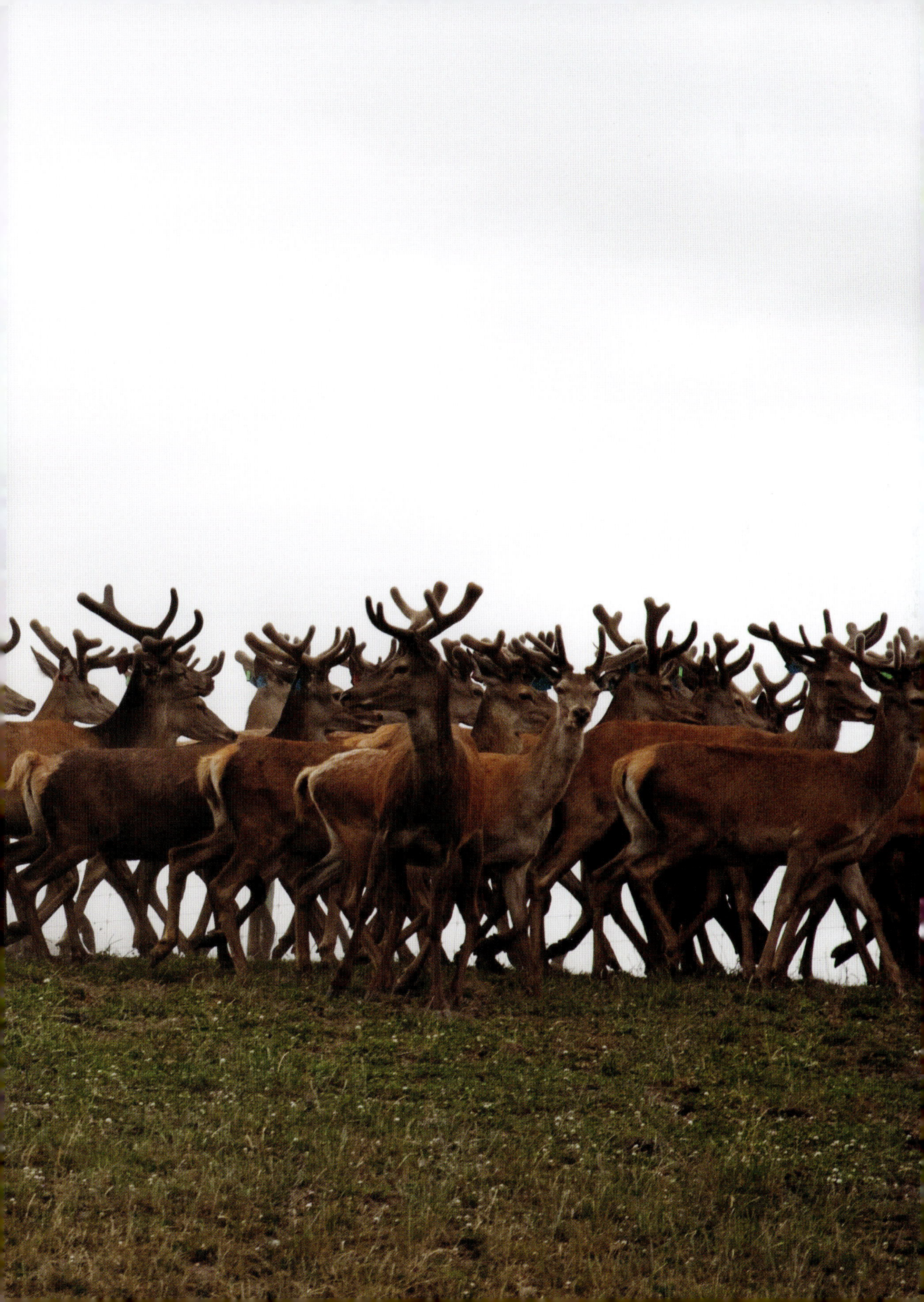

↑ PREVIOUS SPREAD
A herd of young stags cluster together nervously as they're moved out of their paddock.

↑ ABOVE
A dog moves quietly in behind as the stags start trotting down the hill towards the shed.

→ RIGHT
Malcolm, dogs and ute walk behind the herd, not pushing too hard, giving the stags plenty of space to persuade them to move into the race rather than tackle the fence.

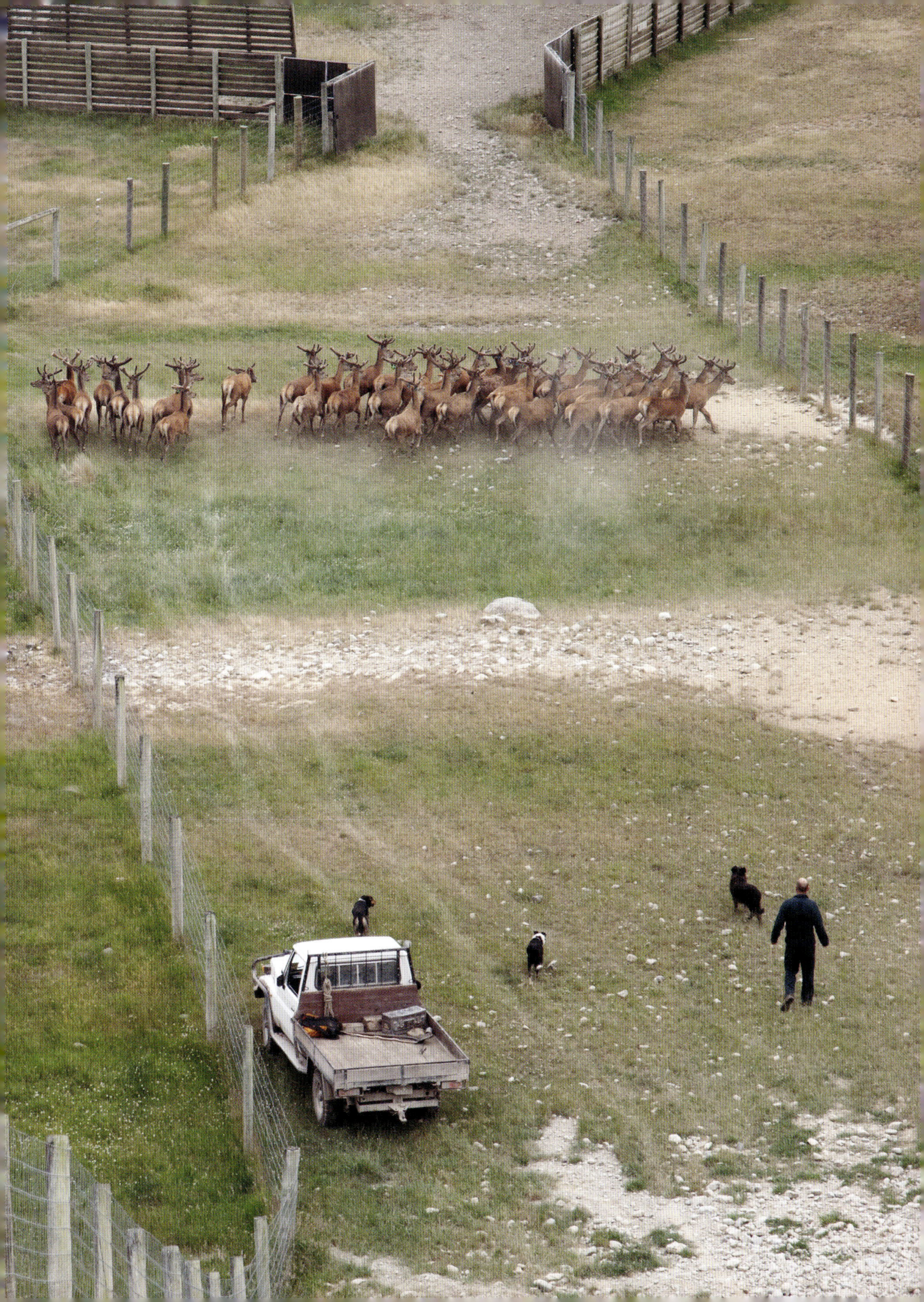

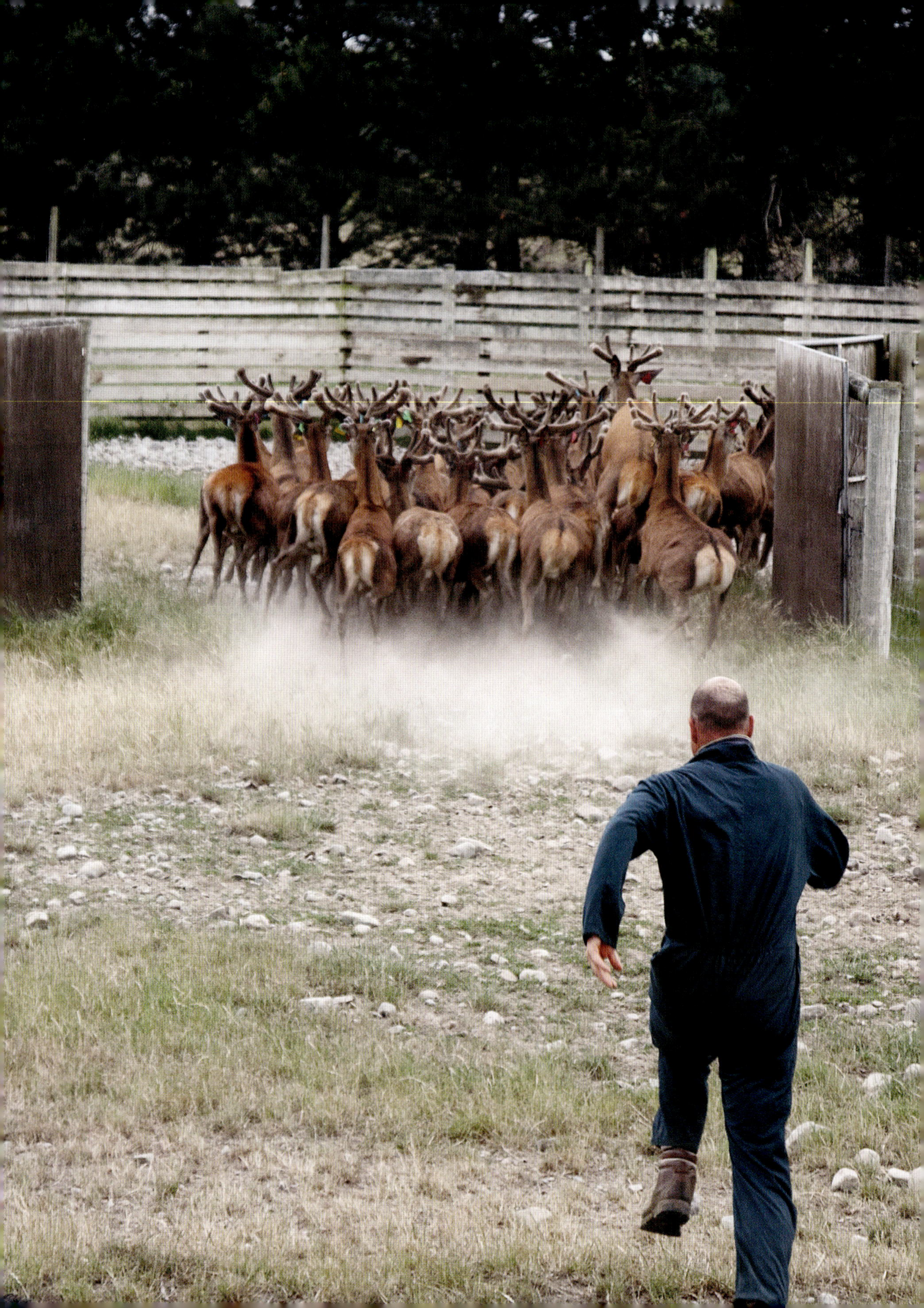

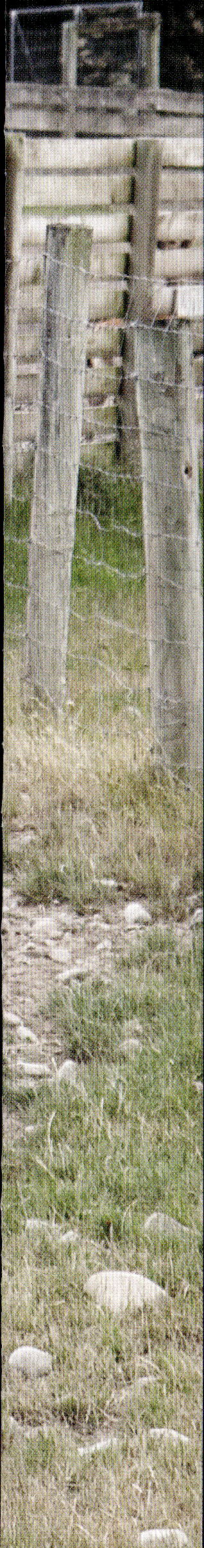

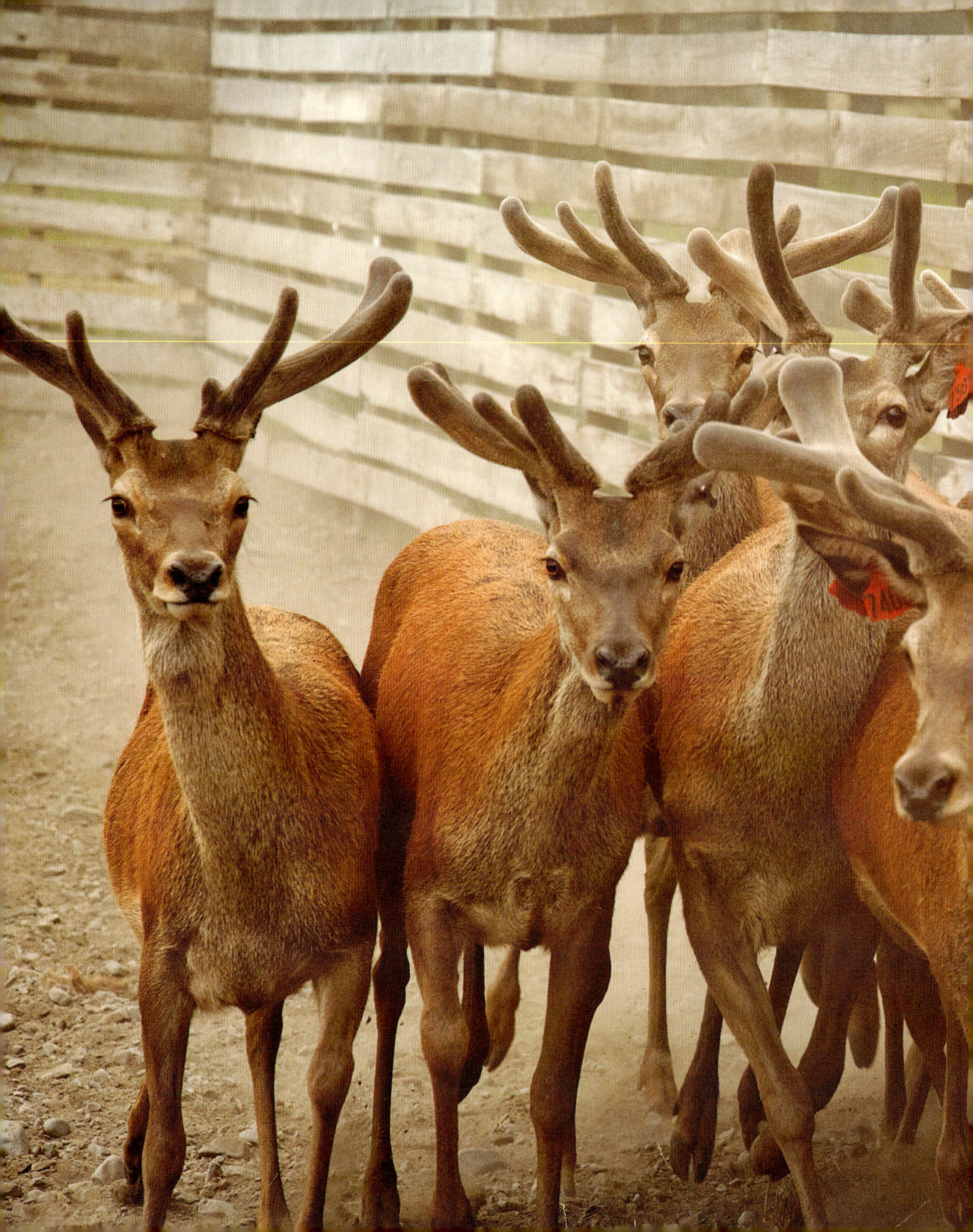

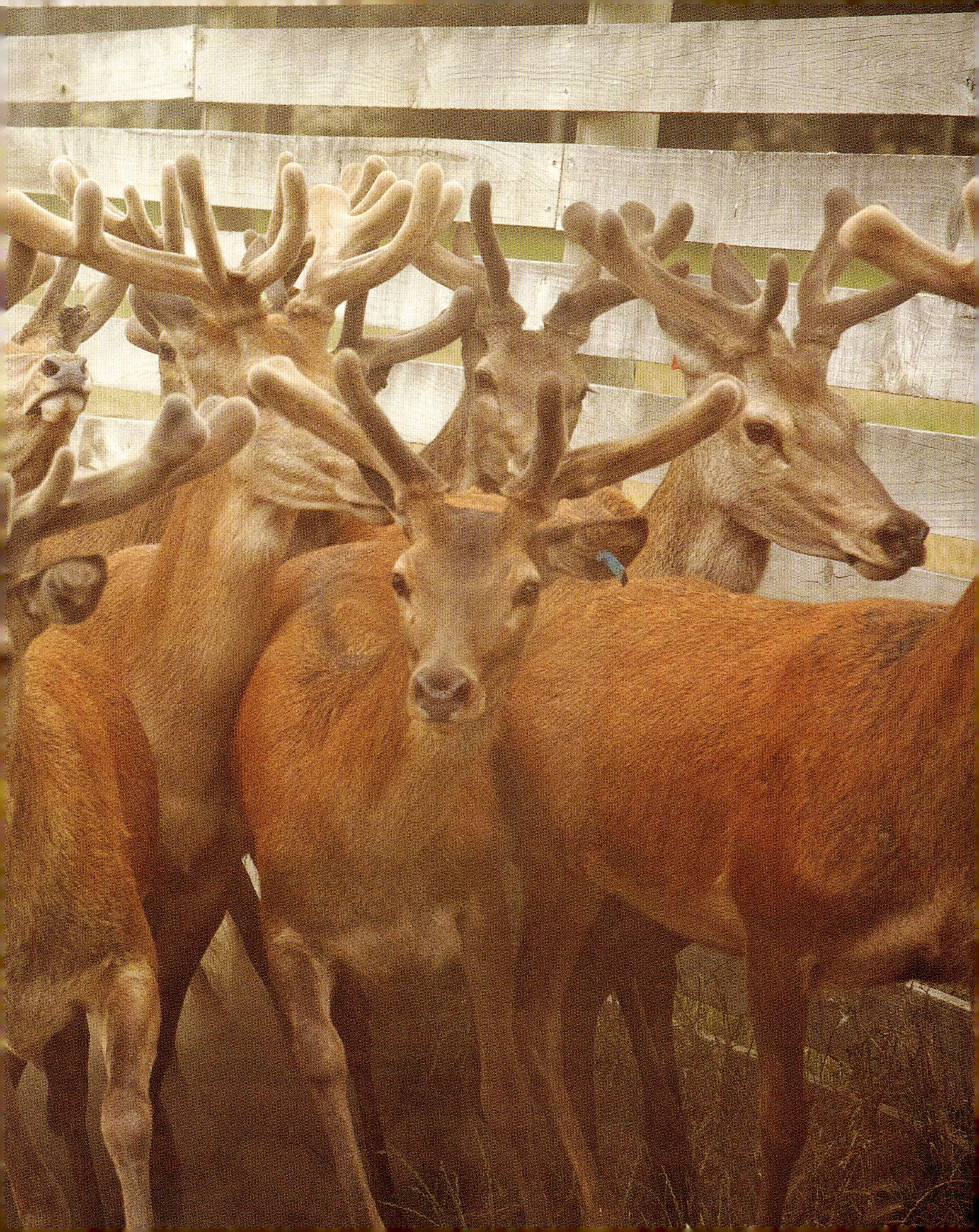

↑ PREVIOUS SPREAD
Young stags penned before being moved into the shed for their velvet to be taken off.

→ RIGHT
Sticks of velvet removed from the stags and stacked along the tray of a ute before being taken to the freezer.

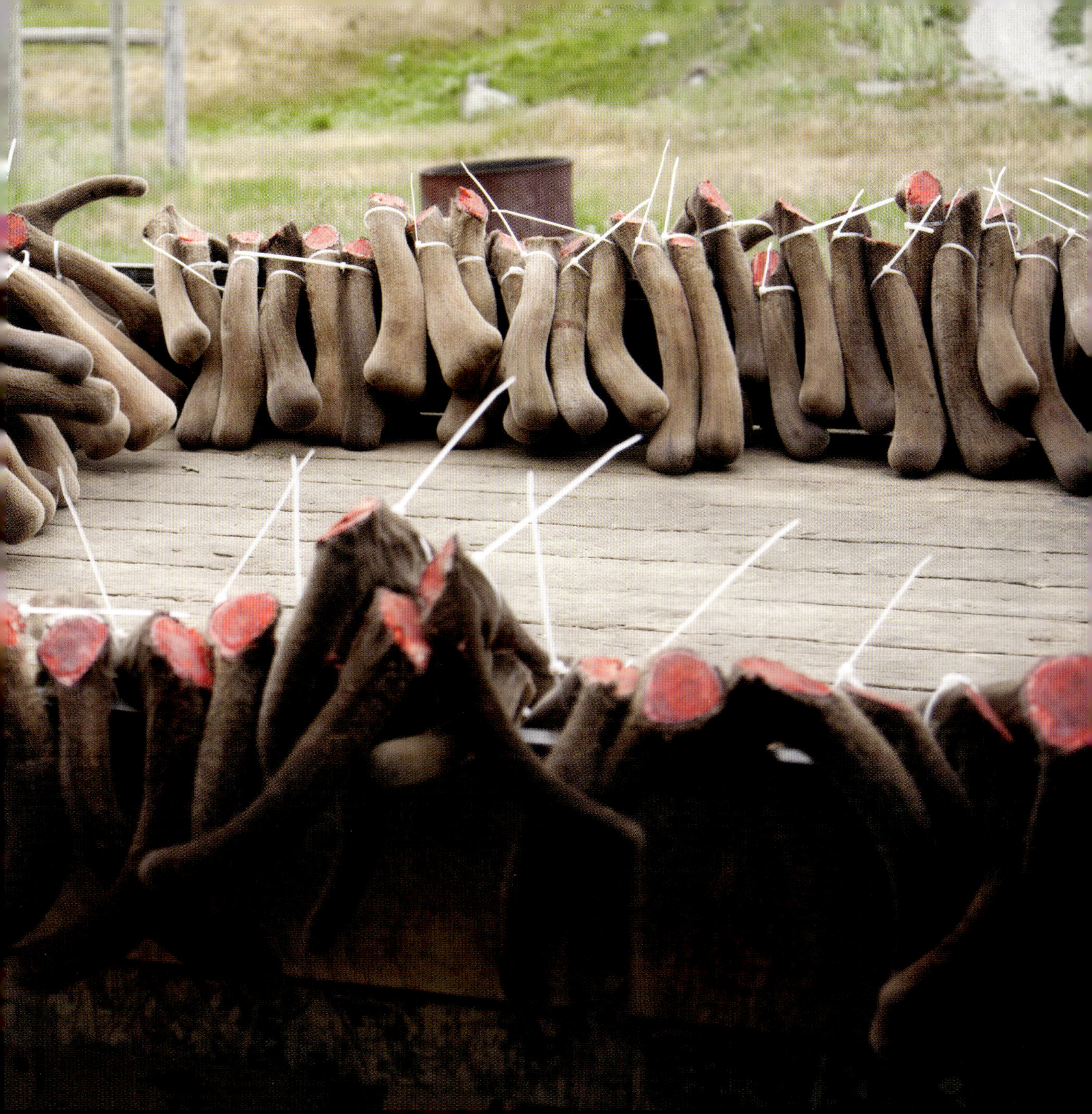

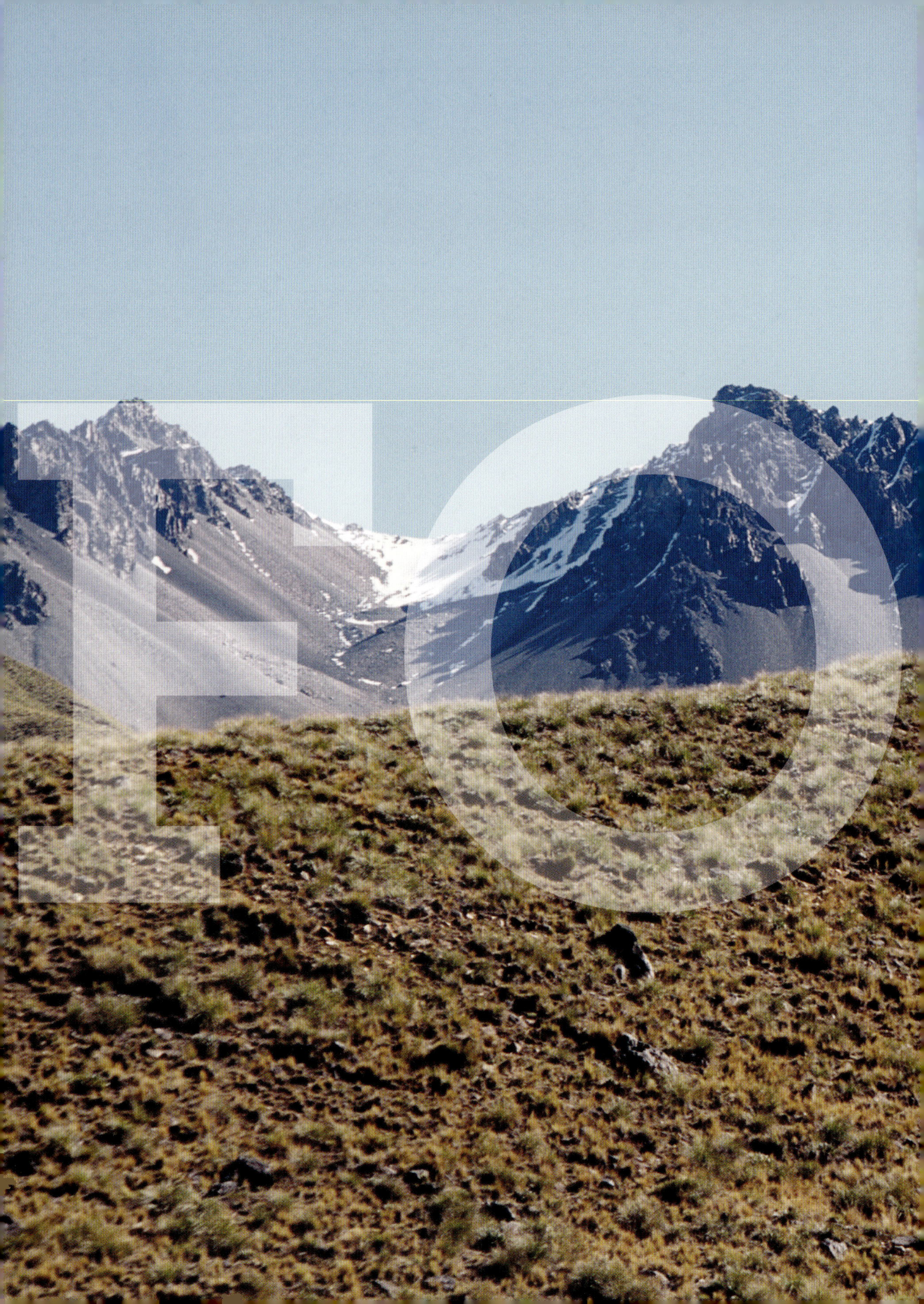

UTR

ACHILLES • THE TWO THUMB RANGE • D'ARCHIAC • CROOKED SPUR • HOGGET • THE GROWLER • BRABAZON • NEUTRAL SPUR • CLYDE RIVER • ROCKY RIDGE • BLACK MOUNTAINS • LITTLE SPUR • FINLAYS • FORBES RIVER • BIG BUSH • BLACK BIRCH STREAM • TOP DOWNS • BULLOCK BOW SADDLE • BALACLAVA BASINS • EXETER PEAK • SINCLAIR RANGE • FOREST CREEK • INKERMAN • THE ROCKS • MOUNT SINCLAIR • SUGARLOAF • MOUNT HOPE

MALCOLM PROUTING WAS buried in the little graveyard on the Rangitata riverbed. For a time, it seemed that the Proutings' hold on Mesopotamia might die with him. Under his care the property had grown rich. Now, that curious tide of extremes that ruled the station's affairs took over once more, for history seemed to have come full circle.

Back when Malcolm Prouting senior took over Mesopotamia Station it was broke. The 1951 wool boom saved him; the station prospered. Now Malcolm was dead. His son Laurie took his place. He found the station, if not broke, then at a low ebb, for Malcolm had been concentrating on developing the two blocks he'd carved off the home property for his sons.

Laurie took stock. He thought Mesopotamia in such a precarious position that even now, his blue eyes narrow when he thinks about it, which in itself is a feat. Getting him to sit down is like packing a spring into its box. He needs to be *doing,* rather than sitting here in his living room, looking through the French doors, the Rangitata running below in its deep valley until it turns a bluff and vanishes.

'No one realised that the home place had been left almost high and dry. A huge amount of funds and development had gone into those two blocks, and there wasn't a fence that would hold stock left on the home property. Footrot had got onto the place and it was a seething mess. In the short space of time after Dad got ill and couldn't run the place any more you couldn't believe how it had skyrocketed — backwards.'

Now the family had to be paid out, and death duties were enormous. The

Inland Revenue Department had both hands out for cash. 'My brother Frank made a start on it, rescuing the situation. He was a fastidious and very good farmer, well liked by everyone in the family, whereas perhaps I had my hang-ups; I could be a bit fiery, probably my grandmother coming out in me.'

All of the surviving brothers were now settled on their own farms; Laurie deep in the mountains at Mount Arrowsmith on the other side of the river. Mesopotamia might be a privilege, or a burden. Either way, the task was to fall on him.

WHEN LAURIE WAS a child the fifty-kilometre journey from Mesopotamia to Peel Forest took more than an hour, sometimes far more. Mesopotamia's own school started in 1956, first in the Nosworthys' old cottage, then in a new building of its own.

Until 1956 the nearest school was far down the road in Peel Forest. So Malcolm's children lived with their grandmother Maggie Gifkins at Peel Forest during the week and went home to the station at weekends. Laurie thought Maggie a tough old bird. 'She had Irish in her and if she lost her temper, look out. I can't believe my mother was so even-tempered.

'Granny had her idiosyncrasies. She didn't mind us fishing. So every time we went away we said we were fishing. If we did anything else it was bad. She made us work. We had to dig the garden, turn the cocksfoot over and turn it into lawn. Some of the other village kids when they got home did nothing. We asked them, how did they get away with that?

'Once she was making what I called jelly jam. She put everything into it, from leaves to laurel berries. It's a wonder we weren't poisoned. And she'd strain it. I happened to be sitting on a chair with an old shovel handle holding the brew to let it drain into the bowls and I upset the lot of it. She flew into a temper, grabbed the shovel handle and she smacked it on the table and swore. I was round the table like a startled rabbit. Holy Nora! I knew if she got me with that stick I wouldn't be here telling the story today.

'In a blind rage she ran round the table to get me but I was out that door like greased lightning. I always had the bike leaning against the tree pointed the right way for such occasions. I leapt on and pedalled off as fast as I could.

→ RIGHT
Laurie Prouting: holidays were things other people went on.

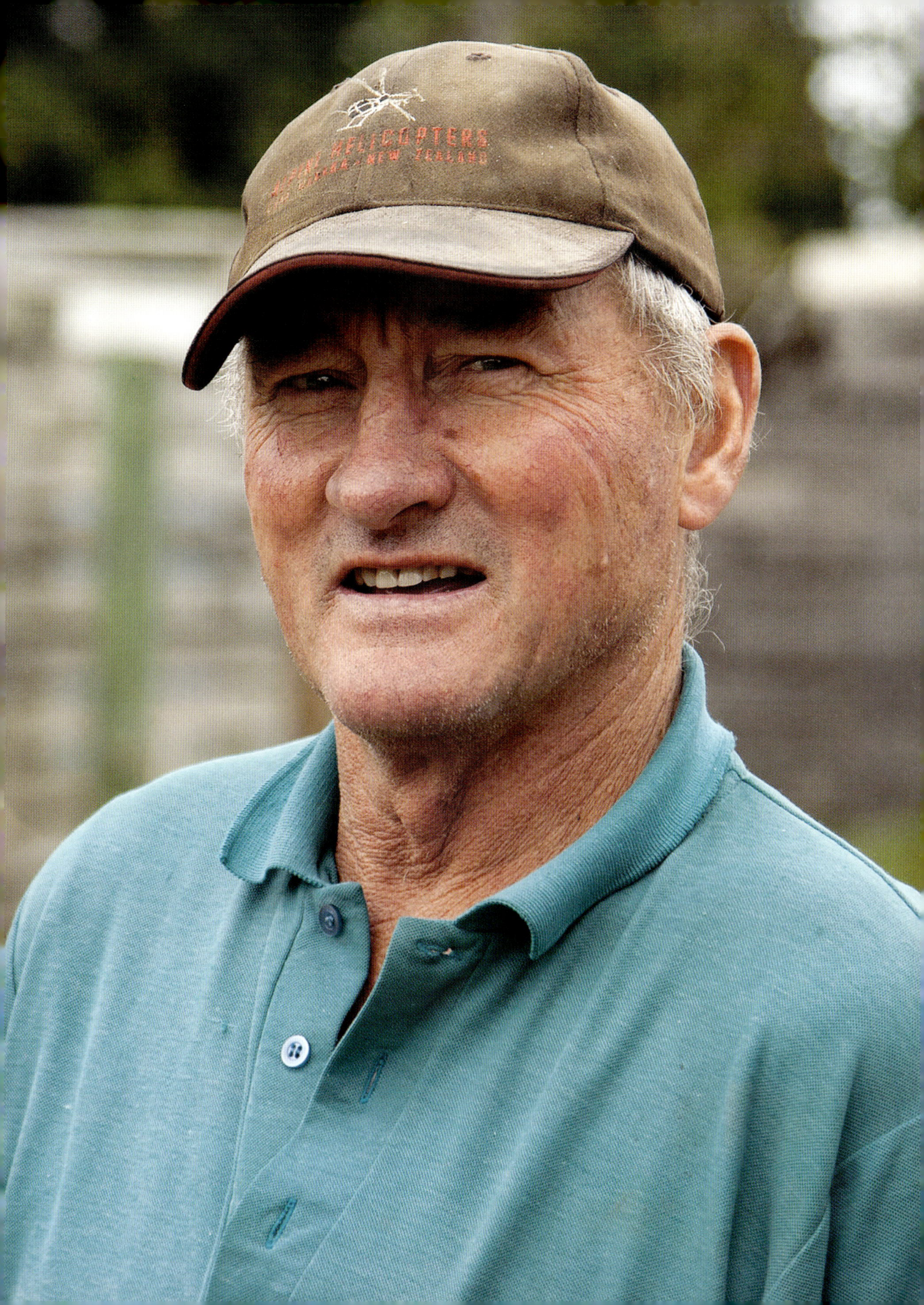
HELICOPTERS
NEW ZEALAND

But I had to go down the back of the section and up the lane at the side and she tried to cut me off across the vege garden and picked up a boulder and heaved it at me as I went past.

'I was really going for it. The rock went between the wheels. I got the speed wobbles but I made it. There was a small bit of bitumen outside and I'd go out and pedal up and down it. About twenty minutes did the trick. I'd come back and she'd be cool. The subject would never be raised again. So we were lucky to survive.'

Every child in the family was destined to become a farmer. They grew up, went to boarding school in Christchurch, left as soon as they could and went farming. Laurie returned to Mesopotamia. He married Anne, who was born in Westport, raised in Akaroa then lived on the family farm near Halkett near Christchurch, commuting to high school in the city. She left school for a dressmaking apprenticeship and, in the days before Chinese-made clothes rendered the craft all but obsolete, became a dressmaker. She still makes clothes for her grandchildren; beautifully tailored, neatly sewn.

Laurie's uncle lived not far from the Halkett farm, and Anne played hockey with his cousin. That was how she met Laurie. 'Some called him a tearaway.' She was a farmer's daughter, she knew farming, she could ride a horse and bring in a mob of sheep. Laurie planned to be a farmer. It was a relationship made in green pastures and they married when Anne was twenty-two.

The newly-weds lived in a cottage at Mesopotamia called Laurels, near Rowans, the cottage where Laurie spent his early years. Laurie continued to work on the station with his father. Then, in 1974, he and Anne bought Mount Arrowsmith Station. Anne sums up these huge shifts in her life in a few words. She is laconic, like their son Malcolm, Laurie as talkative as their daughter Neroli.

Their new station was then called, prosaically, Lower Lake Heron Station. The farm lay beside Lake Heron in a wide, gentle basin, which in spring is vivid with wildflowers, dotted with smaller lakes, laced with streams and on a sunny day seems the brightest place in the world.

They renamed it Mount Arrowsmith, after the mountain range that swoops and soars behind and cradles a quartet of glaciers in its spurs, the great jagged peak of Arrowsmith itself just visible from the quiet picnic spots along the lake where the skylarks sing. It is wonderful, beautiful country, awe-inspiring, terrifying, the kind of country city people go to and admire and shiver then carry their photographs back to warm living rooms.

Laurie and Anne thought it magnificent too. The difference was that they had to live there and farm its flanks. Even on the tough scale of high country stations this one ranked as extreme. On a scale of difficulty, Laurie put it among the hardest.

Such an isolated community had to be self-reliant, and the Proutings had to take care of themselves. They made their own clothes, conserved their food stocks, and outside Laurie battled the snow. Anne taught their two children, Malcolm and Neroli, by correspondence. The nearest school was far away by a road threading through the basin to the vast shearers' quarters and old stone cottage at the Hakatere corner then through the Ashburton Gorge to Mount Somers. They survived.

They bought Mount Arrowsmith as a going concern for $320,000, a lot of money in the day. Of that amount they had the twenty thousand. All the rest was borrowed. They could borrow machinery and equipment from Mesopotamia but otherwise they were on their own.

Mount Arrowsmith rated highly only in terms of altitude. It was shadowed, and cold. 'I knew that of all the high country runs, mine was at the bottom,' Laurie said. 'I had my mind set on Mount Algidus Station [even more isolated, lying in the fork of the Wilberforce and Mathias rivers, hard up against the Southern Alps and the subject of Mona Anderson's famous book, *A River Rules My Life*]. I couldn't manage it; so I took the other place.'

Perhaps fate played its part. Had they owned Algidus Laurie doubted he would ever have gone back to Mesopotamia. Why would they buy such hard country? Because a flush of optimism was sweeping the countryside at that time. Wool prices were rising again and farmers predicted a return to the good times. But the lift proved to be only a bounce.

The year before they bought the farm, wool was selling at 300 cents a kilogram. Laurie based his farm budget on wool fetching half that price, 150 cents a kilogram. His breakeven point, below which he could not survive, was 130 cents.

In their first year on the station the wool price went down to 128 cents. 'I was left gasping. Then we struck some hard winters when the snow just kept falling and falling . . . I reached a low ebb in my farming career two years after we bought it, when I felt I didn't have the coin to rescue my stock from the snow. I'd used the horses for making tracks to try and snow-rake the stuff then one morning I woke and there'd been another foot of snow which meant every track I'd made was covered.

'My bank balance was empty. I had three hundred sheep in desperate straits. The guy I had helping me had the heart of a lion. He was only a small guy, over fifty, and he suffered from epilepsy and I'd marched out that morning thinking, "I will do something, I will do something," and this guy had an epileptic fit on the track we'd cleared. I looked at him writhing on the ground and thought, "What the hell am I trying to do?" I felt cornered, a rat in a trap. That was the low point in my farming career.'

In desperation he telephoned Federated Farmers for help. If he could get two others to join him, they said, they'd share the cost of a helicopter to fly feed up to trapped sheep. 'I rang my neighbours, arranged the helicopter, had all my hay bales ready when it arrived. My neighbour Bill Dobbs, who was really only doing this for me, said he had no idea the snow was so deep, and he had found hundreds of his own sheep in it. He said I'd saved his bacon at the end of the day. By that evening I was singing a merry tune. If your sheep are suffering you're suffering as well. If your sheep are okay it doesn't really matter too much whether your pocket's empty or not, you're feeling a hell of a lot better. It's when your pocket's empty and your stock are starving that you're really up against it.

'Then wool prices got a little better. I wrote to my financiers. They said they knew they couldn't get blood out of a stone and they'd let me off the principal repayment as long as I paid the interest. *Phew!*'

Throughout the crisis Anne kept the home running — which, at Mount Arrowsmith, rather understated the job. As well as the farm routine, and running a homestead where everything had to be brought up in bulk and cooked or made on the premises, and a hundred jobs on the farm to cope with, she was solely responsible for her two children's schooling.

She was an untrained teacher thrown into the job. 'Then, you weren't allowed on correspondence unless you were far away from a school; and there weren't that many of us who qualified. Now, there are people just up the road from the Mayfield School on correspondence. Our correspondence teacher in Wellington was amazing. You could ring her at any time and you'd get an answer. That's all gone now.'

Mount Arrowsmith was a very long way from her parents' Canterbury Plains farm near Christchurch city. Yet Anne never wondered what she'd signed up for. 'I just got on with it,' she said simply. 'Everybody did in those days. It was a great life. And the children had a great life. If you went to the doctor, or the dentist, the accountant, the lawyer, you had to take the kids with you, because they didn't go to school, and because there was no one to look after them. No matter what you did, the children were always around. There was nobody to babysit. We were very hard up initially. But I never felt life was hard. I was so busy with correspondence school and everything else. We had a wonderful community.'

Holidays were things other people went on. 'Some people packed up and went away every Christmas,' she said, and decades later there was still no envy, just wonder. Their first-ever holiday was a trip to Nelson. 'I remember borrowing a tent. We were scarcely there when someone who had worked for us for years and years died. So we packed up and went home. By train. The ride was fascinating. So different.'

The second holiday? 'I don't think we ever had another family holiday. 'Laurie would take the children walking over passes and that sort of thing, a lot. I stayed at home and did the home jobs.'

THEIRS WAS A precarious home. Laurie said, 'We were fighting for our lives. Funnily enough it wasn't until Robert Muldoon came out with his subsidies for farming that we turned the corner. Muldoon for better or for worse was a benefactor of mine. You wouldn't hear many guys saying that.'

After eight years of hard work on Mount Arrowsmith the Proutings were back in the black by courtesy of New Zealand's wrangling prime minister. The farm was making a profit. The property market did the rest. The value of their farm had risen from $320,000 to $1.32 million: 'A hell of a capital gain, tax free. A million dollars today doesn't sound much; back then it was huge. Before then, if somebody had come to me and said they'd give me five hundred thousand for the farm I probably would have readily sold it just to get out of the bizarre position I'd found myself in.'

It was just about then that Peter was killed. A year later his father Malcolm died. When the family had buried both, the Inland Revenue Department demanded death duties. There was no money in the Mesopotamia accounts to pay. Malcolm's will demanded a unanimous family decision on whoever took over the home property; otherwise the property would be sold. It was insurance against disruption, for how many families would agree on such a contentious issue? Yet the Proutings did.

Everyone agreed on Frank. He would sell his property in the Awatere Gorge and return to Mesopotamia. Laurie turned to his own business. He went to Asia to learn about producing deer velvet, returned keen to expand his deer farming, had business deals lined up. At that moment his accountant called: Laurie should talk to Frank.

Laurie did. Frank wasn't going back to Mesopotamia. Furthermore, Frank said, he thought someone should be paid to take it over, for Mesopotamia was in dire straits. Laurie: 'I was absolutely speechless.'

The question was, would Laurie sell his and Anne's holdings to go back to Mesopotamia? He wanted to. 'Mesopotamia is a brilliant place. I knew every boulder.' But Mount Arrowsmith would not sell. Worse, prices were starting to drop. Meetings were held to find a solution. At one of them, Pyne Gould Guinness, then the big Canterbury stock firm and farm financiers, came up with a proposition: would Laurie be prepared to take on both properties?

'I was absolutely staggered. I felt myself in the same situation my father was in when Bob Buick came home and told him he was the new owner of Mesopotamia. I was humbled. But that's what we did.'

So the wheel turned. Laurie and Anne brought their family back to Mesopotamia. He and Anne moved into the big white homestead. Malcolm junior and Neroli knocked off correspondence school for boarding school.

The move was not as simple as that, of course. Matters remained outstanding. Laurie stood firm on one of them: he told his father's trustees that he would not go back unless he held *all* the shares in Mesopotamia. That is, he would not share ownership. His father had set up a company in 1957, Mesopotamia Station Ltd. As each member of the family went farming on their own they would sell their shares back into the pot. Eventually his father would have held them all.

Now that plan had been turned on its head. For it to work, Laurie would have to

→ RIGHT
Winter on Mesopotamia, looking up to the Two Thumb Range, implement shed in foreground.

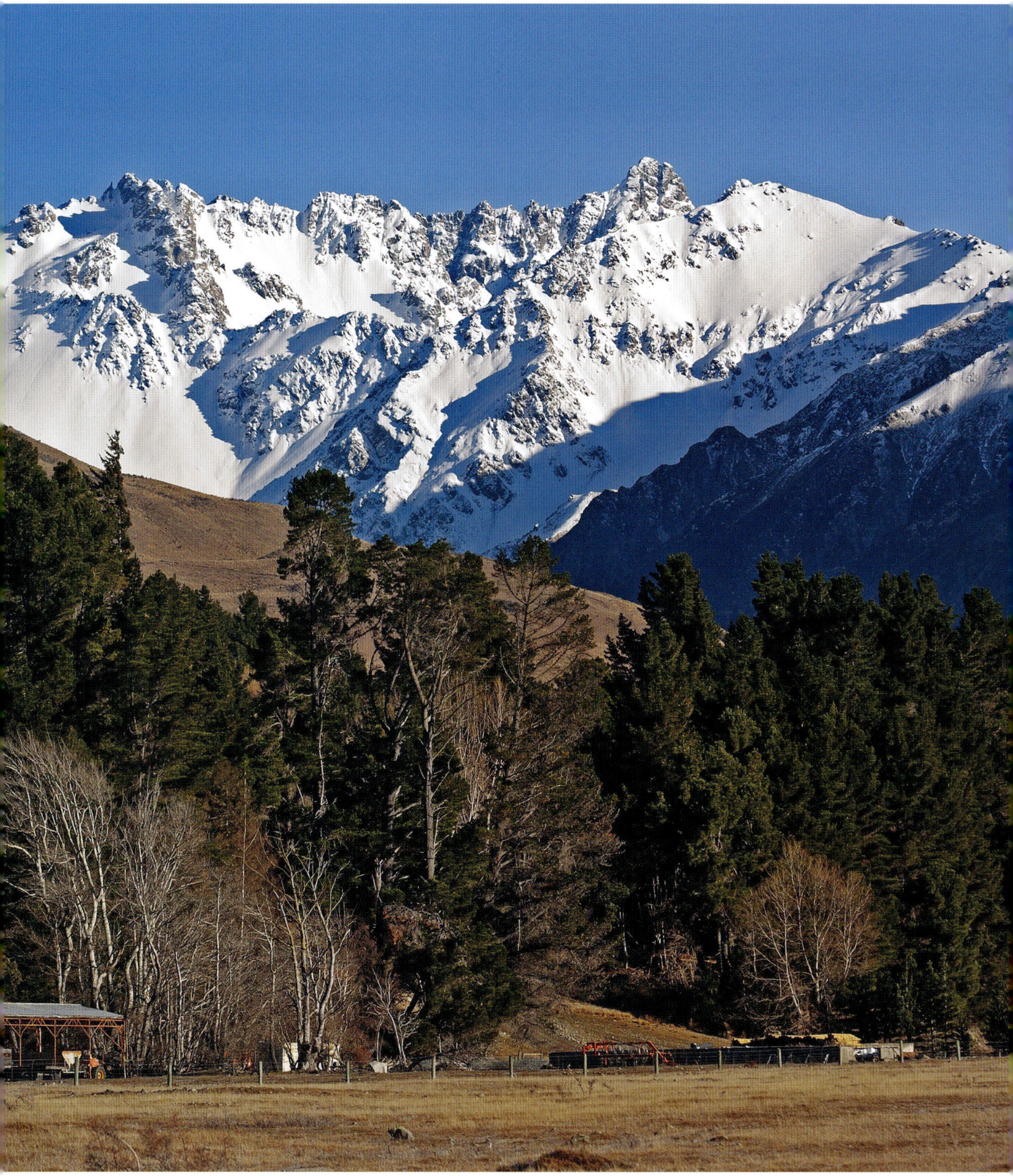

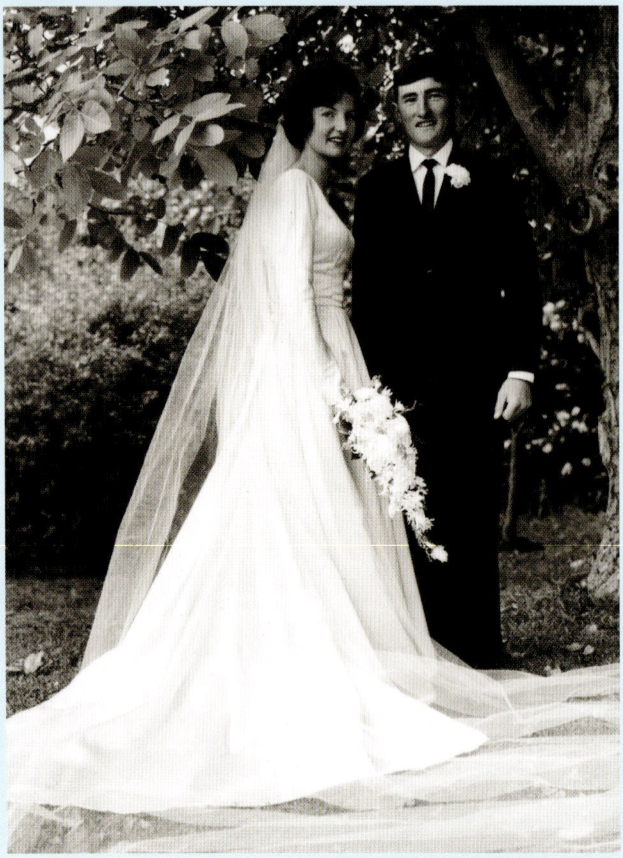

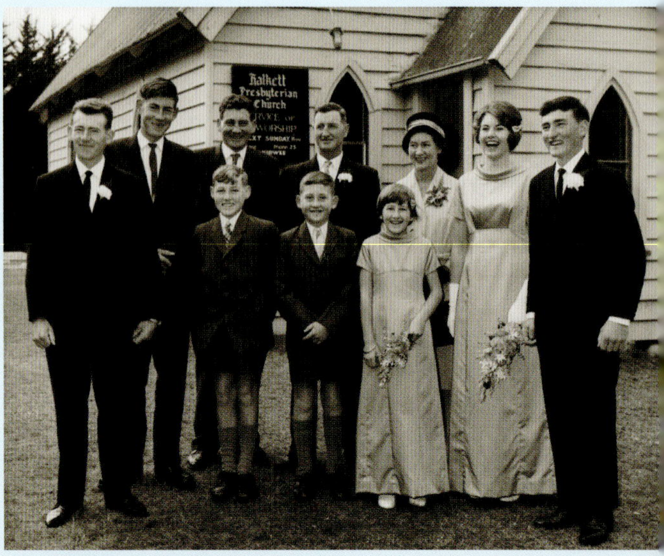
Halkett
Presbyterian
Church

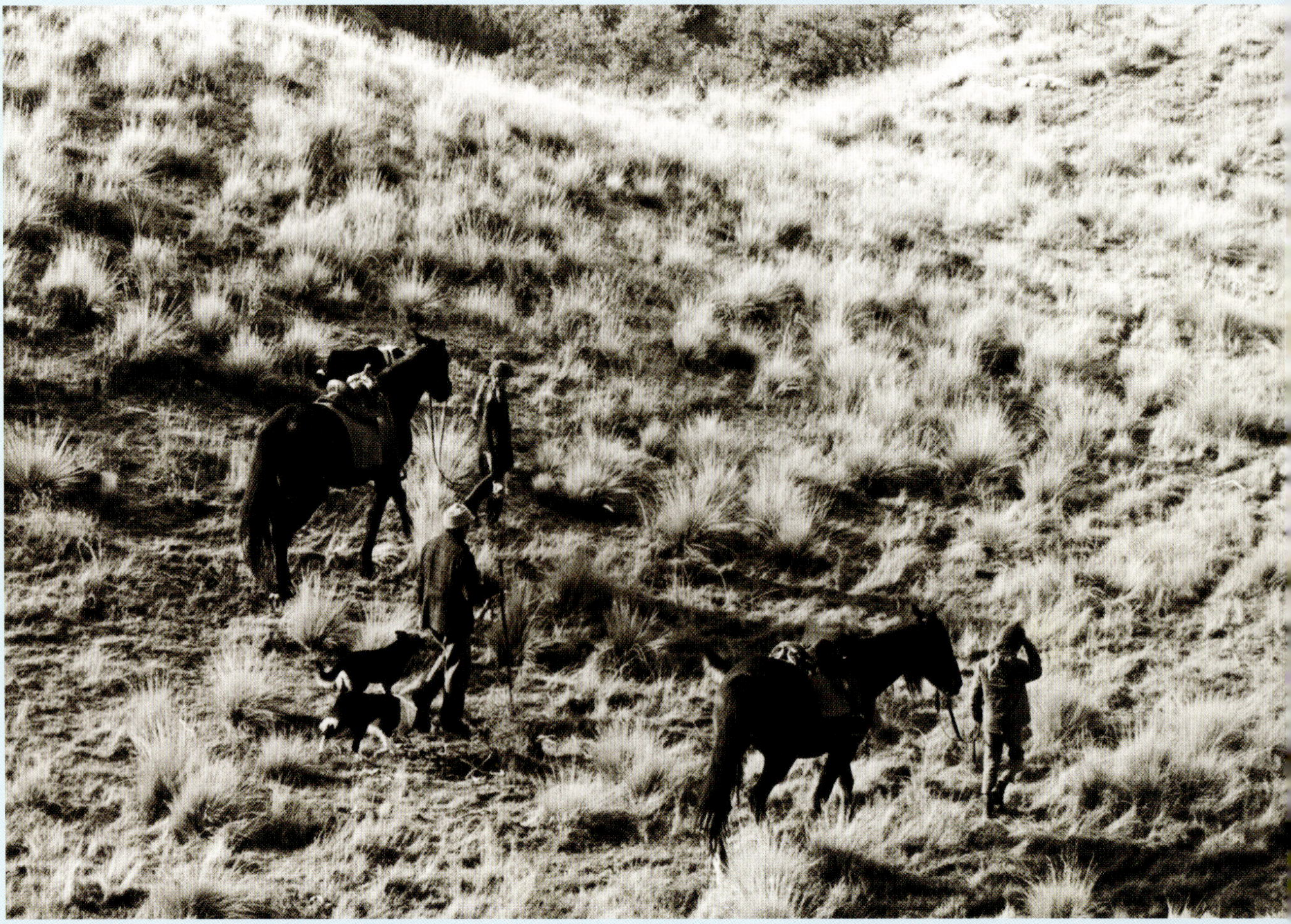

transfer everyone else's shares into his name and owe the family the value of those shares. Effectively he would be buying the farm from the rest of his family on credit, and Mesopotamia had appreciated a little since Malcolm senior bought it for £27,000. Now, it was worth millions of dollars.

The family readily agreed. One obstacle had been overcome, but death duties remained outstanding and there was only one way of paying them: more borrowing. 'I was borrowing money until it was making me dizzy in the head. I thought I'd reached the stage where I could see myself making it at Mount Arrowsmith; and here I was plunging back into it, deep. I knew exactly how my father had felt.'

Laurie still had to deal with an even more fundamental problem: nature. The unruly river had to be checked. The term 'river' is far too simple for the Rangitata. It is formed by two powerful rivers, the Clyde and the Havelock, both of them deep and dark and running off glaciers on the Southern Alps, the Rangitata four kilometres wide at their confluence then swelled by rivers and streams flowing down from the mountain ranges along its way.

The river is a vast avenue directing the might of the mountains to the sea, and the prospect of ordering that 'desolate pathway of destruction' in any way seemed a superhuman challenge. Laurie's mother had worried about the money his father was spending on those riverbanks. Yet the work was essential to keep the river on the straight and narrow and stop it from ravaging the adjacent paddocks critical to the farm's productivity.

Malcolm had built what they called hook groynes: boulder banks in the shape of the letter C, so floodwater was ponded in the middle and its force channelled around the points. A huge amount of work went into constructing them. The Rangitata just tore them down again in a truly heartbreaking way: when the flood passed its peak and the groynes seemed to have survived the worst of it, the receding water undermined the work and destroyed them.

← CLOCKWISE FROM TOP LEFT
Anne and Laurie's wedding day, 14 May 1966. *Prouting Family Collection*

One of the few photos of the family together, the Prouting clan at the Halket Church on Anne and Laurie's wedding day. Front row from left: Allan, Peter, Jen. Back row from left: Frank, Ray, Don, Malcolm Snr, Thelma, Valmai and Laurie. *Prouting Family Collection*

When, in 1975, Laurie and Anne were facing financial hardship, Neroli and Malcolm were a tremendous help on the farm. They were only too keen to leave school work and go out with Laurie. Neroli is on the left, Malcolm on the right and Laurie in the middle.

'My father didn't despair. He said, "We'll build another one on top and beat this." So we built another one on top. The same thing happened. Then another one.'

When Malcolm died in 1981 the riverbank problem still had not been solved; the groynes simply kept blowing out whenever there was a flood. 'It wasn't my father's fault. There just wasn't the equipment in the country then to lift a rock of twenty tonnes and it was the twenty-tonne rock that seemed to tilt the balance in our favour. We changed the style on the nose of the groyne and used those twenty tonne rocks. That stabilised the stopbank. The rocks you see there today are only the tip of the iceberg. The bulk of them run well down into the shingle and now it is solid.'

Laurie and Anne's children Neroli and Malcolm worked as hard as anyone, although they were still at school. Laurie planted willows in the land behind his new stopbanks. That was the children's job. Day after day they followed their father in his crawler tractor as it towed steel claws cutting two deep furrows into the stony ground, the two children following close behind with armfuls of metre-long willow wands which they had to bury half their length into the dirt, holding them upright until the shingly ground fell back into the groove.

The two small figures trailed the bulldozer, both of them concentrating on the job, knowing its importance. Nearly every wand took root. 'They stuck to their guns and we kept at it hour after hour after hour. They helped us enormously.'

In later years that kind of work was to become controversial. The Rangitata is one of New Zealand's great, largely unmodified braided rivers. Willow planting was seen by many as interfering with the river's natural character. It was the last major refuge for three threatened bird species, the wrybill, the black-fronted tern and the banded dotterel, each depending on its wild, unrestrained riverbed for nesting. Conservationists and farmers had sharply opposing interests: the former in leaving the river exactly as it had always been, the Proutings in stopping it from ruining their farm.

In the event the hook groynes and the willows were to have little impact on the upper Rangitata's reputation as a largely unmodified ecosystem, but at the time the discussion was not even on the horizon. 'We didn't need resource consents then,' said Laurie. 'In fact, the catchment board as it was then was prepared to assist us with the cost. The hook groyne idea wasn't ours; it came from the catchment board. They had good common sense and no resource consent. If you only use rock it just stays that way until it's blown out. But using trees as well, year by year the bank grew. We put up netting fences to catch the debris and add to it. The sand has washed in and over the bank and doubled its size. Brilliant. I was spending fourteen thousand dollars a day, day after day, to get those riverbanks set. And we jolly well nailed it.'

Around that time Laurie's sister Jennifer and her husband John decided to branch out into a farm and needed funds. Laurie paid out her share, then bit by bit paid out his sister Valmai the $75,000 he owed. His brother Frank said he could pay him back when he could ('What a brother to have!'). The last two brothers had taken their share when they were settled on their farms by Malcolm.

'We got each family member paid off and that really left my mother who I owed so much to, including money. I paid her fifty thousand each year. I didn't want her to feel cash-strapped because of me. It wasn't making a huge dent in the amount I owed her but it kept her in cash. She thought she was going to be a big spender, but she never was. Couldn't change her lifestyle. She was very moderate. But at least it was whittling down the loan and she'd let me have that at a pretty generous interest rate. As mothers tend to do.

'So things were starting to look a bit better. Wool was selling quite well, although no one knew then the deer were going to spark up and treat us so well.' For like his father, Laurie's fortunes were to turn on another quantum shift in world prices. Malcolm senior had been saved by the wool boom. Now Laurie would be borne up by another boom. This time it was deer.

'They went to as high as five thousand dollars an animal. *One animal, five thousand dollars*. That was good news. By the mid-eighties we were looking very good and I had the break of a lifetime. Roger Douglas [the reforming Labour Government's Minister of Finance] delivered his budget, turning farming on its ear. I listened and sat bolt upright. I thought, *Holy Nora*! Here am I, stretched out like a shanghai. So I turned my farming ideas round. I paid off capital, because I had the funds to do it with the deer.

'I started farming on income then. I found that I was churning up virtually a million dollars in my farming year and I'd have a huge amount in the bank. I was getting huge interest on my money, and I was getting another hundred or two hundred thousand dollars rolling in. I paid Frank, I'd managed to get all the family paid back, and I couldn't believe that this happened in such a short space of time.'

Suddenly the tawny Rangitata landscape grew rosy. The Proutings were in clover, literally, for Laurie turned the money around and invested in his farm. 'We did enormous development on the flat. Why? Because we'd nailed that river. We couldn't touch the flat before that. Now we ripped into it and it produced hugely well for us. I poured so much back into the farm, built a new deer shed, remodelled the deer farm, went to a lot of deer farms to get all the good ideas I could possibly get.'

One good idea, however, owed a great deal to his father. Laurie built a new bridge, as Malcolm had done before him. This one was over Bush Stream, which gouged out the Valley behind the Sinclair Range at the back of the farm then cut a gorge through the rock to reach the Rangitata River. 'That was fun. I could imagine how my father felt when he built the one over Forest Creek. I thought to myself, jingos, how can I get this bridge straight? I've got a mate, Murray, who's very good with a digger. I said to one of his mates, "What worries me is that he has very good intentions but one of his eyes is just a little bit off-centre," and even though I told him not to tell Murray I knew he would.

'When Murray heard that, there was no way even one pile was going to be out of line. When we had a bridge opening he turned up wearing an eye patch. So far the bridge hasn't budged.'

It stands today, a delicate-looking structure but immensely strong, like good furniture, with a little plaque announcing that it was built by the L. Prouting Construction Company and opened on 25 November 1989.

'We weren't farming stretched out like a shanghai any more. We had a lot of the principal paid off. I knew that a bad time was coming, it always does, but unlike a lot of our farming colleagues I had time to put the show in order.'

His family had gone in their own directions. Laurie and Anne still owned Mount Arrowsmith and Neroli was running it, on her own. Malcolm was working on surrounding deer farms, gaining experience. The two were farmers born and bred but very different, and their father delighted in their individuality.

'Malcolm is very independent. For example, I wanted both of them to knock off smoking. I said to Neroli, "Fifteen hundred dollars if you'll knock off smoking, cash." She couldn't resist the cash. 'Malcolm wasn't going to be paid off. He's got that sort of nature. I tried it. It didn't work. Then he knocked off — for nothing. Daughters are hard on your ready cash, sons on your assets. And on your ego too. Yes!

'The pair of them were a couple of damn good kids. When I needed a hand — as I did because I was trying to do everything on my own — they were in there like big dogs to help me. They never said they were sick of it, they worked every holiday, work was all they did, they went back to school exhausted. There were probably a lot of times when they didn't want to go out and help, but they did.

'And after all, what does anyone want to do if they've built up an asset? They want to sit on it. We are all, as my father was, fiercely proud of the property that we've been lucky enough to be able to tend to during our watch. It's more than an asset. It's almost a living thing. So I'm delighted that they feel passionate about it.'

FARMING IS ALWAYS volatile. An old joke describes a farmer winning Lotto. He is asked what he will do with all that money. He doesn't know, he says. 'I suppose I'll just go on farming until it's all gone.'

Deer had their day then dwindled into what proved to be a very long twilight. In 1989 the deer boom ended and the market dropped abruptly. Mesopotamia sank back into the familiar struggle. The station always marched to an odd beat. Agricultural markets are cyclical, like most markets. They rise and fall, but in Mesopotamia's case the drop was compounded by a shift much closer to home, like fronts crossing the Tasman from different directions and clashing into a disproportionately greater storm.

Early in the new millennium Laurie handed Mesopotamia over to his son Malcolm. Each one of the Proutings took over the station at the bottom of its cycle and fought their way up. The shifts had a grim rhythm to them, each new family facing their own struggle.

Malcolm senior had taken over Mesopotamia when it was broke. Laurie took it over when it had again fallen upon hard times. Now it was his son Malcolm's turn and sure enough, the balance sheet was looking bleak. Malcolm took over Mesopotamia on its descent. 'Somewhere,' Laurie said, 'near the low.'

Malcolm had more than just market doldrums to deal with. He faced a revolution in the high country, a return of leased land to the government, and Mesopotamia was at the sharp end of it. Yet Laurie believed in the good fortune that nurtured both himself and his father.

'I can see things starting to turn. Why, I haven't got any good clear idea. I'm just absolutely certain Sue and Malcolm will get a break. Each one of us has had his own hill to climb. Malcolm is still climbing his. But I think he's on the way up.'

PHOTO ESSAY
TAILING

In summer the lambs are tailed in one of
the station's big working days. Long ago, the
sheep were mustered into temporary yards
by people using dogs and horses, using long
lengths of scrim stretched behind the mob
to keep the lambs and ewes together. On the
modern Mesopotamia it is a more mechanised
operation, using a helicopter to bring the sheep
down into a contractor's efficient portable
yards. One thing hasn't changed though:
the heat, shimmering off the mountains
and down the valley.

→ RIGHT
The new sound of the high country — Malcolm's helicopter works behind a mob of sheep in a great amphitheatre of mountains.

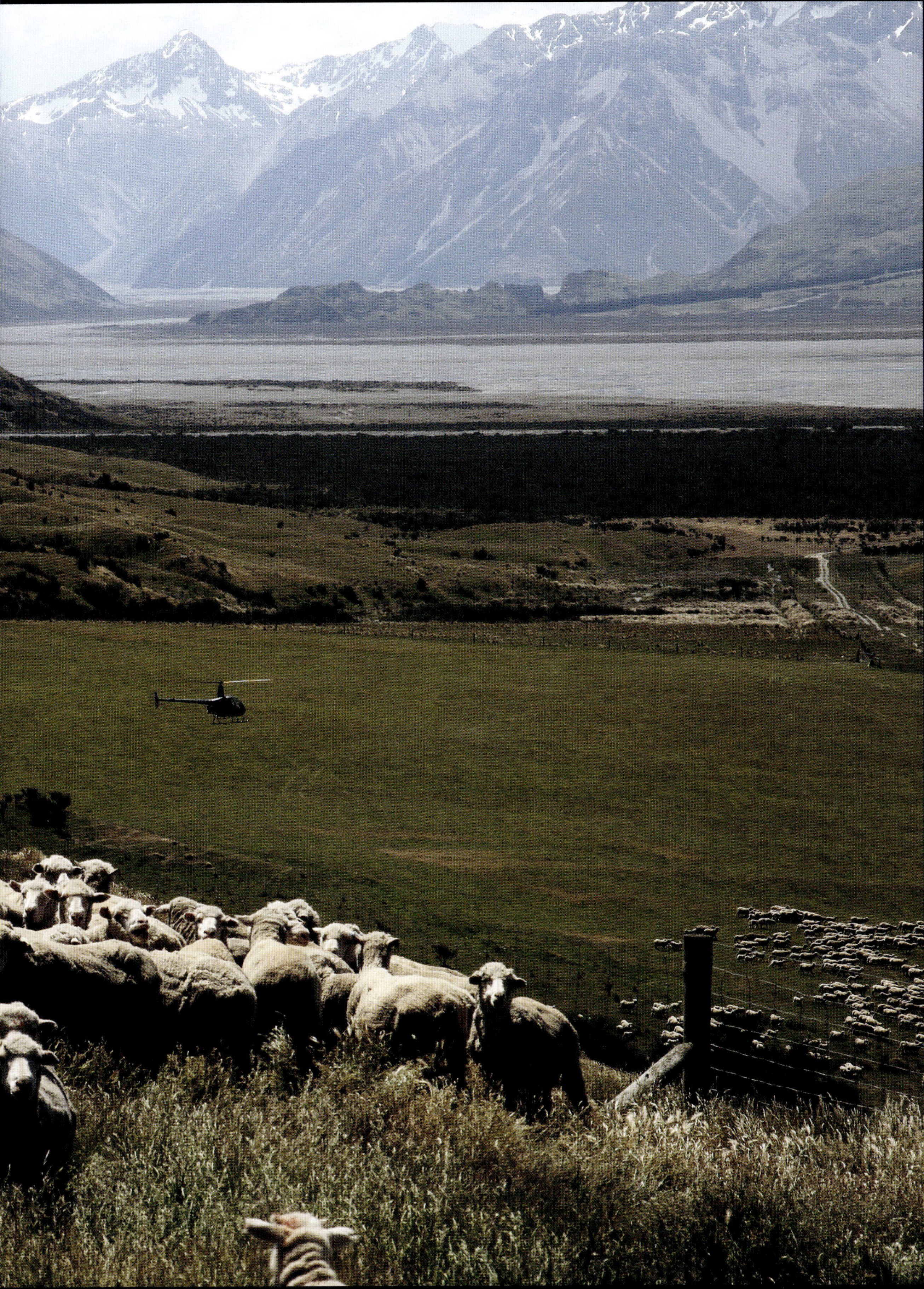

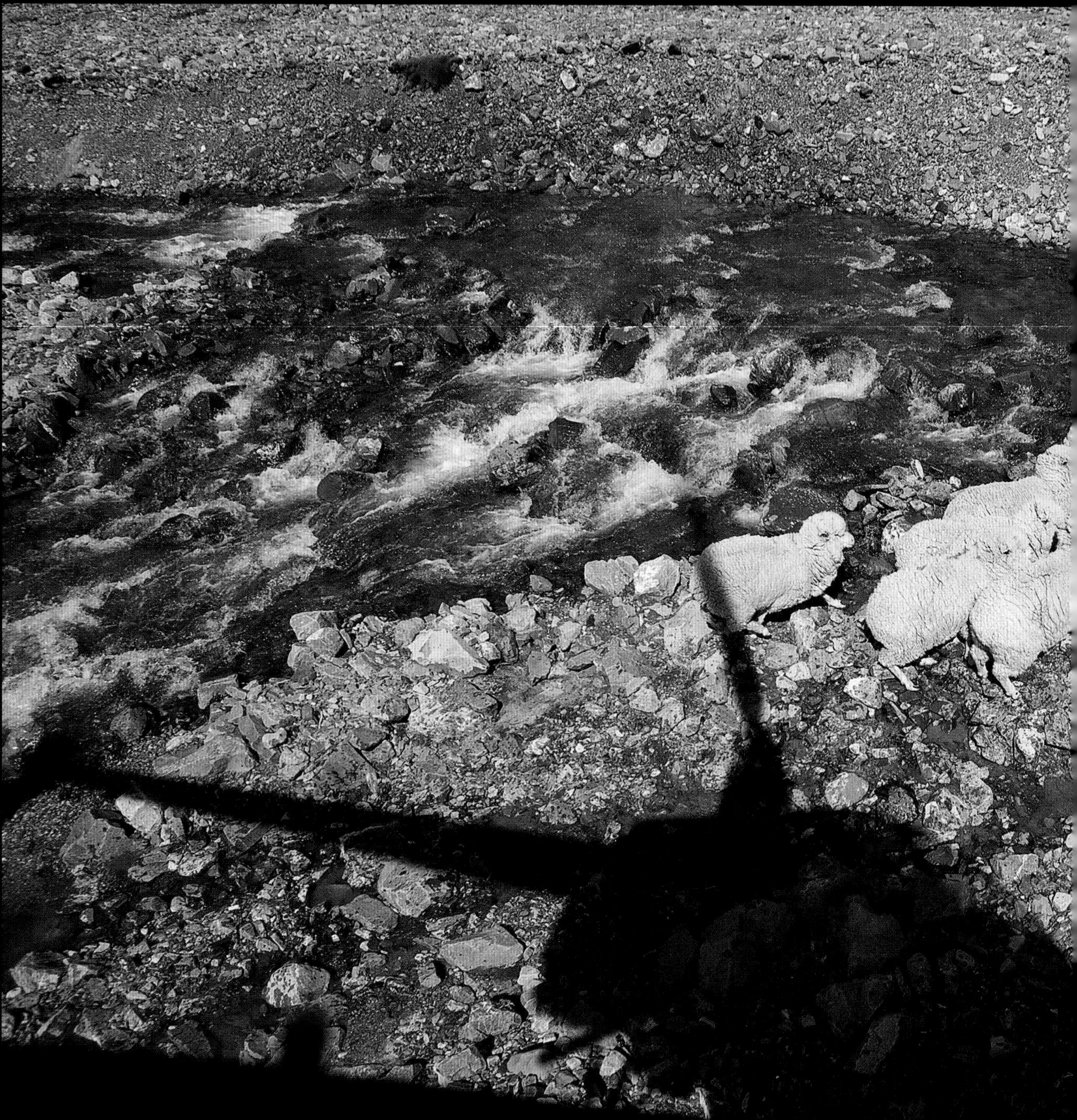

← LEFT
The helicopter's shadow tracks the mob across a stream in the river-bed: mustering by helicopter is now routine.

↓ FOLLOWING SPREAD
The ewes and lambs are in; now to close the gate!

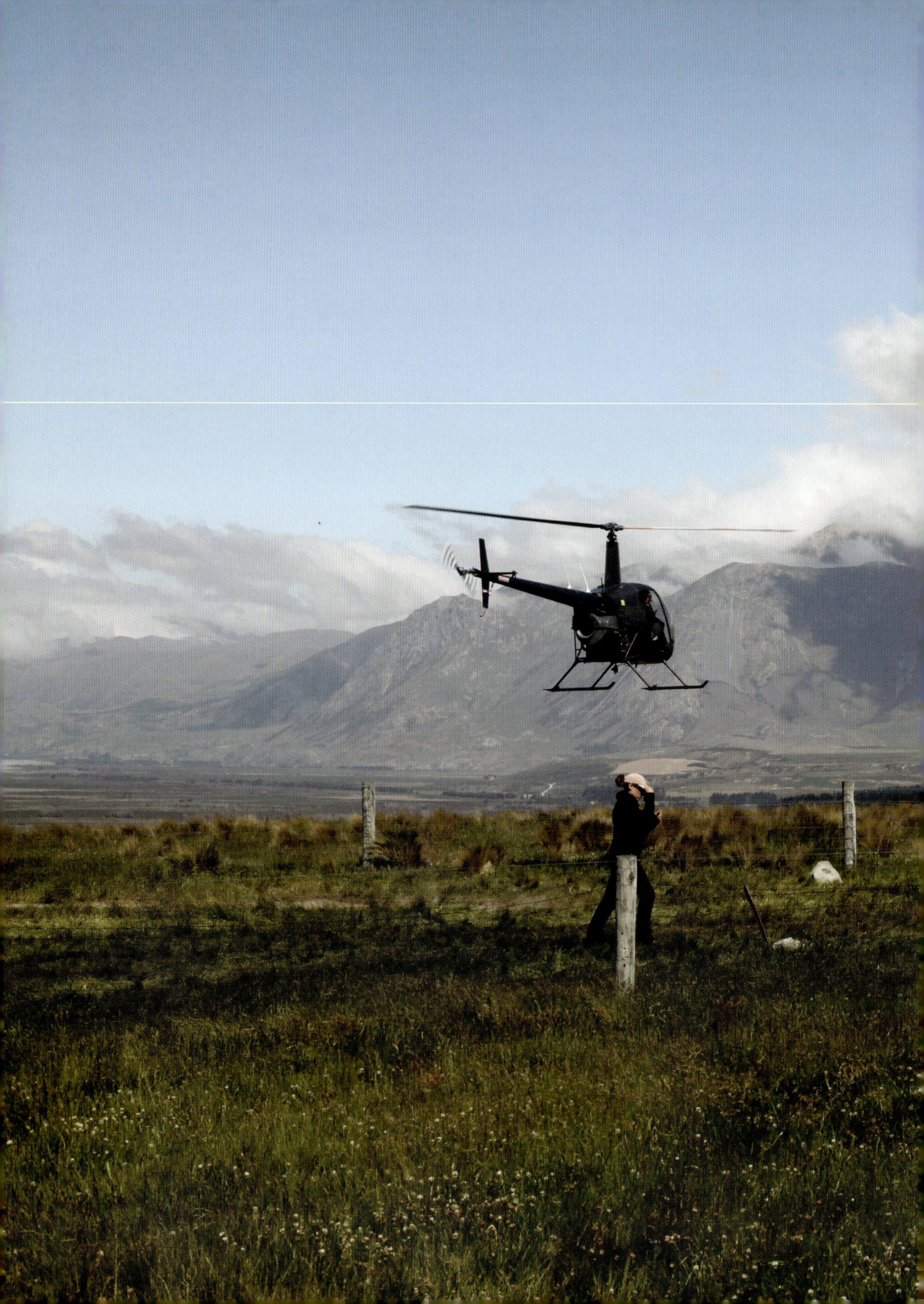

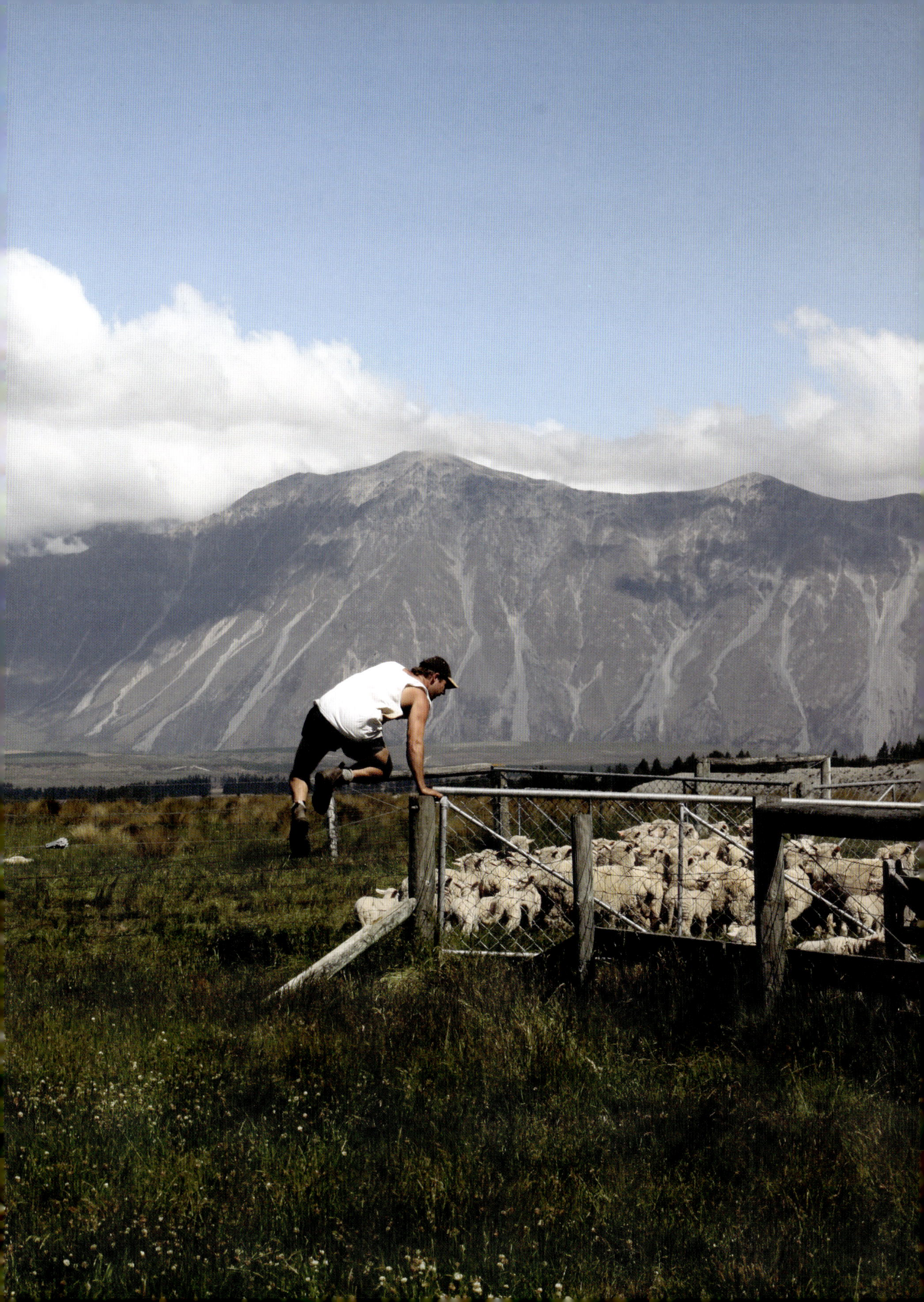

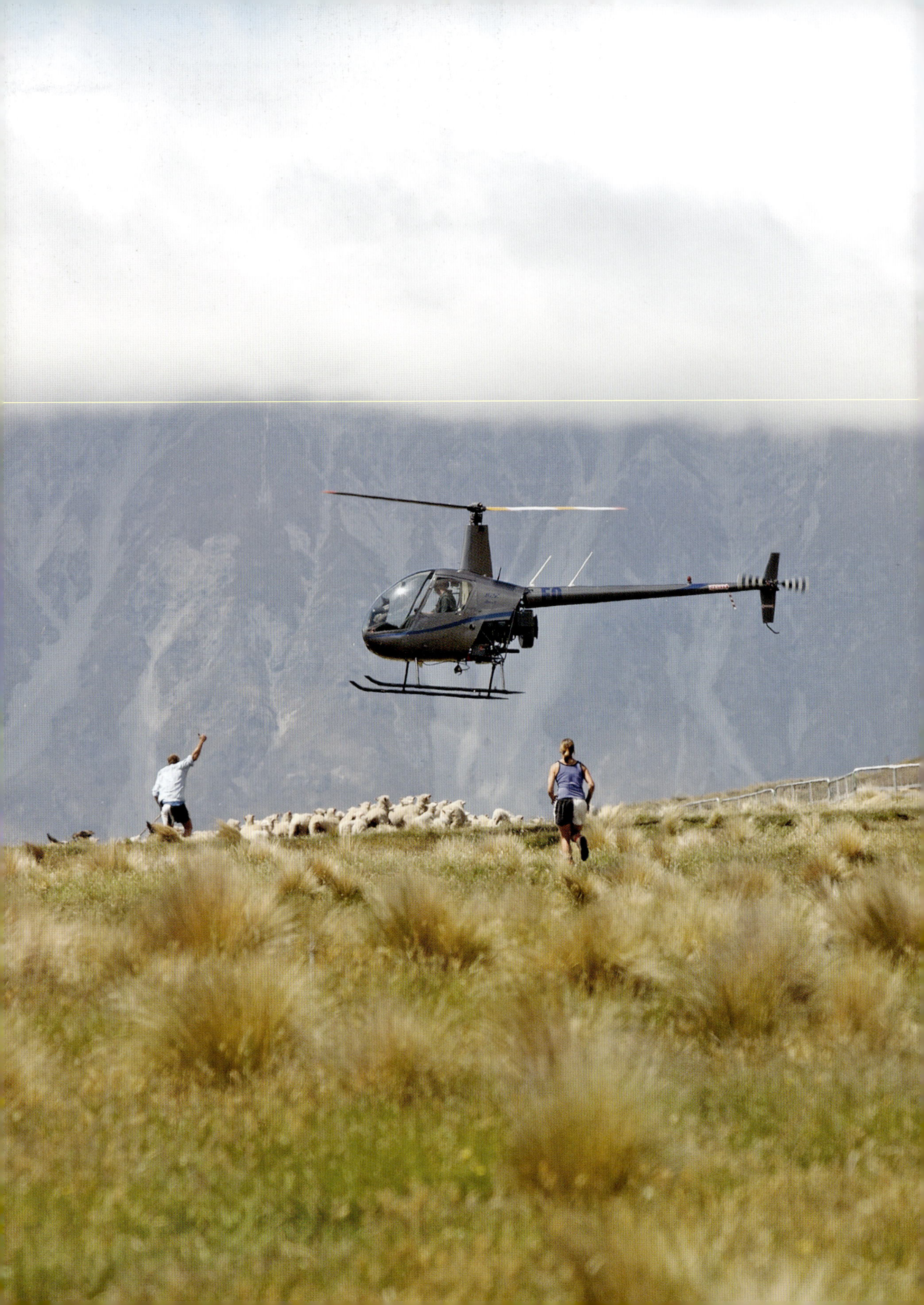

↑ ABOVE
Assembling the aluminium tailing yards brought up by Nic, the contractor, in a neat trailer-borne operation.

← LEFT
Malcolm's helicopter hovers above the mob, while earthbound musterers and dogs move in.

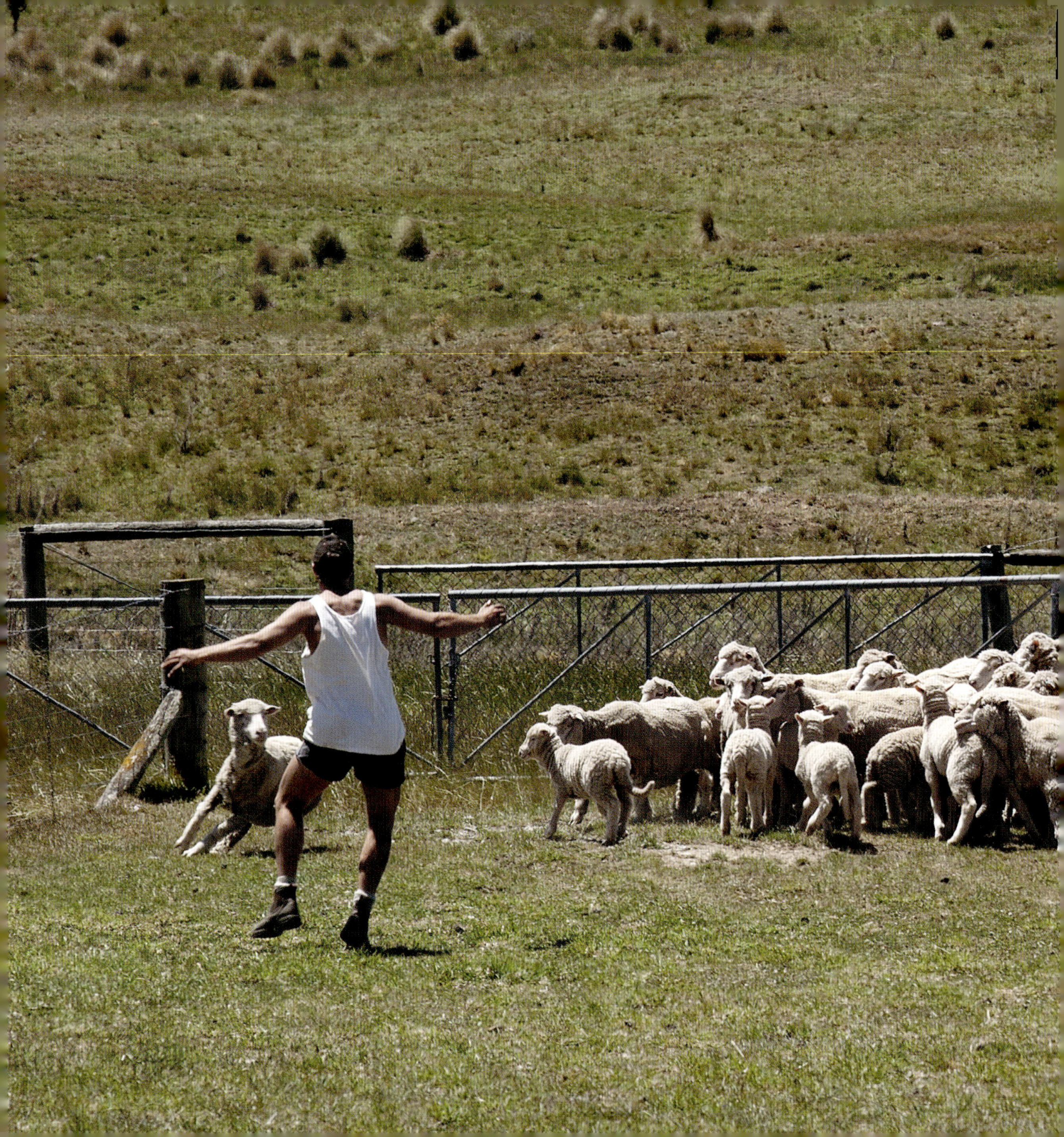

↑ ABOVE
A balletic performance as musterers and dogs push ewes and lambs through a gate.

↑ **ABOVE**
Even sheep can be non-

↑ ABOVE
The lambs are flipped onto their backs, rubber rings go around testicles and tails, the lambs are vaccinated, and the summer heat rises off the valley floor.

↑ **ABOVE**
A lamb gets the full treatment on the cradle, 'a smooth production-line operation.'

↑ **ABOVE**
Sophie and a very young lamb.

↑ ABOVE
Lunchtime: chicken, potato salad, green salad, sausage rolls.

→ RIGHT
Rowie drafts off the lambs from the ewes.

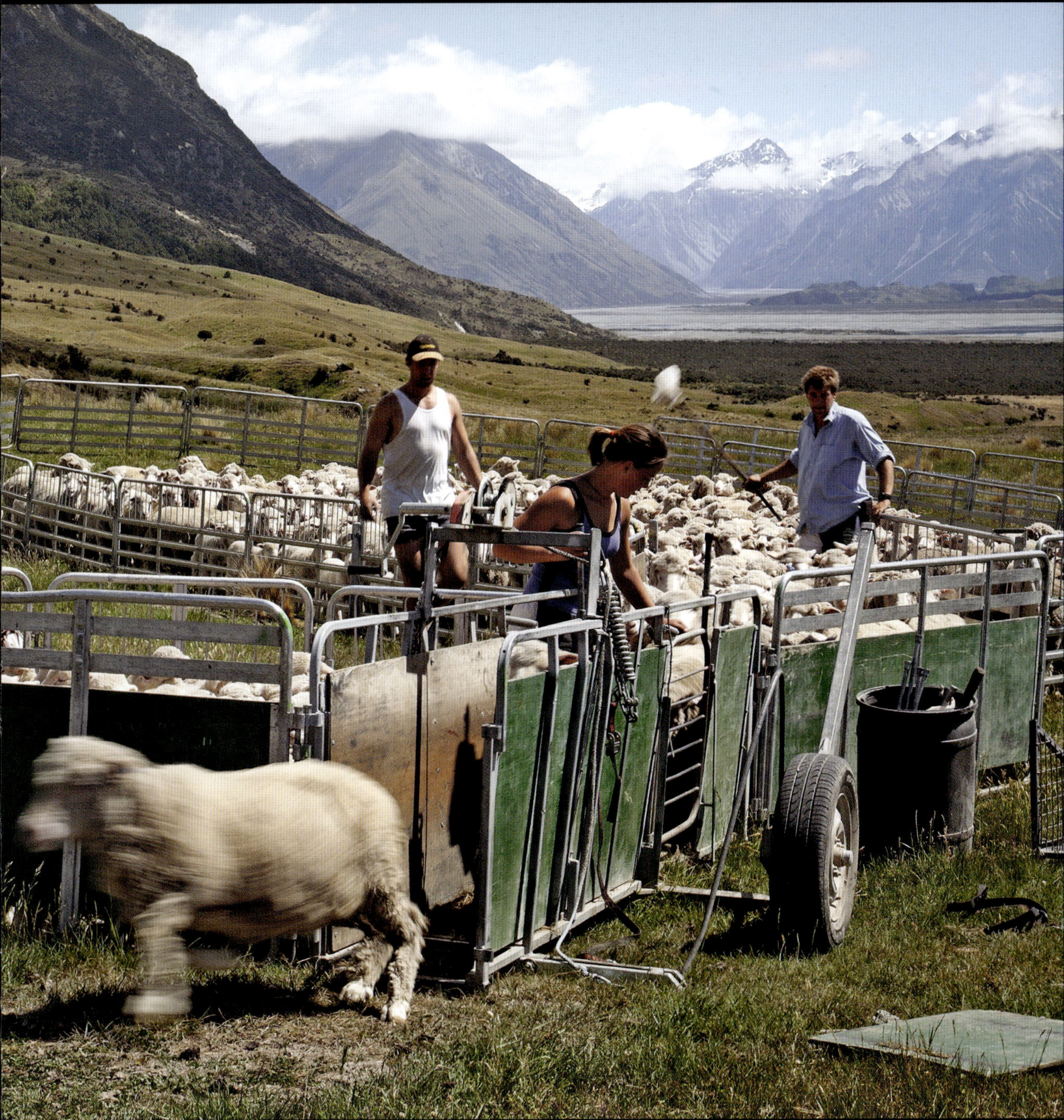

FIN

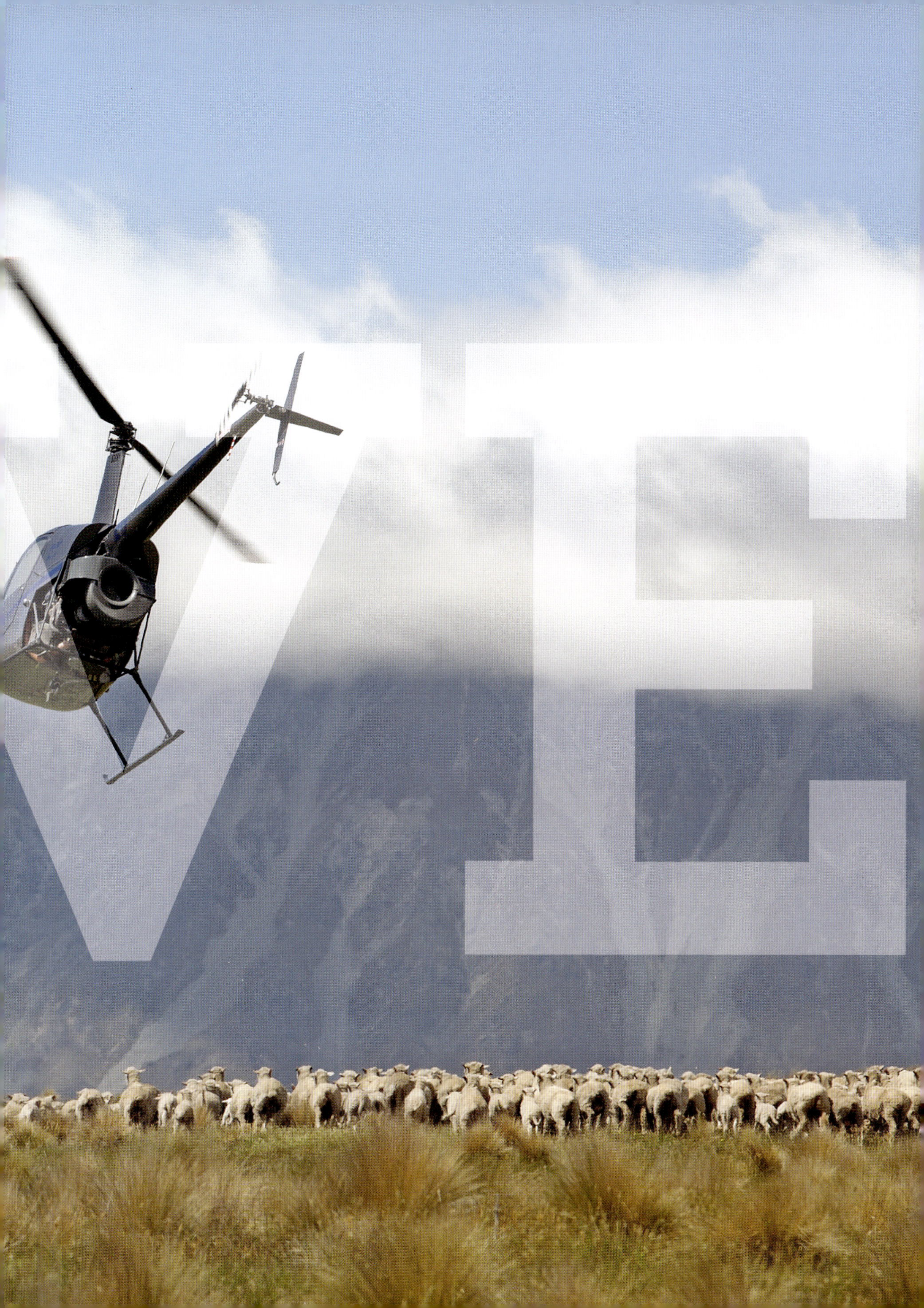
VE

ACHILLES • THE TWO THUMB RANGE • D'ARCHIAC • CROOKED SPUR • HOGGET • THE GROWLER • BRABAZON • NEUTRAL SPUR CLYDE RIVER • ROCKY RIDGE • BLACK MOUNTAINS • LITTLE SPUR • FINLAYS • FORBES RIVER • BIG BUSH • BLACK BIRCH STREAM • TOP DOWNS • BULLOCK BOW SADDLE BALACLAVA BASINS • EXETER PEAK • SINCLAIR RANGE FOREST CREEK • INKERMAN THE ROCKS • MOUNT SINCLAIR • SUGARLOAF • MOUNT HOPE

EVEN IN HIS late sixties Laurie Prouting's life is full of derring-do. He has sharp, bright blue eyes which squint when he makes a point. His easy laugh rings out often. His only real concession to age could be heard rather than seen. A replacement operation left him with a squeaky hip, loud enough for an Earthquake Commission assessor inspecting the house the Proutings kept in Christchurch to blame the noise on the staircase. Laurie tells the story with a huge laugh. He gives the impression that he has faced down most things that worried him, and they weren't so bad.

He claims to have trouble keeping himself busy, but to an outsider the problem is not obvious. He looks most at home in his flying overalls. He has two helicopters and a light aeroplane. One week he might have a huge bulldozer sitting in his yard while he reconditions it for sale, the next a grader whose failed brakes he is fixing. There's even a vintage car back on the farm awaiting restoration.

Laurie left the farm in 2002 to concentrate on the station's 500-hectare safari park. It carried herds of tahr, deer, chamois and fallow deer to be hunted by paying visitors. He ferried hunters and trampers around the mountains in his helicopters, guided wealthy Russian and a declining number of affluent American hunters and in between flew his family and visitors up and down the Rangitata Valley as if he were driving a suburban hatchback.

A high country farmer's life is perilous by any city standard. There are bluffs to slip down, swollen rivers to ford, snow and ice to freeze in, angry or panic-stricken animals to avoid, vehicles to keep upright when the laws of gravity demand they should not. All of them suggest that a proper leisure activity might be to sink into a deep, safe sofa and watch *Antiques Roadshow*.

Laurie, though, is a man whose idea of a holiday is first, not to have one and then, if he were pushed, to take his kids over the Whitcombe Pass to the West Coast, a rather terrifying route precisely described by Samuel Butler in *Erewhon* and named after the Canterbury Surveyor who became one of the first two Europeans to take it, drowning in the attempt. Or not to walk but to *run* over the Milford Track, or do any one of several things most of us take care to avoid.

Anne Prouting is the calm in the centre of the vortex, the super-rock of the family according to her daughter Neroli. 'She backs everyone, she's there for everyone. She's super-gran. She doesn't play golf or anything, she's just here in case she's wanted for the children. Family is number one. She exhausts herself with our children, exhausts herself with Dad.'

Nor does Anne waste time worrying, just as well, for Laurie went well out of his way to do things she might otherwise worry about, excessively. He was a deep sea diver, of course, for how might he miss venturing into such an alien environment?

> **I enjoy being totally in control of my own life. You cock it up, you cock it up. You're in charge of it all.**

'I enjoy being totally in control of my own life. You cock it up, you cock it up. You're in charge of it all. Diving is like that. If you make a mistake then you're going to pay for it. That's the way I like it. You're not reliant on a whole lot of others.'

LAURIE HAS CLIMBED many of the major peaks in the South Island, beginning with Aoraki Mount Cook. 'It seemed like the place to start. I asked this guy Shaun Norman, a guide, about it. Next day he calls me: "Mmmmm. Look, I've just been looking at the weather and I think tomorrow might be good." I found myself saying, "Why not?"'

Beneath the nonchalance, Laurie was worried. He did not like rock-climbing, nor steep snow and ice, and he did not know much about crampons. Aoraki Mount Cook meant all of those things. Nevertheless, next morning found him climbing up to the Plateau Hut, the starting point for Mount Cook climbers.

'There were guys wandering around willy-nilly, there could have been twenty guys all going and coming, all hours of the night. I never got to sleep.

Midnight came and Shaun's out getting dressed. I think, "What the hell . . . ?" He says, "Come on, we're going climbing."

'We left the hut at one in the morning. It was black as. Around four we stopped and had a drink. We were having a yarn and there was an almighty crack and a damned avalanche came down. My eyes bulged. It sounded as if it was right next to me. I knew we were climbing up the Linda Glacier, renowned for its avalanches. It was a bit unnerving. We'd just set off and *whack*! There was another one. And this one, I reckon I could have put my hand out to touch it. Both the guides now were steadily peering into the dark. They were as anxious as I was. But nothing happened.

'By now we were at the top of the Linda ice shelf. I wasn't feeling good. Altitude sickness, but I didn't know it. I felt rotten. We got up to the summit rock and Shaun being the professional guide he is was making sure I was not going to fall off that hill. I thought he was overdoing it to be quite honest. I was thinking "Come on Shaun I can scramble up there on my own, there's nothing to it."

'But my head was threatening to fall apart. I knew I was in bad shape. I got as far away as I could, dug a hole in the snow and spewed up. Straightaway Shaun was on my back, shouting that I'd been pushing him, and now I had altitude sickness, and if I didn't slow down we weren't going to make the top. "I'm OK," I said. And I was too. Eventually we scooted up on top. The avalanches and the altitude sickness worried me. But the steepness of the ice and rock, well, I was good.'

A series of peaks followed. Mounts Aspiring, D'Archiac, Tasman. D'Archiac scares even experienced mountaineers: one party, which could not reach the summit, wrote in a subsequent account of 'three hours of terror'.

Now there was only one more mountain he wanted to climb. Strangely enough, it was Mount Arrowsmith, the mountain that gave his first station its name. He lived beside it, never climbed it.

Climbing, diving and adventuring were sideshows in the theatre of his life, however. The headline act was always flying. A sign at the entrance to Mesopotamia Station proudly announces the airport. A cluster of buildings stands beside an airstrip on the river flat, a hangar, a fertiliser shed, and possibly the smallest airport terminal building in the country, a one-roomed hut.

The airport's prime position reflected its role both in the station's affairs and in Laurie's and Malcolm's lives. Aircraft were used for sowing, top-dressing, mustering, hunting and tourism, as mountain taxis and personal transport. Laurie Prouting was fascinated by the early pilots who came to the station in their Tiger Moths and Austers. The Auster's yellow throttle engraved its image on his young mind. He was hooked. Mentally, he has had that yellow throttle in his hand ever since.

He got his chance in 1960 when he left boarding school in Christchurch and started work on the farm. Both he and his brother Frank wanted to fly and in 1963 they began learning. Their grandmother's iron discipline helped them along. They stayed with her while they took flying lessons in Timaru. After dinner she wouldn't let them do the dishes. She'd clear the table, put down their books in front of them, insist on concentration and demand silence in the house.

Starting from cold they began flying on 18 December 1963 and sat their licences the following January. Both passed. Private pilots' licences required forty hours' flying and they accumulated the hours in just a month and a half.

HE AND FRANK would saddle up their horses, ride out and hack landing strips in the matagouri. 'We thought we were so far advanced. To be able to fly up to one of the huts, land there and do the work we needed to do and get home, whereas it used to take so long on horseback or walking.'

Time has made some of those rough airstrips redundant. They use helicopters more often now. But then, the airstrips led to another innovation: they decided to do their own top-dressing. 'What a way to really get the hang of an aeroplane. You're doing maybe a hundred takeoffs and landings each day. That was brilliant. We were putting out about five hundred tonnes of fertiliser in a year in a little Auster. Ripped the seats out of it and put a hopper in. We just did so much with the aeroplane, even seeding on cultivated ground and making a very good job of it. Now it has become specialised. We get other guys in. The modern-day top-dresser can lift so much and it's so efficient and those guys are good, professional. Whereas we were all eye-ometer.'

Peter and Don learned to fly too. Flying killed Peter, and the events of that day ran and reran in Laurie's mind. 'Peter had a problem with his flying, the problem that killed him. He let his speed deteriorate and he let the bloody thing stall. He was trying to turn away from the high ground. I would have dropped my load but kept going straight ahead, wings level, knowing that if I turned I'd stall, and taken what was in front of me, crash-landed without a moment's hesitation.

'It's lovely to be in the air but you've got to concentrate on the job in hand at all times. If you're not fiercely interested in flying, passionate about it, then you're not going to be able to give it your best shot. I didn't want

Malcolm to feel obliged to fly. It had to come from him and it took him a while. Eventually he wanted to.

'As a family we're probably not over-endowed with a lot of brain power when it comes to academic stuff; the very reason why we're not in an office making a lot of money sitting on our bums. But if we're going to get a flying ticket we've got to go back to the schoolroom. In maths we get by but we're not good at it, although I think I've turned that round to my advantage. I know I'm not good at maths so I do it all twice.

'Malcolm would always err on the side of putting himself down a bit in case anyone thought he was a bit of a smart-arse. He did much better than probably he thought he would and passed his exams without too much bother.'

IF LAURIE EVER got a report card on his life, it would probably be dominated by three Fs: Family, flying and farming. And keeping himself busy at all times, so that day we were bowling along the highway in his ute, one of those vehicles that fit farmers like uniforms, and talking while he was driving towards Ashburton to refill the big tank on his trailer with aviation fuel.

After he moved back to Mesopotamia from Mount Arrowsmith in 1982, he said, he began flying helicopters, becoming an extremely experienced pilot. That led to one of his great adventures for, in 2003: 'Out of the blue a good friend in the North Island rang and almost pleaded with me. He was taking his helicopter to the Antarctic but his girlfriend was due to have a baby just about the time he should have been there. He knew I had the right-sized helicopter and he was almost crying on my shoulder asking if I'd fill in for him. *Holy Nora!* My body was tingling with excitement.'

Anne readily agreed to his going. Laurie was in his early sixties. He became the oldest man on the expedition, a New Zealand-owned ship heading for the Antarctic for *National Geographic* magazine. No one in the ship's company, eighteen on a boat forty-three metres long, had been there before.

'To be honest, well, a lot of the guys on the boat were American film crew, the boat was an ex-Japanese research vessel and it had been designed for small people, and I was one of the few who didn't have to crouch as we walked along the gangways and so on. Some of the seas there were wild, they could throw you out of your bunk. If you had to stoop as you walked and the boat lurched violently, well, pretty well everyone on the boat suffered from a crook back. Very often you couldn't stand up to have a shower. You had to sit in the tub to avoid being thrown out.'

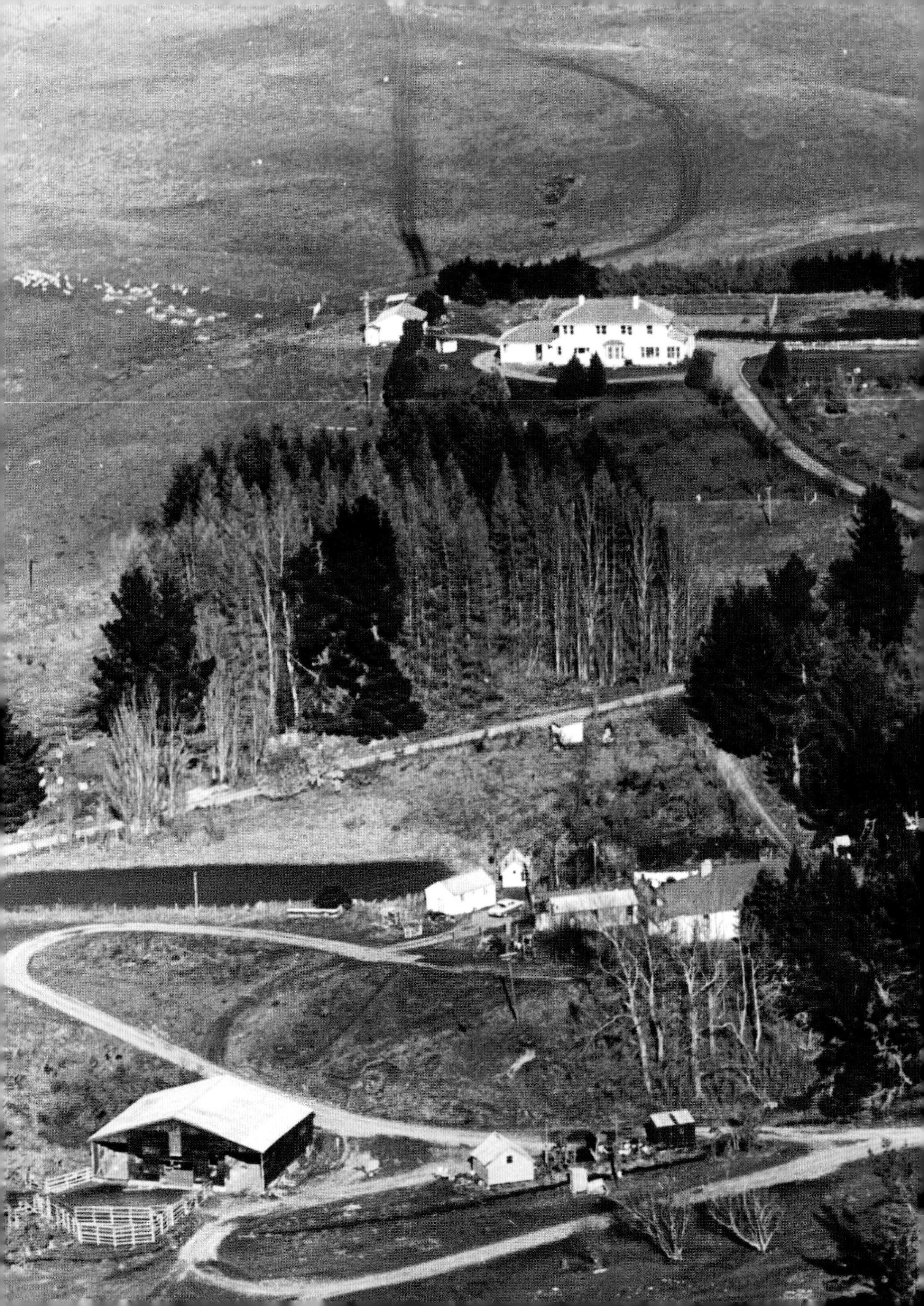

← LEFT
An aerial view of Mesopotamia homestead and station buildings taken by Peter Bush on his first visit in 1970. The stable, built in 1948, is shown lower left; above and slightly to the right is the cookhouse along with various shepherd huts. The implement shed and the old smithy is off to the extreme right.

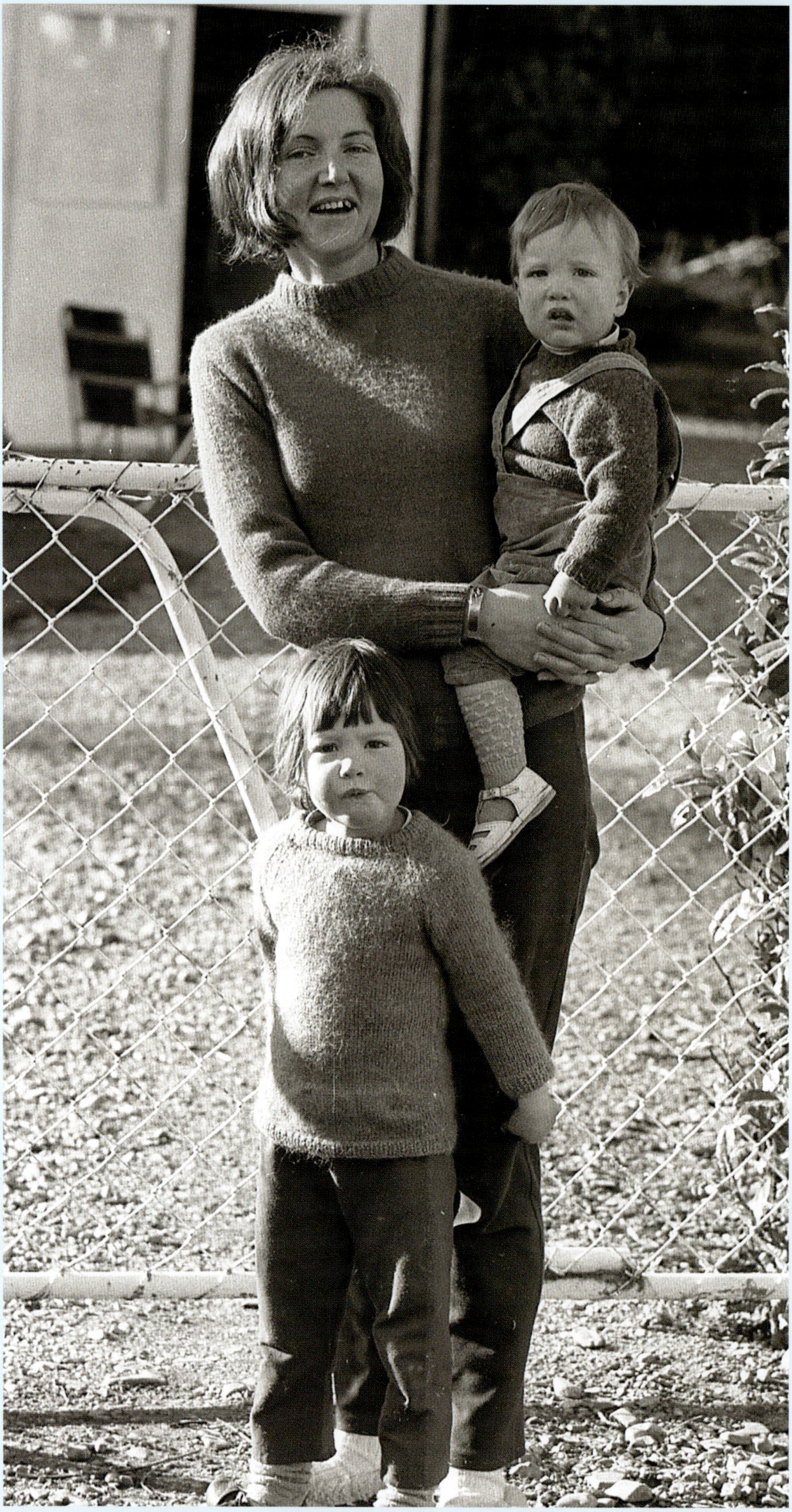

It was his first time at sea. It could easily have been his last, too, for he was almost lost in an incident which even on a continent known for bizarre episodes was unusual. 'One day I took off with two hours and a bit of fuel. Fluctuations in the magnetic fields rendered the magnetic compass almost useless so I was totally reliant on the GPS [a navigation system which fixes position by locking onto satellites] to come back to the exact dot I'd taken off from. This time I came back and the boat simply wasn't there. I was worried, because I had little fuel left. The boat was sitting in a vast area of pack ice. It was painted white and was very hard to see anyway. I called up on the radio and asked where they'd gone. They gave me a vague answer. It really said that they had no idea.'

The sweet-smelling South Canterbury air whistled past the ute, the clean countryside glistened in the sun, green as grass can be green and a very long way from an anxious man trying to find safety in the white wastes of the Antarctic.

'"Well," I said, "you're not at the place where I left you. Can anyone hear the helicopter? Can you help us a wee bit here?" It seemed like half an hour later and my fuel reserves were down to minutes when they came back and said they couldn't hear me. I told them I'd turn on all my lights. "If it's not too much bother to you," I said, (I was getting a wee bit sarcastic) "would you look for them." I was slowly turning the helicopter up and down and around and eventually one of the guys came back and said, "Yeah we can see you." That's one of the moments I remember most.

'I asked which direction I should head. There was a moment of silence. Then they came back and told me just to head off and they'd tell me if I was going in the wrong direction. So I headed off. And they said, "Hey Laurie, turn left," so I turned left, and they said, "*No no no* turn right," because they were looking at me and got it the wrong way round. And I was wondering if I'd ever see the boat again. Because quite honestly I'd have flown nineteen kilometres before I saw it. I didn't believe it. I was getting pretty skinny on fuel. My next option was putting down on an iceberg and saying, "Look guys, you'll have to find me now."

'You can ask why I didn't just feed in my GPS co-ordinates to tell them where I was. But it's a bit difficult to do when you need both hands to fly the thing; for me to have done that I'd have to have settled down somewhere.'

← RIGHT
Anne Prouting holding the young Malcolm, with Neroli in front, 1971.

WHEN HE GOT back to New Zealand Anne had shifted house. She'd moved out of the homestead at Mesopotamia and into a new house further down the valley, almost directly opposite Mount Peel Station but on the other side of the river, more than an hour away from Mesopotamia by road but a few minutes by air.

She did not tell Laurie until she had picked him up from the airport and he was about to turn off towards the Rangitata Gorge. 'Oh,' she said, 'we don't live there any longer.'

And that was how he learned he no longer lived on the station where he had spent most of his life. They moved off Mesopotamia, and his son Malcolm and his wife Sue were on their own.

→ RIGHT
Anne and Laurie Prouting not long after moving from Mount Arrowsmith into the homestead at Mesopotamia, 1982.

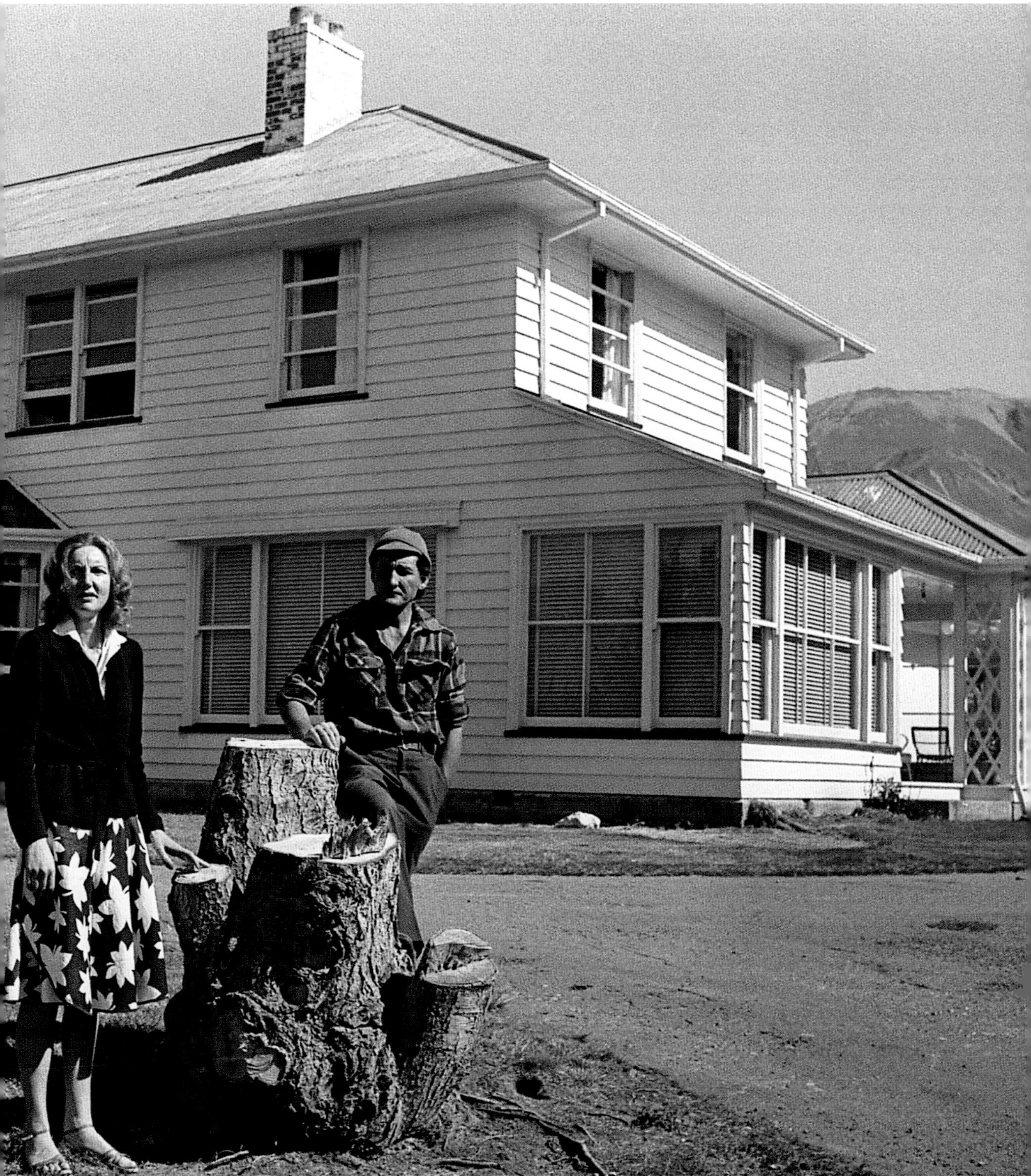

→ CLOCKWISE FROM TOP LEFT

Laurie on top of Mt Cook 'before the top fell off' in 1988.

Visiting the Nordenskjold Hut, Snow Hill Island, Antarctica, 2003.

Laurie in the 'middle of nowhere' on sea ice, Antarctica, 2003.

Bush Stream Bridge, built by the station, 1989.

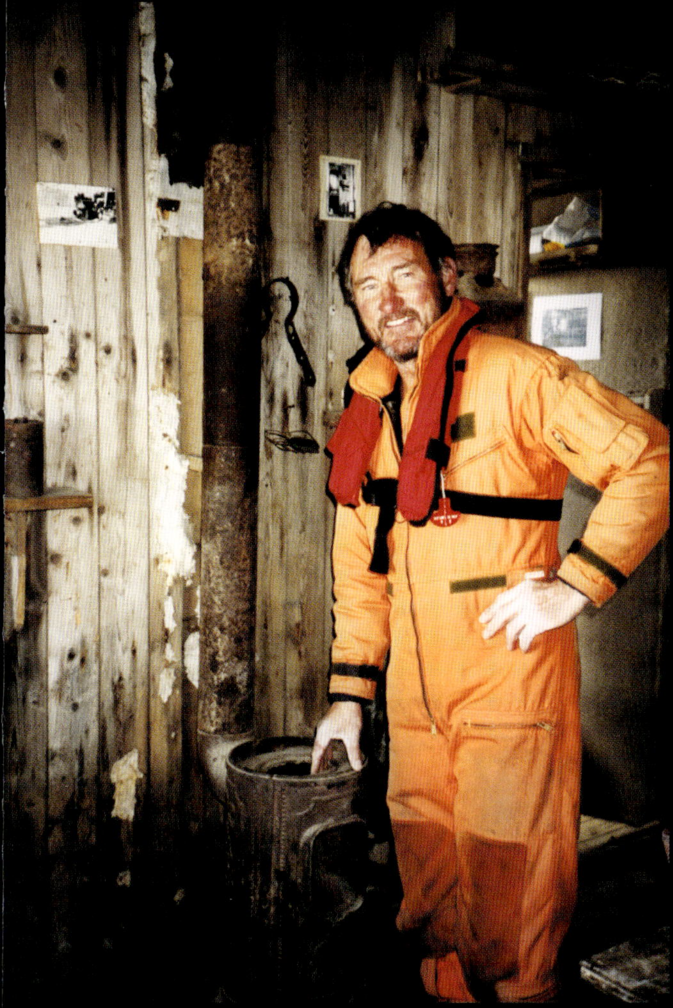

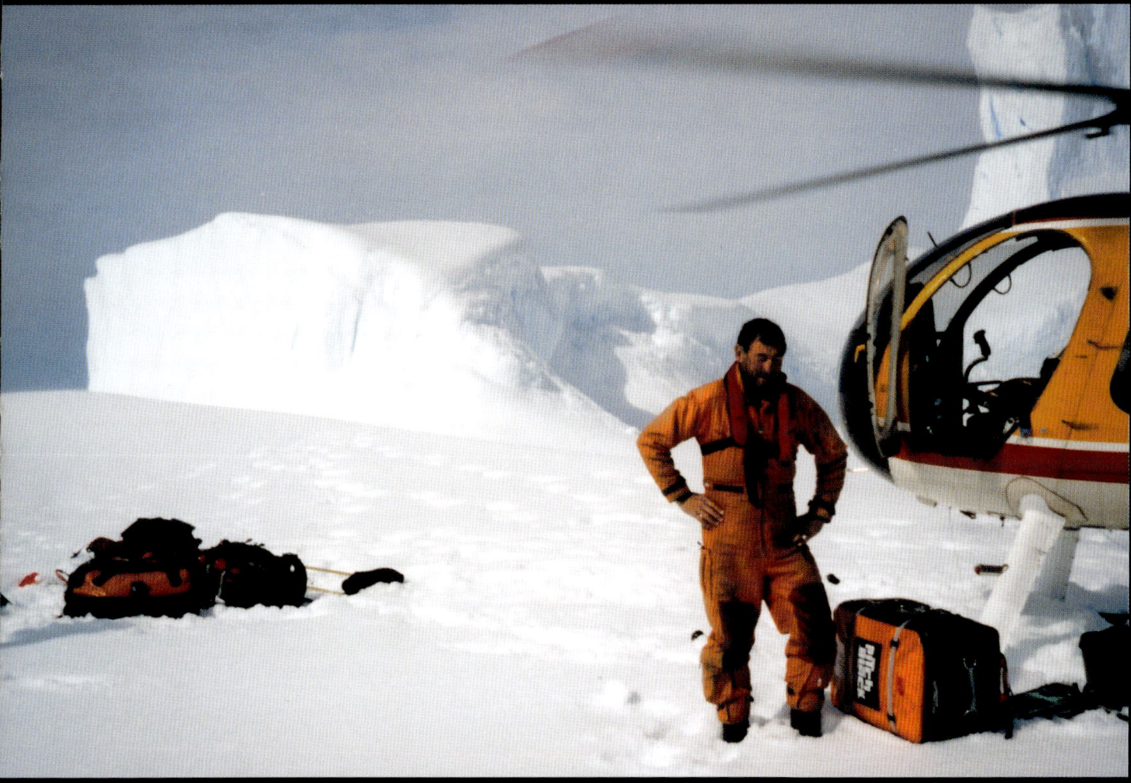

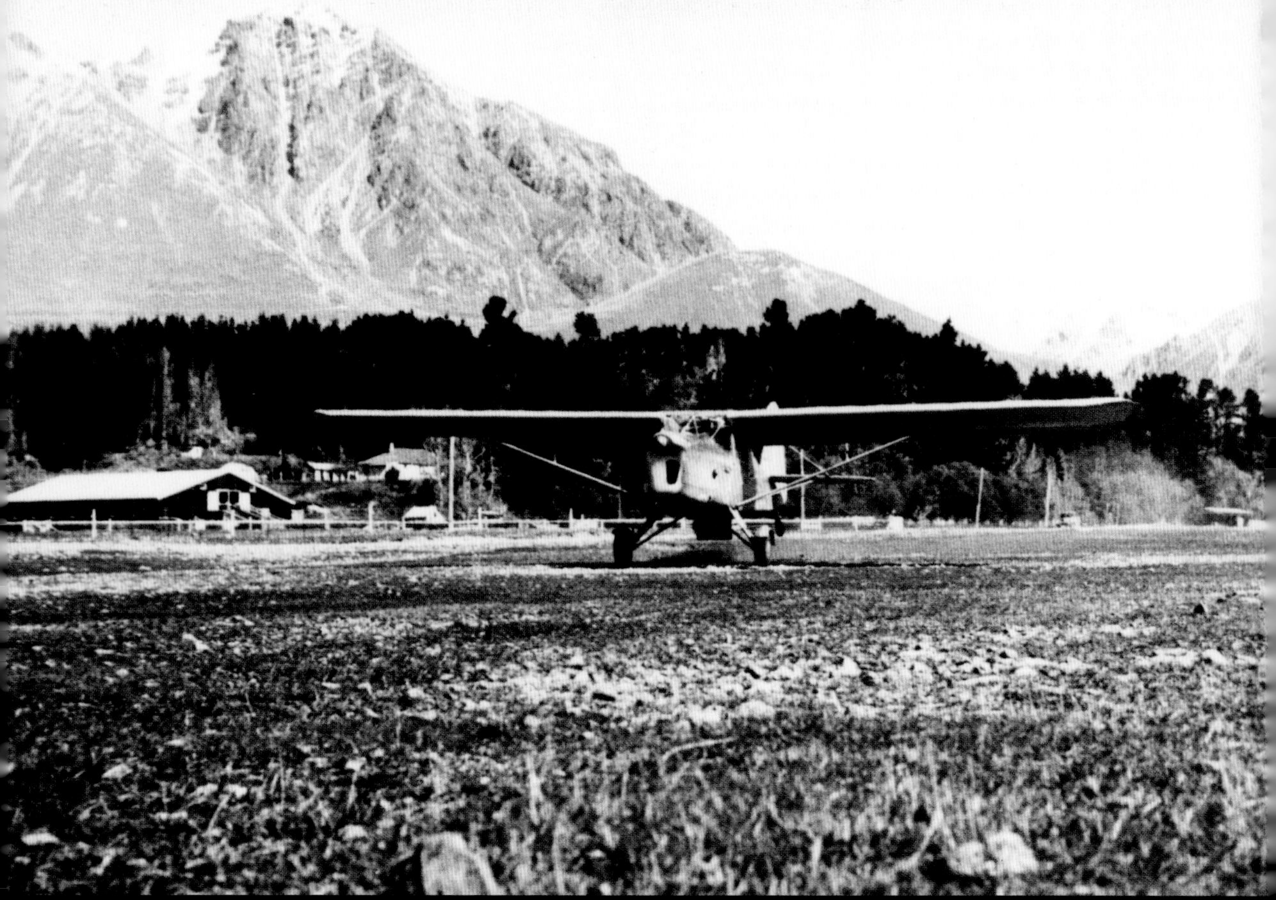

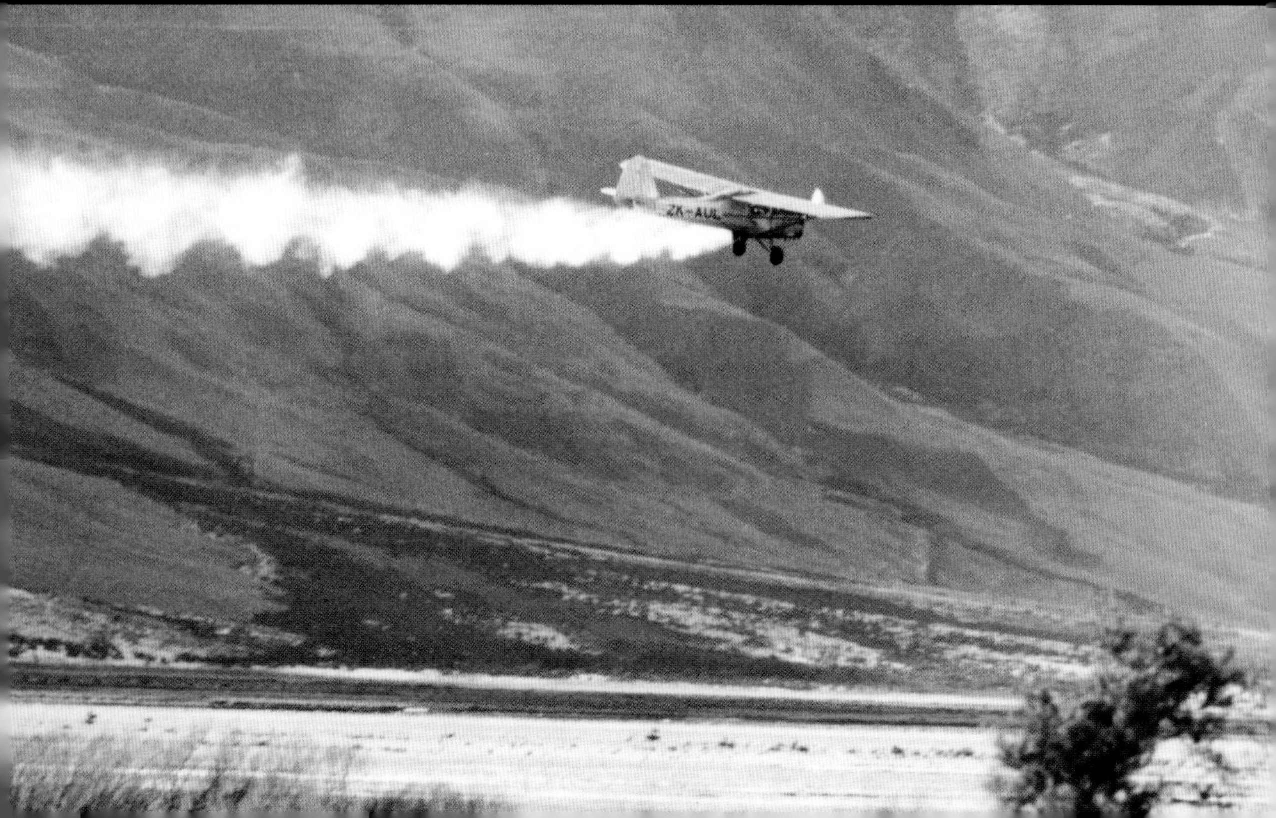
ZK-AUL

↖ **CLOCKWISE FROM TOP LEFT**
The Auster Topdresser, ZK-AUL on take-off at Mesopotamia, 1970.

The Cessna reaching the summit of the taxi ramp at Thornycroft.

Laurie doing what he loves best.

Topdressing at Mesopotamia in 1965. Laurie is at the controls.

PHOTO ESSAY
DIPPING

On a torrid nor'wester day, preparing for dipping starts before dawn. George, Sam, Nic, Rowie, Jess and helpers have filled the plunge dip, and are pushing seven thousand ewes and lambs into the yards. A dozen men and women and one boy, Ferg, work in fierce heat, pushing sheep through the race, into the concrete dip and dunking them to get rid of lice. The first sheep are moving by 5.30am and the whole job takes seven hours. It's finished by lunchtime — leaving the afternoon free for other jobs.

→ LEFT
In the yellow dawn light of a nor'wester day the first sheep are yarded ready for dipping. Malcolm second from left, Sue and Ferg at right.

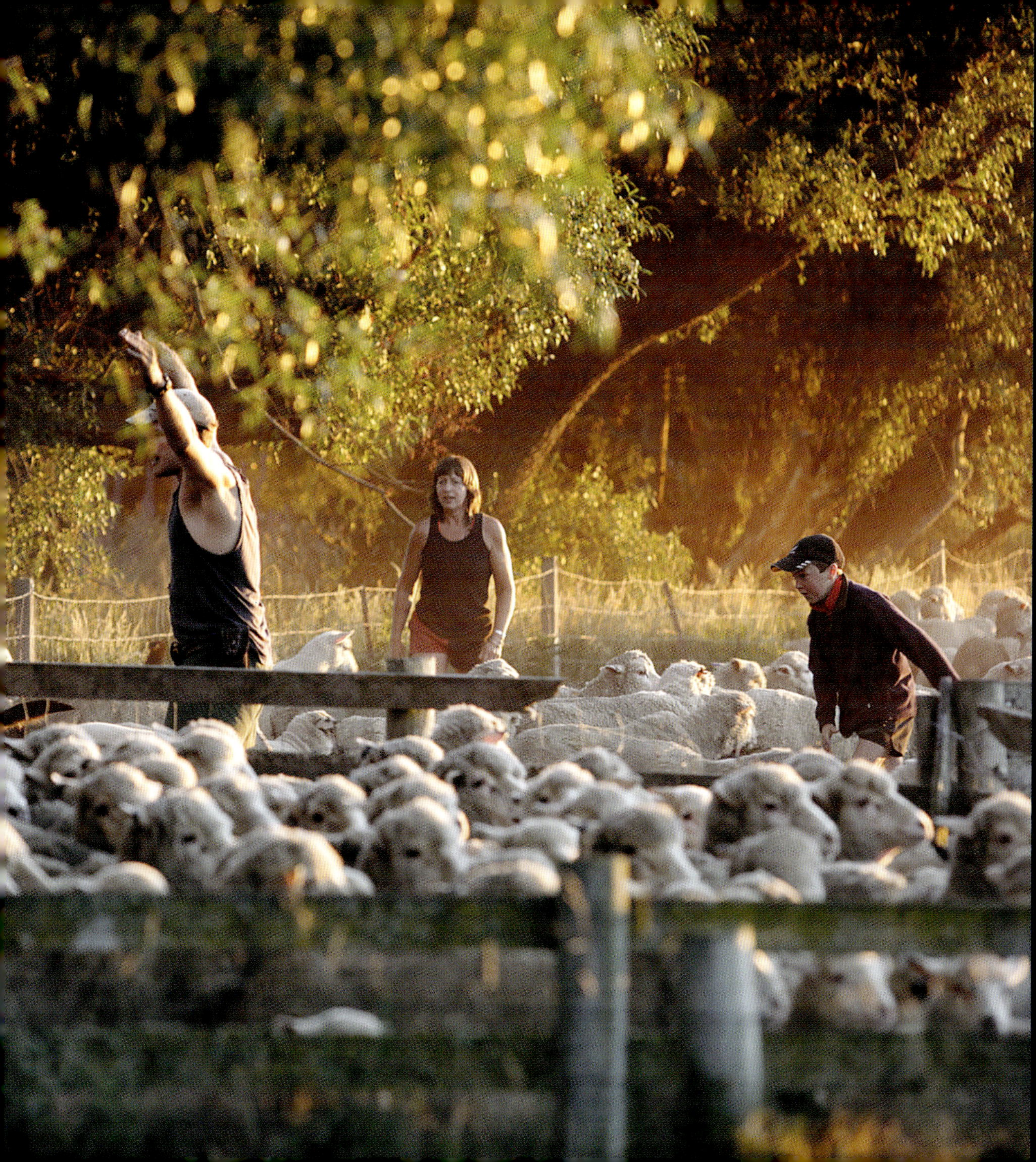

↑ CLOCKWISE FROM ABOVE
Mixing chemicals in the long dip before the first sheep take the plunge.

The surface of the dip is whipped into foam as a steady stream of sheep swim from one end to the other, each of them completely immersed at least twice by workers standing on the sides.

A lamb takes a flying jump into the dip as sheep already in the water are forced below the surface.

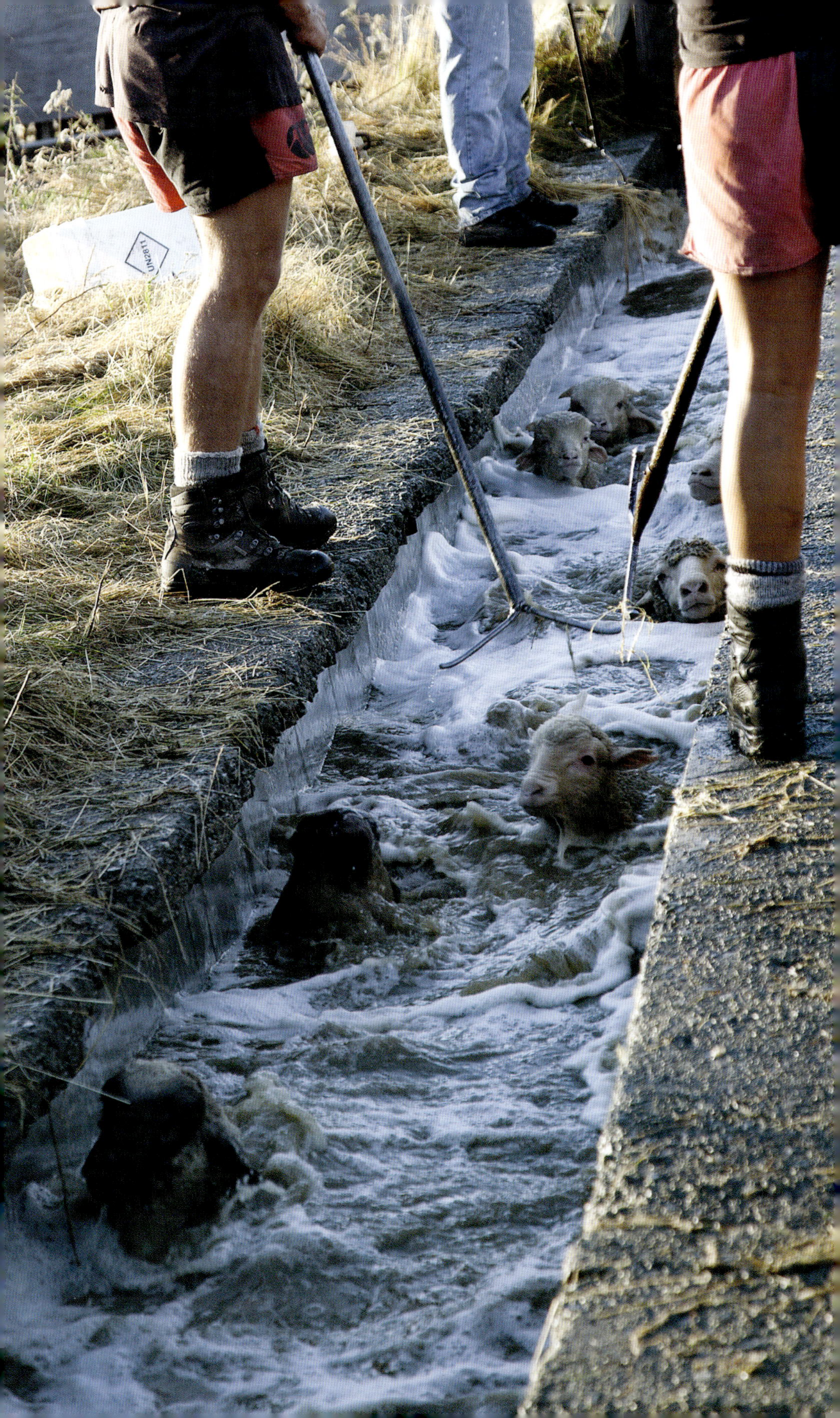
UN2811

↑ ABOVE
The occasional runaway sheep has to be chased, caught and thrown in.

→ RIGHT
Rowie (left) works alongside her brother Slee dunking the swimming sheep.

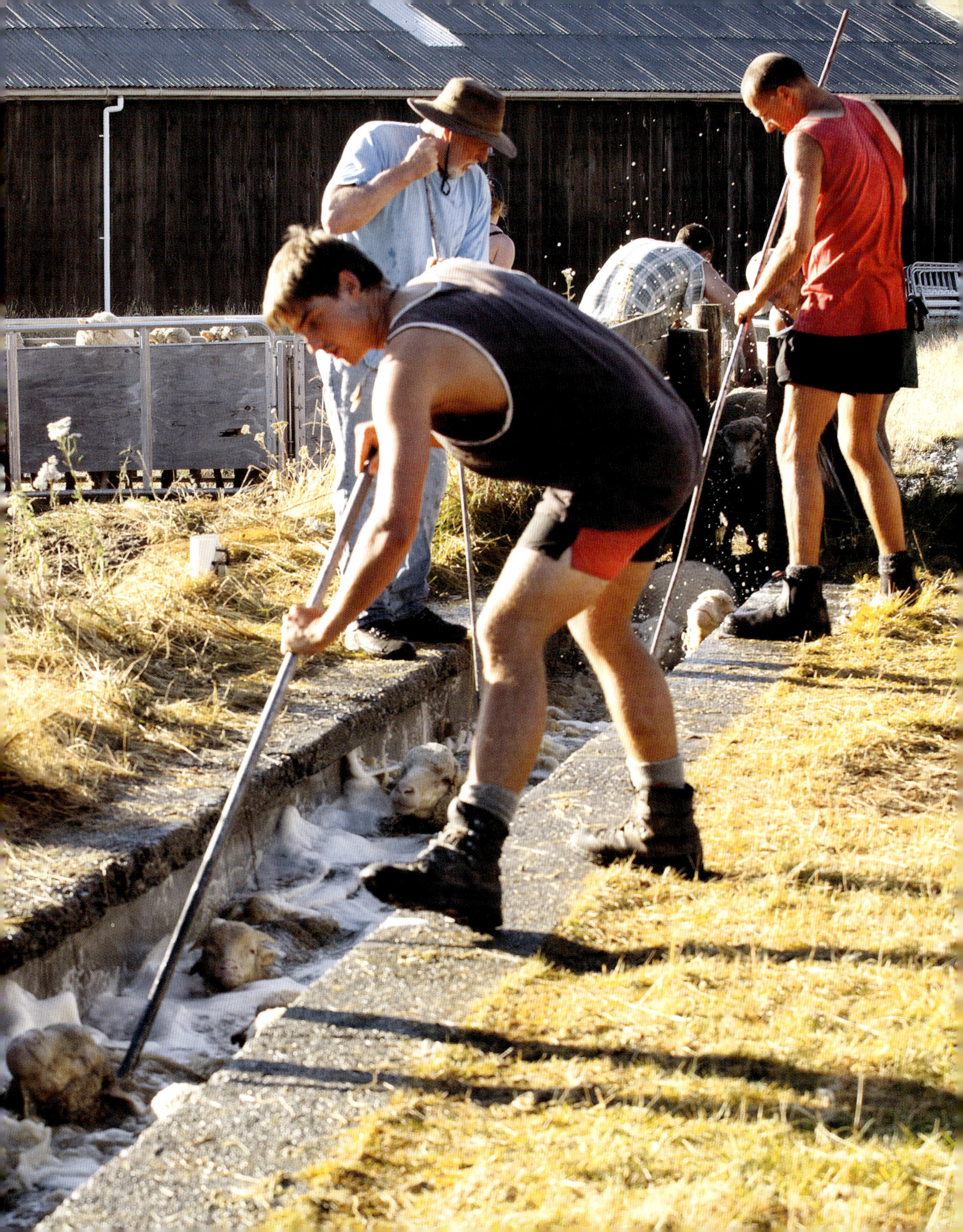

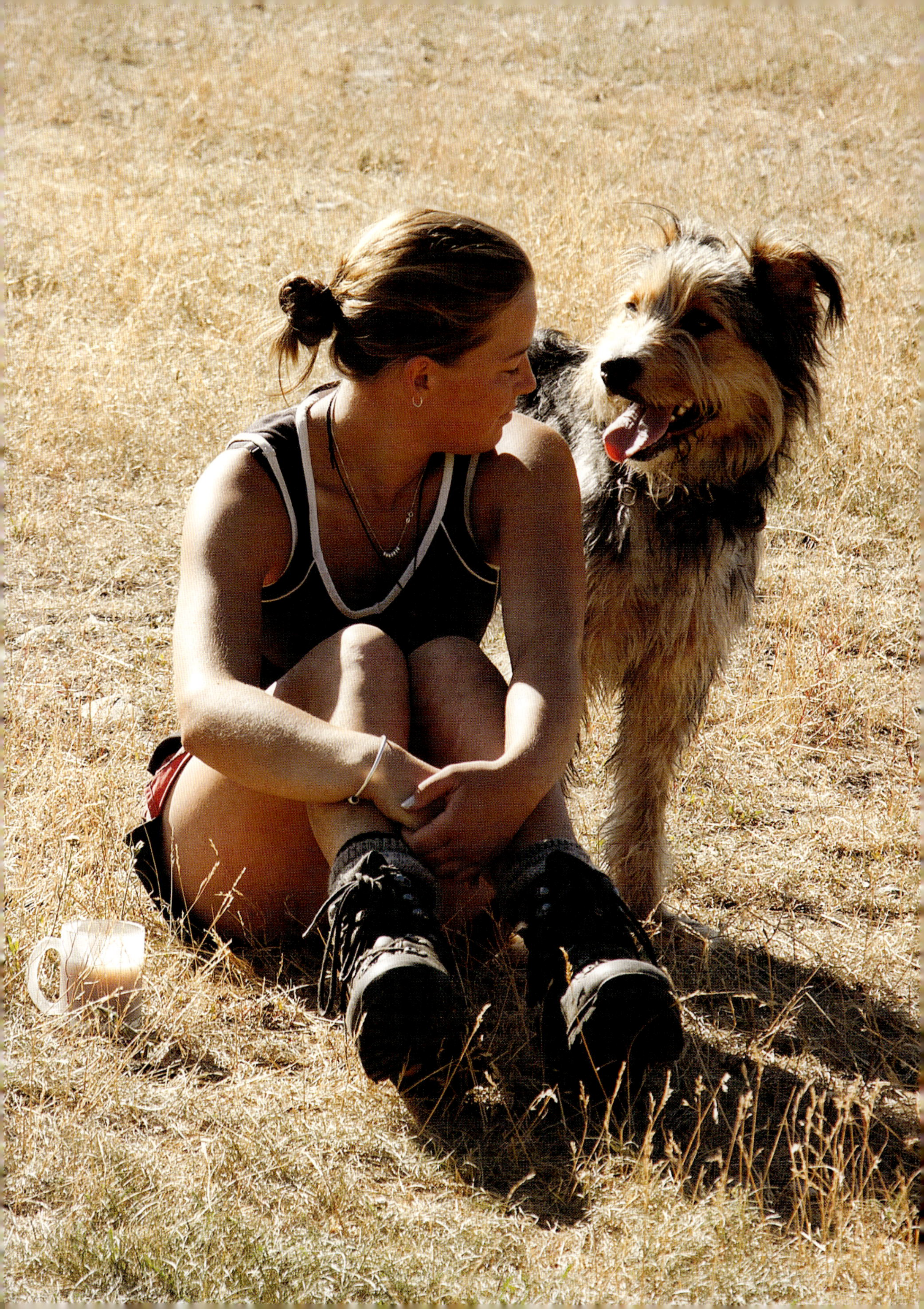

← **CLOCKWISE FROM FAR LEFT**
Rowie and dog chat at morning tea.

Smoko. Relaxing on the sun-burned grass with tea and chocolate slice, half the sheep through, the other half still to go.

Finished! The dip is covered over with old farm gates and wire mesh.

→ LEFT
Lunch at the big table under the pergola beside the homestead, served by Wendy the Wwoofer (in the blue singlet). The caserole is merino slow-cooked in orange juice, honey, garlic and soy sauce, served with lots of vegetables.

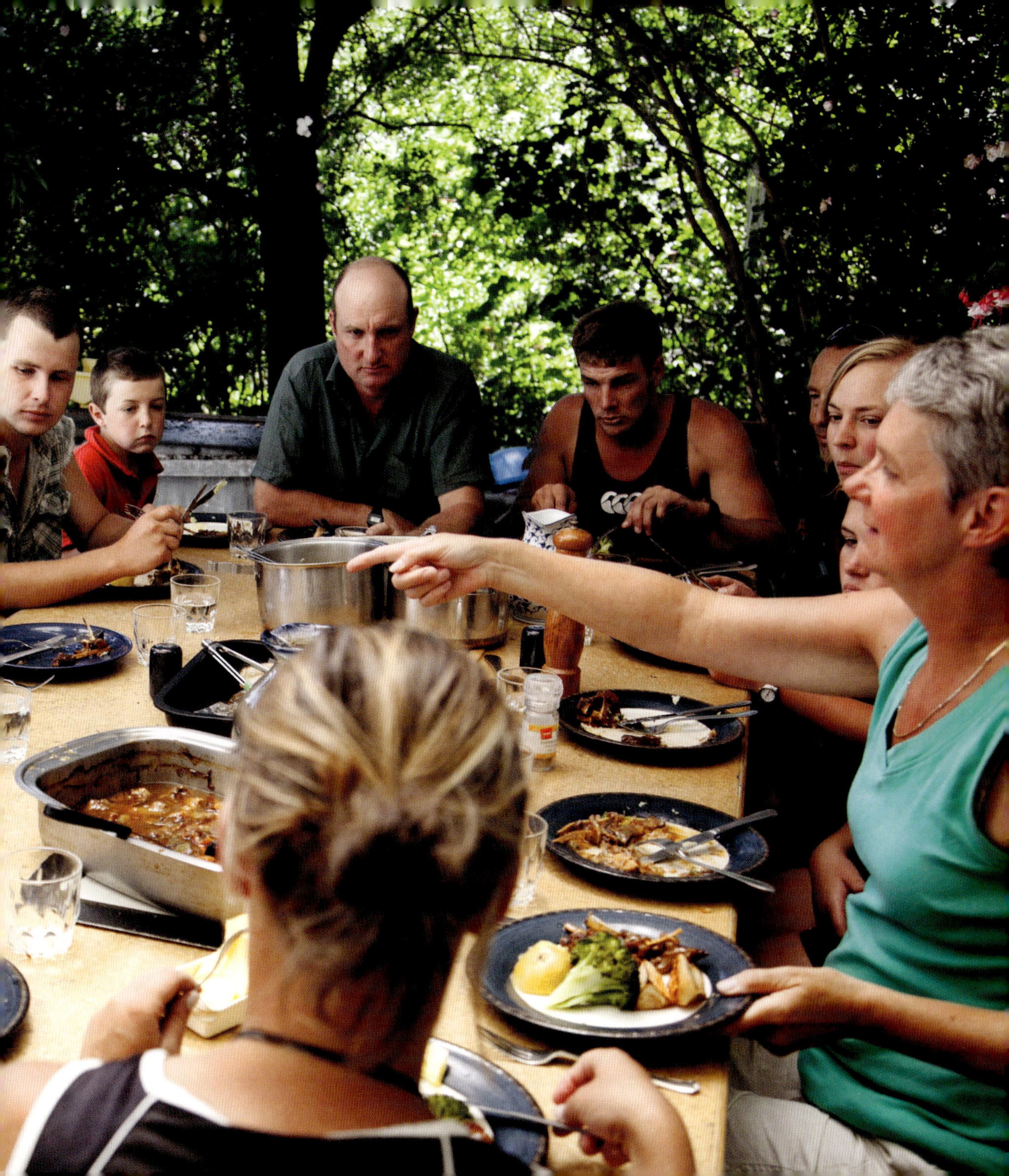

S1

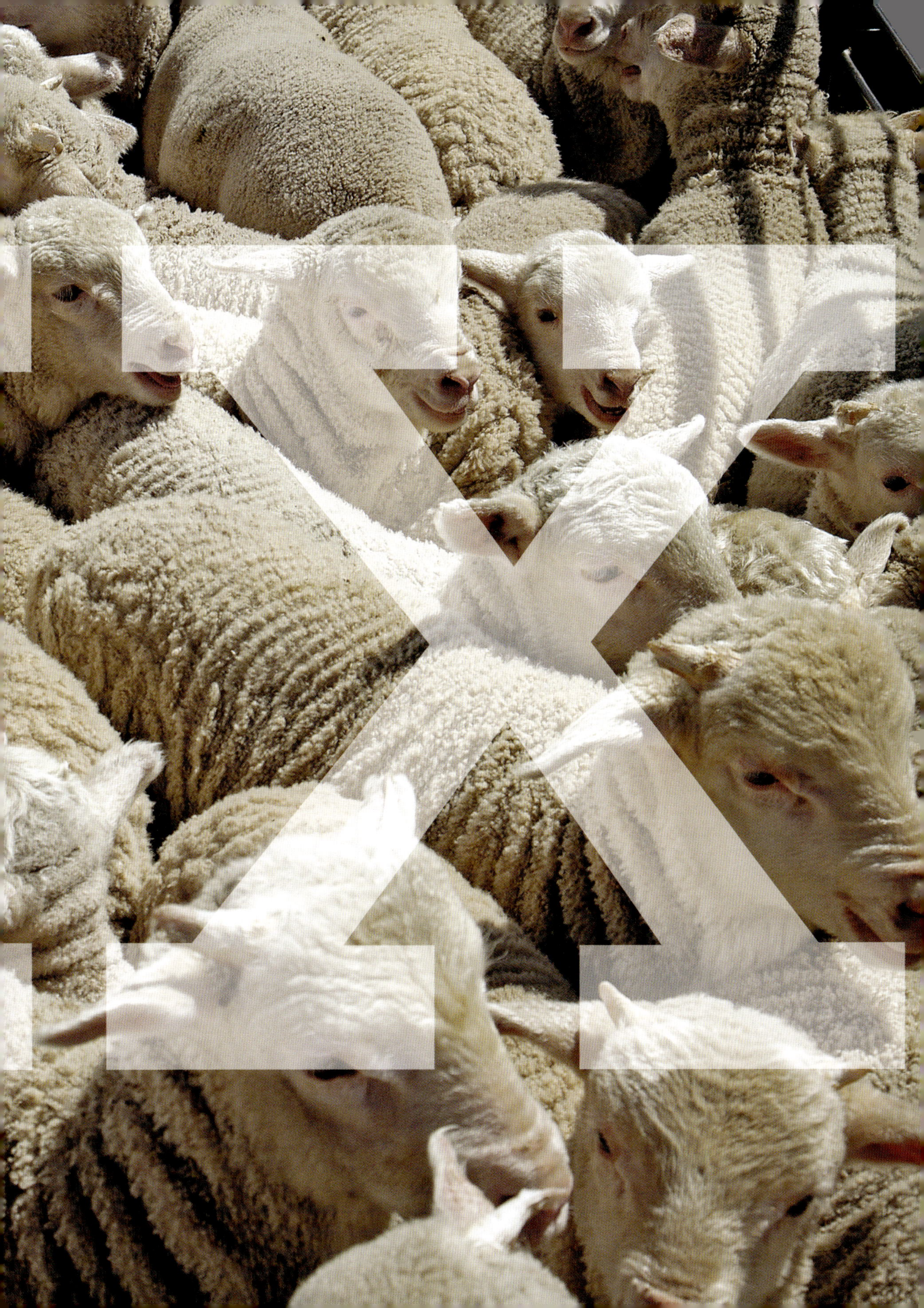
X

ACHILLES • THE TWO THUMB RANGE • D'ARCHIAC • CROOKED SPUR • HOGGET • THE GROWLER • BRABAZON • NEUTRAL SPUR • CLYDE RIVER • ROCKY RIDGE • BLACK MOUNTAINS • LITTLE SPUR • FINLAYS • FORBES RIVER • BIG BUSH • BLACK BIRCH STREAM • TOP DOWNS • BULLOCK BOW SADDLE • BALACLAVA BASINS • EXETER PEAK • SINCLAIR RANGE • FOREST CREEK • INKERMAN • THE ROCKS • MOUNT SINCLAIR • SUGARLOAF • MOUNT HOPE

THE NEW PROUTINGS in the Mesopotamia homestead were not so sure they were on their way up. Laurie might have been certain the dice would roll right way up but lucky breaks did not feature in Malcolm and Sue Prouting's farm plan. Nor could they hear so much as the distant echo of a boom. The future of this legendary station again hung somewhere in the void between hard work and hope. So far omens were conforming to the family pattern.

When Malcolm senior took over Mesopotamia it took eight years and a war to turn it around. When Laurie moved into his father's boots after eight years of fighting to make Mount Arrowsmith pay, he and Anne faced another six tough years with Mesopotamia before fortune turned their way. If the station's finances were plotted on a graph the chart would look like a soundwave, with each incoming generation of Proutings on the low note.

Malcolm and Sue had been eight years in charge of Mesopotamia when Sue found something entirely new in their annual accounts: for the first time their books were in the black. They showed a $13,000 profit for the year. The farm had made a million dollars, but it had cost almost as much to run. A million in from the farm, a million out, and $13,000 left over. Perhaps not so much in the black, more a delicate shade of grey.

The Proutings had not paid themselves a wage, so their year's income for the two of them was less than a joint unemployment benefit. But it was a profit, definitely, and it was their *first*. The third generation took only a tiny bow. Malcolm said, 'We'll see.'

Malcolm is rather more laconic than his father. He has a good deal of his grandfather about him, the look of a man butting into life head-on. He has the Prouting capacity for work; in fact, he has no option *but* to work, for it is impossible to overestimate the labour demanded by this famous station. Sometimes he feels the weight of a dynasty on his shoulders.

He has the same veneration for his father Laurie as Laurie had for his own father, Malcolm senior, and he remembers an old farming adage: 'The first man makes it, the second man breaks it in and the third man buggers it up. I don't want to be the one who screws it up.'

BOTH MALCOLM AND SUE had wanted to be farmers since they were six years old. They did not know about their shared ambition until much later, however, because they were then half a world apart. A world apart, actually.

Sue came from the little Hertfordshire village of Gosmore, living in the woods with her schoolteacher mother and electrician father and her two sisters. They kept dogs, and ducks, and geese, but Sue quickly realised that it would be all but impossible for her to get a farm in England. Her parents were supportive. They tried to help her achieve her ambition. 'They were desperate for me to stay at home. They offered to help me into a farm. But we'd have got twenty-five hectares at the most. It wouldn't have been economic.'

She studied farming at the University of London's agricultural college in Kent for four years, along with 900 mainly foreign students. She learned how to manage her time, get along with a lot of different people, to work alone; skills that were to be useful in the high country. She also found out how to keep a cash-book. 'I was terrible at that then. I'm a damn sight better at it now.' She manages Mesopotamia's finances. Malcolm, she said, proved allergic to the office.

Her route to the South Island high country was circuitous. When she left college she worked on a farm in England. There, chance took over; or rather, two coincidences turned her life upside down, literally.

The first coincidence found Neroli Prouting travelling around England with some New Zealanders, one of whom had been working on the same farm as Sue. They visited Sue on the farm. One of the Kiwi men became friendly with one of Sue's friends. They left on the note familiar to Kiwis travelling abroad: if you ever come to New Zealand, they said, look us up. Sue and a friend came to New Zealand on a working holiday. They *did* look up their friends. They missed Neroli however, for Sue was fully occupied elsewhere.

'We had a blast. It was probably the most amazing year of my life. We picked up lots of illegal jobs, starting with blueberry picking. We were absolutely dreadful at that. We spent our earnings on about three jugs. Then I helped with some polo horses. And we came up to Mesopotamia to collect some hay.' That gave coincidence number two its shot: 'We drove past a water trough and there was a chick fixing it. She looked up and said, "Sue, what the hell are you doing here?" And I said, "Neroli, what the hell are *you* doing here?" Neroli: "I live here. Come and stay."'

IT WAS AN offer Sue could not refuse, although others might have, for as she said, 'There were about seventeen thousand sheep to be tipped over and treated for footrot. I remember Laurie saying, "Pommy sheila, last half a day." Blue, the head shepherd at the time, bet on a day. They were wrong.'

Neroli said, 'Those two girls kept poking sheep until we'd done more than 17,000 of them and from the first day they were screaming and yahooing and they were still the same at the end of it. We couldn't believe it. I thought we'd wear them out, they'd be stuffed, they'd be crawling back; no, they stayed for the whole time and they were very good.'

Sue made an indelible impression on the Proutings. Laurie said, 'This pommy sheila was certainly a live wire, worked as well as any man, and it's better to surround yourself with bright-eyed bushy-tailed people than people who've got their hands in their pockets.'

'Oh. You couldn't get better than Sue,' said Anne. 'She hasn't got a lazy bone in her body. She's just go go go *go*.'

Sue: 'And I sort of stayed.'

Malcolm was in Marlborough working for his Uncle Frank at the time. Sue went to Australia for a year, then dodged back and forth between England and New Zealand trying to get enough points for residency. Once she got a single point away from succeeding, went back to England to do a year's relevant work and earn the critical point, then returned to find immigration authorities had revised the system and she was still one point short. For six years she dodged back and forth between the two countries to win the right to live in New Zealand. In the meantime she had met Malcolm. They fell in love. They decided to marry, but Sue refused to use marriage as her ticket.

'You've truly got to get married for the right reasons. Yes, we knew we were going to get married, but we weren't going to use that to get me into the country.'

That principle made the journey a very long haul. She first came to New Zealand in 1988. She won residency in 1996. The two were married in Hertfordshire, in a church tiny by English standards but which the Proutings thought big as a cathedral. Wedding photographs show Sue blond and beautiful, Malcolm looking surprisingly at home in a suit.

IT WAS A long way, a lot of coincidences and a forest of red tape between a quiet village in the English countryside and a remote mountain valley in New Zealand and Sue, quite unconsciously, had followed in the footsteps of Mesopotamia's first permanent resident, Samuel Butler.

Malcolm took a much shorter route. From early in his life Malcolm's ambition was to farm. He never wanted to be anything other than a farmer. He and Neroli were taught at home but their hearts were in the farm outside the homestead door and their mother Anne found herself doubling as both teacher and guard. 'I had to be there all the time,' Anne said, 'otherwise they'd run away.'

> From early in his life Malcolm's ambition was to farm. He never wanted to be anything other than a farmer.

When Malcolm boarded later at South Canterbury's Waihi Primary School his teacher was puzzled. Every time he pointed at Malcolm with a question, Malcolm ducked. After a few days the teacher asked him why. Well, Malcolm replied, whenever his mother raised her hand she was either going to give him a hiding or throw something at him.

Anne laughed. 'It took a term for him to stop ducking. I couldn't have been that bad could I? It was really that he didn't want to learn. Neroli wasn't so bad. She wanted to get on with it because she wanted to get outside. But Malcolm would debate everything. "That's stupid. Why would I want to learn that?" Then he got the idea, "I better do it quickly then I'll get back outside." For instance, we'd start learning the three-times table. If Malcolm counted sheep by the three-times table he'd have learned it by the time he left school in the morning because he was interested.

'Malcolm was as clever as a cartload of monkeys. Times were pretty hard when we were at Arrowsmith and the beginning of every term began with the old question, where did you go on your holidays? Malcolm wrote one sentence: "I have never been on a holiday." Sent it in. Got away with it.

'It was true. If they did go anywhere it would be to Mesopotamia.'

Malcolm remained terse. Even much later, if he were asked whether he liked Waihi, or for that matter Saint Andrew's College in Christchurch where he was a reluctant boarder, he would answer with a single word: 'No.'

He only ever considered one alternative career: he shared his father's love of flying. 'I was thinking about leaving school and making a career of it. But, well, too much mucking around when I was a young fellow. I went farming instead. I've never regretted it.'

Sue neither. Her mother was upset about her leaving home forever, her father accepting. But Sue had no doubts. 'England is only a day away. I've been back twice in the last two years. But before that it was seven years. I love my parents dearly but they brought us up to live our own lives: "Once you leave home you're on your own," and we were.'

In theory it is a good policy but most parents live to regret it, and so did Sue's mother. 'She said, "I meant in the next town, not on the other side of the world." They've been over here four or five times. They love it. Dad loved Geraldine. He thought he was going back in time. But they're getting on a bit now. Travelling is hard for them. And money. And last time they came out Mum's kidneys failed. We spent the entire time in Christchurch Hospital.'

Now, cemented in by a husband and two children, Fergus and Pieta, Sue's life lay firmly in the high country. 'When I come back from overseas I can't wait. I sit in the plane thinking, we're going home! But it's the same the other way. It's exciting to see Mum and Dad and my sisters. I've got the best of both worlds.'

For they *were* two worlds. It was impossible to get much further from the gentle English countryside, physically or spiritually, than this grand, solemn valley. 'I notice huge differences back in England. The people. The traffic. The fact that you're just a number rather than an individual. I can go into my bank in Geraldine and they'll say, "Hi Sue, how are you? You forgot to sign that cheque three days ago . . ." Whereas I went to a bank in England and they said "What's this number, what's that," they treated you as a potential thief. I call both places home now. I can talk about home here *and* say "when we go home to England". But I would never live back in England again. Never. Ever. I've made the right choice. Everyone asks whether I get lonely. I say no. This is the busiest place I've ever lived and worked.'

It seemed a strange thing to say, on a high country station at the end of a dusty road blocked by New Zealand's highest mountains. Yet in the space of a few days she might have a couple of the busloads of elderly people who come up from Christchurch, tour the station buildings and have a picnic. Sue would ferry those who couldn't walk up and down the hill, where the bus couldn't go. Then she would clean up the cottages after paying guests. Next, the shearers' quarters and cookhouse. Students had booked it for an end-of-year party and left it in a mess. Following that, prepare for a visit by a tour bus company which regularly brought in groups of people. They would use the cottages while a large family group took over the cookhouse.

The station is remote in its mountain valley, but well within range of modern four-wheel-drive vehicles. Cars travel the road up the valley to the Te Araroa national pathway now passing through the farm. Visitors, contractors, tourists, picnickers, trampers, hunters ply the tracks.

'Sometimes,' Sue said, 'I'll take the dogs and go and hide because I don't want to answer the door to anyone else. And, this is a better place to bring up children. I mean crikey, look at it.'

Certainly it is a *different* place to bring them up. Outside, Ferg was kicking a football around the lawn, waiting for his grandfather to pick him up and take him down the valley, by helicopter.

For Ferg's ninth birthday Malcolm loaded his ute with hay bales and set them up in a greasy paddock. He got out the farm rally car, a nondescript green machine fitted out for the rough ride. He gave the kids crash helmets. They were excited. Wow! Ferg's dad was going to hot-rod them around the paddock, real fast!

Wait, said Malcolm. He was not going to drive. *They* were. Their eyes widened like golf balls. *Whoa! Choice!*

They took off one by one. Some of them got up to eighty kilometres per hour. Some spun through 360 degrees, others even turned two full circles on the greasy surface. Everyone had a great time. Malcolm awaited the calls from outraged parents. None came.

It was more successful than another birthday party where Malcolm got a lot of balloons and gave the children slug guns to shoot them all down and was astonished when most of them missed. What was wrong with today's kids?

So for Pieta's birthday he made a target so big they could not fail to hit it. Then a bunch of little girls in their party frocks got a spot of firearms training.

↗ TOP RIGHT
Sue and Malcolm married in the UK at St Ippolyts Church, Gosmore, Hertfordshire, on the 19th August 2000.

→ BOTTOM RIGHT
The Prouting family at Mesopotamia, from left Malcolm, Ferg, Sue and Pieta.

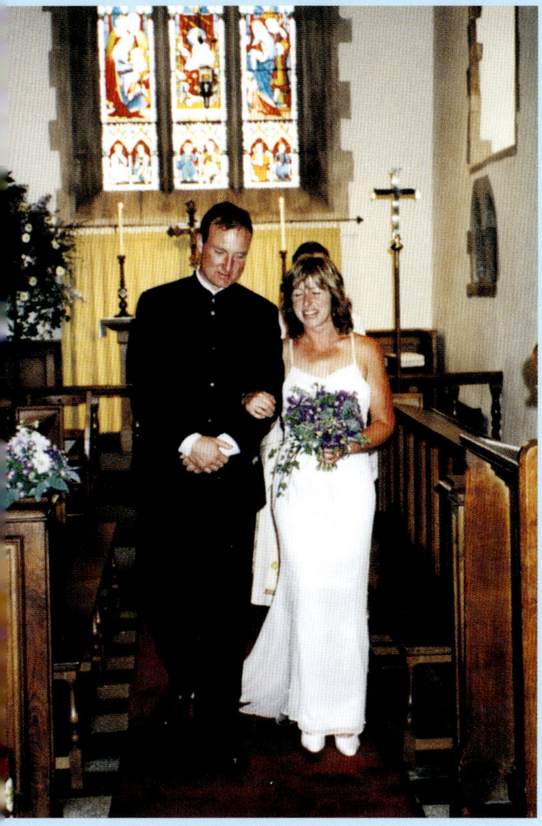

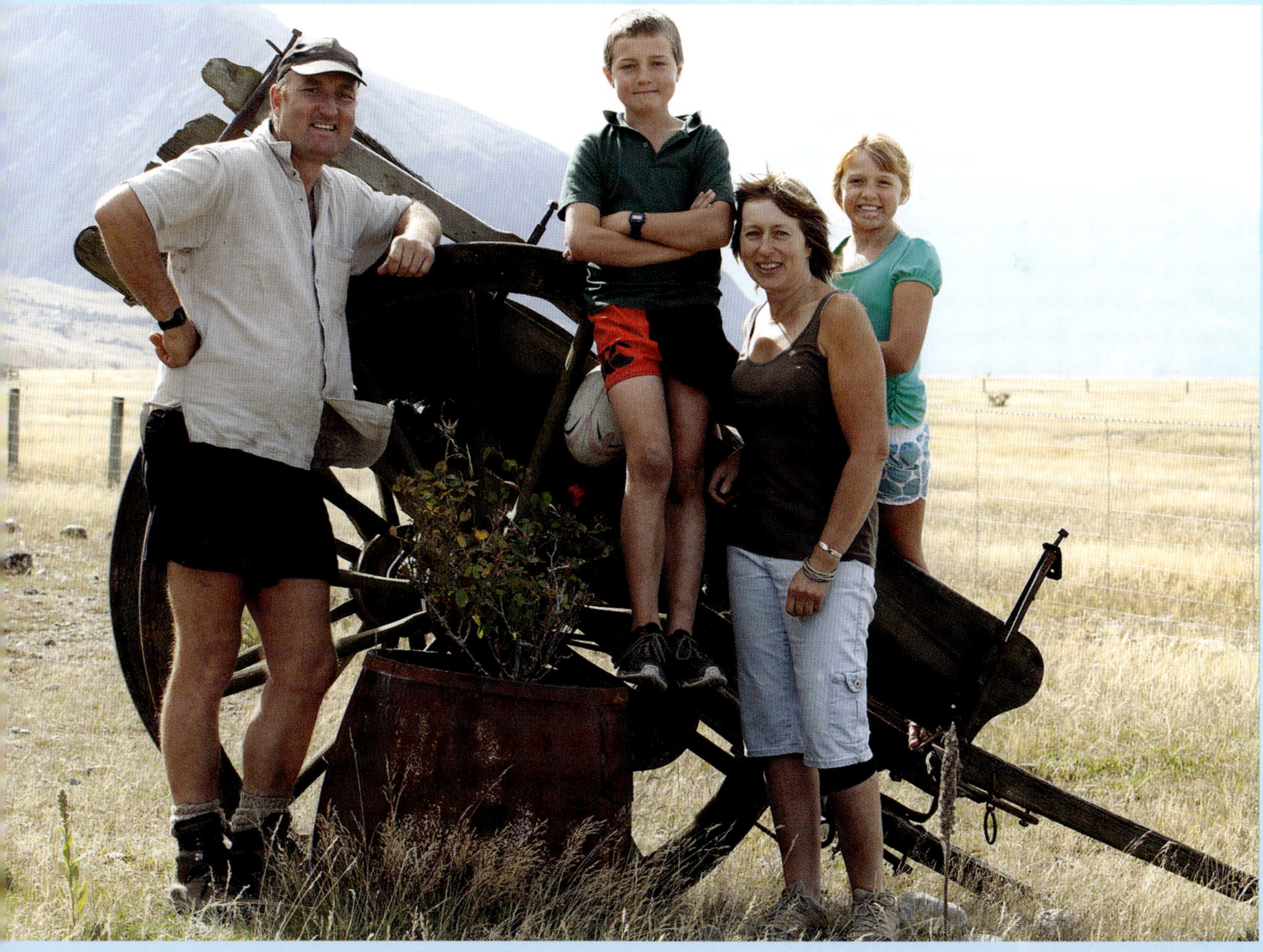

One parent would not let her kids take part. She was a pacifist, she explained.

Malcolm thought her children looked downcast. He considered telling them that next time they came, they should leave their mum at home. But he did not.

Fergus and Pieta were enmeshed in the high country routine. They spent three hours a day going to and from school in Carew, a pretty little place near Arundel. It was a long way away, but still the nearest after both Mesopotamia and Peel Forest schools closed.

Sue had to be out of bed at six o'clock and have them out of the door by seven to take them in her ute in time to catch the seven-thirty school bus at Forest Creek. The bus arrived back at four-thirty in the afternoon and the children were home by five unless Sue stopped to do a little work, perhaps move the deer.

Pieta was born with birthmarks inside her trachea, her windpipe, stopping her from breathing. Auckland's Starship Hospital performed a tracheotomy, opening a little hole in her neck and fitting a tube to breathe through. The tube remained in place for five years, Pieta needing constant attention. The courage a child needs to endure such discomfort for so many years can only be imagined. On one great day in March 2010, it was taken out at last.

That summer Pieta went swimming for the first time and put her head under the water. For most children swimming and

→ RIGHT
Malcolm Prouting junior, the latest of the farming dynasty, at home on his favourite place, Mesopotamia Station.

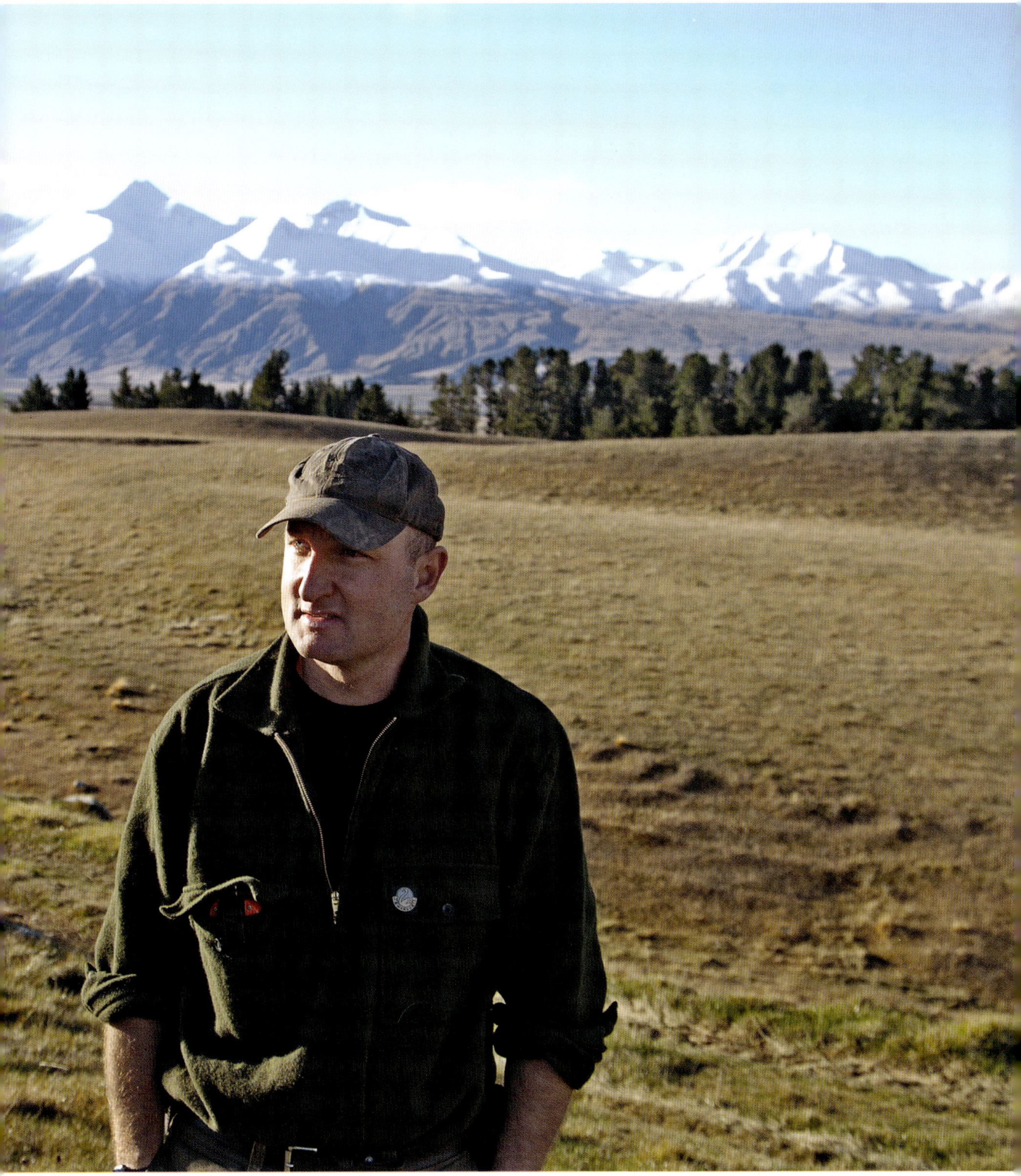

diving under water are as much a part of their summer as ice-cream. For Pieta it was a triumph, shared by her delighted parents. Though she is sometimes solemn, her smile lights her face like the sun. She got a sewing machine for her seventh birthday. Her grandmother Anne, the former dressmaker, helped her make clothes. Ferg wanted a rotary hoe for Christmas; he is a keen vegetable gardener. But, oh joy, he received a motorbike instead.

The children spend hours on their school bus, Sue and Malcolm countless hours driving them to and from the bus, into the towns and Christchurch city. It is simply a part of farming Mesopotamia, hard-wired into their lives. 'You know that wherever you go it's going to be an hour before you start getting anywhere,' said Sue. 'An hour to the Rangitata Gorge is just part of your life. Then you think how long it's going to take to get to other places. But you don't meet any traffic, you don't have any hassle, so . . .

'When we went through tenure review [see chapter eight] there was the option of selling and going somewhere else and I remember being told by Laurie to think about it. We asked each other where we would go if we weren't here. Malcolm said he couldn't think of any place he'd rather be than here. Me neither. This is the best, most beautiful place you can be in. When I come back and go around *Wow!* Corner at White Rock and I see the Two Thumb Range, I think, "I live up there, and it's pretty special."

> **I still stand and stare at it. It's amazing, it's so silent. I'm in awe of it. It's forever changing. The weather can change in two seconds. It brings different shades to the place. This place is a great adventure.**

'I'd love to have time to ride my horse a bit more. I always feel that doing something just for pleasure is wasting time. I'd like to find more time to use the horses for work so that I'd have an excuse. But with the farm, the kids, that takes a back seat.'

Even in her third decade on Mesopotamia, for she first came here in 1988, she remains still captivated by the place. 'I still stand and stare at it. It's amazing, it's so silent. I'm in awe of it. It's forever changing. The weather can change in two seconds. It brings different shades to the place. This place is a great adventure.'

Malcolm is so wedded to the high country he has no real interest in leaving it for any reason, even a break away. He is making a lake on the farm, filling it slowly on a terrace behind the homestead, its lip bulldozed from the hard ground, wide enough for Sue to hope that one day she might learn to water-ski there.

Beside it stands a small bach, corrugated iron of course, with a verandah and sliding doors set into its front. A couple of comfy armchairs inside bear the impressions of Sunday afternoons spent with a quiet drink overlooking the embryonic lake to the valley. Malcolm wants to work it up a bit. He plans something a little better, a bigger bach, a wider lake.

Why? Well, once the rush of Christmas work on the station is over, and autumn hoves into view, he looks around for somewhere for the family to go on holiday. Nothing flash, four days away from the farm is what this family calls a holiday. Yet at heart Malcolm is not eager to go anywhere at all. His favourite place is right where he is. He wants to take his holidays without leaving home. Ergo, the lake, the bach.

Perhaps Malcolm is even a romantic at heart. He woke one morning on his and Sue's wedding anniversary and asked Ro, an Irish chef with a beautiful, crooked face then working as a stationhand, if she could cook something extraordinary that night, something suitable for an occasion. Another thing, said Malcolm. Could she lay it all out in the bach by the lake in the back paddock? Ro agreed. She did her day's work then climbed into a ute and drove the three hours or so into Geraldine and back for the menu she had planned.

After work Malcolm came home and told Sue to get dressed. They were going out. Sue changed her habitual shorts and work shirt for a dress. She put on makeup and heels. Malcolm ushered her into the ute and drove through two gates up to the shed by the water.

But that night, it was no longer a shed, nor was the water busy graduating from a pond. It was a pavilion, by the lake. Cat Stevens wafted from a stereo powered by a portable generator. Sue gasped at the white cloth on the table, the glasses, the cutlery all laid out. Ro served dinner by candlelight. The meal was superb: stuffed chicken breast, asparagus tips, chocolate mud cake with raspberry sauce. Sue loved it.

'The thing was,' she said, 'it wasn't actually our anniversary. He got the date wrong. But I didn't care. The chocolate mud cake was to die for. It was such a beautiful night. And it was all on our own place.'

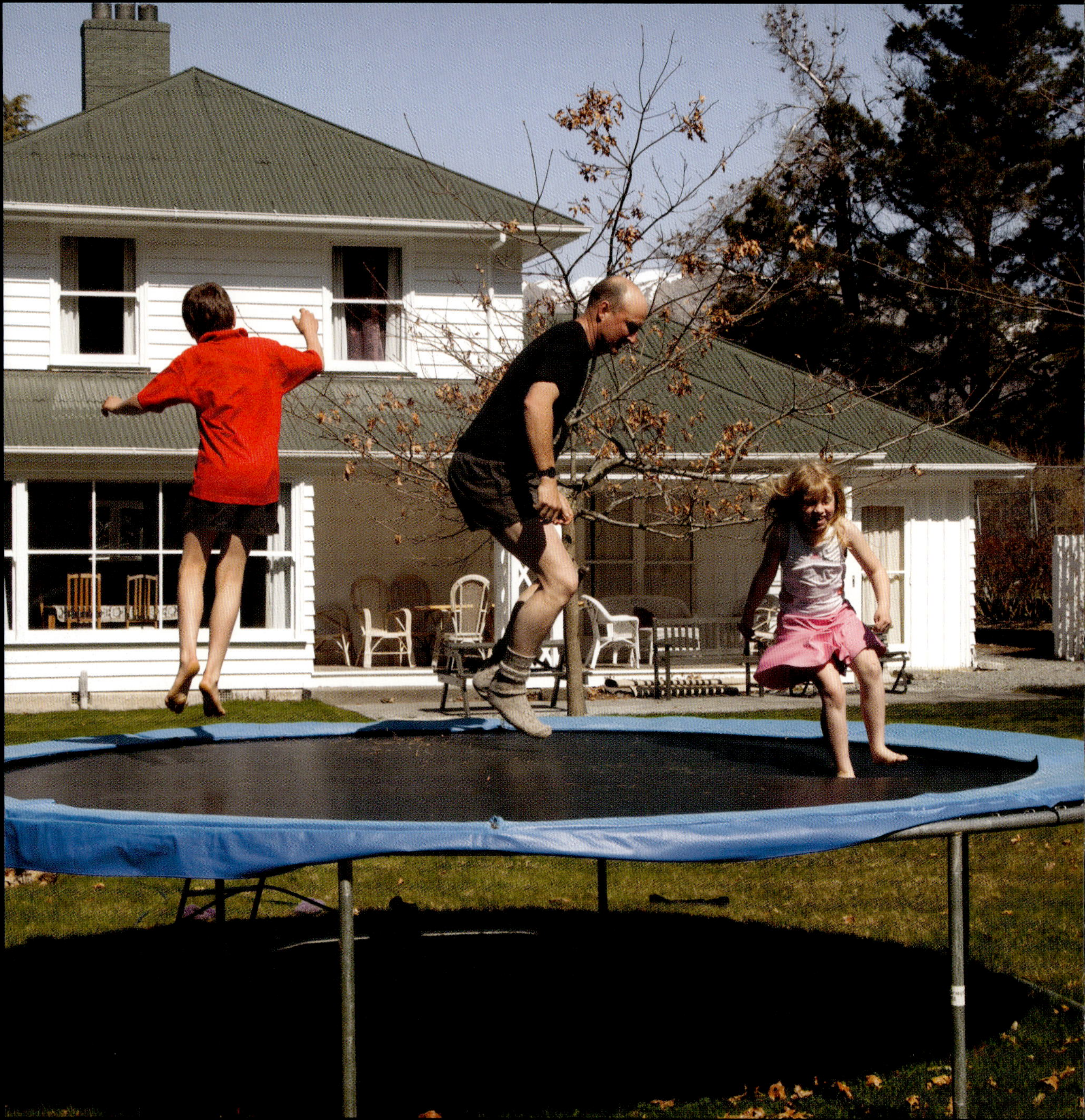

← CLOCKWISE FROM FAR LEFT
Some family time: Malcolm, Ferg and Pieta on the trampoline.

Pieta and her cat, the intelligent mouse-catcher.

Malcolm and Pieta.

SEX

TEN

ACHILLES • THE TWO THUMB RANGE • D'ARCHIAC • CROOKED SPUR • HOGGET • THE GROWLER • BRABAZON • NEUTRAL SPUR CLYDE RIVER • ROCKY RIDGE • BLACK MOUNTAINS • LITTLE SPUR • FINLAYS • FORBES RIVER • BIG BUSH • BLACK BIRCH STREAM • TOP DOWNS • BULLOCK BOW SADDLE BALACLAVA BASINS • EXETER PEAK • SINCLAIR RANGE FOREST CREEK • INKERMAN THE ROCKS • MOUNT SINCLAIR • SUGARLOAF • MOUNT HOPE

NEROLI PROUTING BURST upon the New Zealand public in an early *Country Calendar* television programme. She was an unusual woman, for she was running a high country station all on her own, and she was then barely twenty-three years old. It was not just any high country station, either. Its name, Mount Arrowsmith Station, probably did not mean much to most viewers, but anyone could see it was hard country. It seemed to consist entirely of mountains and rock.

Here was this slim blonde woman all alone. She looked as if she could cope, already so used to squinting great distances into the sun and snow that she looked a little fierce, and you might imagine that given the right circumstances she could be. She had an upside-down grin and white ankles below her sock line, so that even without her socks on she still looked as if she was wearing them. This, she explained, was a problem when she went somewhere poncey, a wedding for example, in a short skirt and high heels, because 'I've got these lush brown matagouri-scraped legs and then I've got these white sock-marks and people think I sunbathe with my socks on'.

The *Country Calendar* programme showed her jumping from a helicopter, letting her dogs out of a sack dangling below it, shearing the odd sheep in a white singlet, with and her blond hair tied up on top of her head. She looked brown and tough and her grin gave her a wry look. She looked, in fact, as if she had been born to thrive on the high country, and of course she was.

Neroli was five when her family left Mesopotamia to go to Mount Arrowsmith, and she was at school in Christchurch when they went back to

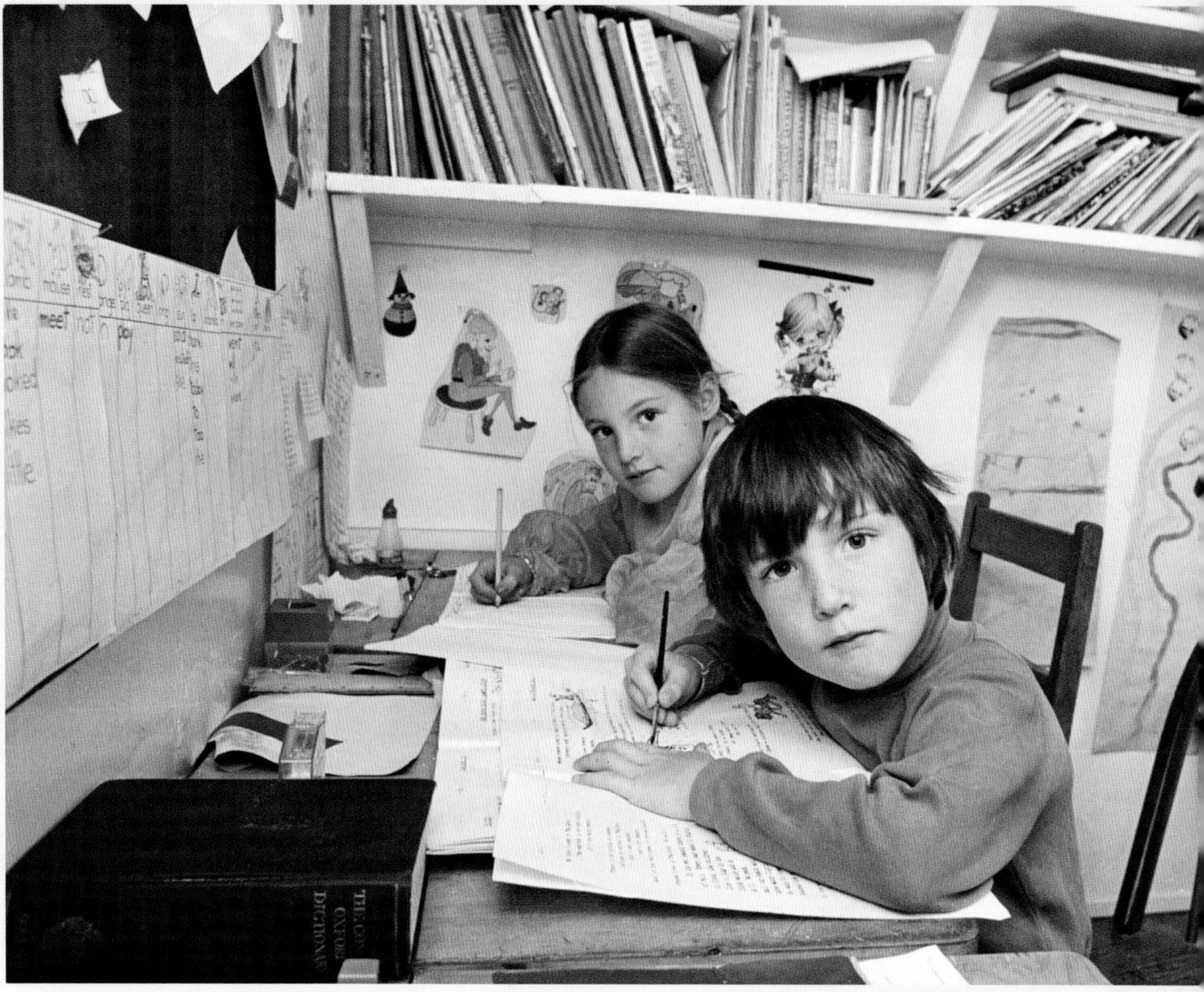

Mesopotamia. She boarded at Rangi Ruru Girls' School, and summed up her schooling succinctly: 'I hated living in a city. Disliked school immensely. I was no good at it. Shocking. I got School Certificate. Then I left.'

She totted up her education's balance sheet. 'I learnt how to judge character pretty quick, because the things I wanted to do were totally illegal and I had to work out how the hell I could get to do them. I was useless at sport. You'd think I'd be good at it because I was so fit and feisty. But I'd never been in a netball team, never played tennis. Never been in a hockey team. Netball I was hopeless at because I didn't know the rules and I wasn't prepared to tell anyone because I'd look like a dick. I was absolutely shocking at catching a ball. So I played hockey. I was buggered if I knew why they kept saying offside.' For all that, at least one of her teachers remembered her fondly: 'She was great. I liked her.'

Sometimes, as a young girl, Neroli rode between the two stations on horseback, a long journey through the valleys and across rivers and fording the dangerous Rangitata where so many had drowned and for part of it at least travelling in Samuel Butler's footsteps, 'the country crumpled up in an extraordinary manner'.

'My mother really wasn't worried if I didn't turn up,' she said. I asked Anne if that was true. 'Absolutely,' she said. 'They knew how to be safe. They knew everything. She had a horse which she'd taught to put out its leg so she could climb onto it and we only found out what she did when Peter Bush sent down a photo of her standing on the horse's back holding the reins and galloping up and down the airstrip.'

The only thing the Proutings would not allow their children to do, she said, was go near the lake, Lake Heron, unless they were with an adult, preferably one who could swim, for the family were then non-swimmers. While it was comforting to know that the family weren't perfect all-rounders, the stricture was curious too, for the children were free to roam over a station that offered all sorts of ways to injure or kill oneself. Perhaps it was summarised like this: water was out of bounds unless it was frozen into snow or ice, when it was okay.

Still, Neroli said, 'I wouldn't let my kids do what I was allowed to do. It's too dangerous. Too scary. I'm a worry-pants. Mum's pretty amazing. All the years Dad's flown aircraft, if he hasn't come back after dark or something she

← RIGHT
Malcolm and Neroli doing their Correspondence School work at Mount Arrowsmith Station.

remains very calm, very positive, doesn't panic. I wish I could be more like that.

'Once we were supposed to be going into town and I was riding bareback up the road and I thought I'd just go and get the wild horses in. So I snuck out there. They gave me a bit of hassle. There were twelve wild horses and they cut back on me. I was so mad. I turned my horse, Bill, round at a hoofing pace and dear old Bill slipped on the ice. So here we were skidding along the ground at a hundred miles an hour and the horses were going past me, blimmin heck!

'When old Bill got up he'd skinned a bit off his shoulders and I'd skinned most of the skin off my legs. And just then Mum came roaring up in the car and yelled, "Where are you, we're supposed to be going to town!" She made me take the bridle off Bill and leave him with the wild horses, and I was very worried someone would let them out and Bill would be gone. I was a bit sore in the car, pretty sore that night.

'We generated our own power at Mount Arrowsmith for a long time and it was my job to clean out the plant. Dad believed I was going to be careful and I wouldn't end up going round and round in the wheel. I wish I had that same trust — or is it just belief? — in children.'

Her own children don't live in the mountains. Instead they play on gentle downs near the string of villages lining the bottom of mid-Canterbury foothills, where people can get a latte and a slice of tiramisu, and in every respect quite a long way from the country Neroli grew up in.

'Once Dad was landing an Auster in a howling nor'wester. We'd have to go and hold the tail of the Auster when it was blowing because it was so light he couldn't steer it in the wind so we'd hold onto the tail to help. He'd fly over the house to tell us he was coming in and this day we hopped on the back of the Land Rover and Mum drove us down (I'd never let my children be on the back of a truck at that age) and bounced through the gate at the camping ground and she yelled "get down", she'd forgotten there were no brakes in the Landy and *karboompah!* through the gate we went, wood chips everywhere, and Mum goes, "Oh well, we're away, and Laurie is waiting for us," two little dots and a stick figure.

'Times were hard and we used to pluck dead sheep for Christmas money. We never had a holiday. The one time we did, the guy who worked for us died. We'd just got to Picton and Dad had to go back. I never remember another holiday. We'd go and do something like walk over the Whitcombe Pass and we'd do it as fast as we could because Dad had to get back. But we did a lot of other cool stuff. Well, cool stuff is working. Working hard. Dad still doesn't know what the question is but the answer is work work work.

'When we went back to Messie and Dad was making that place hum, putting up fences and he was so driven, still is a driven man, and I just admired him. I had twangs of guilt because I felt I hadn't worked nearly as hard as him and it's through his hard work that we've got what we've got.

'Sometimes I feel bad if I sleep past six o'clock because I feel I'm not working hard enough because that is what Dad did and what he still bloody does, gets up at six o'clock every day and is doing something, always achieving something. When Dad asked if I'd like to have a go at Arrowsmith, I said "Oh, yeah". I was twenty-two.'

'She was keen,' said Laurie. 'Furthermore she was capable. She could drive that old loader and it was a prick of a thing to drive because it had no brakes.'

Neroli was taking on one of the hardest farms in the country, 9000 hectares of cold country. But, 'I never thought about that. There wasn't anything that I wasn't going to handle. So I was keen as. Some of Messie can be even tougher. But why Arrowsmith is so tough is that it's just so bloody cold and it doesn't grow anything in the winter to feed stock. Turnips would grow about the size of an egg and you'd be all year growing the bloody things, planting them with all this old machinery then the Canada geese would come and in a night they could take out sixteen hectares of my turnips. It was not that I liked living by myself, I just did it. I didn't get a lot of visitors.

'There was a camping ground by the lake and that was really cool. People would always be friendly and some of them would use my shower then they'd have me down there for dinner. Great!'

> When we went back to Messie and Dad was making that place hum, putting up fences and he was so driven, still is a driven man, and I just admired him. I had twangs of guilt because I felt I hadn't worked nearly as hard as him and it's through his hard work that we've got what we've got.

THE COUNTRY IS beguiling, at first. Visitors drive in from Mount Somers, a picture-book little town, and travel along a smooth sealed road to Hakatere, where the old stone buildings and huge shearers' quarters of Hakatere Station mark a crossroads. This station, bought by the Nature

Heritage Fund, lies at the heart of the Hakatere Conservation Park and as evidence of the country's often-harsh nature, there's the story of Jesson Davis.

Davis in 1862 set out to walk from Mesopotamia to Hakatere but ran into snow. It got worse as he went on, until he had no alternative *but* to continue. When he staggered into Hakatere, stockmen took off his boots but the frozen flesh peeled away with his socks and, as feeling returned, the unlucky Davis was in agony. An alleged doctor living nearby offered to cut off his legs with a carving knife; instead, Davis was taken to Christchurch by bullock dray, endured the journey of several days, had his legs amputated properly by the standards of the time, and survived to work again.

The road to Mount Arrowsmith Station turns off at Hakatere and soon reveals its character, narrow, twisting, turning to shingle as it runs up a wonderful shallow valley, passing the Maori Lakes and heading towards the jagged ridges of the Arrowsmith Range on the skyline. The roadsides are alive with wild daisies, the downs literally fields of gold, lupins in flashes of purple and pink, blue and white. It is benign on a gentle day, easy to imagine it on an unruly one. Lake Heron lies in its bowl beneath the Wild Man's Brother Range. The road passes the homestead, wide and low and looking over the water, curls around the lake then stops, dead.

Sometimes, though, Neroli was not *entirely* alone. Harley Davies, who worked on a neighbouring station, would come over and give her dog-training lessons. The arrangement worked well, so well in fact that a follow-up *Country Calendar* programme many years after the first was able to reveal that Harley had, well, stayed. Neroli married him. They lived happily ever after, or at least seemed determined to. ('I love him to pieces, he's great, he's awesome.')

She'd offered him a job. Evidently the job interview was brief. Harley moved into Mount Arrowsmith. 'We learnt a lot together. He taught me not to sulk. We'd be driving along in the truck and next thing *boompho!* He's hit me in the arm and I'd yell, "What did you do that for?" and he'd say "Oh, just so I could hear your voice again." He's just simple and straight up and I'm so lucky to have him. He's the most amazing father and we work well together.'

When someone showed up with an offer to buy Mount Arrowsmith, Neroli did not think much about it at first. 'I loved Arrowsmith. Dad loved Messie because he grew up there, but I grew up at Arrowsmith. The house has a sixteen-metre hallway and it was Summerhill stone and it was very nice and pink, and big, and Mum had made this amazing garden. So it was only in passing that I mentioned the offer to Dad. Harley was very careful, not saying much because he didn't think it was his place to. It's isolated up there at Arrowsmith. For me it was about teaching children by correspondence, being so far away from everything.'

The family debated. Laurie said that if the two wanted to stay on the property, it was theirs. But he favoured selling. 'I said to Neroli, "All the problems we have at Mesopotamia you are going to have at Arrowsmith, the snow, the hardships of the property." And Arrowsmith was leasehold. The government owned it. I'd had trouble with that since the day I took on farming. It had been a huge issue.

'In the hard light of day, it made good sense to have a freehold property. I said, "Think about it." She did. Then she said, "Tell the guy we'll sell it." The guy came up with the cash, we sold it.' Neroli said, 'I guess I didn't realise Arrowsmith was gone until after it was sold.'

She and Harley moved out and began working on another farm as a married couple, but the money from Arrowsmith was earmarked for another property. Eventually one came up, a farm called Gawler Downs, 1215 hectares of rolling country just above the Plains, freehold, now running 10,000 stock units compared with Mount Arrowsmith's 4000.

Every time the family looked at it, Gawler Downs seemed a better place. They resolved to buy it, but with this family everything was an adventure. The farm was to be sold at auction and on auction day Laurie and Anne were in Singapore on their first-ever overseas holiday together. Instead, an agent bid for them, with instructions to go up to two million dollars, no more. At the last minute Laurie said they might go to an extra bid, if they'd miss out on the property otherwise.

Neroli knew nothing of that last-minute arrangement. Nor did she know the agent who would be bidding for them.

The bidding went up to $2 million. Then an extra $20,000 bid took it past the mark. The auctioneer stopped the bidding. The property had not reached its reserve. He talked with the vendors in another room, returned, announced that the farm was now on the market and was there a better bid?

The crowd in the auction room was silent. Farm auctions are an occasion in the country, and the audience recognised the drama.

'I was starting to sulk,' said Neroli. 'I thought we'd lost it and we were just about to leave. Then they said the property was on the market at that price. There were no more bids. The hammer came down and it was sold. Though, who'd bought it? Everyone was looking around.

'The next thing this guy is walking towards me. He's someone I don't know and I hate not knowing peoples' names. He puts his hand out to shake my hand and goes, "Congratulations." "Sorry?" I say. "Who are you?" "I'm your agent," he says, "and I've just bought Gawler Downs for you." *Oh my god!*

'I'm grabbing him by the lapels and shaking him and there's a roar of laughter and everyone is shaking our hands. It was such an awesome thing. I really wanted this place but it seemed out of reach. It was certainly a beautiful property but I was careful not to fall in love with it too much because I thought it wasn't going to be, it was just too magic. I grabbed a phone and called Mum and Dad in Singapore. Dad was so stoked. He was laughing away and he said you better go and sign it then.'

> **'I was starting to sulk,' said Neroli. 'I thought we'd lost it and we were just about to leave. Then they said the property was on the market at that price. There were no more bids. The hammer came down and it was sold.'**

Laurie said, 'She was one deliriously happy child. Two or three years later I asked her how she was feeling, when they were having difficulty making the place pay, because the mortgage was enormous. She said "Dad, I feel every bit as happy as that day we bought it."'

Neroli and Harley spent a lot on development. They were aiming at turning their 10,000 stock units into 12,000. The farm became profitable, handled its debt, and appreciated in value so much it was now a huge asset. 'We could pay off our debt at any time but we're developing it so much. It's a big balancing act.'

Neroli and Harley have two daughters, Grace and Ella. The children have the same friendly, proud directness of their mother, and their handshake has more than a little of Harley's grip. Raising them was not easy for Neroli. 'I wondered what the hell had happened to me. I couldn't get out the door, I didn't feel important, I felt useless, I hated it.

'I was a great mother, loved my children to bits, but I couldn't do anything, every time I did something on the farm it would take twenty hours, and they were these precious little things, I didn't want them to get dirty, or cold, or run over, or left in the truck. I struggled big time. Mum would come over and look after them.'

Anne found herself in a different age, no daredevil horseback-riding, dark mountain adventures or wild horses and not an ancient Auster in sight. 'We had a girls' birthday party,' she marvelled, 'and a whole lot of us correspondence school mothers were there and we were saying what our kids did and how different it was now. Almost as though their parents don't trust them.'

Neroli and her family live in a long, low brick homestead, graceful, elegant, French doors everywhere, well-tended gardens, the kind of place Neroli might once have called 'poncey.' Perhaps Grace and Ella are unlikely to find themselves carting diesel on a packhorse up a remote mountain valley at night. Yet they race their cross-country motorbikes around paddocks and show every sign of being their mother's children. The only concession to Neroli's new-found caution may be that they wear something she never did — crash helmets.

Now when you find her in the living room or kitchen, she might be a comfortable farmer's wife, mixing the drinks, except for a faint element of larrikin which never seems far from the surface.

'People were sometimes glad to tell my mum and dad that they'd seen their daughter in the pub swearing and cursing and drinking beer (and a lot of the time I was). It takes a lot for people to say nice comments. People tend not to, because it's not interesting to say, "My gosh, your daughter's doing so well."'

But she *is* doing well. The girls are happy. Unlike their mother they love sport. Grace wants to be a physiotherapist, Ella to be a vet or to work in animal husbandry. Neither seems anxious to tread their mother's path. Still, who knows? Neroli doesn't. 'I don't know what I would have said at their age. I wanted to be a truckdriver then.'

The girls were planning some horse-riding for the school holidays. Both could drive a tractor, Grace towing the big roller in the paddocks.

The family has even taken holidays. One to Australia. Another to Takaka in Golden Bay. 'Awesome. Gorgeous.'

Then: 'Done talking? I'm having a glass of wine. How about you?'

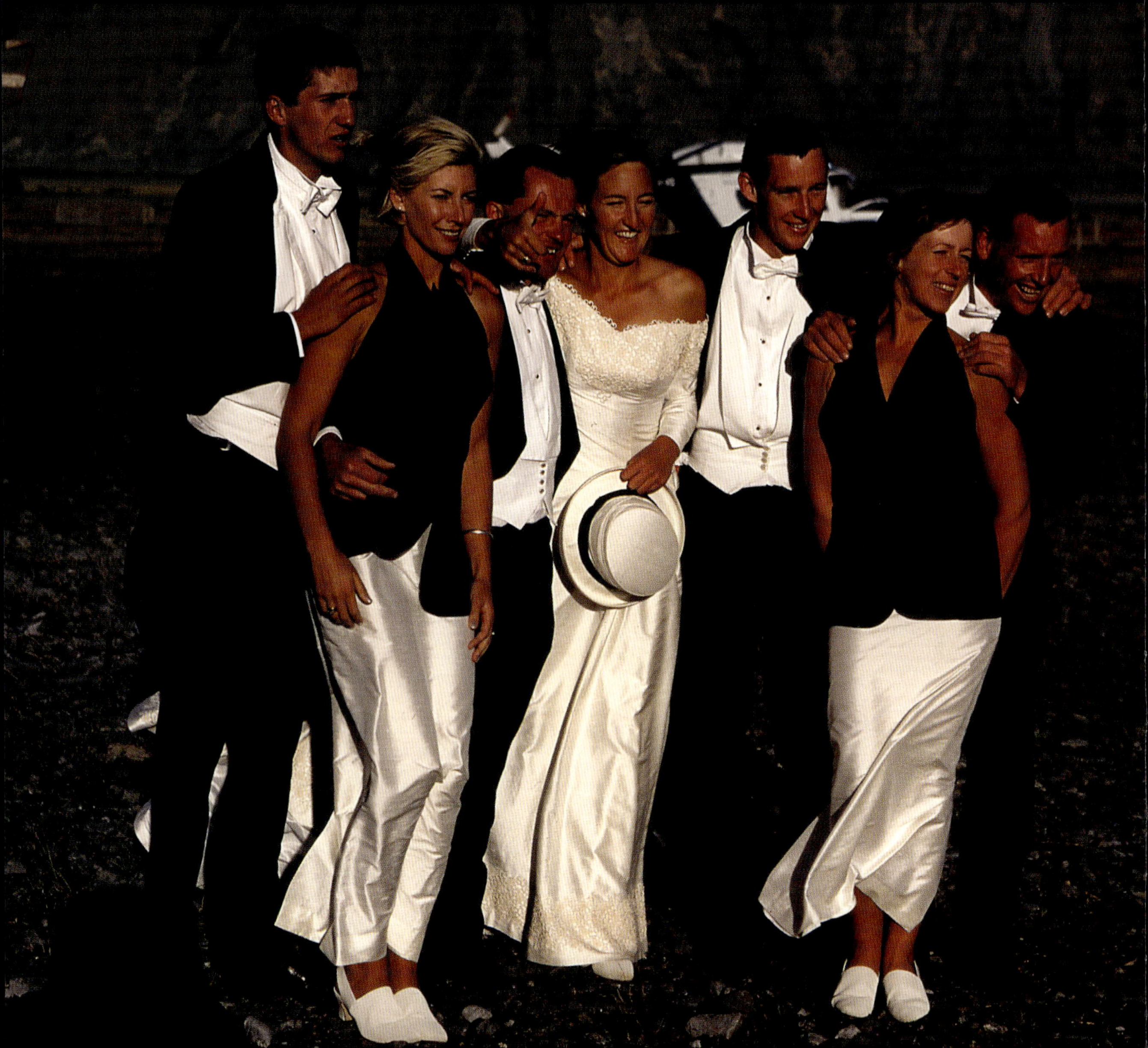

BUSHY ON NEROLI'S WEDDING

Neroli's wedding was a magnificent occasion.

The airport at Mesopotamia was as crowded as Los Angeles International.

There was every kind of small plane. There was even a DC-3.

The bridal party all looked so young and dashing and brilliant.

We stayed in the cookhouse.

Hustle and bustle.

The ceremony was on the lawn.

Neroli came in riding side-saddle. It looked like something out of old Spain.

Then towards evening the bridal group and others were taken by helicopters up to the Two Thumb Range. Such a spectacular chopper ride, one of the most wonderful I've ever had.

And in the evening the champagne corks popped and the table groaned under the food.

Down in the late evening to dancing, music.

And the sadness that the day had to end.

← **RIGHT**
The wedding party, from left: Guy Martin, Kerryn Sloss, John Templeton, Neroli, Harley, Sue Prouting, and Darren Elstob.

PHOTO ESSAY
SHEARING

Of all the events on Mesopotamia's farming calendar, shearing is the single biggest, longest, most critical. The value of the annual wool cheque ebbs and flows in the world's economic tides, but it is still the big one. The Mesopotamia merino flock has been shorn by a shearing gang which reaches back through all three generations of Proutings. The only real changes have been the declining size of the flock, and the gang's recent practice of commuting to the station rather than staying in the huge, venerable shearers' quarters and cookhouse. Otherwise the methods, practices, the traditional shed mystique, even some of the faces, remain the same.

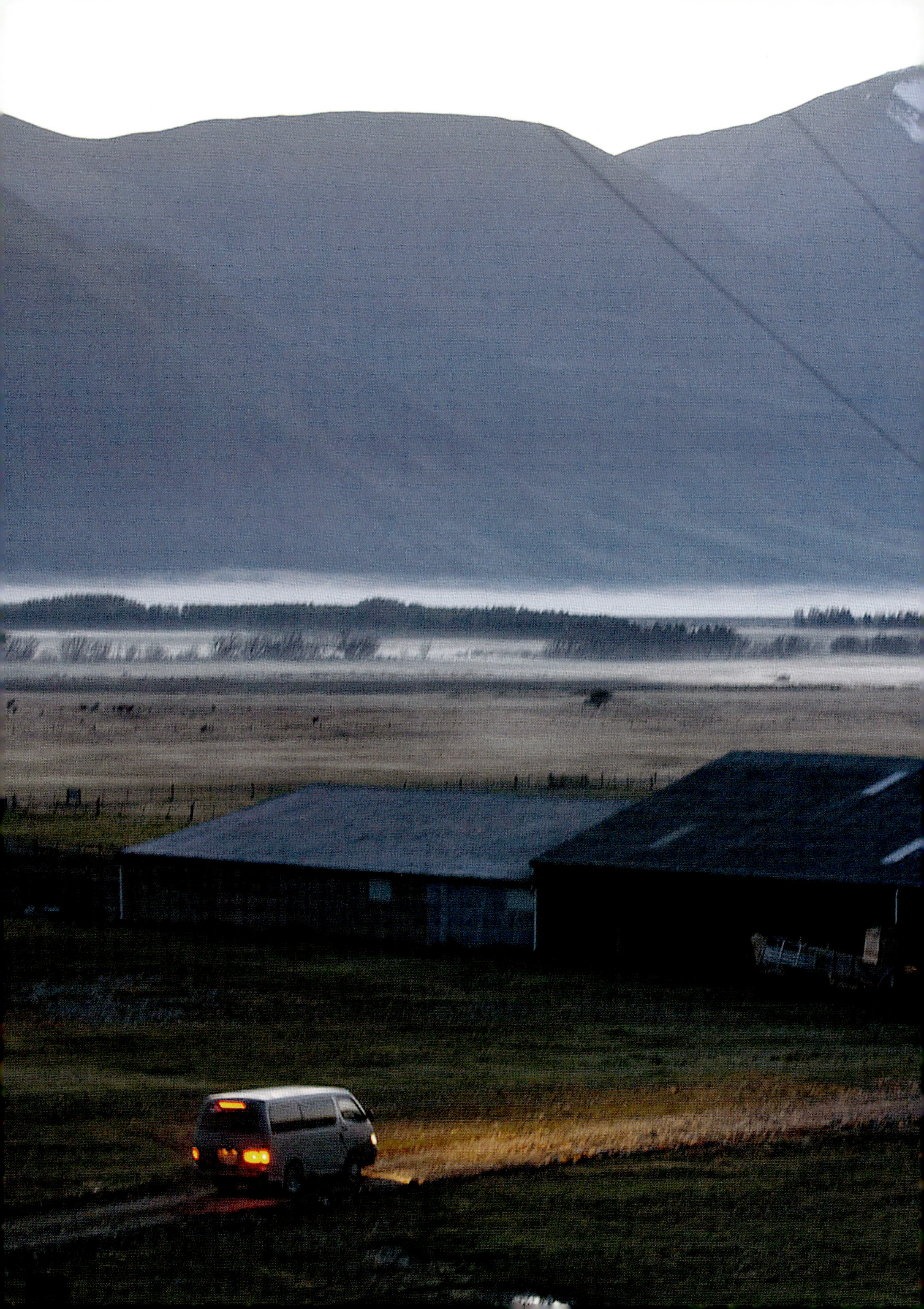

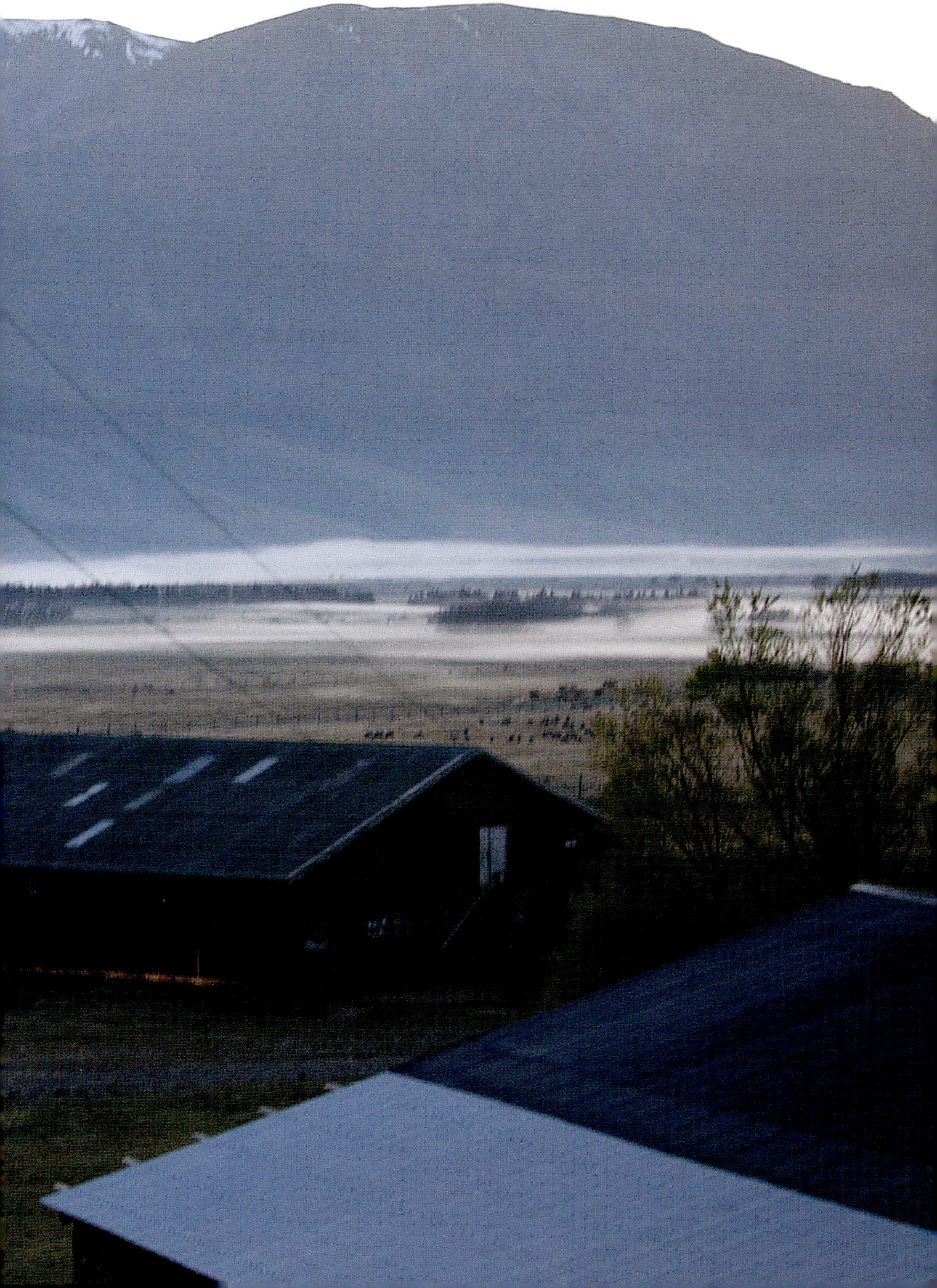

← **PREVIOUS SPREAD**
A fine mist hangs over the Rangitata River in the first light of the new day as the shearers' van arrives at the woolshed.

↑ **CLOCKWISE FROM ABOVE**
In a shed whose interior glows bronze in the morning gloom shearers organise their gear and limber up for the day's work.

Wool peels cleanly off the sheep: grey outside, soft cream on the inside, one of the shearers in a bungy harness to save his back.

Shed hands clear the fleece from a floor glowing from sixty seasons' polishing with soft shoes and lanolin.

Malcolm keeps count.

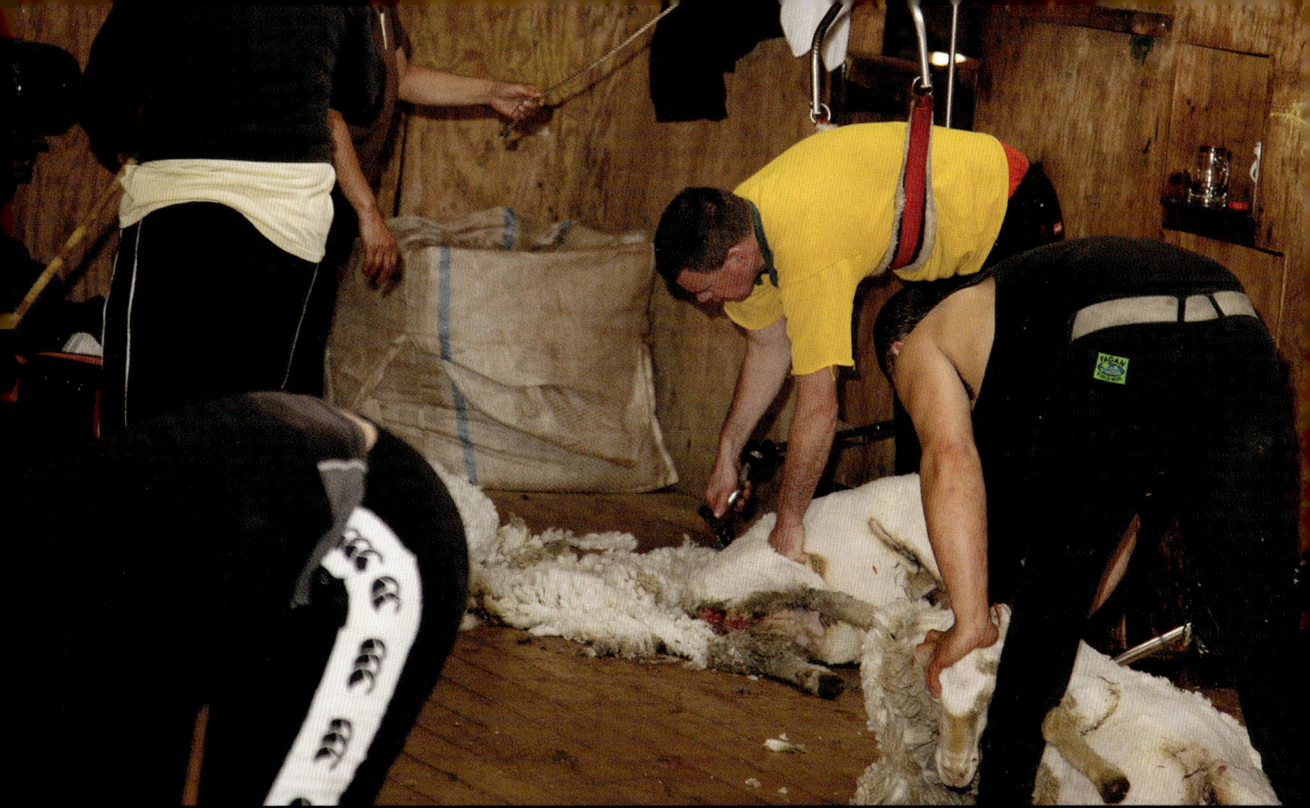

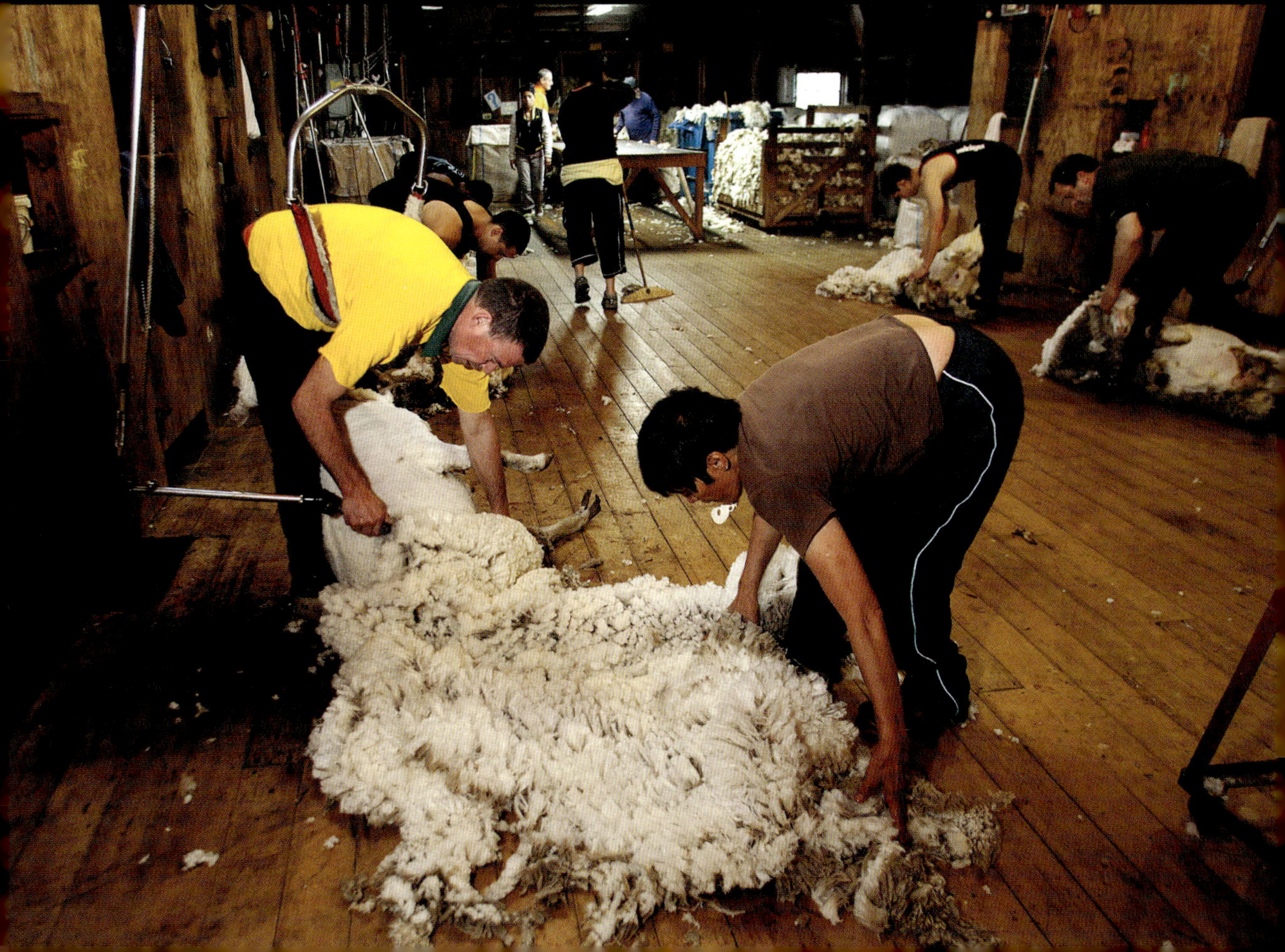

←↑→ LEFT TO RIGHT
Another merino is dragged into position by a shearer, his handset at the ready.

The fleeces are carefully lifted off the floor and carried to the wool-classer's table.

The fleeces are flicked like a blanket onto the classer's table, dropping in one clean spread.

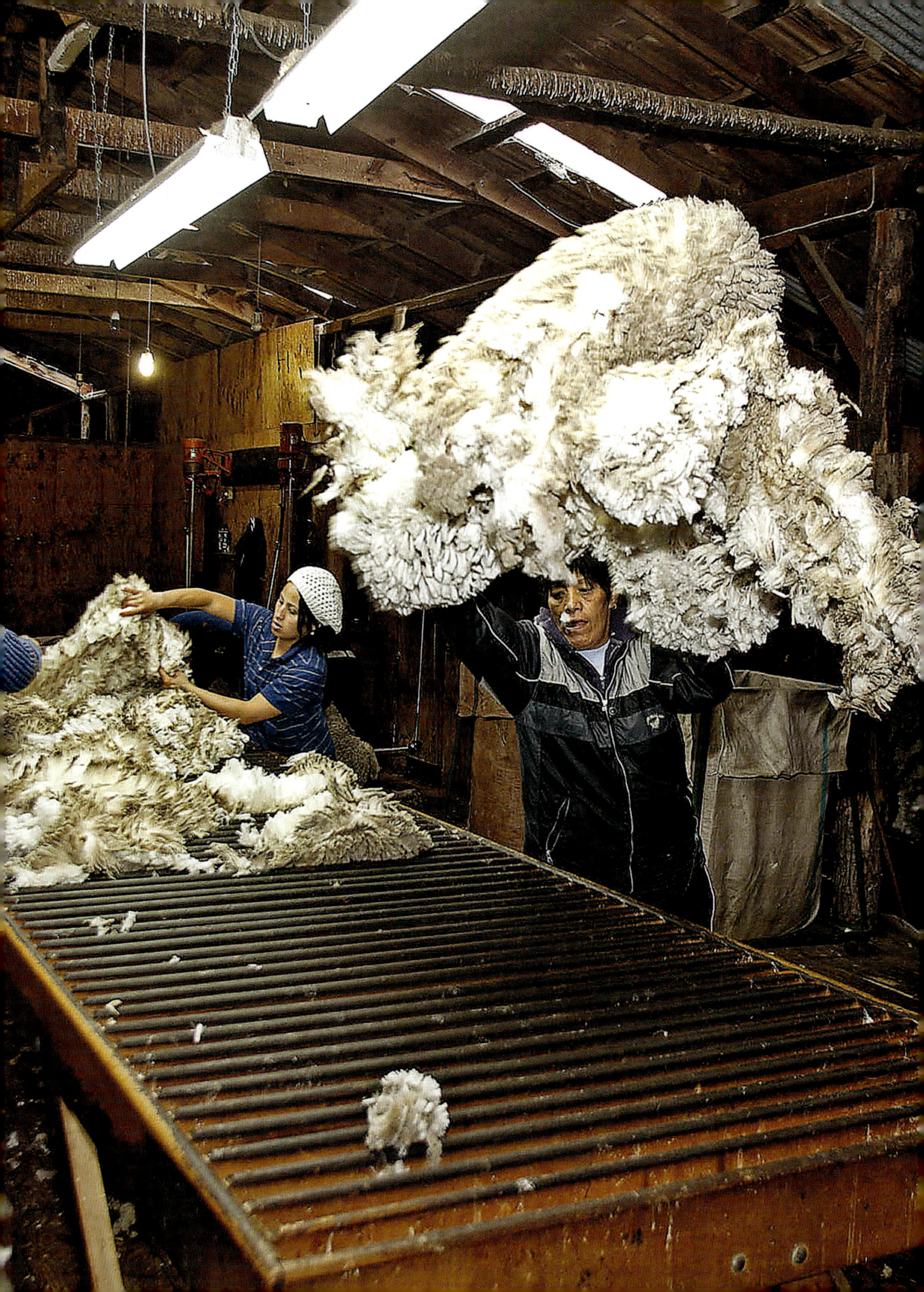

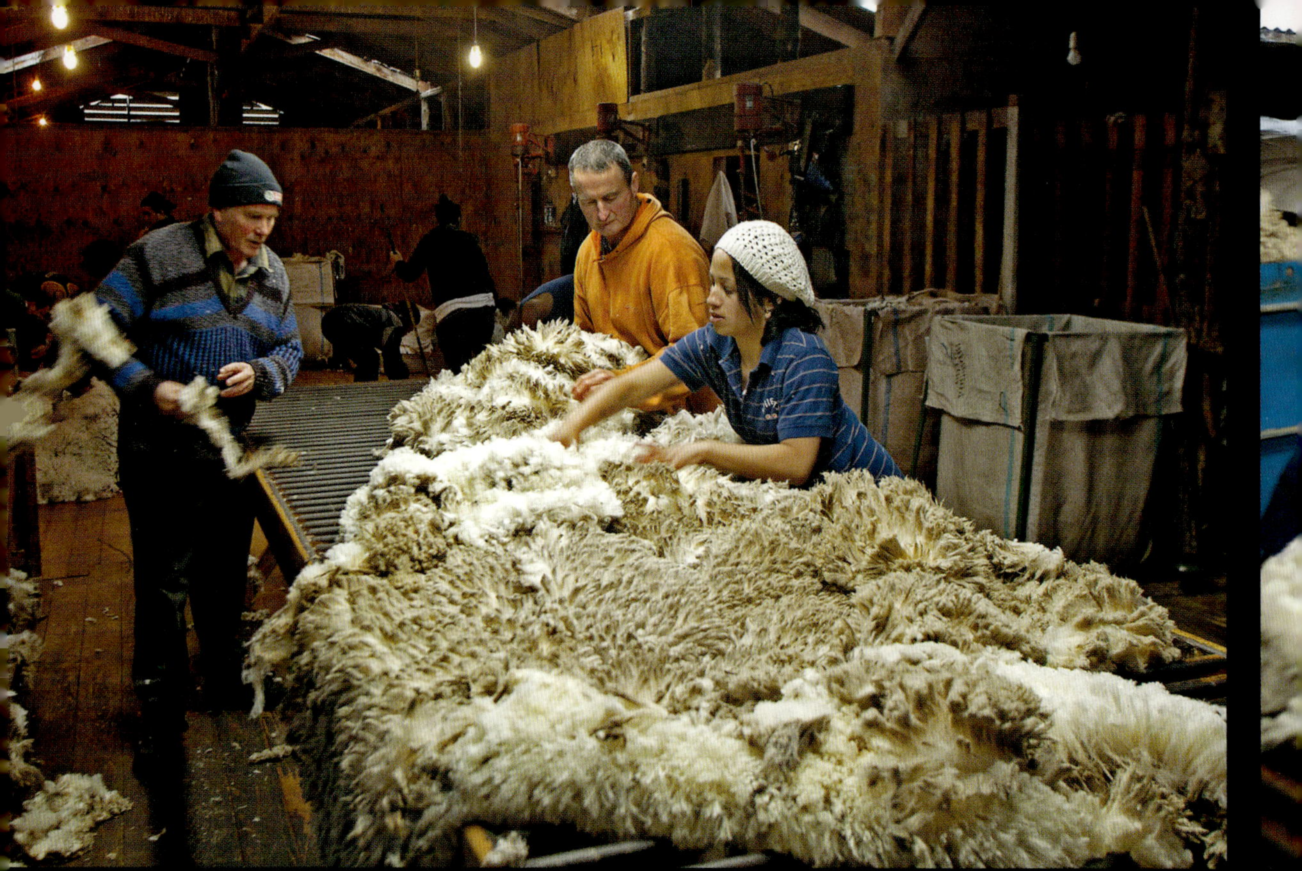

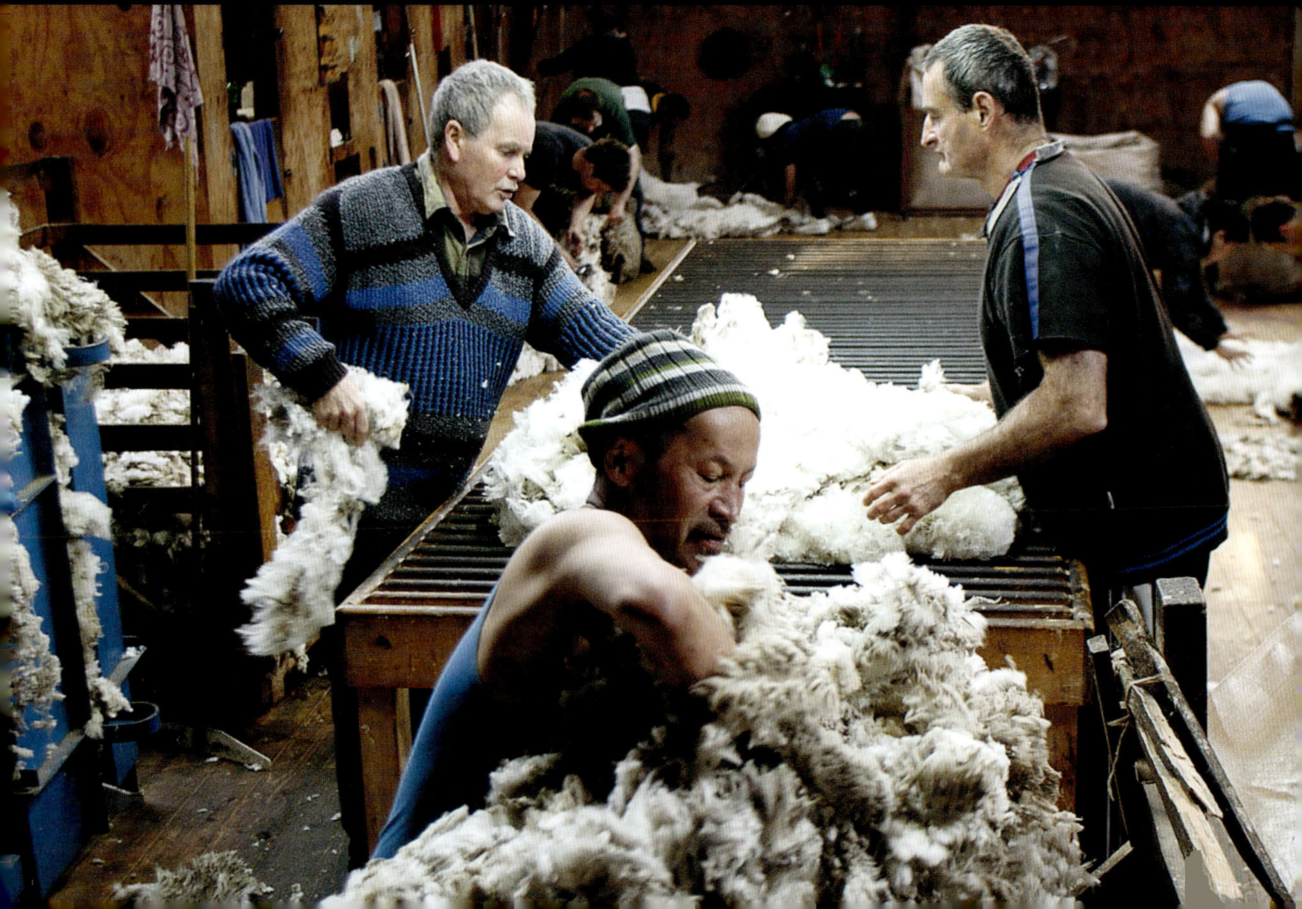

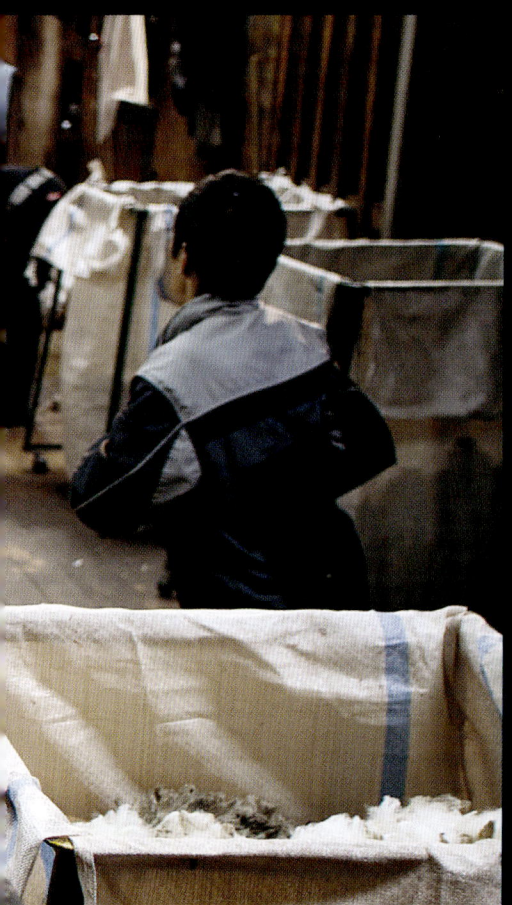

↑ **CLOCKWISE FROM ABOVE**
Kim (left) moves around the fleece, plucking off a bit here, a piece there, feeling the wool with his fingers and classing it by touch.

Kim works across the table from his longtime shed hand Mark.

Fleeces laid on the table for Kim, the classer and leader of the shearing gang, to begin work.

→ **CLOCKWISE FROM RIGHT**
Making the filled bread rolls for lunch.

The shearers take a break every hour, the woolshed falling silent.

In their breaks the shearers lie backs flat on the floor, legs up, like fast bowlers saving their backs at tea during cricket matches.

The fleeces are packed into hydraulic presses, some fifty at a time packed into a bale weighing around 150 kilograms.

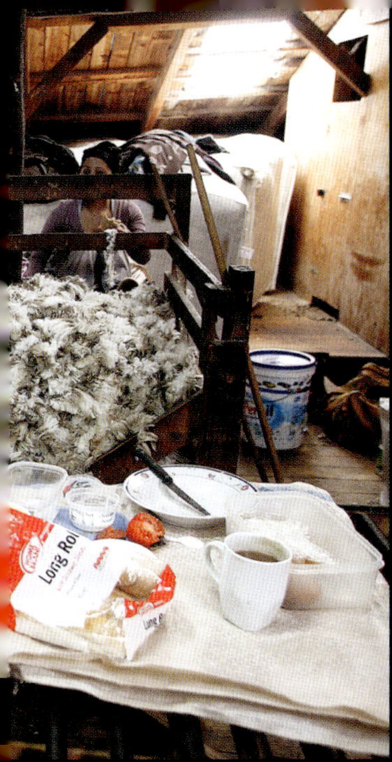

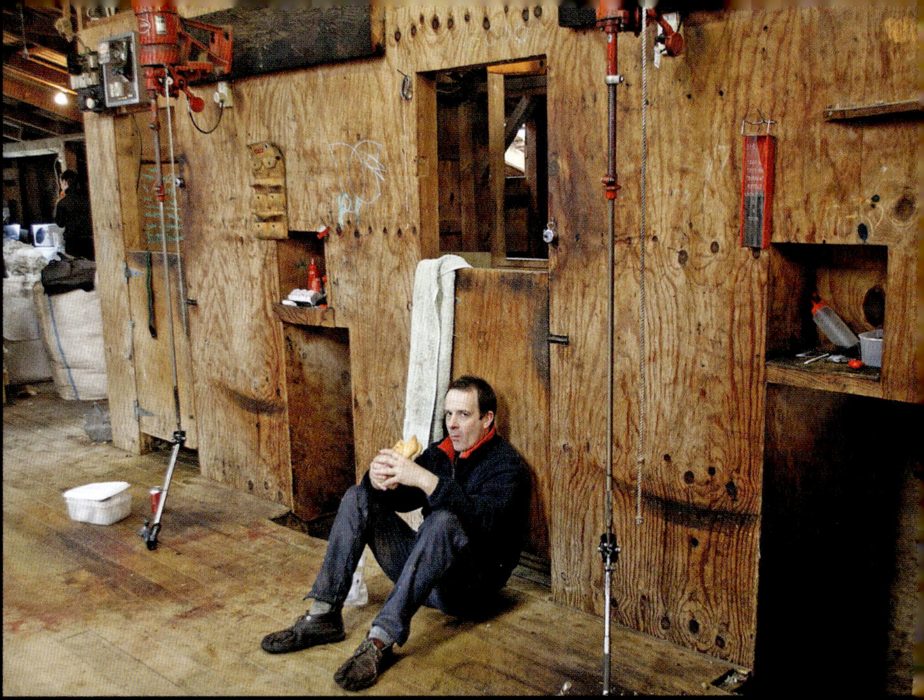

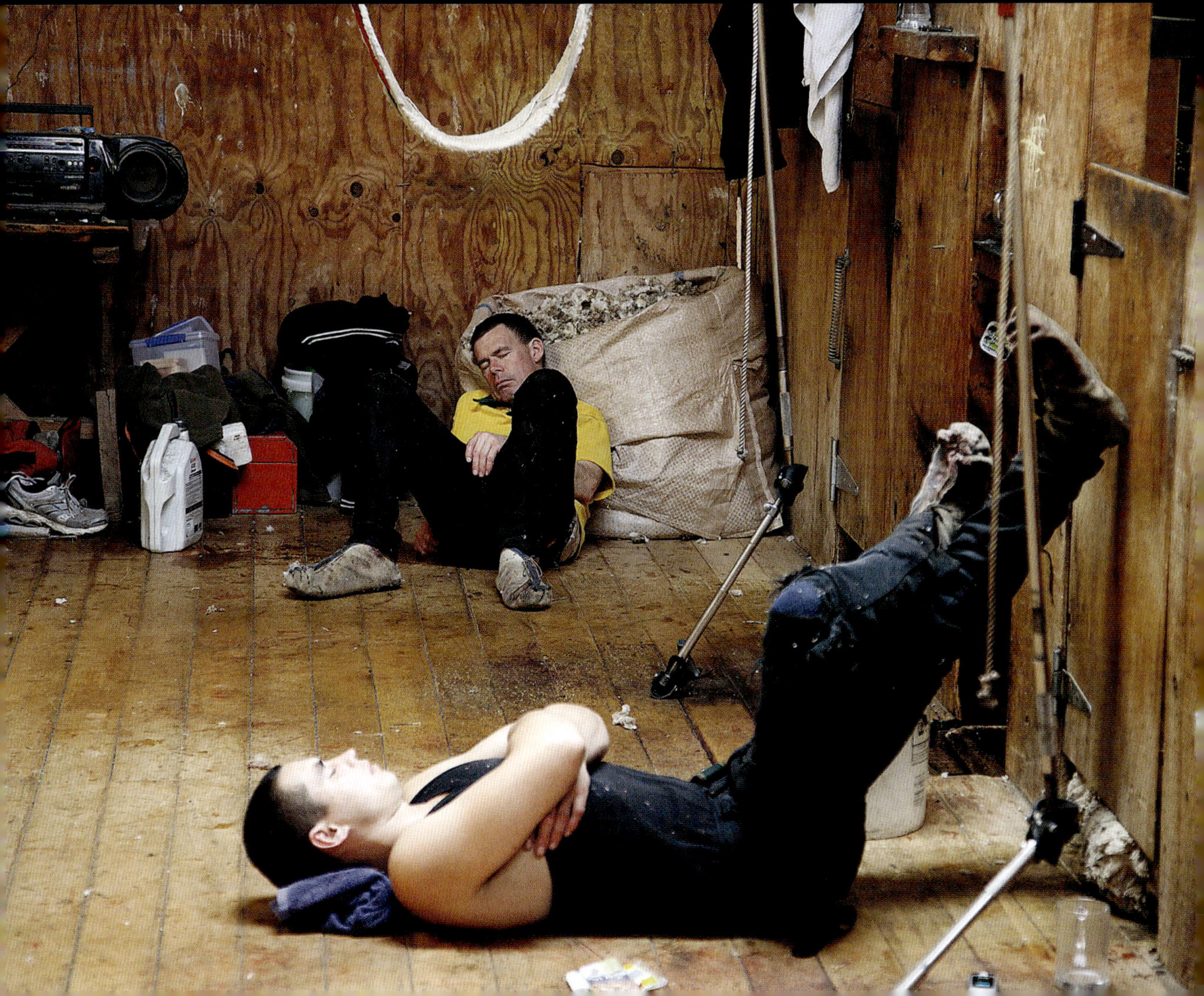

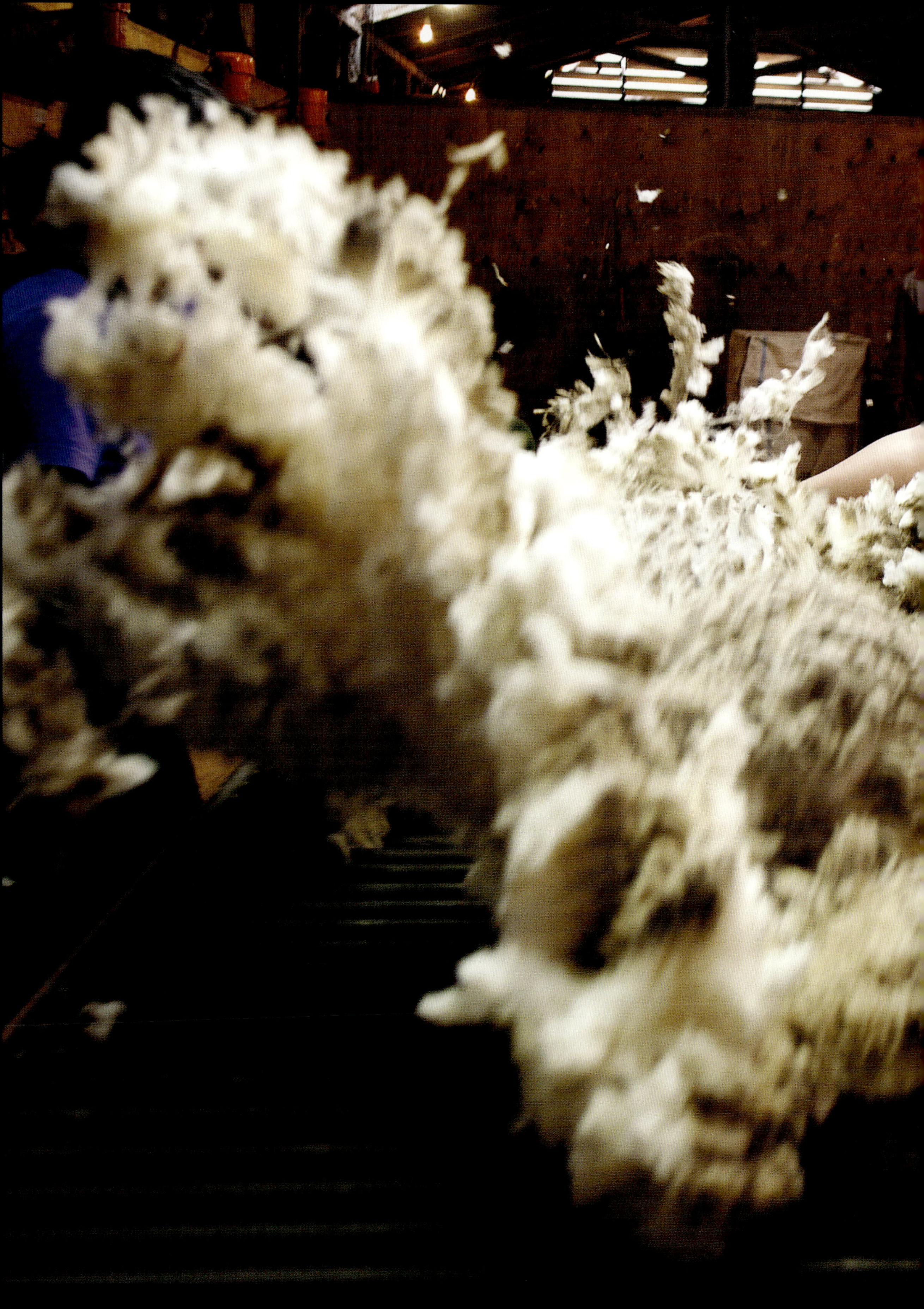

← LEFT
Another fleece lands on the classer's table in one piece, a skill that takes a good deal of practice.

← **LEFT**
Another fleece comes off the table after classing and is carried to the hydraulic press.

↓ **BELOW**
The shearers' floor is kept perfectly clear of any wool except the fleece then coming off the sheep.

↑ **ABOVE**
The shearers wear soft leather shoes.

→ **RIGHT**
End of the day, gather the gear, climb in the van and go home. A few hours sleep and back before dawn tomorrow.

→ **FOLLOWING SPREAD**
The woolshed, the building in the rear, was built by Malcolm Prouting senior in 1949, then state-of-the-art and still functioning perfectly. The building in front is the stables, its walls clad in steel from oil drums hammered flat.

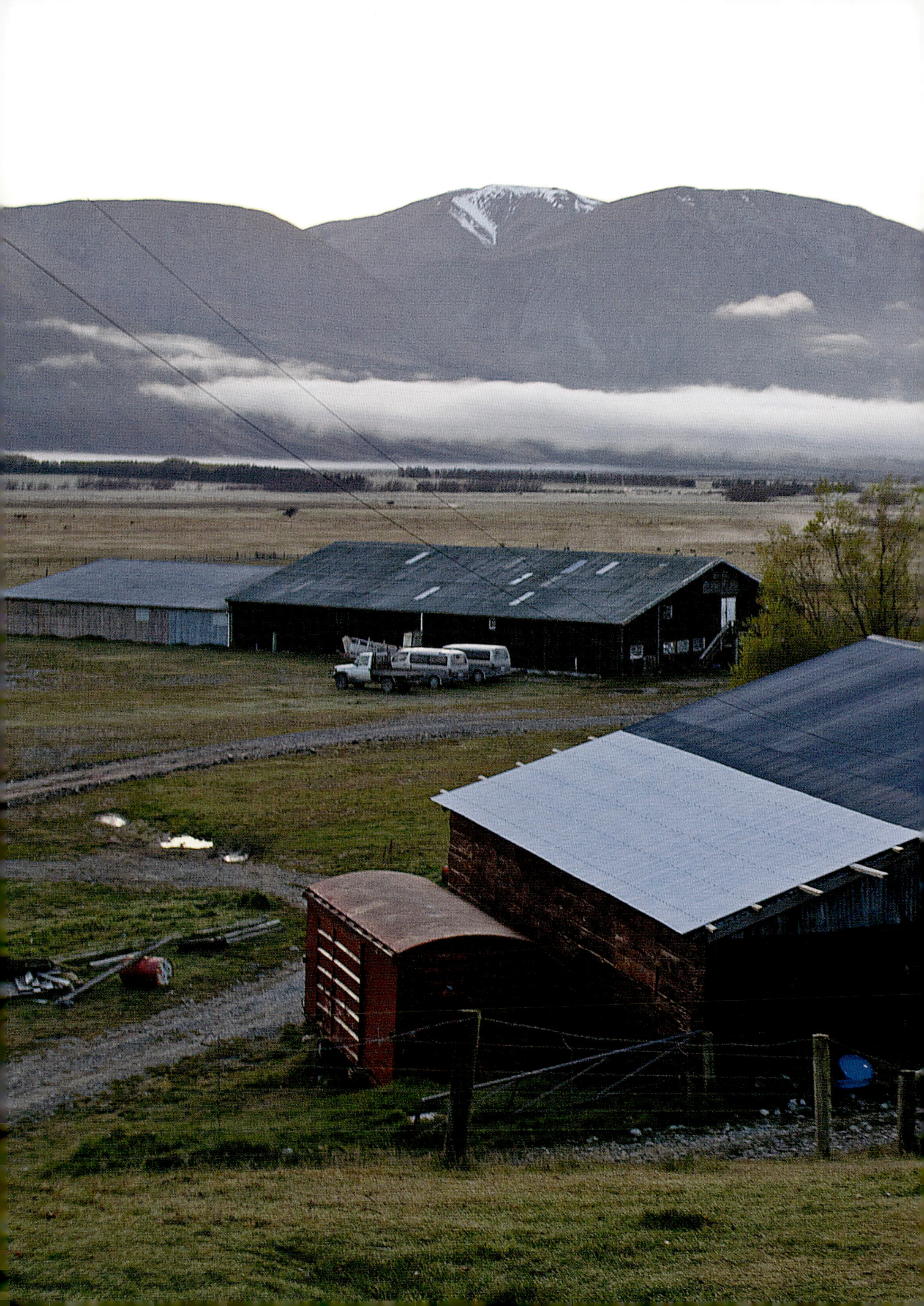

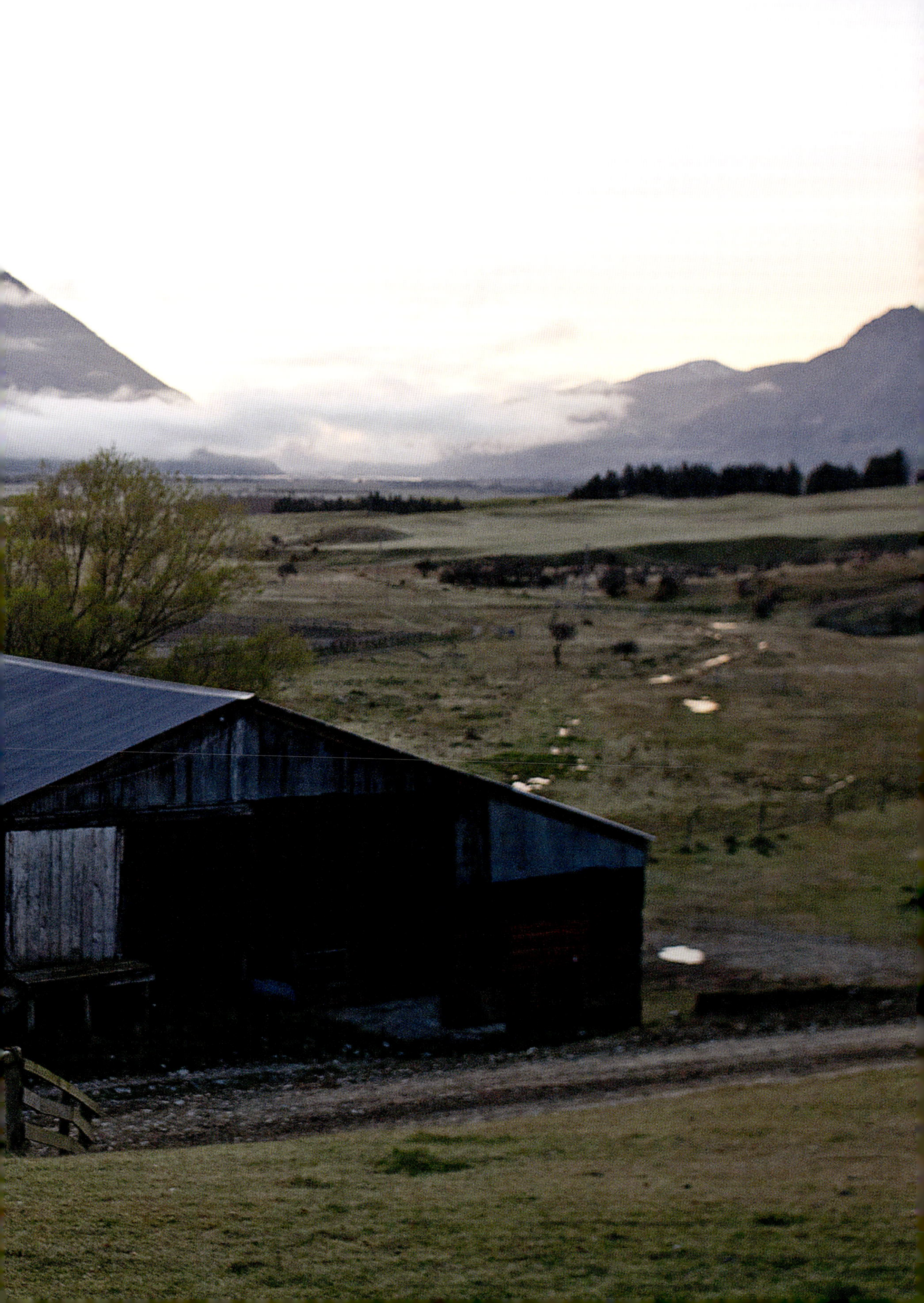

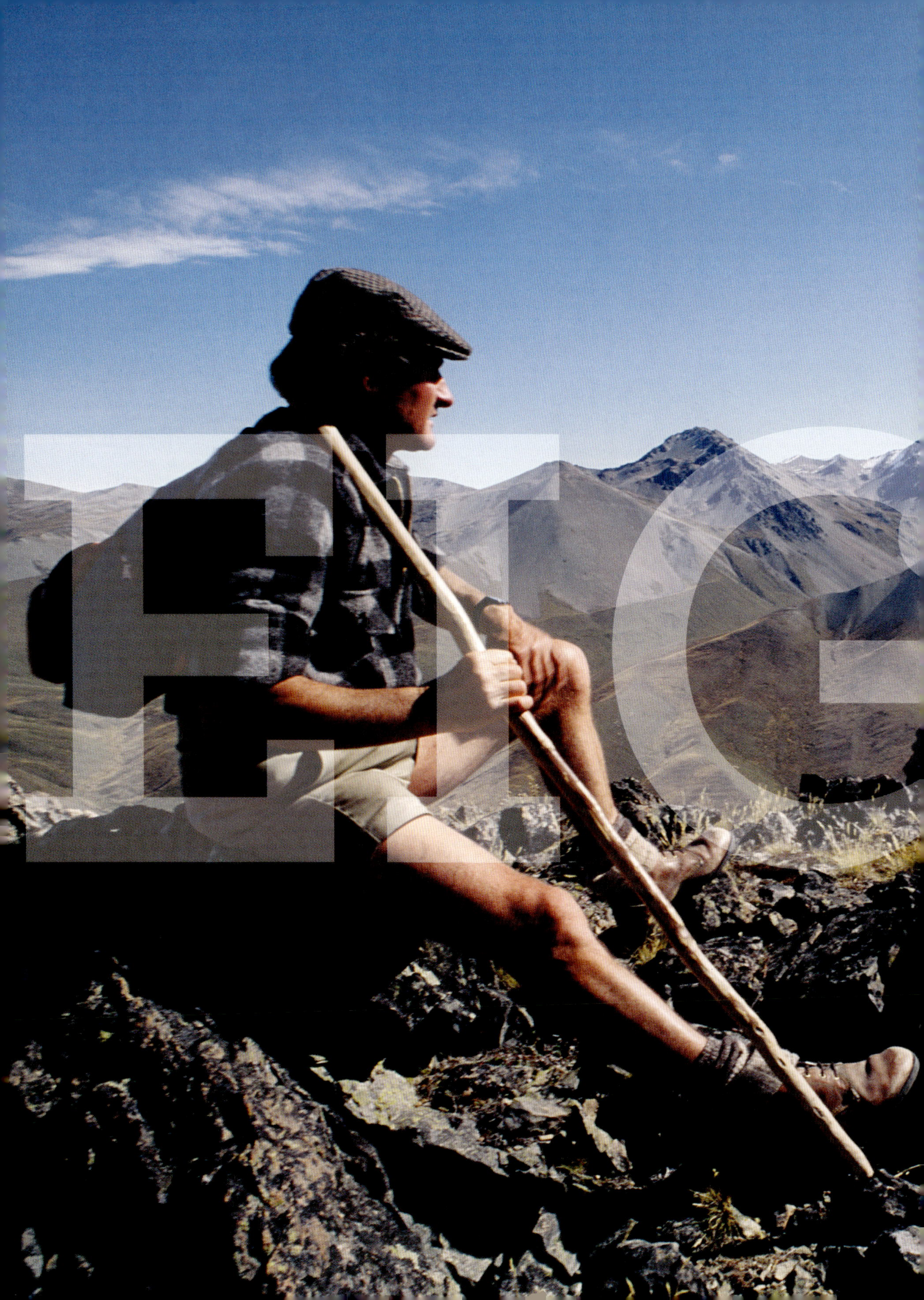

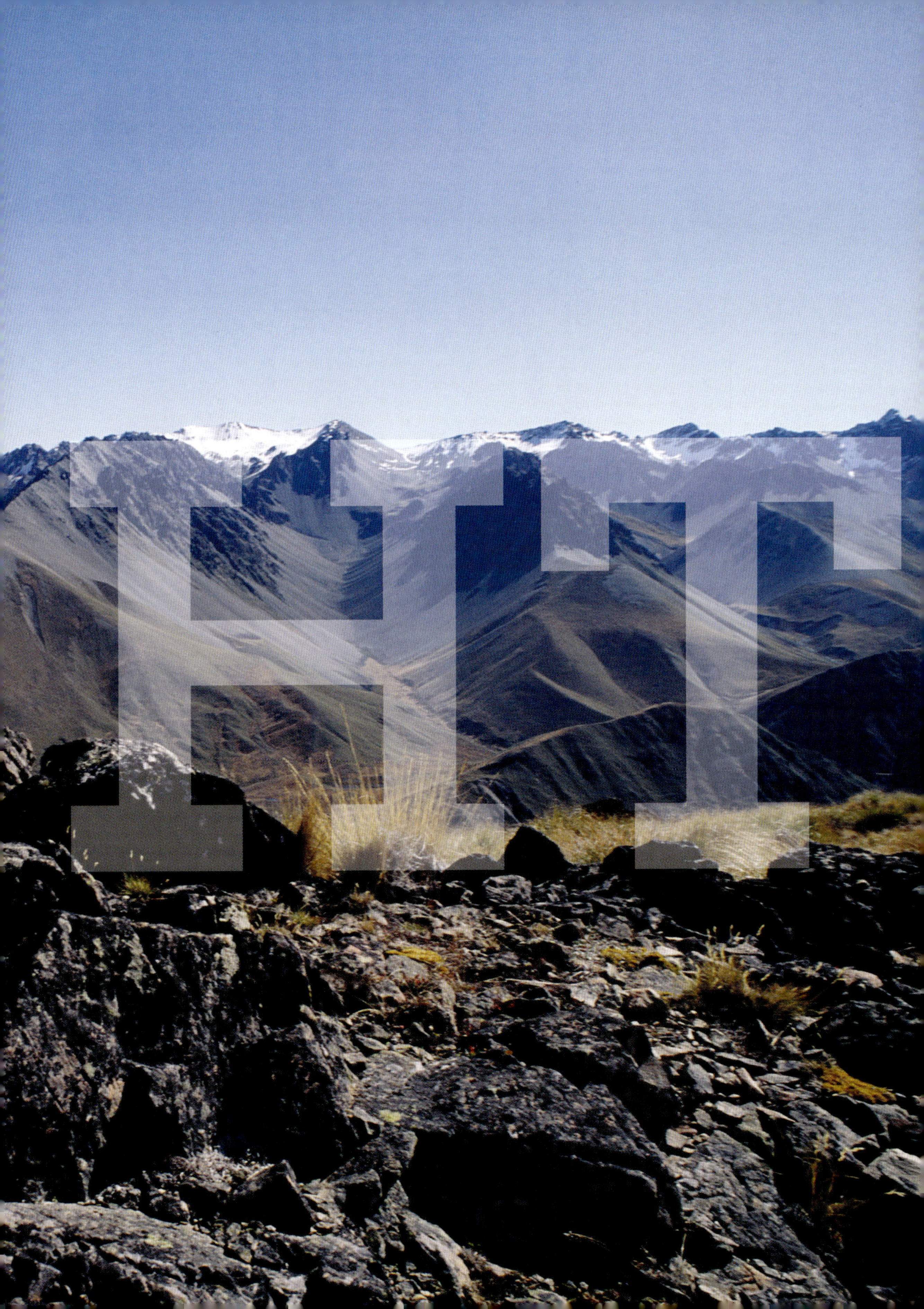

ACHILLES • THE TWO THUMB RANGE • D'ARCHIAC • CROOKED SPUR • HOGGET • THE GROWLER • BRABAZON • NEUTRAL SPUR • CLYDE RIVER • ROCKY RIDGE • BLACK MOUNTAINS • LITTLE SPUR • FINLAYS • FORBES RIVER • BIG BUSH • BLACK BIRCH STREAM • TOP DOWNS • BULLOCK BOW SADDLE • BALACLAVA BASINS • EXETER PEAK • SINCLAIR RANGE • FOREST CREEK • INKERMAN • THE ROCKS • MOUNT SINCLAIR • SUGARLOAF • MOUNT HOPE

EVERY SQUARE METRE of Mesopotamia holds a story, for this is a fabled land in the most literal sense, home to novelists, romancers, historians and people who weave fairy tales around mountains and mists. And it has played host to the generations of New Zealanders who have come to gaze, wander, climb and make movies.

Its European history began with one of the world's great storytellers, Samuel Butler. Butler filled diaries and letters with tales, and followed them with his novel Erewhon. A century and a half later Peter Jackson used the valley as the location for Edoras, capital city of the Rohan people, in his version of the best-known fable of all, *Lord of the Rings*.

At its peak Mesopotamia ranged over more than 41,000 hectares. Its boundaries resembled a giant leg of lamb with the foot at Mount D'Archiac, the edges marked out by the Rangitata River on one side and the Two Thumb Range on the other and the meaty end rolling around from Forest Creek to Mount Hope.

Mustering 18,000 sheep on this land could take a gang of nine men a week, sometimes longer if the weather was against them. Peter Newton, a famed musterer who wrote a history of Mesopotamia Station in 1960, told of one gang held up in the old Stone Hut for two days by heavy snow and high-running creeks. Their dogs had had no food for five days. Eventually two men risked the ice and hiked over the top of the Sinclair Range for supplies. They returned to find their mates surviving on kea soup.

THEN A REVOLUTION overtook the high country, sweeping many of the old traditions before it. Once, people such as the pioneer, mountaineer and author John Pascoe and his climbing mates shared the place only with high country farmers. The second half of the twentieth century found many more New Zealanders tramping, climbing, hunting, horse-trekking, skiing, kayaking, gliding, para-gliding, mountain biking, photographing or simply admiring the mountains.

With a four-wheel-drive vehicle in every second garage and more helicopters per capita than anywhere else in the world the means of getting to the high country was no longer restricted to the small elite of sinewy men and women who, like Pascoe, once tramped long distances, thumbed lifts on trains and trucks, forded rivers and endured foul weather to get there.

> **At the same time high country farmers became embroiled in their own revolution as recreation and adventure tourism displaced sheep. Running tourists alongside merinos saved many a farmer's bottom line.**

An insistent public began demanding not just greater access to mountains but more control over them, for recreation, or to preserve their grandeur and fragile ecosystems, or because people believed, following a major review in the nineties, that the way the high country was being farmed was unsustainable, accusations the farmers stoutly denied.

At the same time high country farmers became embroiled in their own revolution as recreation and adventure tourism displaced sheep. Running tourists alongside merinos saved many a farmer's bottom line. Foreign and corporate ownership became increasingly common, and controversial. For all that, most stations were still farmed by the independent, wilful, resourceful, staunch group of families who, generically at least, had always ruled the high country.

Mesopotamia accommodated hunters, trampers and climbers from its beginnings. Deerstalkers, for example, helped Malcolm Prouting senior build his bridge over Forest Creek. The station had carried their hut to Mistake Flat on a trailer, and they knew they would be using the bridge to get to the hut, so they lent a hand. All the Proutings asked in return for access to their land was common courtesy and respect for their property.

Laurie Prouting spelled out their approach like this: 'Various people call us land barons and want to go marching over our property. Well, they always can. Even the young fellers who go up there in their Land Rovers and Toyotas, loaded to the gunnels with booze, some of them just out there to waste themselves. But why not do it properly, talk to us, treat the runholder like a human being? I remember one guy coming up, a teetotaller who owned a garage in Belfast in Christchurch. He said he'd love to go hunting. And later he gave us a case of lemonade as a thank you. Well, first time anyone did that. We wound up good friends. Whereas you have a lot of crusty young guys today who think they have every right to hunt and tramp wherever they want to. It has always been a bit of an issue.'

The issue, however, was rapidly coming to a head. Pastoral leases once covered twenty per cent of the South Island and ten per cent of New Zealand. Some 304 South Island high-country properties covering more than two million hectares were farmed under Crown pastoral leases.

The leases meant that the people who farmed these high country stations did not own them. Instead, they were owned by the government and rented to the farmers. The pastoral lease system had served for a century and a half, but now the government and the public demanded change. In summary, they wanted their land back. The South Island high country became embroiled in a giant land swap. In a process called tenure review, runholders were to gain freehold title over part of their properties in exchange for land handed back to the Crown for conservation.

The government took the more remarkable, ecologically valuable and scenic parts of the stations and put them into the conservation estate. They became public land, open to the public. In return, the farmers got the more valuable farming country on their runs to call their own. They were no longer lessees. Instead, they became fully fledged freehold owners of their land.

The idea first emerged from government offices in the early nineties, the swap being heralded as the high country solution. Its advocates called it win-win: farmers shed the more troublesome parts of their land and became outright owners of the rest to do as they pleased with it: fence, subdivide, develop, sell. The public won a protected conservation estate, which they could roam or look at, or which simply made them feel comfortable that some of the most beautiful parts of the country were theirs.

A few agreements were struck before the scheme stumbled. The land swaps stalled and did not resume until the late nineties. The South Island's spine then began merging into a giant conservation park running from top to bottom. Some farmers welcomed deals which freeholded much of

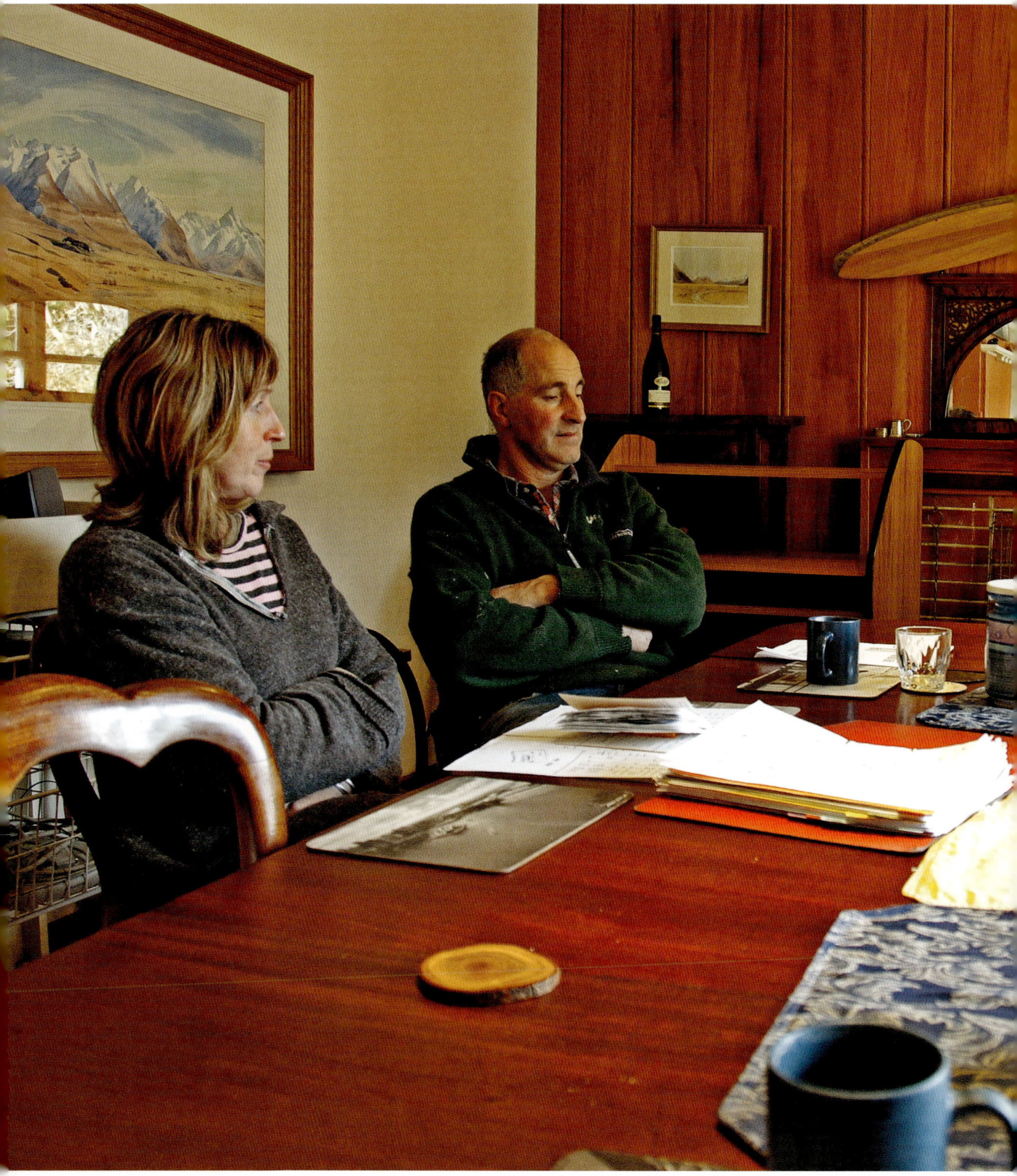

their properties or sometimes made them rich, for the cash settlement could go either way, to the farmer or to the government. Others resented the change, which brought with it a loss of land and often, a way of life. Some did not believe the government was capable of managing its new estates. On the other side environmentalists worried that not enough tussock land was being reserved, and that the exchanges were leaving too much land in farmers' hands and not enough in the conservation estate.

The Proutings never had any illusions about their fate. Much of their land was high altitude, mountainous. By now one guiding principle had been established: the higher the altitude, the more the government wanted. Mesopotamia's wild mixture of peaks and deep valleys, glaciers and ravines, remote country and skyline dominated by near-mystical peaks such as Mount D'Archiac and the Two Thumbs was a siren-call to conservationists. The family could already feel pencils sketching most of their station into the boundaries of a new conservation park.

Officially, the bargaining was voluntary; if they wished, farmers could stay as they were. The Proutings did not believe that retaining the status quo was viable. They saw a double threat: the government of the day could raise rents to the point where a farmer would be forced into tenure review; or it could simply make the voluntary tenure review process compulsory, as one government minister had already suggested.

Compulsion carried a price. It always did. Better, they reasoned, to settle while they were free to negotiate even if, as Malcolm said, 'it's a deal with the devil'. The negotiations were fraught. They started in 2003 and ranged over five years.

The stakes were high, but the negotiations had their lighter moments. Malcolm found himself more comfortable

← LEFT
A round-table conference in the homestead's dining room, Sue (left), Roger Johnston, the manager of Forest Creek Station and Malcolm (right).

dealing with Ngai Tahu, the leading South Island iwi, than with the Department of Conservation. He once swept his hand along the Sinclair Range, over the whole vast landscape once occupied exclusively by Mesopotamia, and asked a kuia, or woman elder, 'What part of the place do you want?'

'None of it,' she replied, 'it's too cold up here for us.'

'Then why don't you take the whole station and we'll lease it back from you?'

'Bugger that,' she said. 'Then *we'd* have to deal with DOC.'

At one stage the government side was offering the Proutings only 3000 hectares of their huge station. 'If that was a car,' Laurie observed, 'you'd wind up with the front right-hand mudguard. How could you accept something like that?'

The family sometimes felt the whole thing would fall over and the parties, Land Information New Zealand and the Department of Conservation on one side, the Proutings and their advisers Meredith Lowe and Alasdair Ensor on the other, would walk away from the negotiating table. But DOC was keen on the putative agreement, and the Proutings' financial advisers believed it was a good one.

'Our people were telling us we'd got a bloody good deal and urging us not to push it to a point that would kill it,' said Laurie. 'And I was still being pretty reckless in saying, "Just a minute, I can still see flaws in this document."'

Despite their differences, the two sides agreed at last. On 7 April 2008, a deal was announced by the Labour government's Land Information Minister David Parker and Conservation Minister Steve Chadwick.

By then, Mesopotamia had already shrunk. Of the original 40,000 or so hectares, the station still leased 26,115 hectares. The rest had gone out of pastoral lease by various ways. Malcolm senior had carved off 4000 hectares of freeholded land for his sons Don and Ray. Don and Helen Prouting called their station Tui and sold it to Canadians Mari Hill Harpur and her husband Douglas for $6.3 million. The Canadian couple had earlier bought Ray and Margaret Prouting's adjoining station for about $3 million. The two stations were now farmed as one, Forest Creek, with the Canadians establishing extensive forestry blocks. The Proutings had already freeholded about 2800 hectares of land on Mesopotamia, and some of the station's original area had previously been surrendered to the government.

An extraordinary result of the deal is that the family now seem uncertain exactly how big their station is. But rough arithmetic takes the 5252 hectares of land freeholded in the negotiations, adds the freehold land already existing, and comes up with some 8000 hectares, ecologically sensitive covenants covering 1487 hectares of them. Or to put it another way, the station started with an area bigger than the Abel Tasman National Park and finished less than a third of its size.

Why would the Proutings agree to give up such a huge part of their grand old station? Because they believed they had no choice. 'We were cutting off our right arm to do this,' said Laurie. 'Malcolm wouldn't have given them one square centimetre of land. But I was absolutely desperate to get rid of the situation where someone was setting the rent for us every eleven years, and those eleven years seemed to come around very quickly. Profitability was so poor at that stage that we had two options: one was to do tenure review, the other was to go broke. Simple as that.'

They foresaw another pressure point. They believed the government was running out of money for such agreements, that future deals would involve more trading and less money. They were prescient. Later, the government began doing exactly that.

The Crown took 20,863 hectares of Mesopotamia for its new conservation park, lying neatly beside the huge Hakatere Conservation Park on the other side of the river. Somewhere in the ether Samuel Butler pounded his keys with a wry smile.

As an incidental public bonus the Mesopotamia deal filled in a twenty-five kilometre gap in the Te Araroa walking track, the national pathway that now runs from one end of the country to the other. Trampers could loop through the old Mesopotamia and stay in huts where once musterers spent nights yarning. They could follow the paths trodden by shepherds over one and a half centuries, amid the grandeur and the loneliness. Or they could walk on up the Rangitata, turning into the Havelock River past the Black Mountain and the great faces tumbling down to the river.

The conservation estate won alpine screes and stonefields, herb-fields, tall tussock grasslands, shrub lands, beech forest and regionally rare upland totara, the habitats of such threatened birds as the blue duck, New Zealand falcon, kea, black-fronted tern and the wrybill with its curious sideways-curving bill.

The Proutings got the five thousand, two hundred and fifty-two hectares and $4.6 million. They won their important hunting concession, and a twenty-year tourism, filming and photography non-exclusive concession over the new conservation land 'for the continued diversification of the family business'.

They also secured an important twenty-year right allowing them to graze stock on 619 hectares of lower-lying conservation land above the Havelock River. The money allowed the Proutings to pay off debt and start afresh, while Mesopotamia was pared down to its best. Yet it was a huge blow to family pride, and they still smart under it. 'It's our business, our livelihood, our passion, our history,' Malcolm said. 'For the guys on the other side of the table it's a job.'

TO SUE, MESOPOTAMIA is still huge. 'The size of the place is mind-blowing. We went rafting on the West Coast one day and we flew back around Lilybank by Lake Tekapo. Then Laurie flew over the Two Thumb Range and said to me, "Sue do you know where we are now?" I said I hadn't got a bloody clue. He said, "Well you're on your own back garden." It was so hard to comprehend that we were so far out and it was still Messie. Even now when the place is smaller you can go up somewhere and you're in the middle of nowhere.'

Even trimmed back the station now ran about 11,000 merinos, 500 cattle and 3000 deer, including 700 velveting stags. For comparison, in 1980 it carried 22,000 sheep, 1600 cattle and 1100 deer.

Traditionally sheep provided the station's main income. Now it was divided almost equally between sheep and deer, with cattle contributing only some seven per cent of the gross. Wool prices had improved, the deer market was picking up.

'The problem is,' said Malcolm, 'that we're getting what we got ten years ago. But all the other costs have escalated. We've all got more efficient. Years ago Perendales doing one hundred and five per cent at lambing were considered excellent. Now the figure is one hundred and forty to one hundred and fifty per cent, and specialised farmers are doing one hundred and eighty per cent. You can't keep on doing that. It's only just treading water. Everyone's gunning for production instead of price increases.'

The station's income seemed huge to outsiders, until they saw the cost of running the place. It earned more than a million dollars a year, 'But we spend over a million dollars too. Last year we made thirteen thousand profit, although we have a development programme costing over two hundred thousand dollars a year. We did very well out of tenure review. It affects every farm in vastly different ways. We're very fortunate because we have vast downs, such huge flats at the front, and tenure review suited this place. Other places will nearly go bankrupt. It would have been too many nails in the coffin for the family not to have gone through it.

'Even if you excluded rent rises the cost of maintaining some of this country can only rise. Looking after this country for what you make off it, the marginal country, the cost was going to be prohibitive. I think the Crown is going to realise that; probably they already have realised it, because I understand they're not so keen on land that has got any issues hanging over it. Our timing wasn't at the big money stage. Yet I think, strictly as a businessman, for a balance we couldn't have had our timing much better. But still, as a high country farmer it's gutting that we've lost the high country. It's still a deal with the devil.'

> **When she looked out of her kitchen window she mourned the loss of Mount Sinclair, looming behind the homestead. The mountain was still there. It still looked the same. But it was no longer part of the station, and she felt a part of her was missing.**

Now when Sue drove around the *Wow!* Corner at White Rock virtually everything she saw was no longer Mesopotamia's. It belonged to the government. When she looked out of her kitchen window she mourned the loss of Mount Sinclair, looming behind the homestead. The mountain was still there. It still looked the same. But it was no longer part of the station, and she felt a part of her was missing. That, said Malcolm, was a very hard thing to get their heads around.

'Because, did you really own it? The family has always looked at it like this, we're just custodians of the land, we don't really own it. We're here for such a minute part of the time the land has been here. But as a high country farmer it's hard to lose so many things.' His arm took in the sweep of the mountains, the musters. 'The whole thing,' he said.

Malcolm believed it likely that the Department of Conservation eventually would allow conservation land to be grazed, where they needed weed control, or they wanted the land to remain as tussock grassland, or simply to earn some money off the conservation estate. 'These guys will hum and hah and say so many weeks and so many sheep and by the time I put them out there and get them back again do I really want to do it?'

Then he laughed. Sue laughed. Alasdair Ensor, who'd been listening to the conversation around the big lunch table on the terrace outside the kitchen, laughed. He said, 'If Malcolm and Sue can use the excuse to line the packhorses up and go out to get the sheep back in again they'll want to do it.'

A year later the new Te Kahui Kaupeka Conservation Park was opened.

FIRST HERE 1959

MARGARET MOSES
BRUCE HARRISON] WORKED HERE
8/9 FEB 1991
TOO OLD TO CLIMB THE

WED 6-1-93
HEADING FOR STONE HUT
R. PROUTING
M. PROUTING
G. PROUTING

The name meant 'the gathering place of waters', for Mount D'Archiac was the font of both Lake Tekapo and the Rangitata River. The park comprised 93,856 hectares of high country with the Two Thumb Range and Mount D'Archiac at its core. Mesopotamia Station contributed almost a quarter of the new park, including the jewels in its crown.

At its opening in April 2009, the National government's Minister of Conservation, Kate Wilkinson, paid tribute to the Proutings' role in creating the new park, given the family's sorrow at parting with its high country. Without their stewardship of the land and their tenacity there would have been no park. Their loss, she said, was the public's gain. That was certainly true, for the new park was among New Zealand's most spectacular.

She said, 'While the mountaintops and tawny tussock basins won't hear the sound of the muster again, the nation will unquestionably benefit from the attainment of this incredible swathe of country now being protected for all New Zealand to enjoy.'

Laurie Prouting spoke at the ceremony too, but he was more blunt. Look around, he invited guests. See the native bush on the front of Mount Sinclair, up the Bush and Birch streams. Note its pristine condition. Observe the absence of wilding pines, broom and gorse, rabbits, wallabies or wild pigs on Mesopotamia land going into the new park; recognise that there were few deer and that tahr were under control. Ask the question, he said: Has this land suffered under one hundred and fifty years of farming? Then challenge the Department of Conservation to do as well.

THE TITLE 'STATION' still fitted Mesopotamia best. The name went with its location, its loneliness, the mountains, valleys and the wild country. They mattered more

← LEFT
History pencilled on the walls of the Felt Hut.

than size, or at least, just as much. The station still ran down to the river but skirted the front of the Sinclair Range instead of rolling over the top and into the valley beyond.

A finger of land now extended to the edge of Forest Creek and peered down at Butler's old hut site where the creek forked below, then ran up to the old Felt Hut. It seemed to beckon at the Bullock Bow, the famous pass where once flowed rivers of sheep. The reshaped station took in the smooth decline of the Brabazon Range as it eased into the river, then it sidled along the lower slopes of the Black Mountain Range as the Havelock River turned into the Rangitata. The Black Mountain Hut still sat within its boundary, solid and squat beside the river, forever the palace in a storm. The Felt and Black Mountain huts were the only two remaining on the station.

The Growler Hut, far up the Havelock River, the last refuge as the old station narrowed on its way up Mount D'Archiac, was now on the conservation estate. The hut was once the bane even of the most hardy musterers. David McLeod, in his book *Many a Glorious Morning*, described it as 'very unpopular accommodation. Built of rough stones, placed in the direct funnel of the valley where the wind tore screaming off the glaciers, it seemed to crouch, its low-set walls and squat chimney barely higher than a large tent. The walls, once plugged with clay to keep the weather out, had opened with the passage of time, so that often a whistling draught was right beside your ear as you lay in your bunk. The bunks were of sagging sacks, the floor was dirt, and of course the chimney smoked.' Its history was now the property of the Department of Conservation, along with the huts in the Bush Stream Valley: the Crooked Spur, Stone, and Royal huts.

The Crooked Spur Hut, rebuilt by Malcolm senior, now welcomed hunters, and trampers who had made the journey through the rocks and ravines carved by Bush Stream between the Sinclair and Brabazon ranges. The Stone Hut was rebuilt by Bob Buick, earning him a toast from the station's musterers. The old hut had been constructed from boulders rolled up from Bush Stream. They formed the hut's walls and chimney, which were innocent of embellishments such as cement to hold them together and keep out the wind.

'There were no bunks or table and all hands simply unrolled their swags on the floor and gazed out through the chinks in the rocks,' wrote musterer Peter Newton. 'However, it had a good corrugated iron roof and that, I suppose, was considerably better than a tent.'

Malcolm senior put in a new hut, well up towards the Bullock Bow. It was called the New Hut, of course. Following a brief visit by Prince Charles and Princess Anne, flown in by helicopter, it was renamed the Royal Hut.

The station always let the public use its huts for the asking, free of charge. Now they were available to anyone who bought a ticket from the Department of Conservation and made the difficult journey through the valley, perhaps thinking of the musterers who had taken refuge there over the last century and a half.

The new park was a wonder, a prize now in the public domain. Yet the public lost something, too. The autumn muster of 2008 was the last of the great traditional musters, the kind that once graced calendars and postcards the world over.

A gap, a bite, a hollow appeared in the national legend, that world of sheep flowing over golden tussock, of armies of lean musterers and armadas of dogs, of sweaty hats and dusty check shirts, corrugated iron chimneys and grilled chops. Now Ash the head shepherd was a musterer without a muster, and he mourned the loss. 'That stuff up there was what I lived for. Getting right out on the tops, playing around up there. I still reckon we'll get it back one day. One day. Probably just not in my time, that's all. For me the highlight of the year was the autumn muster. I looked forward to it all year, to going out for five days. I'm gutted it's gone.'

Ash could be among the last of his genre. He wrote his epitaph unconsciously. 'No walking on the big hills. I can see the whole point in doing it. But it's still a bloody shame.'

Yet you did not look at this land and wonder what it was like, once, for it was the same as it had always been. If he were riding his horse Doctor up the valley today, Samuel Butler would recognise it at once. A little less of his accursed Irishman, the purple matagouri perhaps, more fences, better pasture. But the grandeur of the place could not be changed by men with laptops. Its beauty and its silence go on forever.

> **Yet you did not look at this land and wonder what it was like, once, for it was the same as it had always been.**

PHOTO ESSAY
THE CATTLE MUSTER

On a day which starts with a grey morning and moves on to autumn blue, the black Angus herd comes down from the mountains while the going is good and the nor'west wind stays away. If the rivers come up, calves may be swept off their feet. The cows are brought down to the river flats and herded through the streams and into the home paddocks. Next day, the calves will be drafted off and the cows TB-tested. This is a family affair, and every available hand is called in to help. The calf sale is looming. In the autumn day, everything goes with scarcely a hitch.

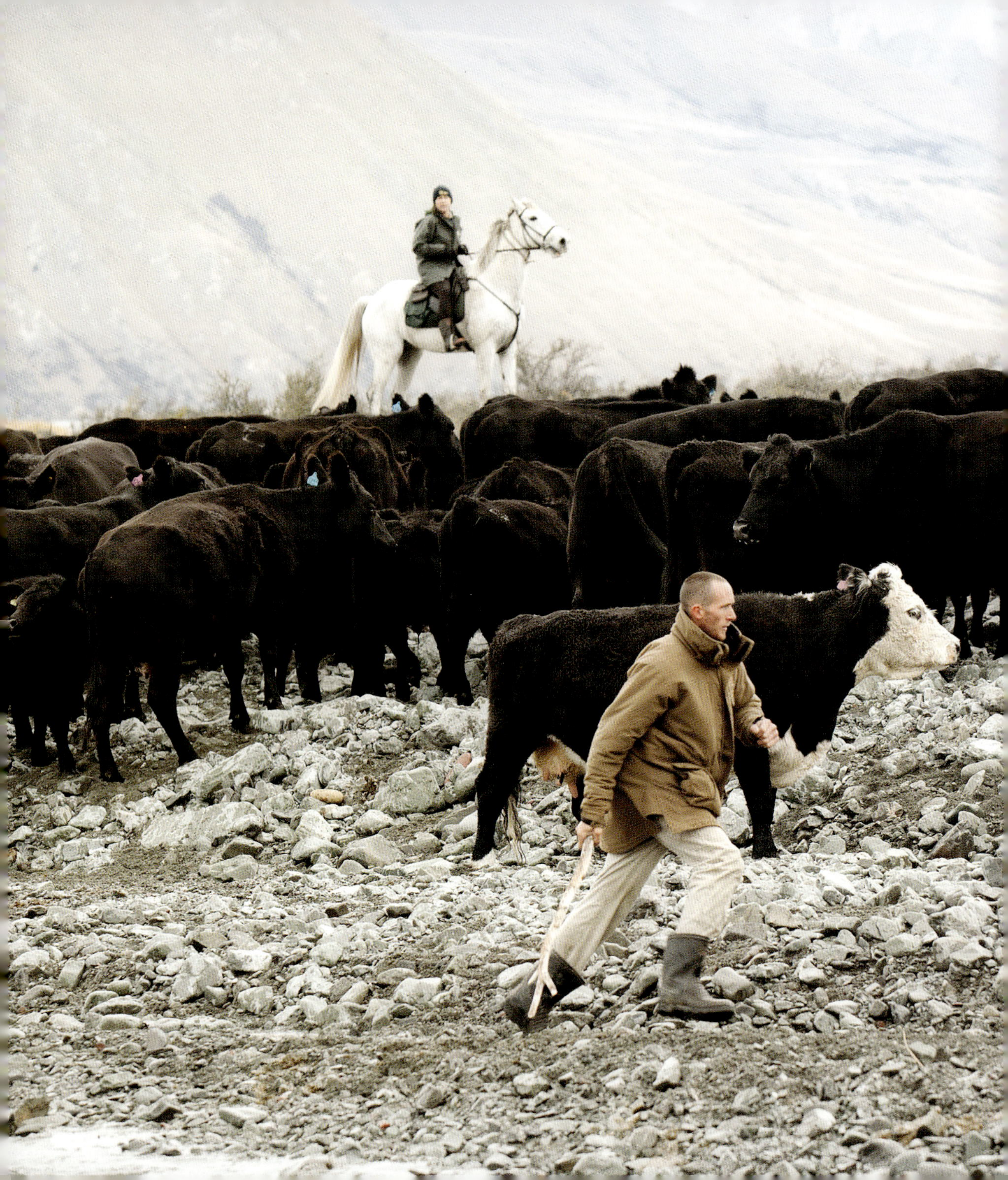

← **LEFT**
Black cows, riverbed shingle and misty hills in shades of grey, Ash O'Donnell, the head shepherd, watches the near side while Sue, on her white horse, takes the other.

↓ **FOLLOWING SPREADS**
Black Angus, white horse: Sue Prouting musters a herd of cows and calves.

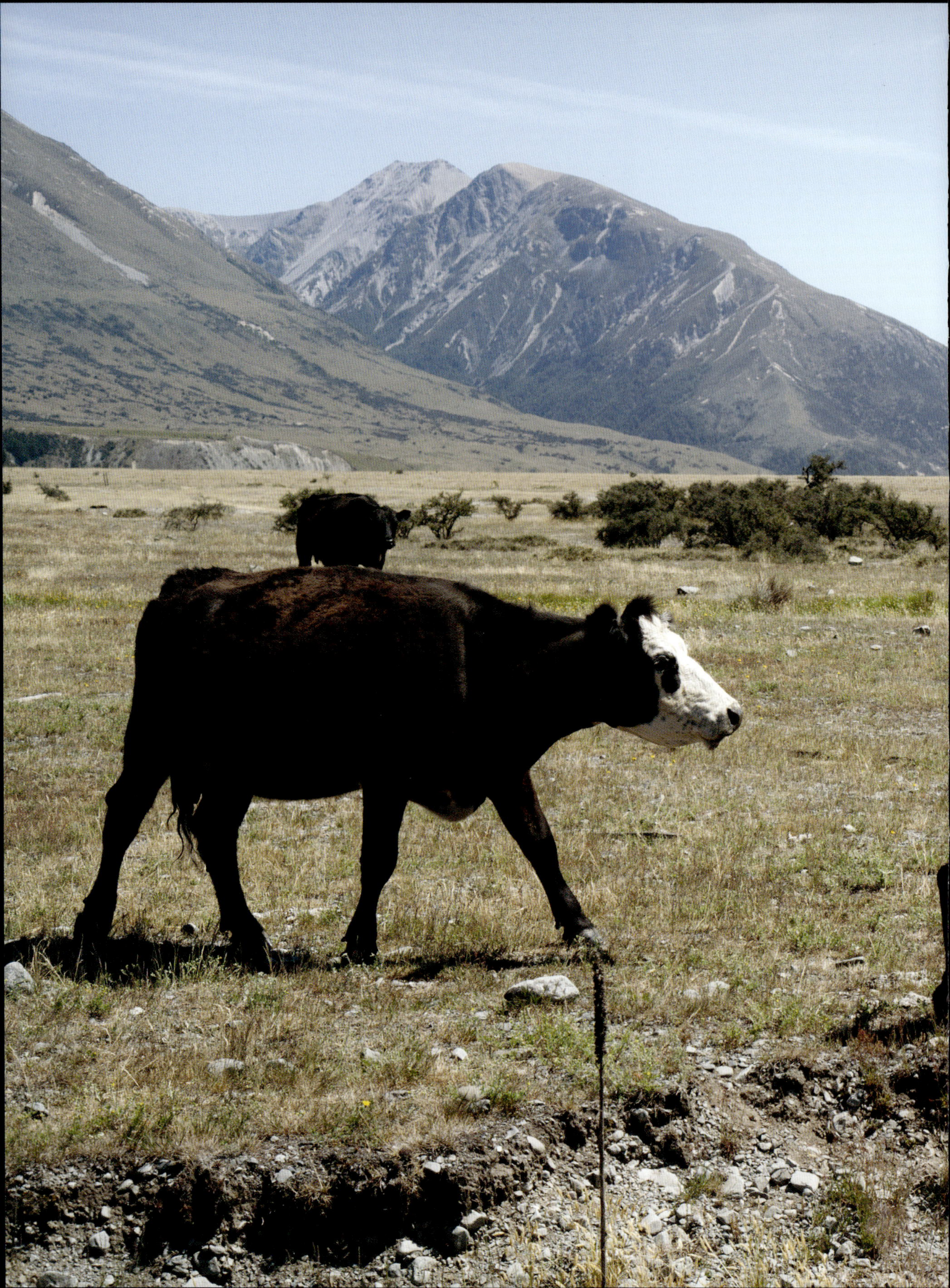

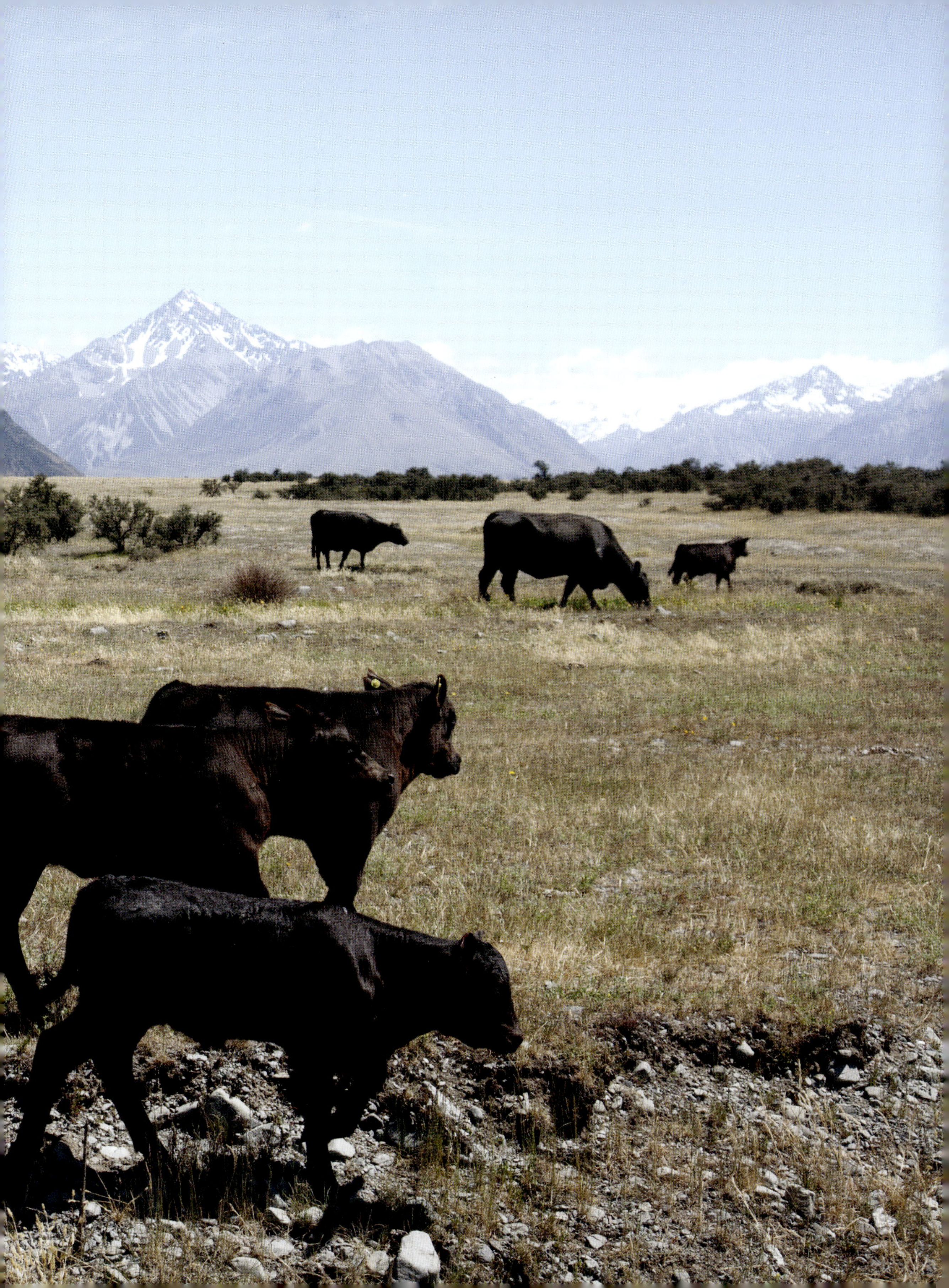

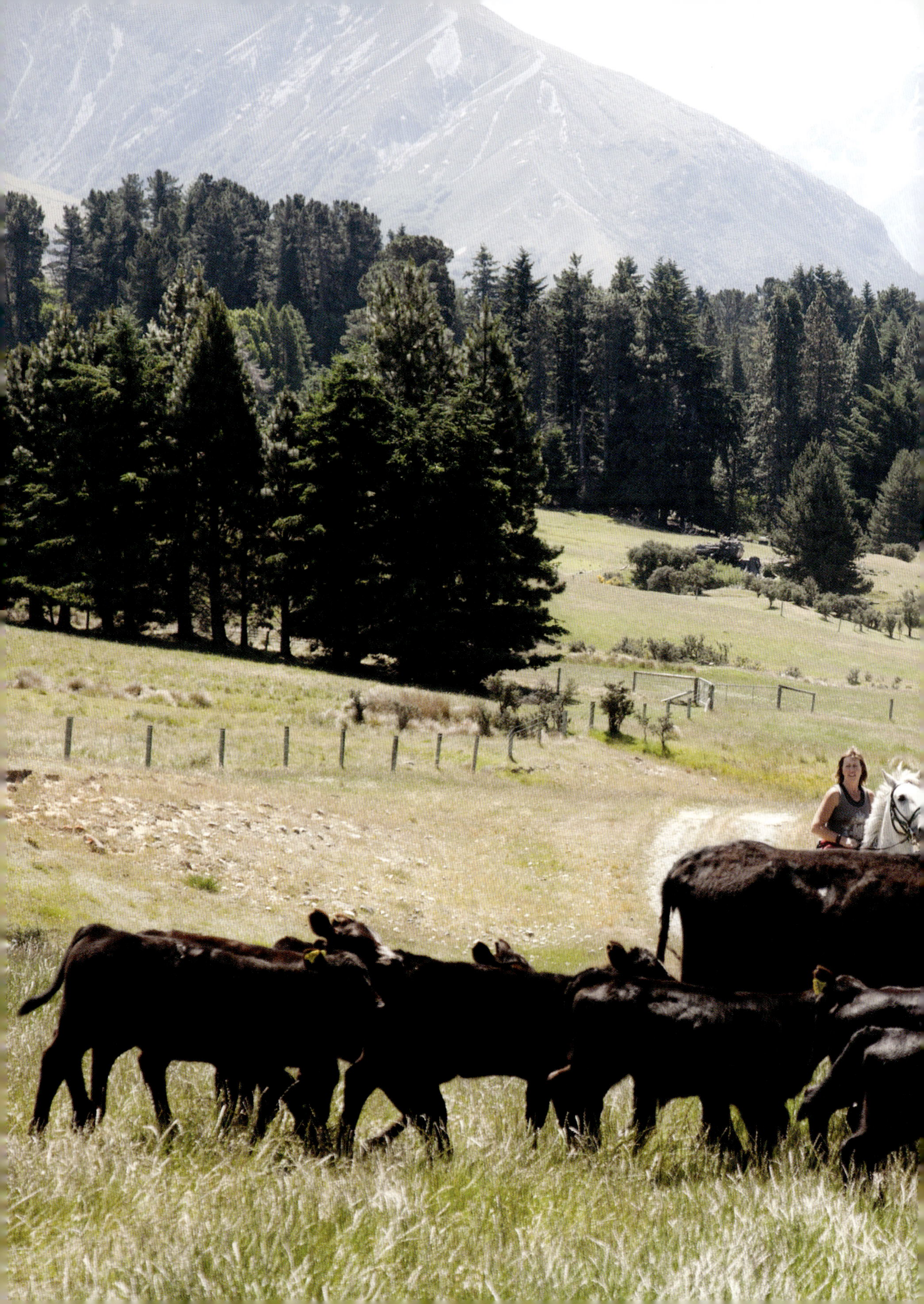

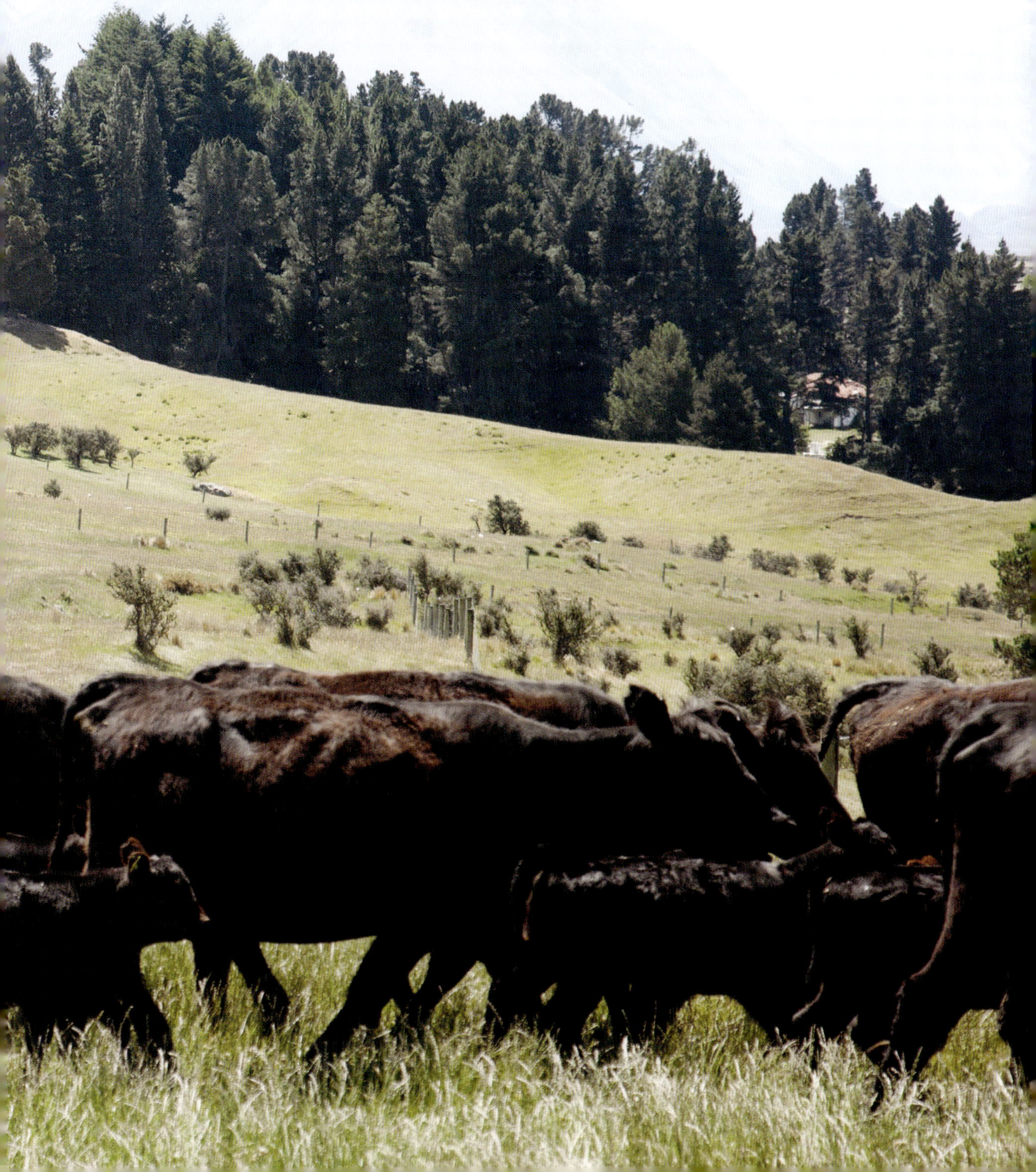

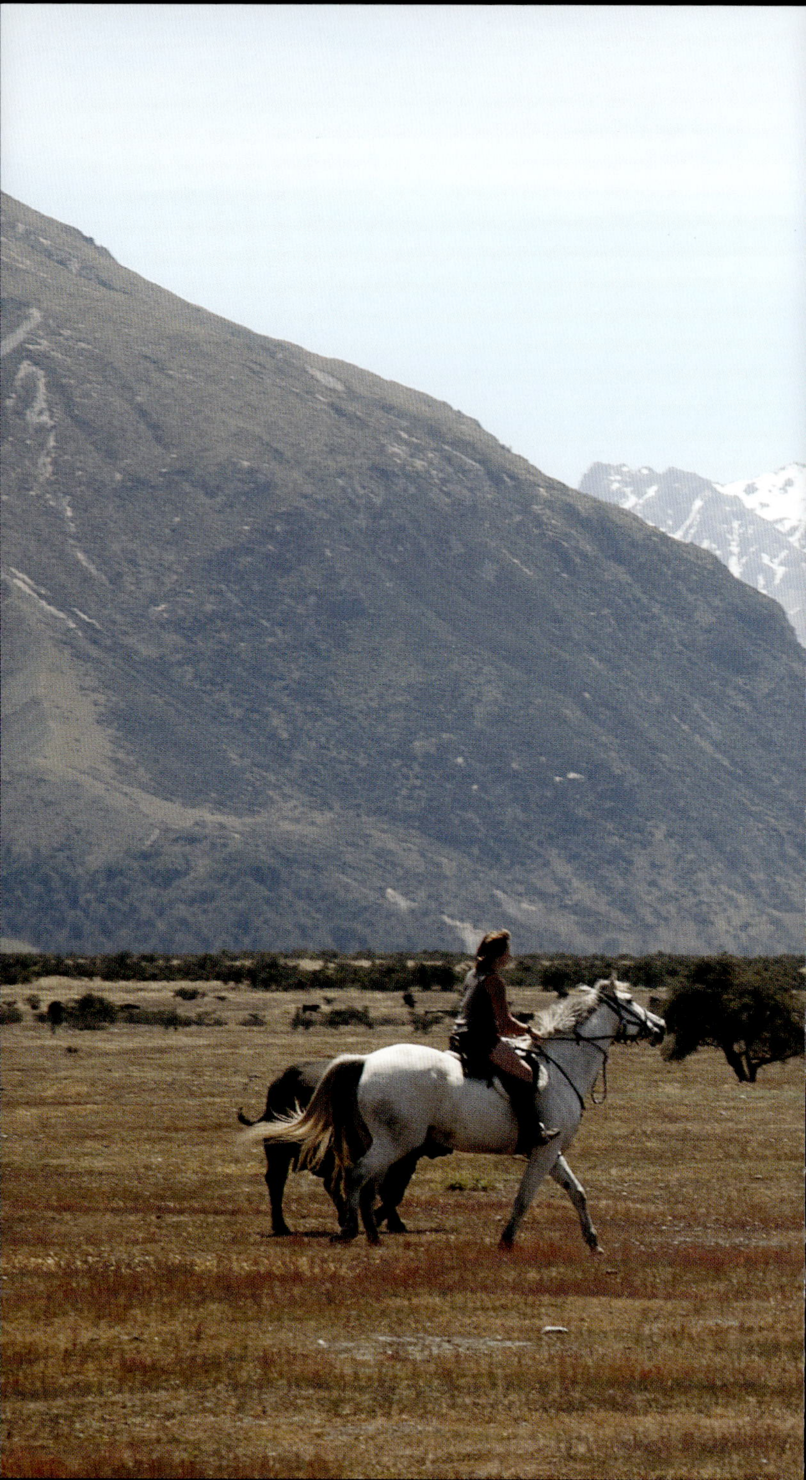

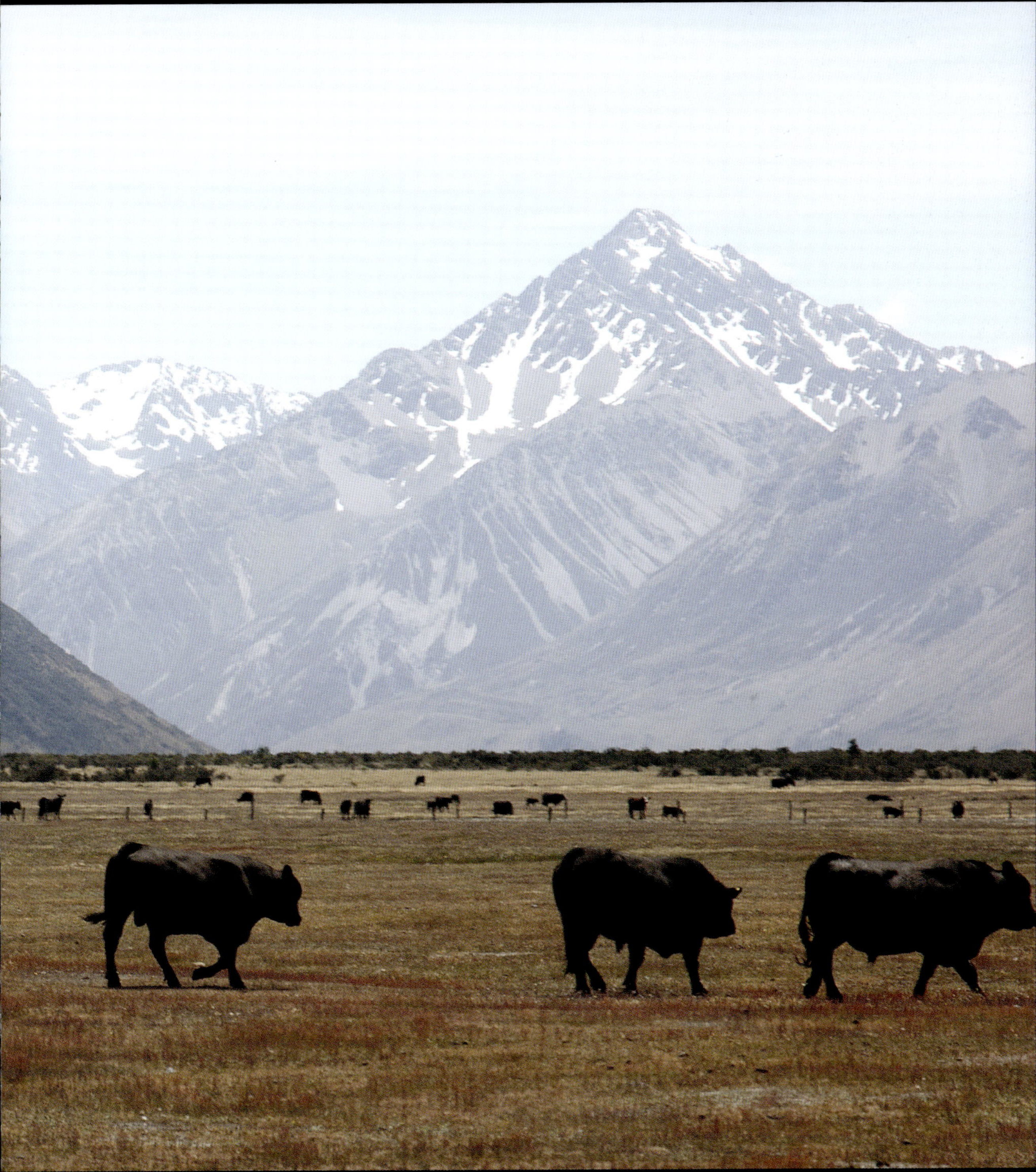

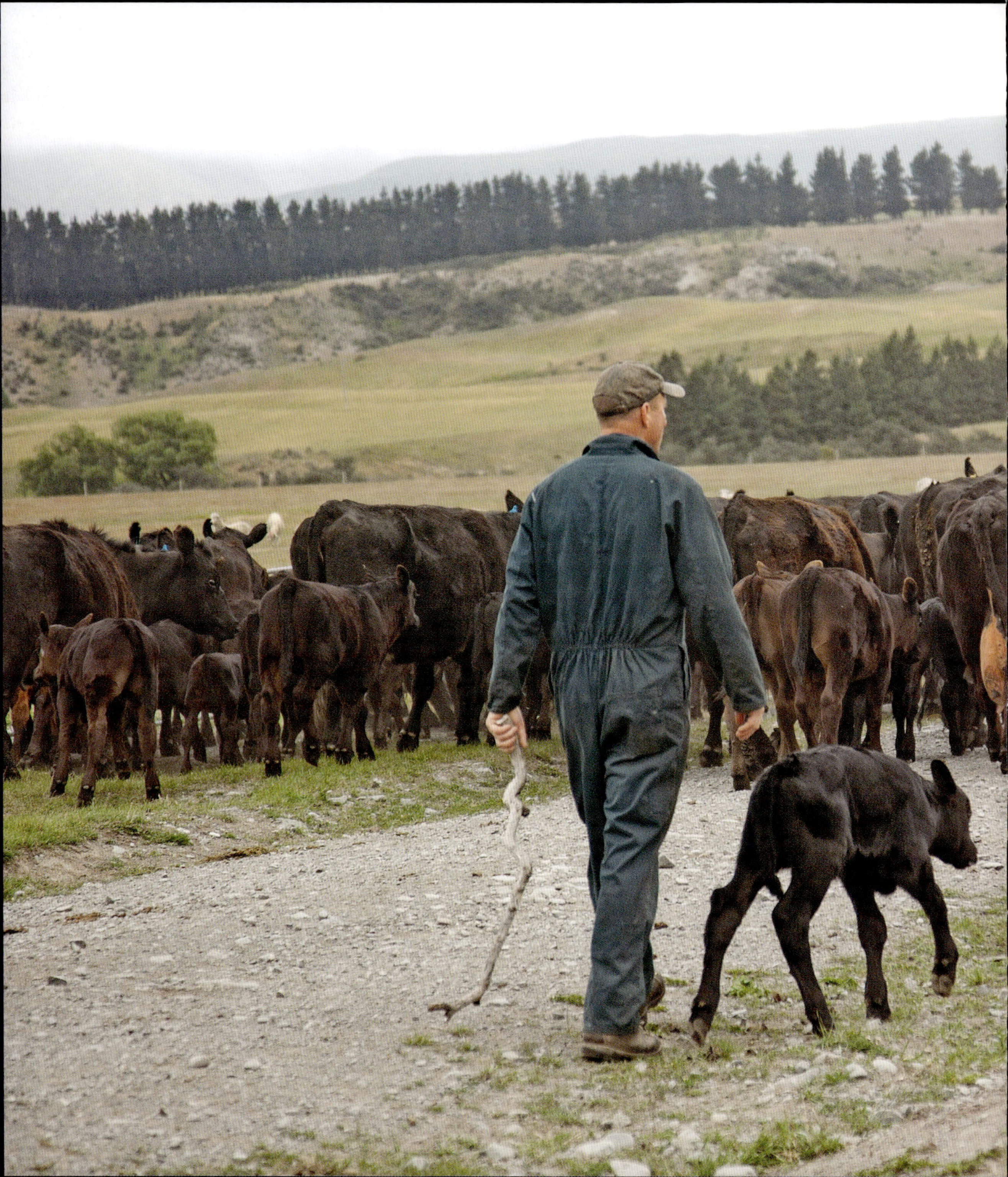

← **LEFT**
Malcolm coaxes a wayward calf back into the herd as it moves downhill.

↓ **FOLLOWING SPREAD**
Sophie, stick in hand, moves a cow and calves into one of the split-beech yards on the river flats.

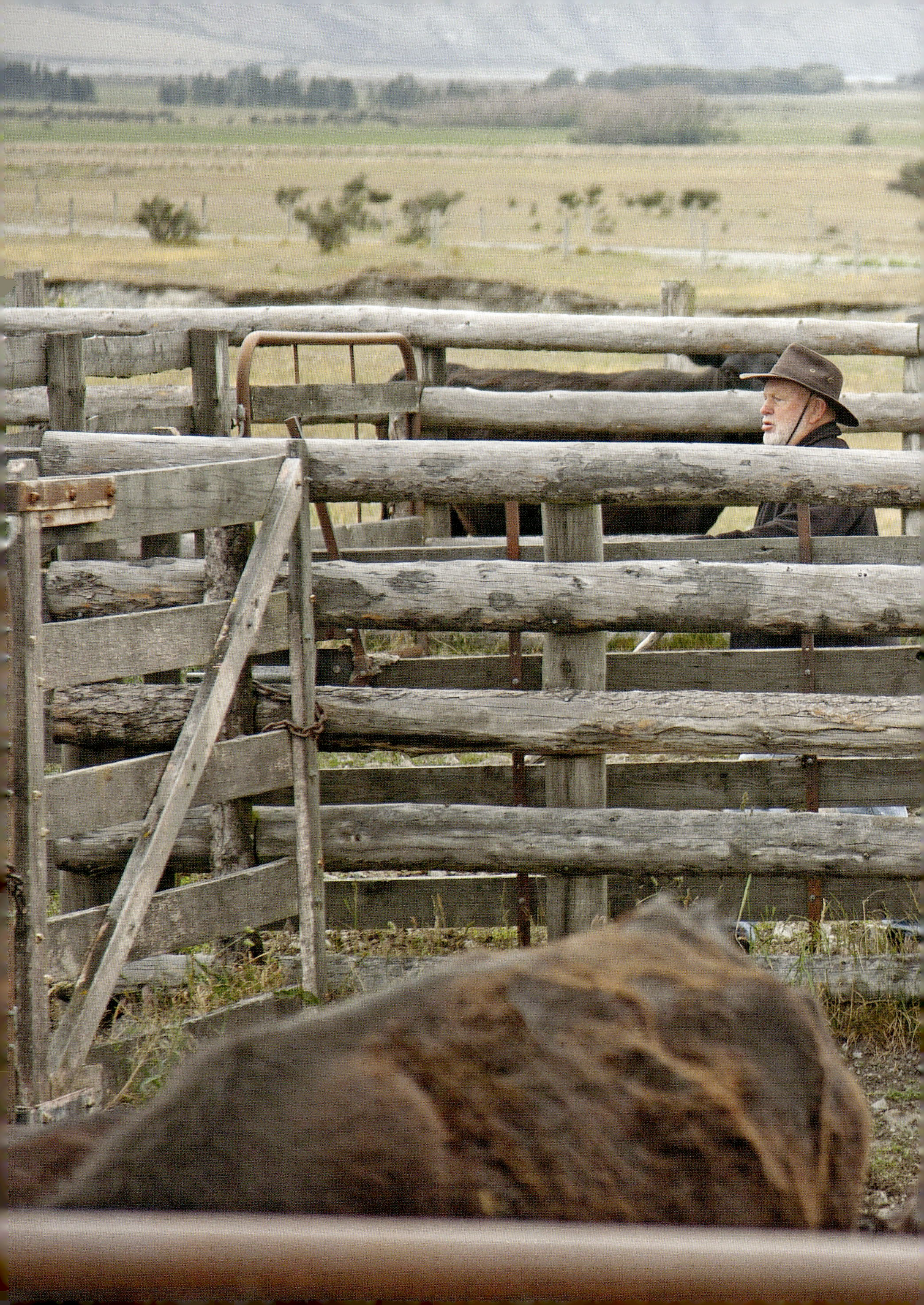

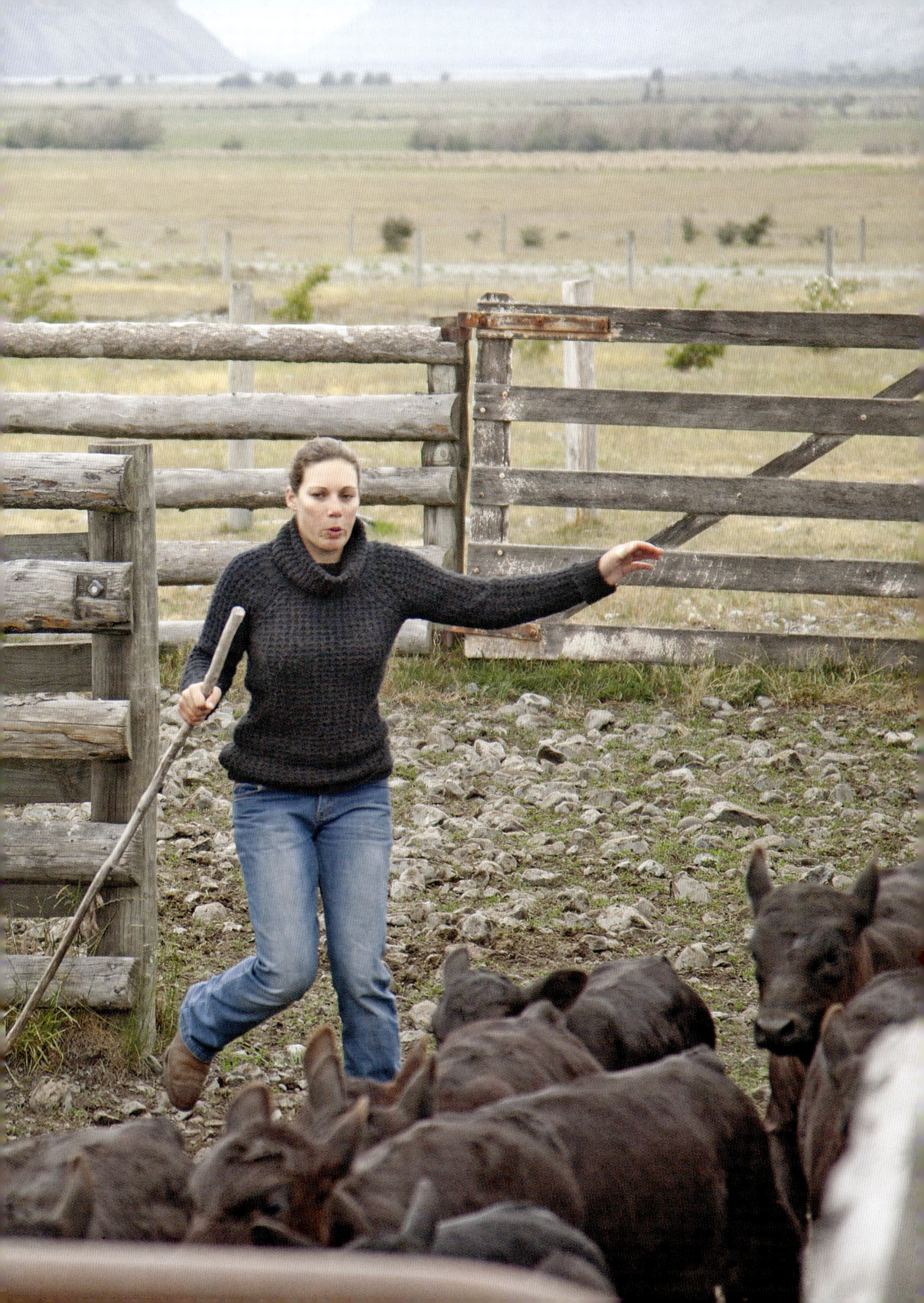

THE FOUR SEASONS AT MESOPOTAMIA

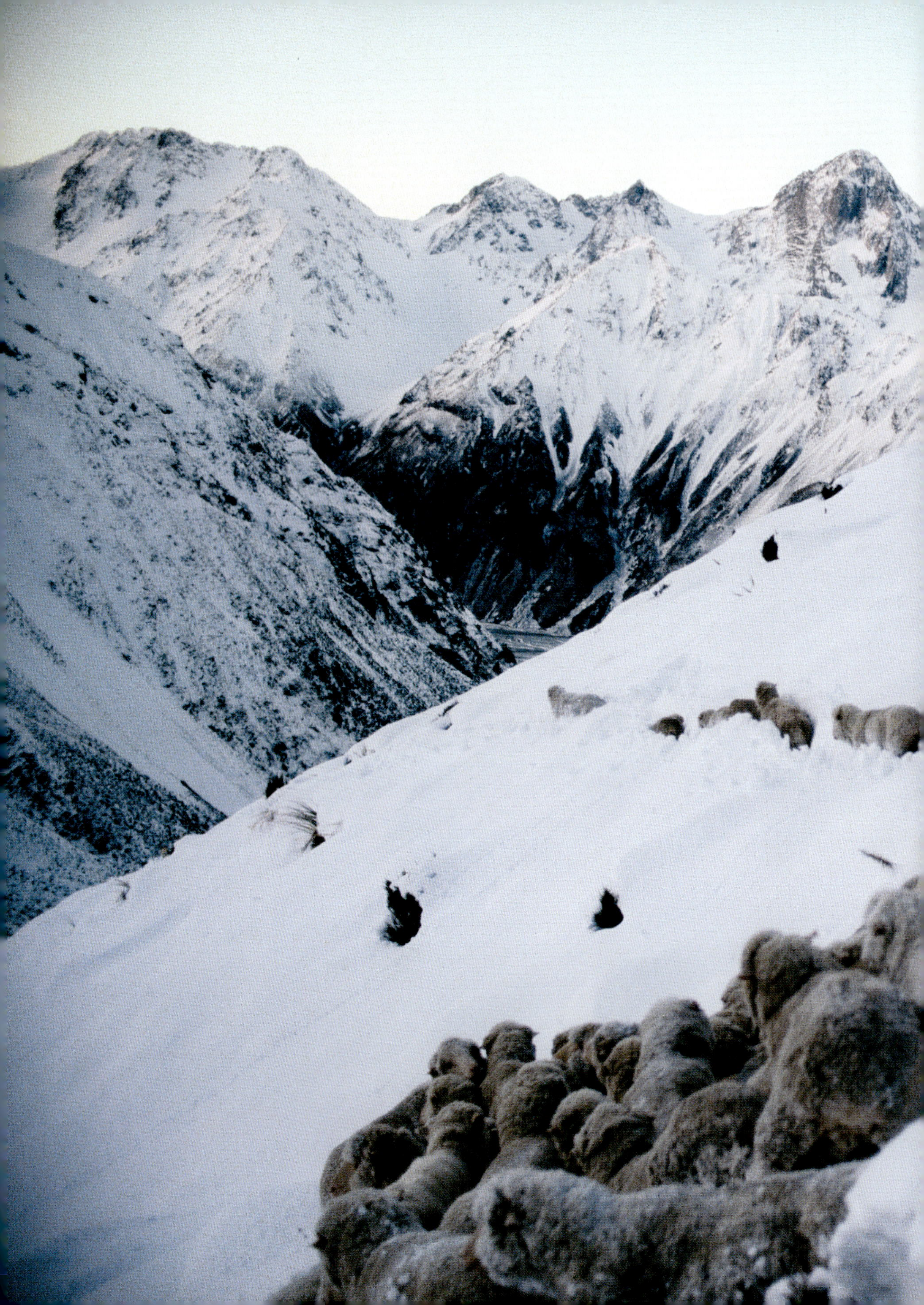

WINTER

ACHILLES • THE TWO THUMB RANGE • D'ARCHIAC • CROOKED SPUR • HOGGET • THE GROWLER • BRABAZON • NEUTRAL SPUR • CLYDE RIVER • ROCKY RIDGE • BLACK MOUNTAINS • LITTLE SPUR • FINLAYS • FORBES RIVER • BIG BUSH • BLACK BIRCH STREAM • TOP DOWNS • BULLOCK BOW SADDLE • BALACLAVA BASINS • EXETER PEAK • SINCLAIR RANGE • FOREST CREEK • INKERMAN • THE ROCKS • MOUNT SINCLAIR • SUGARLOAF • MOUNT HOPE

AT 7.30 THE winter morning is clear, quite light although there is no sun yet. The patch of frost behind the cottage glimmers. It never melts in the winter, just changes colour. It crunches under my boots.

Malcolm Prouting has already left for the day's work and is down at the tractor sheds where the station's first schoolhouse, the old Nosworthy cottage, still stands. He is fuelling up, for Ash, the head shepherd, has come back to work early. He has had an operation on the tendons of his right hand and is supposed to be off work while it mends. He is already sick of doing nothing. There are only the two of them. Malcolm, the tractor driver, has gone off for a knee replacement operation in Timaru. (Malcolm seems a popular name on this station.) He will be on compo for a couple of months and the station has a serious labour shortage.

Ash is going to drive the big tractor pulling the silage wagon, spilling the rich-smelling feed to the stock down on the river flats. He reckons he can do the work without damaging his hand. He trundles off, the red tractor pulling the red wagon, crawling along like a slow train, and we go up the hill in Malcolm Prouting's white Land Cruiser truck to start moving break-fences so the merinos can get a fresh feed of turnips.

Malcolm takes a track angling up one of the terraces that spread between the river and the ranges like the ramp of a ziggurat. On flat ground at the top he parks the truck overlooking the Rangitata River and we sit, Malcolm still for a moment, both of us silent before the majesty. The country strikes right to the cortex, a vast panoply of mountains and snow and huge sky with the

> The sky is bright blue, the snow white, the tussock golden, the river slate. We can see every part of the station except the Brabazon flats and the top pastures further upriver. The Two Thumbs Range spikes up behind Mount Sinclair.

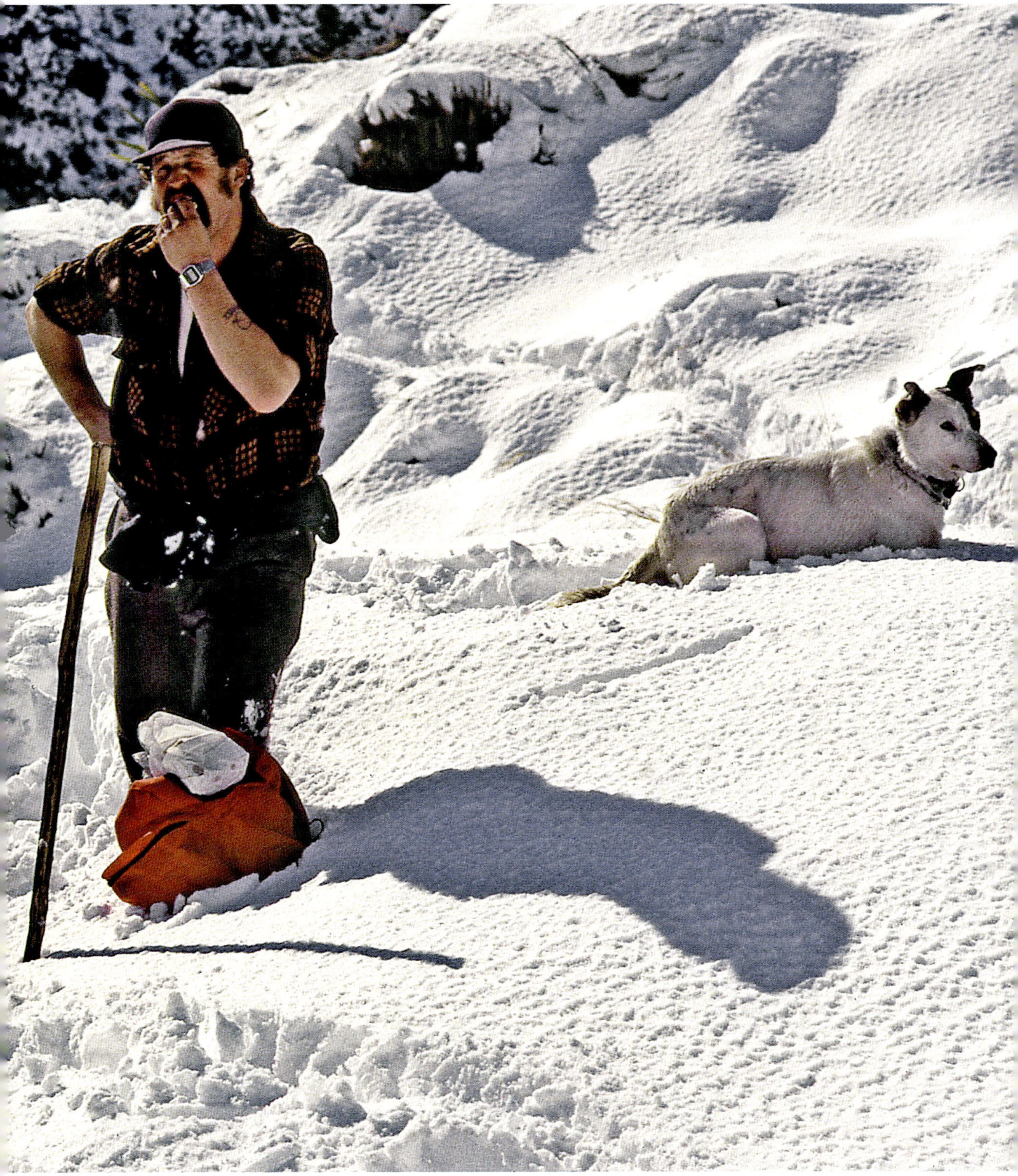

river carving through the middle of it and other, secret rivers spurting behind shoulders of rock through gullies cleft into the hills.

The sky is bright blue, the snow white, the tussock golden, the river slate. We can see every part of the station except the Brabazon flats and the top pastures further upriver. The Two Thumb Range spikes up behind Mount Sinclair. The mountain, and the Sinclair Range, were named after Dr Andrew Sinclair, the former Colonial Secretary, or head of the early New Zealand civil service when it was under Sir George Grey's administration. Sinclair drowned crossing the Rangitata on an exploratory journey in 1861.

A beech forest, carefully preserved by the Proutings, runs up the front of the range. On the far side of the river, Mount Potts and the Pyramid guard the entrance to the Potts River sluicing out of its dark gully into the Rangitata. Upriver begins the startling composition of mountains and snow and forest and rock and rivers which are curtain-raisers for the Main Divide whose looming grandeur cannot merely be seen, but felt too. I shiver looking at it; can human beings survive those faces?

Then I ask Malcolm if he's proud of the country, his life's work, his father's, his grandfather's. He says, 'I see everything that's going wrong.'

'A lot of people would be pretty happy standing where we are now,' I say.

'Yeah, but where are they when the whole place is under a metre of snow?'

Malcolm takes no prisoners. He is iconoclastic, pragmatic, sardonic. He says, 'My mate rang up and reckoned I should come to the ballet on ice.' The Imperial Ice Stars of Russia were performing *Swan Lake* on ice skates.

'He reckoned I needed a bit of culture. I sez to him, when *Guns N' Roses* do a show on ice, give me a call. Otherwise, I'd rather go and sit in the hut with Ferg and kill something.'

His bark is a great deal worse than his bite, but it is still at least as good as a huntaway's. He can be counted on for a fresh and entirely different view on things. 'I go to parties and people ask me what I do. I say I'm the CEO of a multi-million-dollar company. Oh, they say, which one? And I say, I'm a farmer.'

He drives back down the hill and into a paddock and starts shifting a break-fence, a temporary electric fence, across the paddock allowing stock access to a fresh strip of feed. The sheep and deer feed on turnips in winter, a strip at a time, rooting them from the ground and hollowing them and finishing each strip before the fence is moved to a fresh swathe. Behind them they leave ground strewn with the chewed hulks of turnips, which make white circles on the dark soil. On one side of the fence the ground is simply churned-up earth; on the other the purple-and-green crowns of huge turnips are welcoming as city lights on a dark night. The work is repetitive rather than hard, and he talks easily.

Malcolm is wary of government and suspicious of the education system, which he reckons is leading the country into some kind of non-productive purgatory. 'We don't need more lawyers and accountants and shiny-arses,' he says. 'We need people who can *do* something.' This family argues that the real producers have been cast down, that production has become a dirty word in a world dedicated to shuffling paper whose value became apparent in the banking crash.

It is an easy argument to follow up here where Malcolm's next dollar depends on his knowledge and skill and perseverance in the pale sunshine of this day or the heavy snow of the next. So we bat the subject around a bit then turn to the real stuff, moving the mob with one of his two dogs, Bo, who he says is his special needs dog: Bo gets confused easily, sometimes simply gives up and goes home. The other dog is an iron-grey beardie with spooky yellow eyes whose name, of course, is Blue.

Malcolm talks about musters, about musterers' huts. About the New Hut which was renamed the Royal Hut. His father Laurie was posted on a hilltop during the visit by Prince Charles and Princess Anne and told to look picturesque so when the royal helicopter flew overhead he could be pointed out as a hardy shepherd lad typical of the high country. But the pilot took a different route and after a while Laurie got sick of his role as a scenic amenity and went home.

Malcolm pulls out a combination tool, selects a sharp blade, peels a turnip. The purple skin drops to the ground leaving pure white flesh. He bites into it as if he's eating an apple. It looks tempting and Bushy takes a few home and boils them up for dinner. They are so tough mere table knives won't cut them and they taste truly awful. We throw them to the three roosters hanging around the house, whose feathers are as bright and formal as football jerseys. Days later the turnips are still on the ground.

'Karma's a bitch,' Malcolm says. 'From what I've seen it usually catches up.'

He could have been talking about any number of things in a high country farmer's life. In fact he was reflecting on irony. One of his critics had been caught out. He'd spoken out against heli-hunting on a television programme. Then he'd been spotted heli-hunting himself, illegally.

But Malcolm is not gleeful. It might be dangerous. 'Karma's a bitch,' he says again, and starts on a new story, of a group of people who stopped on their way up to one of the huts once owned by the station but now managed by the Department of Conservation. They asked if they should sign an intentions book.

'Are you related to me?' asked Malcolm.

'No.'

'Do I know you from somewhere?'

'No.'

'Then why should I give a damn?'

The story is apocryphal, because Mesopotamia people *do* give a damn. Everyone on the station seems to know exactly who is tramping or fishing or hunting the rivers, peaks and valleys at any given moment. They make a mental note of arrivals and departures and match them with weather and they know if someone is taking a chance, or has simply disappeared.

Later Malcolm has scarcely finished telling me that he is getting tough on public access to the station when someone from a four-wheel-drive club calls and asks if the club can cross their land and stay in their hut. Sure, he says.

Malcolm gives a damn not least because he has to search for people who get into trouble, and sometimes rescue them. He tracked one young man who had been hunting alone, a shepherd on Mount Peel Station who knew his way around the mountains, and found his body at the bottom of a bluff near Mount Peel. His death was one of two that year. Malcolm feels for the boy's parents, is dismissive of his own role: 'It's what we do. It was just a case of tracking. Laurie saw the tracks out of the chopper. We get a lot of that up here. The police are the ones who call out the search and rescue but we try to get it going a lot quicker.

'A lot of official channels seem to grind so slowly and are very good at calling you at the eleventh hour when it's just getting dark and you've got no daylight to manoeuvre in. Pilots can't see in the dark. We'd like to find the guys alive. But a lot of it is just bullshit. The guy's just got stuck. You fly into the hut and he bloody-near abuses you: "I told that silly bitch if it rained we'd be out in two days . . ."'

Laurie almost lost his life on one of those calls. An aircraft with four passengers had been reported missing. Laurie searched the Rangitata watershed for two hours in his Auster aeroplane and found nothing. Later that day the search and rescue people called again. Someone up the Lawrence River had heard an aircraft. Would Laurie fly over for a look? Laurie did not think it a good idea. The wind was roaring around the peaks that day. Flying was dangerous. But there were two young children in the missing plane.

→ PREVIOUS AND RIGHT

Blue Horton, a former head shepherd on Mesopotamia, snow-raking one hard winter in the 1980s.

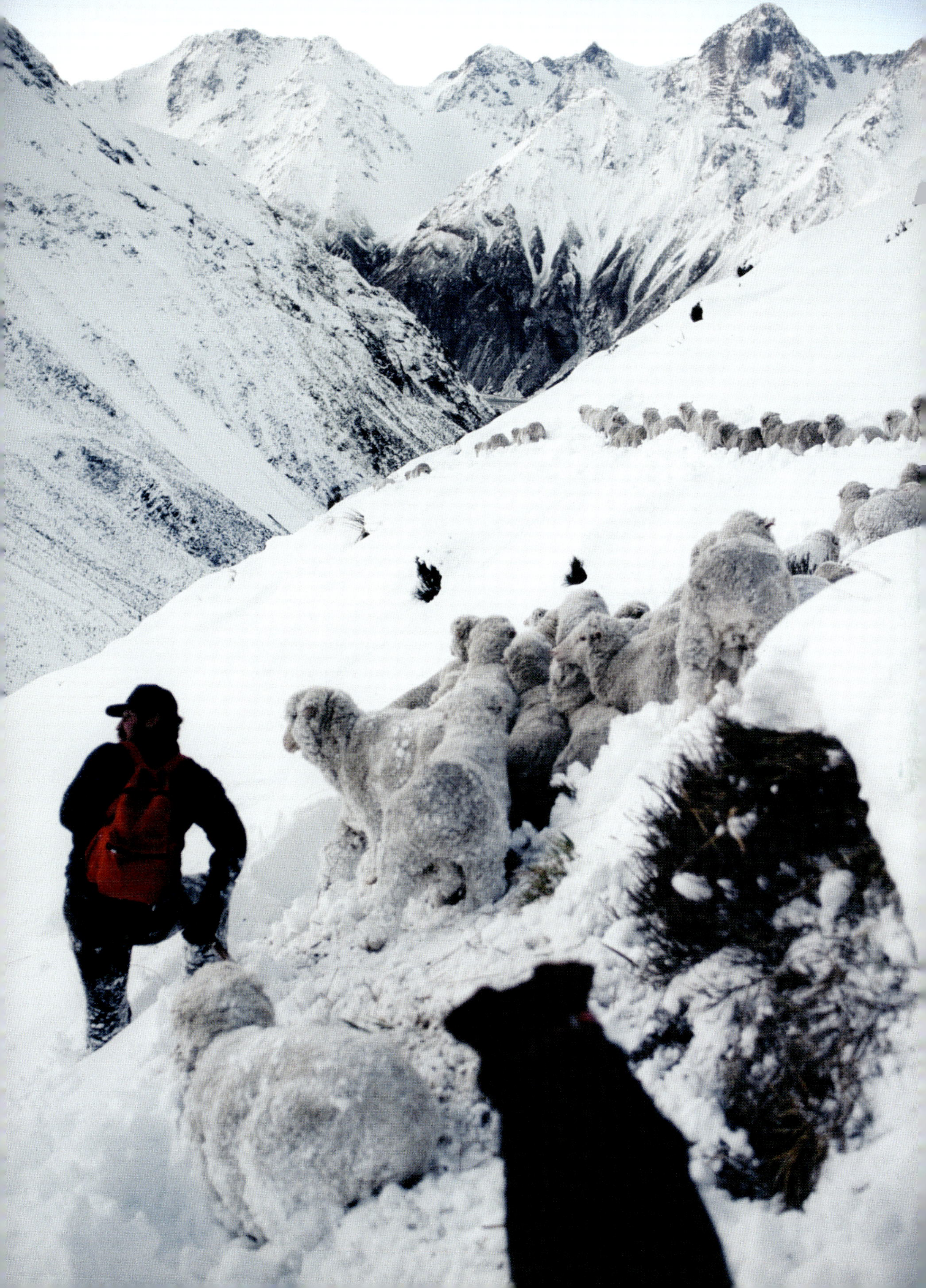

One peril of mountain flying in such weather is that the airflow goes up the mountainside, reaches a certain altitude and forms what appears to be stationary cloud. In fact, it is still in turmoil.

'It doesn't pay to get too close to that,' Laurie says, 'otherwise in a light aircraft you cannot stop. That's what I think happened to this pilot. He got sucked up, pushed up into the cloud. Then you have about a minute before the average guy becomes spatially disoriented and it's all over.'

Laurie stayed below the deceptive cloud formation, but high enough to keep out of trouble in the tight valley. 'And then suddenly, it's as if a hand grabbed the aeroplane and flung it to the ground. We were whipped down that mountain by some almighty force so suddenly that anything on the floor went up and hit the ceiling and stayed there because the acceleration was so fast. Including the fuel. It went to the top of the tank and through the cap and there was a steady stream of fuel going over the top. Not only that, the float of the carburettor went up too and stopped the fuel going into the engine so that now I was without a motor. I pushed the stick forward to keep it going down and kept up the airspeed because if you lose airspeed you lose everything. So it was accelerating towards the ground. The hillside was just whistling by.

'I couldn't turn or I'd stall and my only chance of pulling out at the bottom was if I had flying speed. So I'm thinking I've got to do a crash landing up in the rocks there somewhere but I'm going to hang on until the very last minute. And eventually we hit the bottom of it all and we turned around and the fuel came back down the pipe and the motor was going and I was wondering how much room I had left before the head of the valley, and as soon as I could I began my turn.

'The guy with me was good, he knew that I was struggling but he couldn't believe we were caught in something like that. And we did our turn, got out of there and went home. Called them back and said no, couldn't find any aeroplane. It has never been found.'

LUNCH TODAY IS sole fillet served with a special sauce, leeks and bright orange squares of pumpkin, with lemon tart to follow, all made by Ro, the Irish Wwoofer, a voluntary worker under the Worldwide Opportunities on Organic Farms scheme. Ro is a chef in her other life but looks so at home on a horse that Mesopotamia might have unsettled her forever.

After lunch Sue has her own break-fences to move, this time for the deer, which are her part of the farming operation. The herd of weaners and hinds watch her working. The deer fences are more complicated with their tall waratahs and five strands of electrified tape. The job takes around two hours.

Sue runs her own dogs, collies and huntaways. Some of them are good and some not so good, she says. In fact, one or two of them would probably be shot if they belonged to someone else, but being English, she says, she is soft on animals. Sue works a stag and two hinds along a fence to a gate, with the stag challenging her and wanting to break away but the dogs, good or not so good, do the job all right.

Then we go down to inspect the old ice-skating rink on a frozen pond in the shadow of a bluff planted with cedars to block out the sun. We walk with that nervous tread you get when you can see the bottom somewhere below and wonder how thick the ice really is.

A huge willow spreads over the pond. A brazier still holds the charred ends of logs which warmed competitors in the last curling competition. Beside it are the curling stones, all home-made and a long throw from the smooth, crafted objects seen at the international rink at Naseby. They are circles of concrete in which are set anything that might make a handle: a horseshoe, a tahr horn, a bike pedal, half an electric lantern, an old tap.

Sue has to take Ferg to the rugby next day and organise the station Christmas party. It is June but they do not have time for a party at Christmas, their busiest time. She has to train one of the four puppies which have just found a way to escape through the wire of their compound, the old tennis court behind the homestead. All of that is on top of everything else: the farm, the deer, the cottages, the garden, the cooking not just for her family but also for the farm workers, agents, contractors and the dozens of others who often throng her table. Sometimes she simply works until she drops.

Ferg and Pieta have to catch the school bus at Forest Creek. Schooling is always different in remote communities. The Mesopotamia School closed in 2000, 44 years after it opened as a brand-new school with a roll of eight children. Before the family moved to Mount Arrowsmith Neroli spent a year at Mesopotamia School. She simply wandered down the shingle drive from the homestead to the school, the shortest school journey the Proutings ever enjoyed. Malcolm went to Waihi, a private primary boarding school near Temuka. The defunct Mesopotamia School was given to the upper Rangitata community. Malcolm mourned its passing. 'It's a pity, a country community falling apart. My grandfather fought hard to get a school here, to get the power on.'

The old school teacher's house near White Rock is now privately owned.

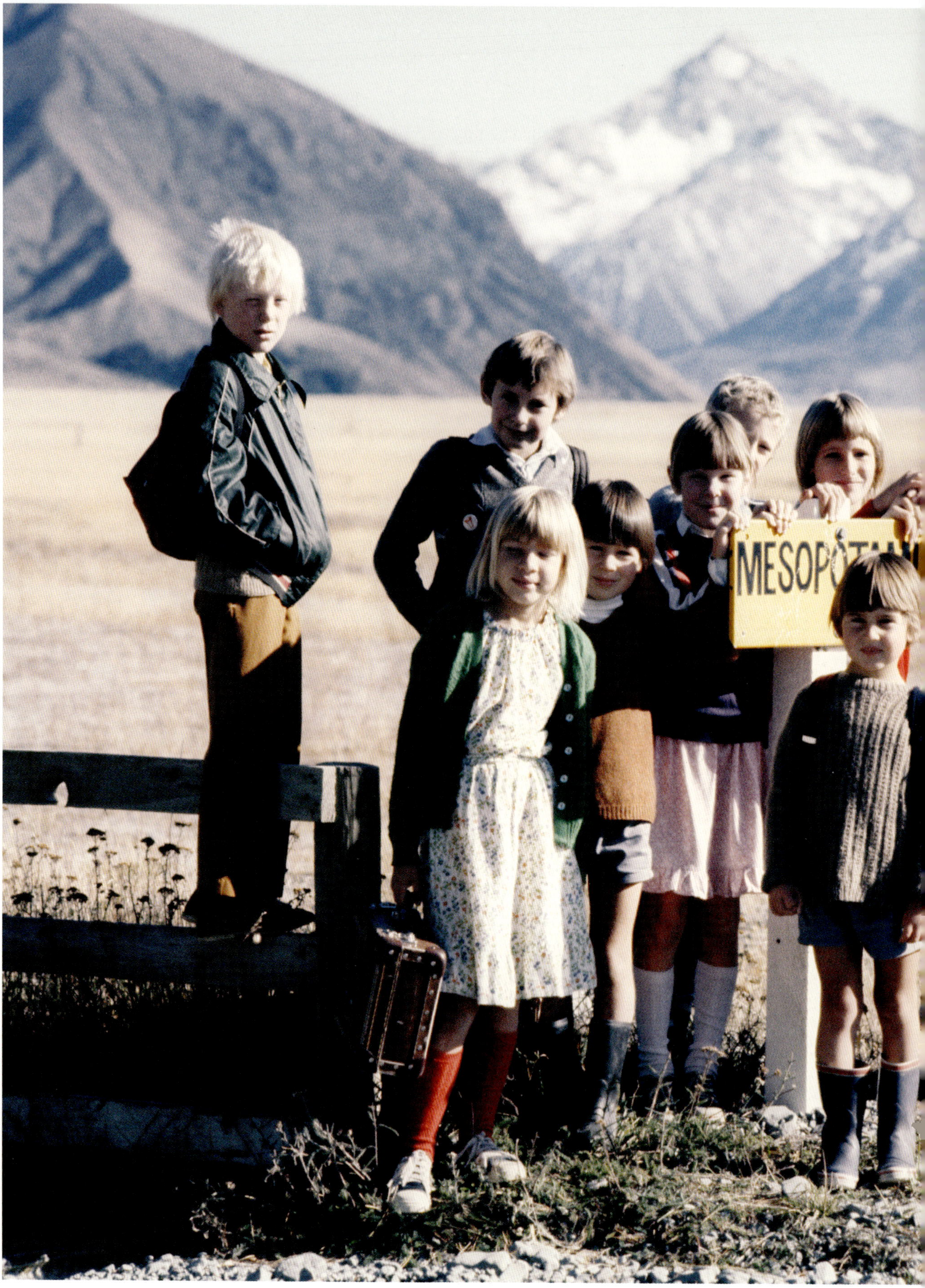
MESOPOTA

> **It's a pity, a country community falling apart. My grandfather fought hard to get a school here, to get the power on.**

← LEFT
Former glories: the pupils of Mesopotamia School gathered at the station's signpost a few years before their school closed. Left to right: Steven Weir, Kyle Burnett, Cathy Prouting, Michael Sowden, Sarah Burnett, Mark Armstrong, Angie Crawford, Nicky Armstrong in front of sign, Gary Prouting, Aaron Prouting, Michelle Galbraith, Bard Crawford.

The school roll reached its peak at twenty-one. Its roll slowly dropped, from eleven to five, then to three. Then it closed, at least as far as the Education Department was concerned.

The school and its playground still have that comfortable, safe feeling of places where happy children once gathered. The playground has a set of rugby goalposts at one end and a soccer goal at the other, which seems to cover the field. It has a kitchen and a tiny library and a big classroom Narnia-like with pictures and postcards and colour, still showing the Mesopotamia School treaty: Respect other people and their things, wait your turn to speak, talk politely, talk ideas through and be responsible for your own learning; the last quite a sophisticated concept. It looks as if the children might return at nine tomorrow, instead of being gone forever.

Charlie Dunstan, the old wagoner, attended its opening in 1956 along with some 200 people. 'It was a howling nor'west day, the ladies on the station put on a bit of lipstick and entertained the gathering to afternoon tea. What angel's food! Such a contrast to the mutton and damper that the old station poisoner used to dish out to us nearly fifty years ago. The afternoon tea at that function, the cream cakes and the ginger snap cones will be remembered long after the windy speeches are forgotten. Samuel Butler would have been amazed at the modern amenities and electricity, but nobody even mentioned Butler — such is fame. The present owner, Mr Malcolm Prouting [Malcolm's grandfather], has built a bridge over Forest Creek and one can push a perambulator to the station today; indeed, the lonesome trail ain't lonesome any more.'

Rowie Larcombe and her brother Slee went to the school when her father was a rabbiter, living in the rabbiter's cottage down the Rangitata Valley. She shows me the Maori kites they made, still hanging from the ceiling beside the home-made balloon with its little gondola she made with Hamish Taylor from Rata Peaks Station along the road.

'We were always in the hills. We always did stuff.' She strokes a glass case with a cricket bat inside, autographed by the New Zealand and Zimbabwe teams. 'Richard Hadlee [the famed New Zealand cricketer] gave us this when he came up here. He played cricket with us. We went to Wellington, to Te Papa and the police station and to Jenny Shipley's office [she was then Prime Minister]. None of my friends from other schools got to do half the stuff we

→ RIGHT

Plaques mark the beginning and end of Mesopotamia School, opened April 28, 1956, closed almost exactly forty-four years later on April 14, 2000.

PRESENTED TO THE MESOPOTAMIA
SCHOOL BY
MR. & MRS. M.V. PROUTING.
ON THE OCCASION OF THE OPENING
28TH. APRIL 1956.

MESOPOTAMIA SCHOOL
CLOSURE FUNCTION
22nd JANUARY 2000
SCHOOL CLOSED
14th APRIL 2000

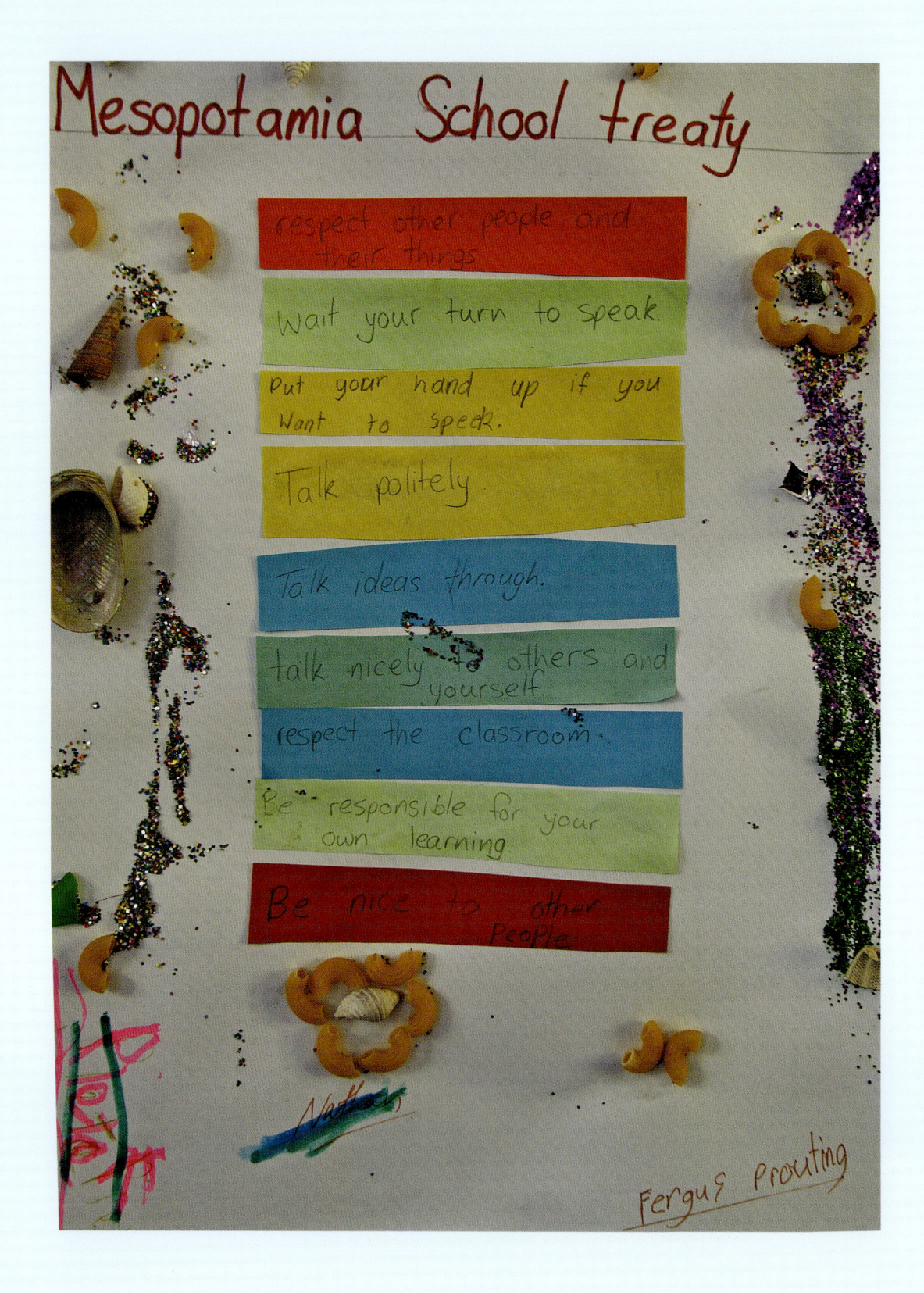

Mesopotamia School treaty

- respect other people and their things
- Wait your turn to speak.
- put your hand up if you want to speak.
- Talk politely.
- Talk ideas through.
- talk nicely to others and yourself.
- respect the classroom.
- Be responsible for your own learning.
- Be nice to other people.

Nathan

Fergus Prouting

did and we lived in the wop-wops.' Sitting on a table is Q-bear, the teddy which went to the Antarctic.

School sports matched Mesopotamia against other schools. They wore blue tops with 'Mesopotamia' sewn on in black velvet. They learned to swim in the homestead's pool. School concerts were a big social event in the area. They had a pet pig, called Mrs Pig, who ate their school lunches. 'It was either her or her piglets.'

Best of all was Mrs Jackson, the teacher, known to all the children as Mrs J. Mrs J lived in the schoolhouse during the week, picking up the children in the school bus on the way to Mesopotamia, dropping them off on the way home, and going home to Ashburton at the weekends. On Mondays she'd bring a pile of cream buns back with her. Rowie loved Mondays. She loved going to school too. Most of all she loved Mrs J. 'She was a friend rather than a teacher.'

The kids wrote down what they wanted to be, Sarah a saxophonist, Phillippa a racing driver, Hamish a gunslinger. Rowie wanted to be a fairy but she became a shepherd instead, handling stock, tractors and farm machinery with easy confidence. Slee became a rafting guide in Norway. She and Slee return to Mesopotamia and help on the station. 'I love it. It's so beautiful. I think it's the most beautiful place in the world and I see it as my home, even though it's not my home. I feel like they're my family.'

Even when the school officially closed, it went on being a school. Effectively, it became the country's smallest private school. Sue taught Ferg and Pieta correspondence classes in the classroom. Then Anna, a primary school teacher and daughter of Wendy who worked on the station as a Wwoofer, came over from England and took over. Nathan, a Wwoofer and a school teacher, taught them for a whole year. He still sends postcards, this one from India, that one from Cambodia.

At the end of 2009 Mesopotamia Station closed its school for good. The valley was accustomed to school break-up parties. They were one of the big social occasions in the Rangitata. But this last party was truly big. Sue says, 'It was the break-up party to beat all break-up parties.' A faint echo still hangs in the air, of laughter and children's voices.

Eight children ride down the valley in the school bus now, travelling in the opposite direction, away from Mesopotamia. The bus picks up more

← LEFT
The Mesopotamia School Treaty, a recipe for respect in the classroom.

↑ **CLOCKWISE FROM ABOVE**
The old and the new: Mesopotamia School, now closed.

Schoolchildren make themselves comfortable for the long drive, Pieta and Fergus on right.

Home again: Sue Prouting (back to camera) and Fergus.

The school bus leaves Forest Creek in early-morning grey, the driver, Jenny Deans, ready for the long haul to Carew.

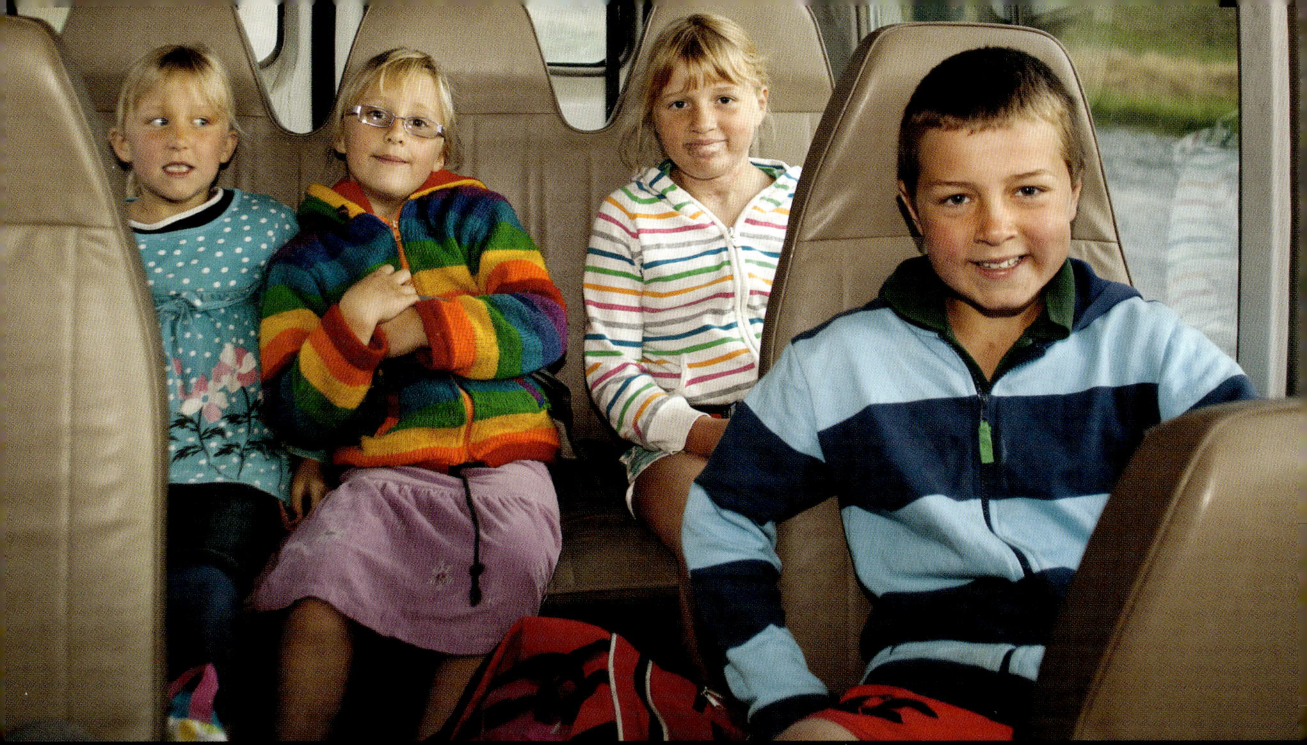

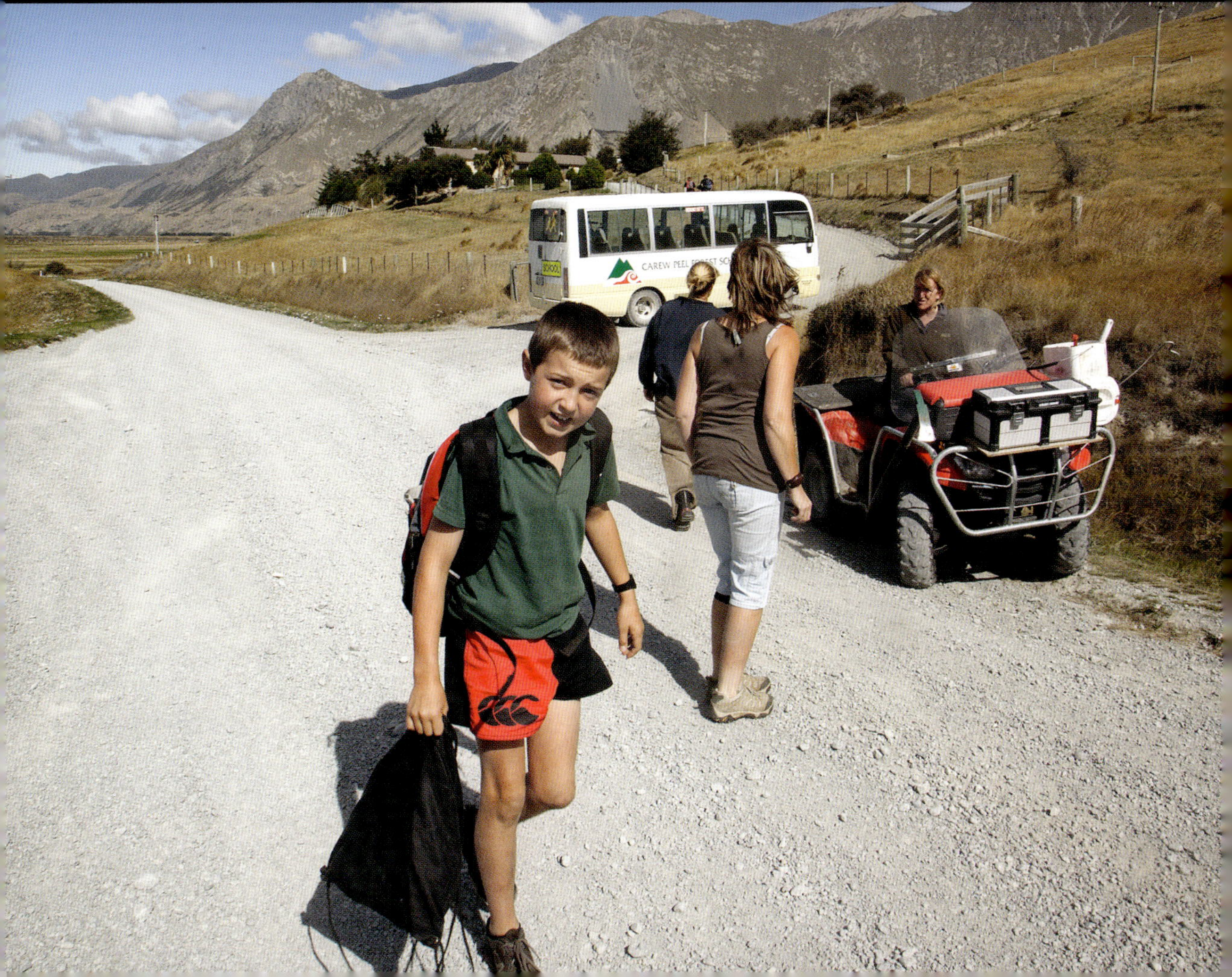
SCHOOL
CAREW PEEL

In Most Loving Memory
of
ELIZABETH S. HAWDON
BORN MARCH 15TH 1851
DEPARTED THIS LIFE AT TIMARU,
SEP. 11TH 1921.
SHE WAS THE FIRST BORN CHILD OF
CHRISTCHURCH, CANTERBURY, NEW ZEALAND.

THEY THAT SOW IN TEARS SHALL REAP IN JOY
HE THAT NOW GOETH ON HIS WAY WEEPING, AND
BEARETH FORTH GOOD SEED, SHALL DOUBTLESS
COME AGAIN WITH JOY, AND BRING HIS SHEAVES
WITH HIM.   PSALM CXXVI. 6.-7.

ERECTED BY THE STATION
IN MEMORY OF THOSE WHO WENT
OVERSEAS FROM MESOPOTAMIA
AND FELL IN 1914 – 1918 WAR.
F. BOUCHER   R. DALTON
J. JOBBERNS   J. McNEIL
A. McRAE   J. McRAE

children in Peel Forest, whose school closed even before Mesopotamia's.

The children now go to a school with one of the longest names in the country: The Carew Peel Forest Mesopotamia School. It is an hour and a half from Mesopotamia, so Ferg and Pieta spend three hours a day on a bus. Secondary schools remain a problem. Neroli and Malcolm went to private boarding schools in Christchurch. But they are expensive. The new generation of Proutings on the station is contemplating breaking the private school tradition favoured not only by their own family but so many Canterbury high country farmers. It would be a controversial decision. But Sue says, 'In days gone by the money was there to send them off to boarding school. It's more of an economic issue now. Besides, I had children to *have* my children, not to send them off to boarding school.'

BESIDE THE SCHOOL stands the remains of Samuel Butler's homestead, a pile of stones and a couple of broken walls which once housed the dairy. The hut was finally deserted in 1911. It fell into disrepair, and although newspapers, societies and individuals argued the case for preserving it, no one actually did anything. The roof fell in, and exposed to the weather the sod walls crumbled. By 1927 it was a heap of rubble. A plaque now marks its passing: 'On this site was Samuel Butler's homestead, 1863.'

The nearby war memorial is more poignant. The bloodbath in the trenches reached into even this faraway crevice of Empire. Eight Mesopotamia men, an entire mustering gang, went to World War I. Only two returned.

I imagine the men lying beneath the Turks' fire at Gallipoli, or crouched in the Somme mud, dreaming of the clean quiet air of home.

↑ TOP LEFT
The Church of the Holy Innocents beside the Mount Peel Station homestead. A few weeks after this photograph was taken the church was badly damaged in the first of the Canterbury earthquakes.

← BOTTOM RIGHT
Memorial to a mustering gang killed in World War I, beside the remains of Butler's cottage.

← BOTTOM LEFT
The gravestone of Elizabeth Hawdon, said to be the first born child of Christchurch, Canterbury, in the church cemetery.

DOWN THE VALLEY beyond the gorge the old stone Church of the Holy Innocents stands beside Mount Peel homestead. John Barton Arundel Acland and Charles Tripp arrived in New Zealand in 1855. The two claimed great swathes of their 'convenient site', accumulating almost 121,000 hectares at their peak including Mount Peel and the Orari Gorge and spreading across the Rangitata to Mount Possession and Mount Somers. Their station ran right up the Rangitata to Forest Creek, where five years later Samuel Butler was to build his hut and found Mesopotamia.

The partnership split up in 1862, the Tripps taking Orari Gorge and the Aclands staying at Mount Peel and building a handsome two-storeyed house of timber and handmade brick with elegant gables, the kind of place that would have fitted into the English countryside yet held its own in this imposing land. A century and a half later Aclands still run Mount Peel Station and the Tripps still own Orari Gorge.

The first of the Acland family built the Anglican church of stone carted from the river, and named it for three children who died in the 1860s. The church is a simple, stalwart building lined with native timber pit-sawn at Mount Peel. Managers, shepherds and faithful servants are buried here, alongside family members and friends whose names reach through Canterbury like the lines on a palm.

Every headstone seems to mark a story. Adam Taylor Clark died in October 1857, one of the many who drowned crossing the Rangitata. His grave in the riverbed was slowly disappearing, and John Acland, one of the succeeding generations, moved the iron cross marking it to the church cemetery.

Elizabeth Hawdon was said to be the first-born child of Christchurch, Canterbury. She was born in 1851, when the city was still a few buildings on its swampy site. Lest the inscription show a colonial arrogance towards the tangata whenua, Maori would have said their children were born in Otautahi.

Here lies the stillborn son of Abner Clough, a giant of a man who worked on the station from its start. Clough became a high country legend even before those legends were written and was said to perform superhuman feats of labour. He was also said to be the son of an Englishman and a 'high-born Maori princess'. Whatever the truth of that, Samuel Butler called him 'a prince by nature and if he had had a good education would have been a polished gentleman'.

Dame Ngaio Marsh's ashes are buried here. She died in 1982. The great crime writer was a friend of the family. She once worked as a governess to the family of Sir Hugh Acland, a surgeon, and much later is said to have asked her former boss over dinner how he'd murder a man in three minutes in a lift travelling three floors. The surgeon advised a knitting needle through the eyeball to the brain, and, using a skewer instead, Marsh immortalised the technique in print.

Two White Russians mysteriously found their last resting place in this Anglican churchyard far from home. Anita and Vladimir (Val) Muling were introduced to the Aclands by their close friend Ngaio Marsh.

Other graves testify to the nature of the country: an unknown man, his grave marked by a boulder, who drowned in the Rangitata. A young Englishman who ignored the rule for crossing the Rangitata and instead of lighting a fire and waiting for help tried to cross alone and was swept away. A shepherd's son, aged eleven, who died when his thirteen-year-old brother threw a poker at him. Eighteen-year-old lover of the mountain life Ryan Jopson who slipped and fell to his death on Coal Hill in May 2009.

There's a kind of cross-pollination with other famous Canterbury families, Barkers, Harpers, Burdons, Deans. Alan Cedric D'Ewes Barker died in British Columbia in 1996 and his ashes were buried at Mount Peel. Every year, on the anniversary of his death, a cheque for $500 arrives from Canada to help with the cemetery's upkeep. Austen Deans, whose landscape paintings grace many a living room wall in the Canterbury high country, lived in Peel Forest and is buried here, near his wife of fifty-seven years, Elizabeth.

Pride of place, in front of the church on the terrace overlooking the Rangitata and scanning the valley, goes to John Barton Arundel Acland: born Killerton, Devon, 1823, died Christchurch, March 1904.

One famous local was *not* buried at Mount Peel. Black Andy was an Australian aboriginal. He was the station runner, a man who, according to John Acland, could run from Mount Peel to Christchurch with the mail, crossing two great rivers on the way, get drunk, go to jail and be bailed by the Bishop of Christchurch (a friend of the Aclands') all in seventeen hours. Then he'd run back again.

Black Andy was deported to Australia for threatening to kill his boss. There, he killed a man who had murdered his mother, and was hanged. Butler is thought to have used him as the model for Chowbok, the companion to Butler's hero in *Erewhon*.

LAURIE AND ANNE PROUTING'S house is opposite Mount Peel Station. The Rangitata River flows between the two, and the nearest bridge is well downriver. To get there by road from Mesopotamia you need to drive down the valley, through Peel Forest and Arundel and on to the town of Mayfield, then back up to the river, the Two Thumbs glistening in the distance.

They have forty hectares here, to accommodate an airfield. The strip runs along a terrace below the house. Beside the long straight South Canterbury roads, oaks and willows are bare against the pale blue sky, frost still lying under the hedges.

'We've been waiting for you,' says Anne. 'Sit down and we'll have lunch.'

I was not expecting lunch, although I knew country life was often more sociable than in the city. If you arrived around midday, you were expected for lunch. In a futile attempt not to take Sue Prouting's hospitality for granted I sometimes waited to be invited for lunch until she told me that every time I didn't turn up, she had to throw food out.

Anne says, 'In the cities, well, I don't really know why some people have kitchens, because they never invite you to a meal. Even with the flashest kitchens.'

There are eight around the table today, a lunch party in a city but an everyday occasion here, where friends, neighbours, painters, plasterers, plumbers, drivers, hunters and a parade of visitors all find a welcome at the table. The sunny dining room is full of light and noise. Through the tall windows I can see far up the Rangitata Valley to the bends and buttresses that hide Mesopotamia. Two paintings of the station hang on the wall.

This farmhouse is one of those rangy brick places which seem relaxed and content with their lot and slip into the South Canterbury landscape as comfortably as the tussock. Anne puts down huge plates of Mexican bean salad and a big bowl of white potatoes.

One of the group is Harley, Neroli's husband. He shakes hands with a grip that makes a vice seem an unworthy implement. He has forearms

→ TOP
Ferg gets a hug from his sister Pieta as he comes off the rugby field in the Geraldine colours, red and black.

→ RIGHT
Family gathering. Back row: from left, Grace and Ella Davies. Middle row: from left, Pieta and Fergus Prouting. Front row: from left, Malcolm, Sue and Anne Prouting, Neroli and Harley Davies. *Prouting Family Collection*

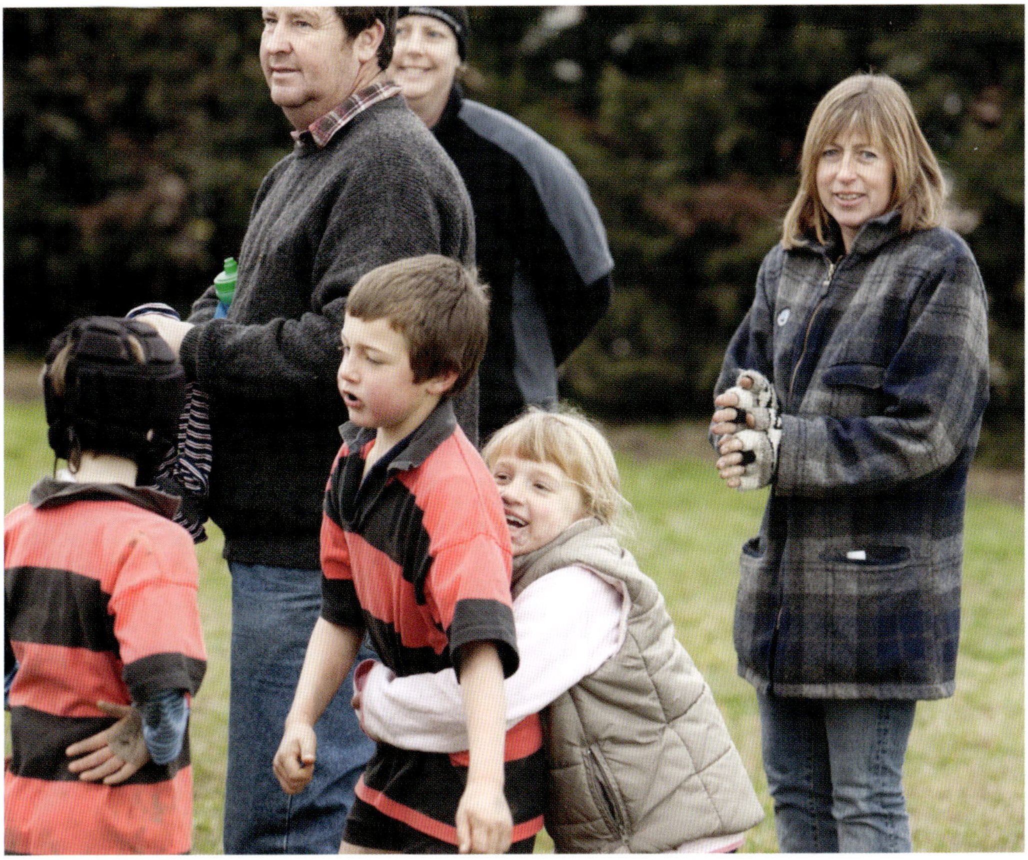

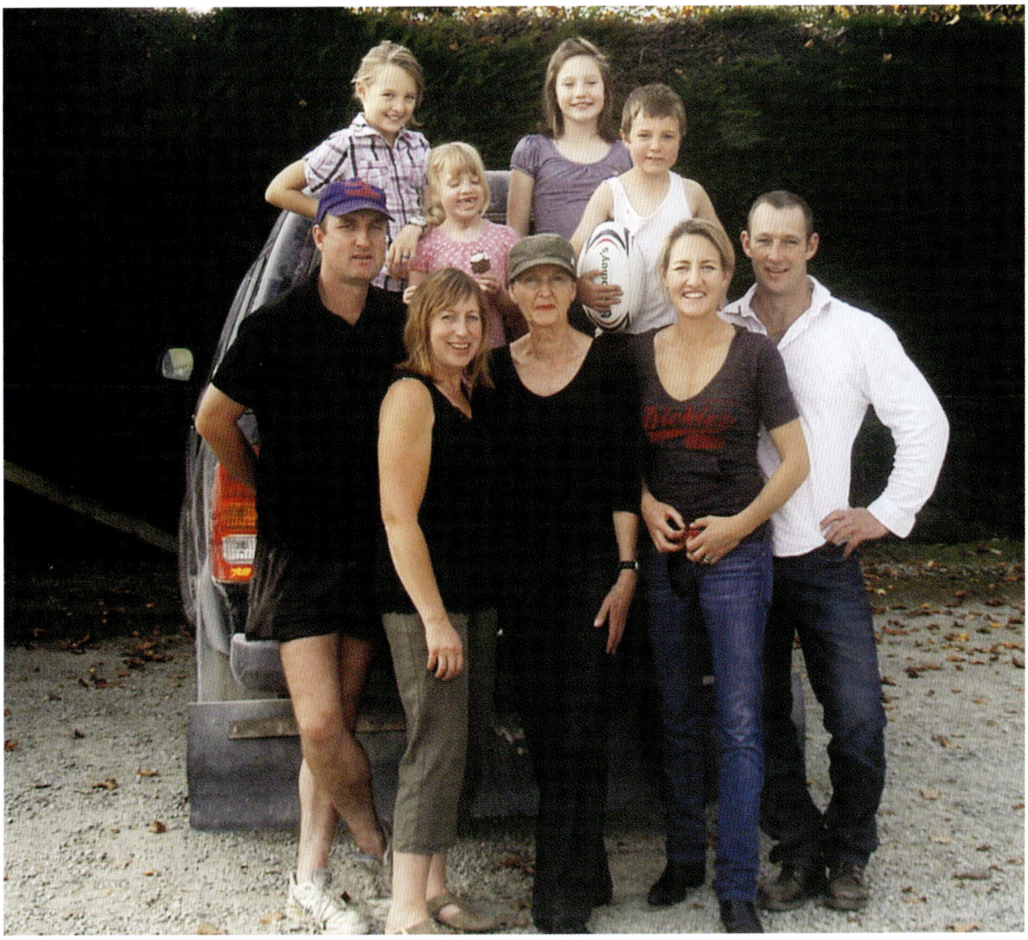

like goalposts and a face which seems a collection of features rather than a composition. Harley is with Troy, a helicopter pilot.

Laurie talks about aircraft. His clear blue eyes narrow when he's making a point. He has a straightforward approach to life which seems largely based on the proposition that if it flies, it's good. Today is the day Harley flies solo.

Laurie flew his helicopter solo after eight hours' flying. Harley's aim is to shave 10 minutes off this time, although Laurie does not seem at all put out by the prospect.

As soon as they can decently leave the table they're off into the garden and down to a tiny helicopter, so well-kept I'm surprised to discover that it's old enough to be onto its second engine. Harley and Troy climb into the cockpit, jammed together as cosily as a couple in a sports car. The machine lifts off and flies around to the side of the house, whose wide glass living room doors open to a broad lawn with a vista extended by a cunningly contrived ha-ha wall. The lawn seems park-like but from the pilot's seat it's probably tiny and Harley says so.

They land, and Troy gets out. Harley is on his own. He lifts off. He is in the air. He is flying solo. His father-in-law watches intently as the machine slowly rises. Laurie insists on a gradual lift. He says, 'You get a metre up too quickly and if anything goes wrong you're in trouble.'

So Harley's first flight is an unspectacular affair, a little off the ground, down again, up, down, up, turn around. Troy walks around the lawn. The helicopter follows him like a dog on a chain. After half an hour or so of this Troy climbs back in and the two of them lift high into the air and buzz over the valley below, zooming into a cornered circuit, speeding along a downwind leg, turning along a base line and turning again into an approach that lines up perfectly with the strip.

They're a dot in the sky. The engine note changes. The engine has been turned off, Laurie says, squinting against the sun. The helicopter is auto-rotating, a survival technique in case of engine failure. The machine dives towards the ground at a steep angle and alarming speed; I feel my hands tugging some imaginary control, pull up, pull up. At the last minute the engine note picks up; the aircraft seems to brake a few metres above the ground, hovers for a moment, then speeds forward and up to do it all over again.

Later I watch Laurie in his white overalls climbing into the big, second helicopter, the machine rising slowly then rearing up and back and disappearing over the edge of the terrace, reappearing far up the valley and zooming towards the Crooked Spur Hut where three hunters are awaiting a lift out. He makes flying look nonchalant, the mark of a careful, skilled pilot.

BEYOND PEEL FOREST lies the gentle, orderly South Canterbury countryside with its triumvirate of perfect New Zealand small towns, Geraldine, Fairlie and Pleasant Point. It is Saturday morning and we drive through Geraldine, Mesopotamia's nearest town. The road skirts a hill where pretty houses bask in the bright day and runs into a main street, which escaped the desolation of many New Zealand small towns in the 1980s and 1990s and now seems thriving. There is even an arcade across the road from its solid Anglican church, next door to what must be the cleanest, most attractive public toilets in all the land. A park lies languid in the morning sun.

We take the road to Temuka, with its fine old hotels lining the main street and run the bypass through Timaru, whose welcoming signs once proclaimed it to be the 'Riviera of the South'. Then through St Andrews, which keeps a respectable distance from the Pacific surf pounding its shingle beach, and on to Pareora.

Pareora's presence on State Highway One has all but faded away. I'd been through it countless times, sweeping along the route, never suspecting there was a community between the road and the sea. Yet the vanishing façade hides a town huddled around a freezing works, the reason for its existence, then stretching down to a grey sea lumping onto its forlorn shingle beach this winter morning.

The journey from Mesopotamia takes more than two hours, a long trip for a routine Saturday morning rugby game. Ferg is playing for Geraldine. The team is in red-and-black jerseys, a tiny echo of the mighty Canterbury side. They are playing Pareora on a muddy ground next to the freezing works.

Ferg has a cut on his cheek. He plays on the wing. His mum Sue says he's not going very well today; he was a doubtful starter because of a bad cold, but here he is, although the temperature gauge on my dashboard stops at three degrees. The coach today is a school teacher. Another coach is a stock agent, a third owns a stock truck company. Ferg has come a long way for the game, but so have others: from Ashburton in one direction, Oamaru in another. They take their rugby seriously here.

The team scores a try and everyone cheers, but the other side has scored lots. What was the final result? No one keeps score at this level, the coach says. The mud sticks to our shoes like glue.

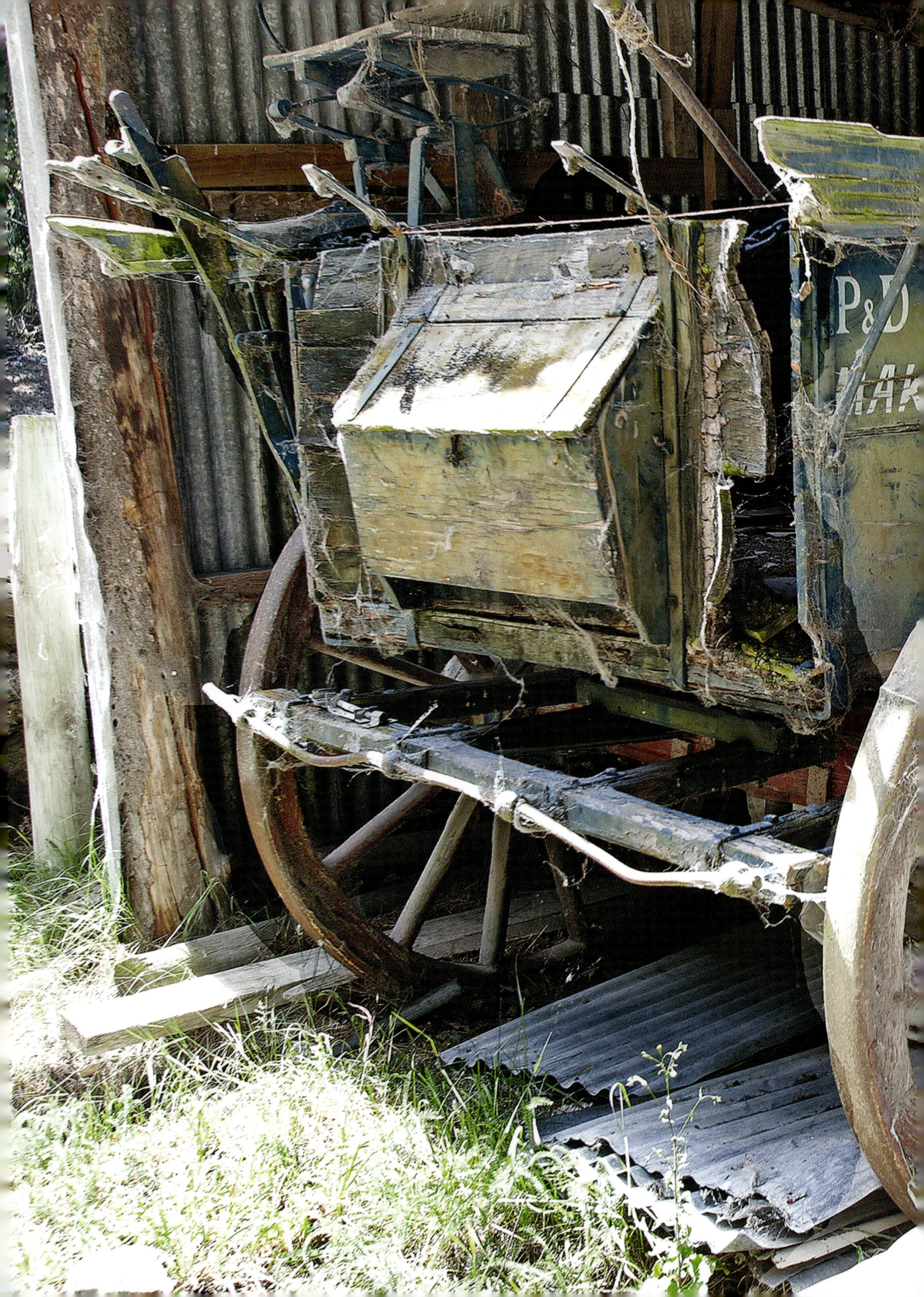
P&D

SPRING

ACHILLES • THE TWO THUMB RANGE • D'ARCHIAC • CROOKED SPUR • HOGGET • THE GROWLER • BRABAZON • NEUTRAL SPUR • CLYDE RIVER • ROCKY RIDGE • BLACK MOUNTAINS • LITTLE SPUR • FINLAYS • FORBES RIVER • BIG BUSH • BLACK BIRCH STREAM • TOP DOWNS • BULLOCK BOW SADDLE • BALACLAVA BASINS • EXETER PEAK • SINCLAIR RANGE • FOREST CREEK • INKERMAN • THE ROCKS • MOUNT SINCLAIR • SUGARLOAF • MOUNT HOPE

IT IS SPRING, but here in the high country the cold likes to stay past winter's closing time. Out on the great Plains warmth rises from new green paddocks where lambs frolic.

Here the sun is warm but the air chill and when you walk, the draught of your passing is rather like opening a fridge door in a warm kitchen. The breeze floats up the valley and arrives like a knife. A chaffinch's long declining chirrup echoes in the dewy silence. Then a magpie's warble, a dog's bark.

Something terrible happened in the city early this spring. An earthquake ripped through its roads and streets, laying waste to the gentle, the venerable, the new and brash alike. The old stone church at Mount Peel Station was torn apart, its splendid window smashed, stone walls awry, limestone carted across country by bullock dray now broken on the ground. The church is buttressed by baulks of timber, awaiting salvation, its guardian angel Rosemary Acland certain it will be restored.

The earthquake faded as it travelled up the valley. By the time it reached Mesopotamia the shaking did not so much as rouse the sleeping Prouting family. They faced problems enough this spring. Weeks of bad weather delayed shearing, and then, just as they were about to start, the news bulletins brayed about the worst storm on the planet right here in New Zealand. On Mesopotamia this came down to a week of nor'westerlies, the wind sweeping down the mountains in katabatic gouts and dumping its load of water before proceeding down the gorge to the Canterbury Plains in a more seemly and much warmer manner.

The shearing gang was late because it was working through its list of farms and the weather delayed those further up the list, so everyone got shuttled downwards.

Mesopotamia has 11,000 ewes and they need eleven clear days to finish. But right from the start there's a hitch: the gang is one shearer down. He simply packed up his gear and disappeared. Went up north, they said. Malcolm and Sue are disconsolate. That's an extra three day's shearing, at least. The chances of getting almost two weeks of reasonable weather — it doesn't have to be fine, just dry — are not good. The peaks are still topped with snow. On Bullock Bow Saddle avalanches grumble down the mountainside.

EVERYONE IS SIGHING over the good old days. Malcolm looks back to the huge musters of the past, so much a part of the high country tradition they've become part of the national legend.

The shearers remember the days when they finished work, walked up the hill to the rambling old shearers' quarters where they slept, ate the huge meal the cook prepared for them, got up to high jinks and went to bed, rising for breakfast the next morning and strolling down the hill to work; instead of getting up a couple of hours before dawn and dozing in a van for an hour and a half's driving from Ashburton. And eating the cut lunches they brought with them instead of sitting around the vast table up the hill, where they'd gather again in the evening instead of climbing back into the van, driving for another hour and a half, and falling into bed for what often seemed a short night's sleep.

The dawn arrives in a pink V shaped by the valley narrowing for the Rangitata Gorge before the river spills out onto the Plains. It pushes a roll of white mist before it. A still, silent world, the mountaintops white against the cut-glass sky.

In this cloudy morning the shearing gang is climbing out of the van and up the wooden steps into the woolshed and puttering and muttering and murmuring in the near-dark and the sheep under their feet below the slatted floor making quiet sheepy noises.

Ash comes over with a black beardie pushing nine years old and heading for retirement. He wipes a purple chalk mark onto the dog's head. 'How'd you like to be culled?' he asks. The dog hopes he's kidding. It wags its tail.

'Your first dog is always the best,' says Ash. 'You put so much work and time into him. He should be pissed off with me. I got a few flea bites so I put him through the dip.' The sheep dip is a filthy soup. But the dog looks at Ash admiringly and goes on working the sheep.

Fine merino wool is always expensive. The clip makes up a big part of the Proutings' income and this year prices are up. Much hangs on the next ten days. Hundreds of thousands of dollars are at stake here. The woolshed shines bronze under the lights. A thick smell of sheep shit and wool and lanolin and sweat creates a bouquet only woolsheds have, fragrant to some, noxious to others, just a fact of life to farmers and shearers.

The woolshed was built by Malcolm senior in 1949, a marvel of its time. It was then state-of-the-art. Shorn sheep from its eight stands shot down chutes into counting-out pens beneath the shearing board, or floor, which was high enough above the ground for a tractor and trailer to be driven under it for cleaning out. Its wool room and branding race were under cover.

> **The shed is an amphitheatre, a dancehall, an arena; it could have been any one of those, because everything within is choreographed, planned, practised, governed by tight rules of etiquette and practice.**

Modern woolsheds with their covered yards include features like these as a matter of course but sixty years after it was built the Mesopotamia woolshed still functions perfectly. It glimmers with antiquity and purpose. The huge uprights supporting the roof are still those beech trees cut from the forest up the valley, hauled down and left in the round, tough as steel. The shed is an amphitheatre, a dancehall, an arena; it could have been any one of those, because everything within is choreographed, planned, practised, governed by tight rules of etiquette and practice. Of course, it is none of those things to those who work here. It is a woolshed, a working gallery for, today, five shearers and eight shedhands including Kim, who runs the gang and is judged one of the best wool-classers around.

The shearers arrange their gear beside them, water bottles, combs, towels. They tune their handpieces as if they are musical instruments — which, today, they are. They rattle, buzz and moan in a symphony broken each hour for a break, taken by all the shearers at almost exactly the same moment, though I can see no signal. They move like dancers around the sheep, almost balletic in their soft leather moccasins, one of them suspended by a harness and a bungy cord to save his back. In their breaks they lie, backs flat on the floor, knees up, like fast bowlers at tea and lunch during cricket matches.

The floor is oiled by sixty seasons of soft shoes. Around the shearers it is polished to a low sheen. Blood smears the slats at their feet. The merinos have distinctive wrinkles around their necks. They get in the way of shearers' combs and cuts are common. The deeper cuts are stitched up on the spot, bright scarlet on the white bodies of close-shorn sheep.

They are curious about me, hiding in the shadows, careful to keep out of the way and not stumble over any rites. My first experience of a woolshed was helping out a farmer when the gang was a man short. My job was to take off the edges of the fleece, keep the board clean and keep up a steady supply of sheep to the two shearers, jamming their pens with stubborn ewes which had no interest in facilitating proceedings.

Letting the pens empty was one of several cardinal sins I discovered that day when the gang boss stayed crouching in a shearing position but with no sheep to shear. His lips moved soundlessly: '*Sheep-oh!*'

Today the shedhands watch me covertly as I scribble in my notebook. 'Since you're taking orders,' says one, 'thirty-five fish and twenty scoops would do us.'

Mark comes over. 'You writing a book mate?'

'Yes,' I say warily. Being written about can arouse any of fifty emotions, some of them involving weapons. But Mark is merely interested.

'I'm a great reader myself. *The Analyst*? *City of the Dead*? Great. James Lee Burke? He looks more like a cowboy than a professor but when he writes you can smell the Gulf. I'm a recovering alcoholic myself so I can relate to him. Lee Child — well, he's done it a bit too often.'

> **Kim moves around it, feeling the wool, plucking off a bit here, a piece there, savouring the wool with his fingers.**

He packs a fleece into the hydraulic press, one of around fifty fleeces it will take to fill a bale weighing 150 kilograms.

The wool peels cleanly off the sheep: grey outside, soft cream on the inside. The shedhands dance around the main players, the shearers. One picks up a fleece and flicks it like a blanket onto the classer's table, greased by generations of lanolin. It floats above the surface for a moment like a parachute, then drops in one clean spread.

Kim moves around it, feeling the wool, plucking off a bit here, a piece there, savouring the wool with his fingers. 'I don't have to feel every bit of it. It's a good length, and sound. Grade average about 19.5 [microns].' That's good.

Kim has been shearing at Mesopotamia for thirty-three years, through all three generations of Proutings, starting as a shedhand. 'Malcolm senior was a real gentleman and a real worker. I couldn't fault the man. He was a role model and that's how all the boys were brought up. Laurie was like his father. Malcolm junior has both his grandfather and his father to live up to.'

Kim can remember when 18,000 sheep went through the shed, from Mesopotamia and the two satellite stations Tui and Garundale, the two blocks subdivided by Malcolm senior for two of Laurie's brothers. Some of his gang, such as Mark and Celine, have worked with him for more than a decade.

'This stuff,' he gestures towards a bale of pieces, 'is either short or tender.' Short is obvious enough, but tender? 'It pulls apart. That's why Malcolm shears before lambing. When a ewe has lambed the wool gets tender, breaks easily.'

Another piece goes into the colours pile. 'This is green brandy. These are your yellows, limes, pinks.' Graded as carefully as living room paint. They're a pastoral fashion item: already dyed in nature's own colours.

Another bale for necks and collars. Then the moit, the bits from the necks stuck with straw, pieces of matagouri, the detritus a sheep picks up as it roams a high country farm, the mess hard to comb out.

A top-grade average comes in at 19.5 microns, medium-fine. Necks are about eighteen, backs about the same but they are high-yielding and less dirty so they are worth more. The market allows a few pieces of lower-yield, shorter wool with the top-grade fleece, a point that too-careful, overhonest New Zealand farmers were slow to take. Kim says, 'They found that internationally New Zealand was seen as too fussy. The mills needed shorter lengths in with the good stuff so now they throw a few in.'

Then the locks. They come from around the backs and they are shorter still, sometimes from the shearer going back over what he has already done, so small they often fall between the bars of the wool table or floor. They go in with the topknots from the tops of the animals' heads, and the socks, from the lower legs. They're known, of course, as the tops, socks and locks.

This year top-grade wool is fetching around fourteen dollars a kilogram. Necks bring nine to ten dollars, backs seven to eight, pieces four dollars and fifty cents, tops, socks and locks two to three dollars. But the prices are rising. Wool is back in favour.

The fleeces go into a hydraulic press, forcing them down into the big square bale until it is packed so tightly the bale stands solid as a block. The top is clipped on with wire hooks and the bale barrowed over to join the ranks at the edges of the shed, one of them tipped on its side to make a table for the microwave and the sandwich toaster.

Kim, the maestro, wears glasses to read with. It doesn't matter. He does his job by feel, not sight: 'The hand is better than the eye.' He feels the fleece with his whole body, like someone listening to good music. His hands are soft, like a pianist's, or perhaps a healer's; fine lover's hands. They can feel down to a quarter of a micron, which is one millionth of a metre, thinner than the wispiest human body hair, thin beyond the comprehension of most human minds. His touch is phenomenally gentle, measurably so, for the wool industry doesn't take his word for it: the wool is micro-tested by machine later because, of course, classers like Kim could be wrong. Except, Kim never is. Or at least, he concedes, 'very rarely'.

His hands are his fortune. He doesn't mix concrete, or shovel shingle, or do anything else that might affect his touch. This is an art form. 'It takes a very long time to learn,' he says. 'We're a dying breed. Ten years from now we probably won't have anyone like us left.'

Kim is fifty-seven. His gang once handled 150,000 merinos in a season. Now they're down to 22,000, 10–11,000 of them from Mesopotamia Station, their biggest single merino breeder. It costs Malcolm around four dollars and twenty cents to shear each animal. Mesopotamia merinos are a special breed, grown to suit their harsh environment, producing medium-fine wool, most of it bought on contract by Icebreaker, the Queenstown-based merino outdoor clothing company.

> **The sheep, white and skinny, disappear down a chute and are seen no more on stage, first the stars and now extras, joining their bewildered fellows in the pen below.**

The sheep, white and skinny, disappear down a chute and are seen no more on stage, once the stars and now extras, joining their bewildered fellows in the pen below. A stream of sheep come down the chutes on their sides, hit the ground, struggle to their feet and stand in a new world of bony sheep and gloom. Ash funnels them off into side pens and vaccinates them against footrot.

The sheep stand in the dirty water of a footrot dip for half an hour. Footrot is the main animal health problem on Mesopotamia. Merinos are susceptible to it. The disease puts them off their feed, weakens them.

This spring Kim's gang spent three weeks on the job for sure enough, two weeks of fine weather was too much to hope for. It turned bad and held them up. It was not the worst year, though. One terrible spring the shearing took almost two months and that, well, that was bad.

THE COOKHOUSE AND shearers' quarters were housed in one rambling wooden building on the hillside overlooking the stables and woolshed, but a respectable distance away from the homestead. It's a labyrinthine building.

Its huge kitchen, the main one of two in the building, has two electric stoves, fridge, industrial-sized freezer, toasters, microwave ovens and generations of appliances, and a thousand cupboards enclosing an entire history of pots, pans, and assorted instruments.

The big table in the dining room beside it will seat around thirty people, alongside armchairs which could have graced, once, the lounge of a respectable country hotel, a mysterious high chair, a woodbox full of aromatic split pine and a bin of cones, a toybox containing stuffed toys, blocks, colouring pens.

The cook's quarters have a bathroom and two bedrooms, each with a queen-size bed and two bunks, and a private sitting room with its own armchairs and sofa and fireplace. In the bathroom the toilet roll holder is a piece of number eight wire twisted into a loop and fastened to a piece of wood with a couple of staples.

The shearers' quarters occupy the other side of the building. They're a maze of bedrooms; twenty or thirty people could live here easily.

The shearing gang once might have spent two weeks or more here. 'Oh,' says Celine, 'if those walls could talk . . .' She thinks for a moment, then, 'We'd all be in trouble.' Mark tells of the shearer who got so angry with the programme on the television set he turned it off — with a shotgun.

The cavernous wash-house has three sinks, two concrete-and-lead tubs, and two washing machines. The bathrooms have open urinals and facing showers and, through a door, a more genteel shower, toilet, laundry tub and sink. There's a flat at the back with its own kitchen and bedroom.

Bare wood floors and wide hallways link everything together and there's a billiard room at the front with a single bed, should fatigue suddenly overcome one of the players.

And one of the best, most amazing libraries anywhere. Hundreds of books line the shelves, all neatly stowed: Stephen Leacock's *Sunshine Sketches of a*

Little Town, first published 1912, once the proud property of the National Library Service. Or the *Extraordinary Entanglement of Mr Pupkin*, who used to come home from his office in the Mariposa Court House, and on some days as he came through the door would call out to his wife, 'Almighty Moses, Martha! Who left the sprinkler on the grass?' Legions of shearers after a hard day in the woolshed must have found relaxation in the pages of Alice M. Chesterton's *Whittenbury College: A school story for girls*, this copy purchased from A.W. Hopkins, Ashburton ('Always the latest in books').

Or *The Return of Tarzan*, just in case they'd missed his departure, by Edgar Rice Burroughs, first published 11 April 1918, with several editions a year following until 1928. And a particular gem: *The Sanfield Scandal*, by Richard Keverne, published 1929, its title page showing it to be the property of the Mesopotamia Library, once a lending institution in its own right and owner of many of the shelved books such as *The Intrusions of Peggy*, by Anthony Hope, which must have entranced many a weary shearer: 'The changeful April morning that she watched from the window of her flat looking over the river began a day of significance in the career of Trix Trevalla — of feminine significance, almost milliner's perhaps, but significance all the same.'

They might have been riveted when the victim's wife fainted at significant news, her neighbour (for reasons best known to herself) undressing her, 'hardly noticing her fine breasts', and: 'Good gracious, she didn't wear a belt, not even a suspender belt; she had on just a flimsy brassiere, one of those half-up things or whatever they called them, and a pair of panties . . . It was almost shameful.'

But these days the shearers have all gone. The curious readers now are trampers, or hunters, or jetboaters. Shearers stopped staying there some four years before, and started commuting instead.

THE RANGITATA FLOWS deep grey and clear this spring. It looks gentle enough. Much of the water that feeds it is still locked up in the glaciers and snows of winter. But the river is a sleeping giant. It can turn into a marauder in hours, breaking its bonds, bounding over the countryside and sweeping away pastures, fences, stock.

→ RIGHT
The grave of Dr Andrew Sinclair, the Colonial Secretary of a very young New Zealand, who drowned crossing the Rangitata River in 1861 and was buried on the river flats.

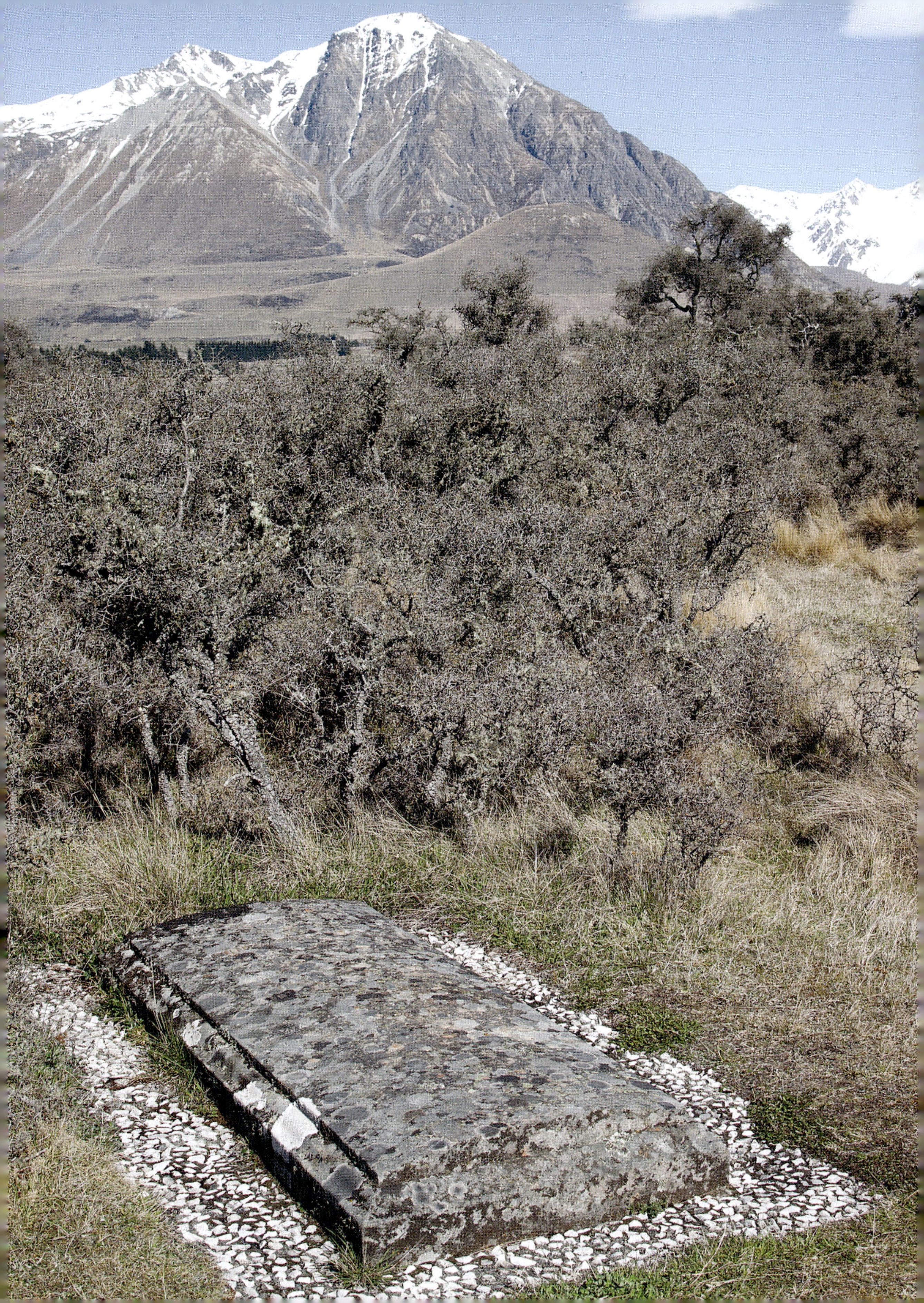

The torrent threatened Mesopotamia's viability as a farm, for the station depends on its river flats. Malcolm Prouting senior saw them as the key to prosperity. To farm them he had to rein in the river. He needed to control one of the biggest, fiercest rivers in the land and keep it from ruining his paddocks. When he died in 1981 the river banks were still being blown out by floods. Laurie took over the task.

On this spring day the water swirls gently around the scalloped edges created by the groynes they built. The massive boulders run far through the water and into the shingle beneath. The wonder is that they were created essentially by a couple of men and a bulldozer. Imagine the to-do of a construction company, had there been one prepared to take on the job: screeds of plans, engineers, squadrons of machinery, a small army of workers, a whole roomful of consents.

Behind the groynes the neat rows of willows planted by Neroli and Malcolm as children are touched lime green by spring. The trees have grown into a forest, lines of them running parallel to the river, trapping silt and debris, building up and anchoring the land between the groynes and the precious river flats. Visitors can stroll along the tops of the stopbanks, the wild river on one side, the gentle green on the other, with never a thought for rage and destruction. They can take a path leading away from the banks and the rush of water and creeping through matagouri until, without warning, they stumble across a tiny cemetery.

Here lies Dr Andrew Sinclair, noted botanist and public figure, the Colonial Secretary who drowned crossing the river in 1861. His grave disappeared into the matagouri and tussock for thirty years until it was rediscovered by a dozen men from a shearing gang, searching the river flat in front of the homestead and finding it half-buried in grass and moss. Perhaps, even now, the slab does not mark the grave: Charlie Dunstan recorded that the riverbed was so rough the dray carrying it overturned and the stationhands left it where it lay. The site grew into the Upper Rangitata Cemetery, last resting place of some seventeen people. A single struggling blossom tree adds a few dots of pink to the matagouri.

Allan Prouting, who died in a car accident in March 1974 aged eighteen, is buried there. Beside him lies his brother Peter, killed when his aeroplane crashed on the station on 6 February 1980, aged twenty-three. Then Malcolm senior, and his widow Thelma who died in 2004. And Thelma's mother and father, Frank and Maggie Gifkins. Some in the cemetery had worked at Mesopotamia, such as Hec Ayers and his wife Esperance, Thelma Prouting's sister. Ayers spent thirteen years at Mesopotamia and was head shepherd. They lie beside others without such connections, people who had simply loved the Rangitata and the high country. There may be other, unmarked graves for the high country life was precarious. Dunstan wrote that a station hand cut his foot with an adze and bled to death. His body, said Dunstan, also lay in the riverbed.

A NEW, EXOTIC face has appeared at the station. It belongs to Sophie Beugnot, from Les Menuires in the French Alps, a ski resort where Sophie worked in the season. She was raised as a traveller. Her parents moved around France, the French Indies, South America, Guadeloupe and Africa, and Sophie moved with them until she returned to University in France, then travelled first to Australia then New Zealand.

She is a Wwoofer, one of the army of volunteers who roam the world's organic farms working for board and keep. Somehow, two years before, she found her way up the Rangitata Valley, almost as far from Les Menuires as it is possible to get, with only the mountains in common.

She worked at Mesopotamia for only ten days but, critically, she met Ash. She could hardly avoid him, for Wwoofers at Mesopotamia are accommodated in Ash's cottage; a constant stream of young people of all nationalities passing through the old cottage where once Laurie and Anne lived. As Sophie tells it, 'I was with a friend, a girl who was travelling with me. So we were really enjoying our lifestyle, having barbecues and things. And we were working a lot, working long hours, and we were happy to go to work in the morning. It's something you don't find in France any more. You don't find people working that hard. Or maybe people stay more in the city.

'Then I went back to France. So I had three winters in a row, winter here, a French winter, then three months working in Wanaka in the winter. Too much winter. So I decided to go to Australia for a year, just to be somewhere warm. My English before I went to Australia was really bad. I picked it up in Australia. It's easier in Australia than in New Zealand. People speak slower there. I have trouble with the slang here. The first time I came to Mesopotamia here I couldn't pick it up. I didn't understand what they were saying. But now I understand it pretty well.'

What brought her back to Mesopotamia? 'Hum. I come to see Ash.'
Ash: 'Me?'
Sophie: 'Who did you think I meant?'
She and Ash fell in love. She looks happy. Ash's smile has grown even wider.

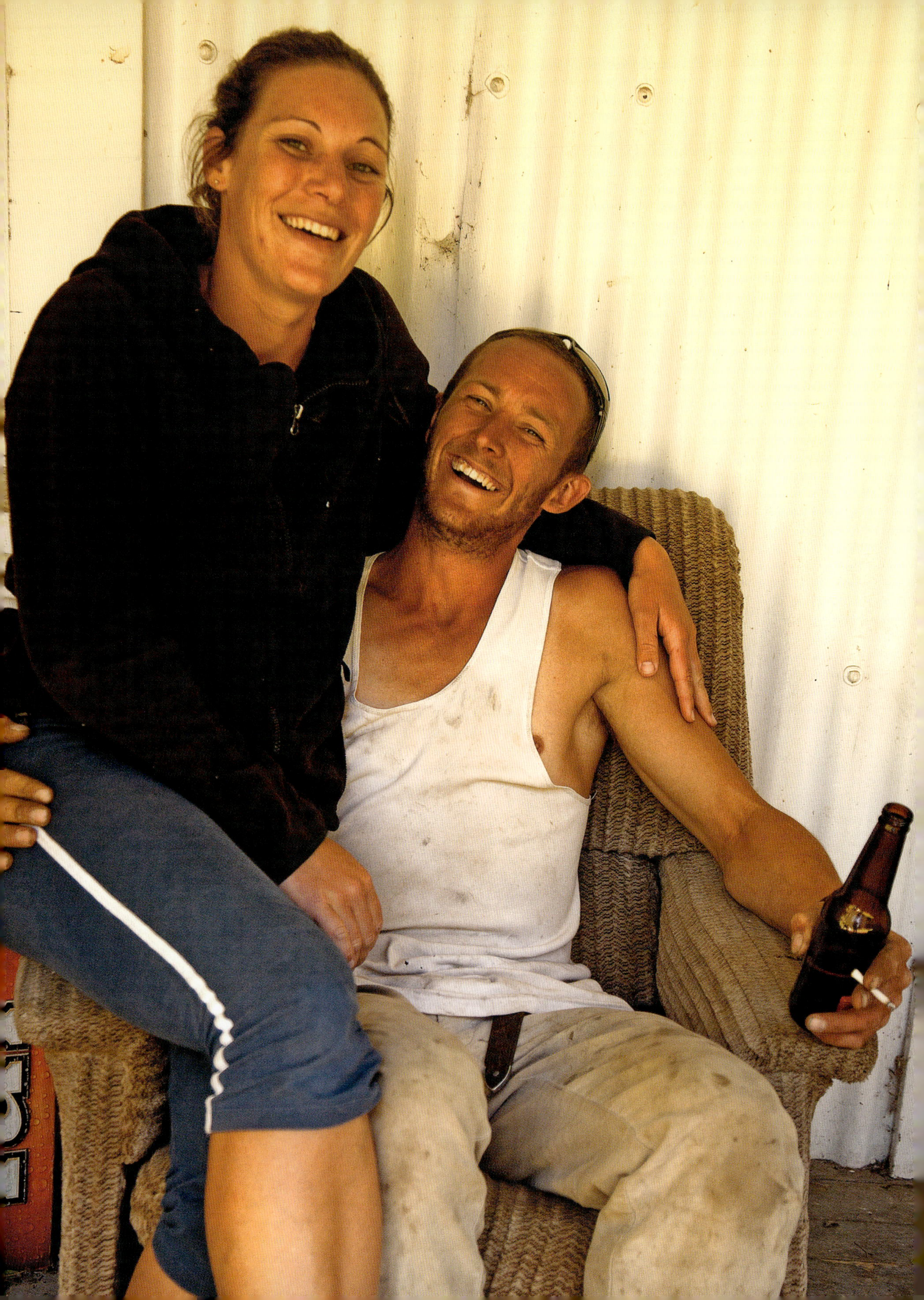

Tomorrow is her twenty-seventh birthday. Yesterday Ash took the day off and went into town to buy her a birthday present. Mesopotamia buzzed with speculation. A ring? Ash returned with a kayak.

Today Ash fetches a beer from the fridge. Sophie has not converted him to wine. It is six o'clock in the evening, but he still has work to do. Never finished, she says, with a touch of resignation. Then: 'I'm going with you.'

Ash O'Donnell came from Darfield near Christchurch, now best known as the epicentre of the 2010 earthquake. His father was a musterer who worked on stations in the valley, Mesopotamia, Erewhon, Mount Potts, and once appeared beside the Felt Hut in one of the outback author Barry Crump's books. Ash's ambition was to be a musterer like his dad. Now he is head shepherd at Mesopotamia. He has been here three years. He works long hours, hard work often on his own. He fits the high country mould perfectly: lean, hard, capable, decisive.

Yet it is difficult to see how the high country appeals to Sophie, an often lonely life in the mountains with extremes of weather and little time off. The nearest town is Geraldine but they go there only when they're out of supplies. They have satellite television, but seldom turn on the set.

'I don't mind being on my own,' she says. 'I like the mountains, I like nature. It's nice here. Quiet. There are neighbours, always friends coming here.'

Ash does not see how he could get a farm of his own. 'I'd like to. But the chances of that . . . competing with foreigners and stuff, is pretty hard to do'.

Sophie: 'I want him to come to France and make some money.'

'We're thinking of going to France for a look around,' says Ash. But, he says, he'd miss his dogs.

He talks instead about a ride on horseback with Sophie. They rode up Bush Stream to the Crooked Spur Hut in the great Valley beyond, then two days at the Stone Hut, then over the range to Lake Tekapo. Sophie delighted in the country, in the way the horses could find their way through the great boulders on the bed of Bush Stream. 'It was so nice.'

This spring, as Tennyson described it, the young man's fancy lightly turned to thoughts of love. The wiry Ash does not fit easily into a fairy story, but what else is it? Here was the solitary shepherd holed up in his mountain fastness when *kapow!* In walks a beautiful Frenchwoman who falls in love with him.

It was as if all his Christmases came at once. In fact, he says, 'They did.'

← LEFT
Sophie and Ash, on the verandah of their cottage at Mesopotamia: all his Christmases came at once.

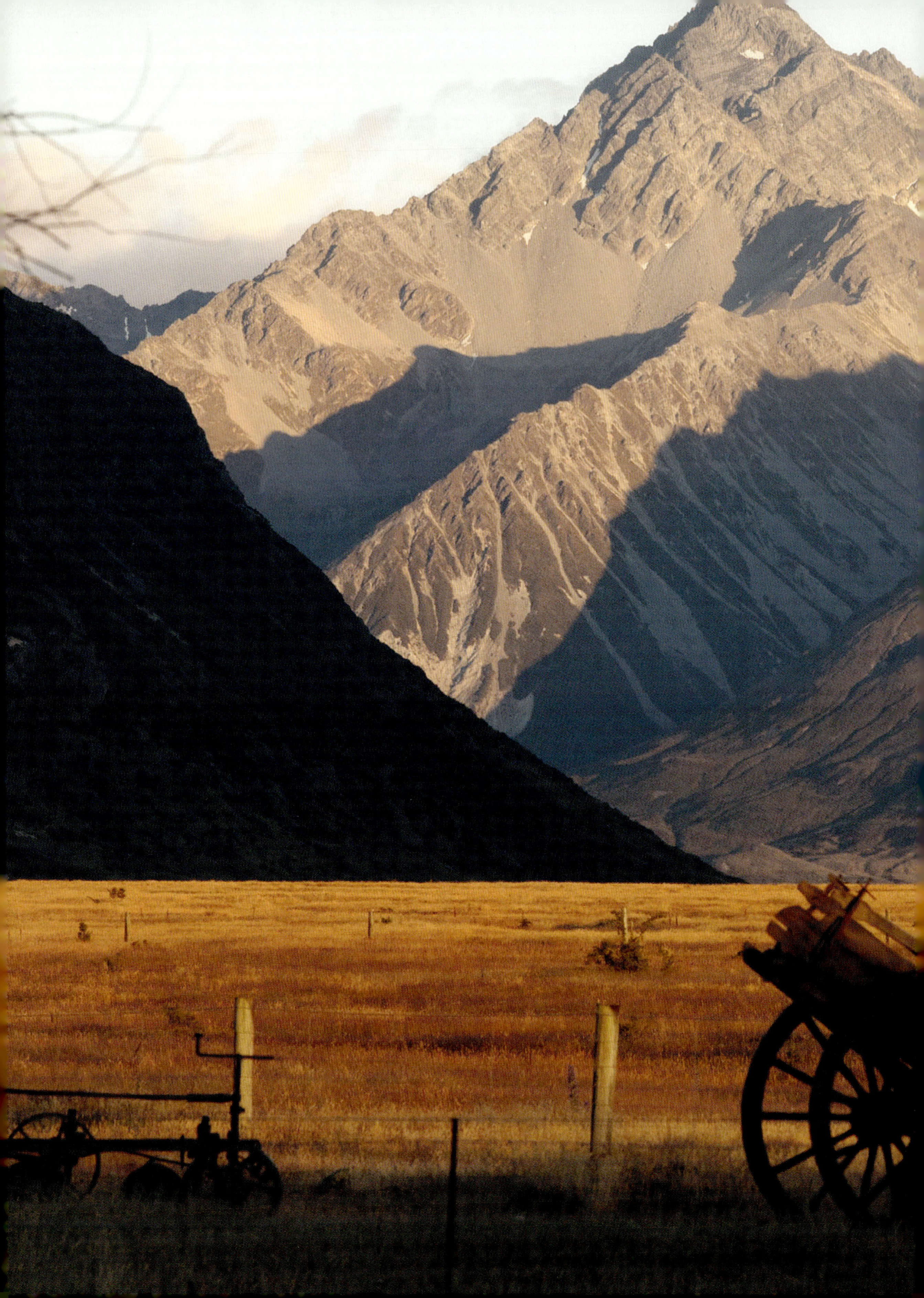

SUMMER

ACHILLES • THE TWO THUMB RANGE • D'ARCHIAC • CROOKED SPUR • HOGGET • THE GROWLER • BRABAZON • NEUTRAL SPUR • CLYDE RIVER • ROCKY RIDGE • BLACK MOUNTAINS • LITTLE SPUR • FINLAYS • FORBES RIVER • BIG BUSH • BLACK BIRCH STREAM • TOP DOWNS • BULLOCK BOW SADDLE • BALACLAVA BASINS • EXETER PEAK • SINCLAIR RANGE • FOREST CREEK • INKERMAN • THE ROCKS • MOUNT SINCLAIR • SUGARLOAF • MOUNT HOPE

THE RANGITATA VALLEY is donning its summer gear. Bright green willows spring along the river, whose thin braids now twinkle happily in the sun, the matagouri sheds its winter purple for a regal green; wild roses and pink foxgloves splash the valley. A nor'wester, still soft, slides down the valley, flicking the tops of pines running in straight ranks down to the river. The three gaudy roosters, bright as the day, gather beneath our kitchen window, crowing as if they've made the morning themselves.

The day is definitely worth applauding. A more delicate, shinier, more subtle sky is impossible. Wisps of gentle white cloud lace the blue, as if every spider in the valley has spun a piece and tossed it high. The river gleams through the lime-green willows and gurgles between its silver banks. Flats become downs which climb to terraces rising into mountains in a great ascending chorus of senses. It is just six-thirty, hot, the sun already seeking rocks and crevices. It boils away the morning cloud and mist and the valley lies still.

The angry bee-buzz of Malcolm's tiny helicopter rises in the clear morning air, echoing off the valley walls, the new sound of the high country, drowning the yells of musterers, the barking of dogs. Helicopters as farm tools have become as routine as tractors. He is using the machine to push the ewes and lambs down the slopes into the tailing yards, faster than dogs but demanding self-control, for impatience with stubborn animals, colourful on the ground, is dangerous in the air. 'If I miss one or it breaks back, I don't get angry. I say to myself great, more flying. And I go back for him.'

Nic the contractor has brought up portable aluminium pens in a neat trailer-borne operation that is a long way from the banged-up tailing yards of old. The sheep are run into the pens and the lambs drafted off. A harness flips the lambs onto their backs. An elasticator slips a tight rubber ring around testicles. Another ring goes around tails. They'll drop off into the paddocks later. Tags go into soft ears. The lambs are vaccinated. It's a smooth production-line operation but hard work in the sun.

Morning tea comes out: big vacuum flasks of tea and coffee, slabs of cake. Lunch is chicken, potato salad, green salad, sausage rolls. They work for thirteen straight hours. Next day Malcolm announces that he is going to lounge around a bit, not go so hard so early.

An outsider would not pick the difference. Work begins at seven-thirty, although Sophie has started an hour earlier: she had to catch her horse, saddle up and ride down to where every able body on the station is bringing in the cows and calves.

The nor'wester is still, lying in wait for the day. In the big paddock between the airport and the river, the animals are bawling and calling and people move in gently behind and drive them slowly towards the yards. Some are on foot, some in utes. Sophie and Sue are on horseback, weaving from side to side, the horses stepping high and the riders sitting straight as picadors.

The cows and calves move into the big wooden pens of split beech fastened to posts with heavy galvanised nails and the steel gates clang shut behind them. Malcolm and Ash draft off the calves and they stay in the pens while their mothers patrol outside and sniff and call and bellow. The calves cry and bray and bark and the whole thing is a huge discordant symphony so loud that when an aircraft takes off nearby its engine is drowned out by the noise.

Smoko. I say to Ash, 'It's full-on at this time of year, eh?'

Ash, who moves with absolute economy, puts a filter in his mouth and slowly builds a cigarette around it. He lights up, blows smoke. 'Mate, it's chaos.'

The calves begin moving through the races, ten or twelve at a time. Malcolm clips the station's mark into their ears. When Ash raises his hand Sophie places a tool in it, like an operating theatre nurse; tag pliers, elasticators. He holds up a hand, she knows which one he needs; he holds up the used instrument and she replaces it with the next. Ash clips bright yellow tags into the calves' ears, a big square number in one ear, a round yellow one in the other. If the calf is male he uses an elasticator to fit a rubber ring around its testicles.

The calves don't like people fooling around down there, or perhaps they resent their future as steers; either way they struggle, so that Ash emerges from underneath each one looking as if he has gone a good three minutes in a wrestling ring. The calves are drenched and released to their sobbing mothers and they trot off across the paddock like kids picked up from school.

For hour after hour calves rattle into the race, struggle with their tormentors, emerge with their ears decorated and their testicles made redundant. The nor'wester gets up, rips down the wide valley in a hot blast.

> **The day wears on. Bullocking, bellowing, blowing, the nor'wester mixing sweat with dust and cementing it into every pore.**

Everyone works in a way few in the city could appreciate, much less tolerate. Sue does not walk around the yards. She runs. Men drafted in for the day leap the yard rails like hurdlers. Ash disappears beneath the sea of animals and surfaces blowing like a dolphin.

We drive up to the homestead for lunch. I ask Malcolm if he follows his father's creed of 'no hands in pockets.' 'Yeah, and no loitering. And I hate blokes who sit on the rails in pens.' He says he has a dog which bites them on their backsides, although he claims he didn't train it; the dog started policing the rail-sitters of its own accord.

'And,' says Malcolm, who has given the matter some thought, 'I hate blokes who sit around and do nothing.'

Lunch is sausage casserole with carrots, kumara, rice, asparagus, super-sized. No truck after lunch. 'If you're not there I'll go without you,' Malcolm says, often, and this time he has. So it's a long walk down the hill, past the woolshed, through a couple of fences, across the road, past the airfield to the yards.

The day wears on. Bullocking, bellowing, blowing, the nor'wester mixing sweat with dust and cementing it into every pore. The calves bucking and struggling, every second one objecting to having his nuts put in a vice and all of them grizzling about getting their ears mutilated.

The last calf emerges from the race and goes off bellowing across the paddock. Everyone knows how it feels. Ash straightens painfully. Thank God for that, he says.

Now the bulls are put in with the cows, much harder than it sounds. The huge animals range from a bull called Mazda, which would excite any matador, down to mavericks that remain aloof from the prospect of weeks of unlimited sex and want to take their business elsewhere, anywhere but here.

I once heard Sean Fitzpatrick likened to a farm animal in the sense that out in the paddock he looked quite normal but up close, he was huge. Up close, bulls are even bigger. They have one thing in common with the former All Black captain, however: they do not like being pushed around. So there is more tagging and drenching and shoving and sorting out the cows and bulls into their paddocks and by then it is around six o'clock so Malcolm and Ash vanish to do some sheep work and return at seven-thirty, another twelve-hour day and it has been as hot as hell throughout, long clouds lingering around the peaks but not moving.

Even Ash looks weary. His body is the colour of his canvas chaps. Every inch of him is covered in the pale milky shit of young calves. He rests on the rail, lights up. I ask him what he does at the weekends and his bright blue eyes regard me for a long moment. 'What's a weekend?'

THE TWO THUMBS are completely bare now, black against the blue sky, the snow gone. The morning is painted shades of grey. Streaks of silver are shot through with coils of iron-grey rising to plump balls of slatey cloud hanging over the peaks like cushions in some god's boudoir.

Up on the terraces it is high summer and the tussock is golden and the skylarks celebrating. The spaniard sends great gouts of creamy flowers into the sky from its orange throat, like smoke from fire.

The day has already lost its calm. The nor'wester has climbed out of bed late, stretching, flexing its muscles and ready to go. Downriver a patch of mist hides the V of the gorge lying between its hills like a Rubens painting.

Malcolm unchains Bo, his special needs dog with a penchant for disappearing, then Blue the beardie with the spooky eyes, and Jock, a black, tan and white heading dog which Malcolm does not entirely trust: 'Farmers have their likes and dislikes. Some like dark roof mouths, or brown. I never liked three-coloured dogs. Jock's a good dog but he's flighty.'

Whether it is his colour or not, Jock does not have a good day.

Malcolm climbs into his truck. 'Welcome', chirps the sign on the radio he cannot turn off. Bo jumps onto the back of the truck but Blue and Jock are filled with the spirit of the morning. The Land Cruiser rolls along the shingle road at forty kilometres an hour. The aging Blue is at maximum speed but Jock just stretches out and lopes along.

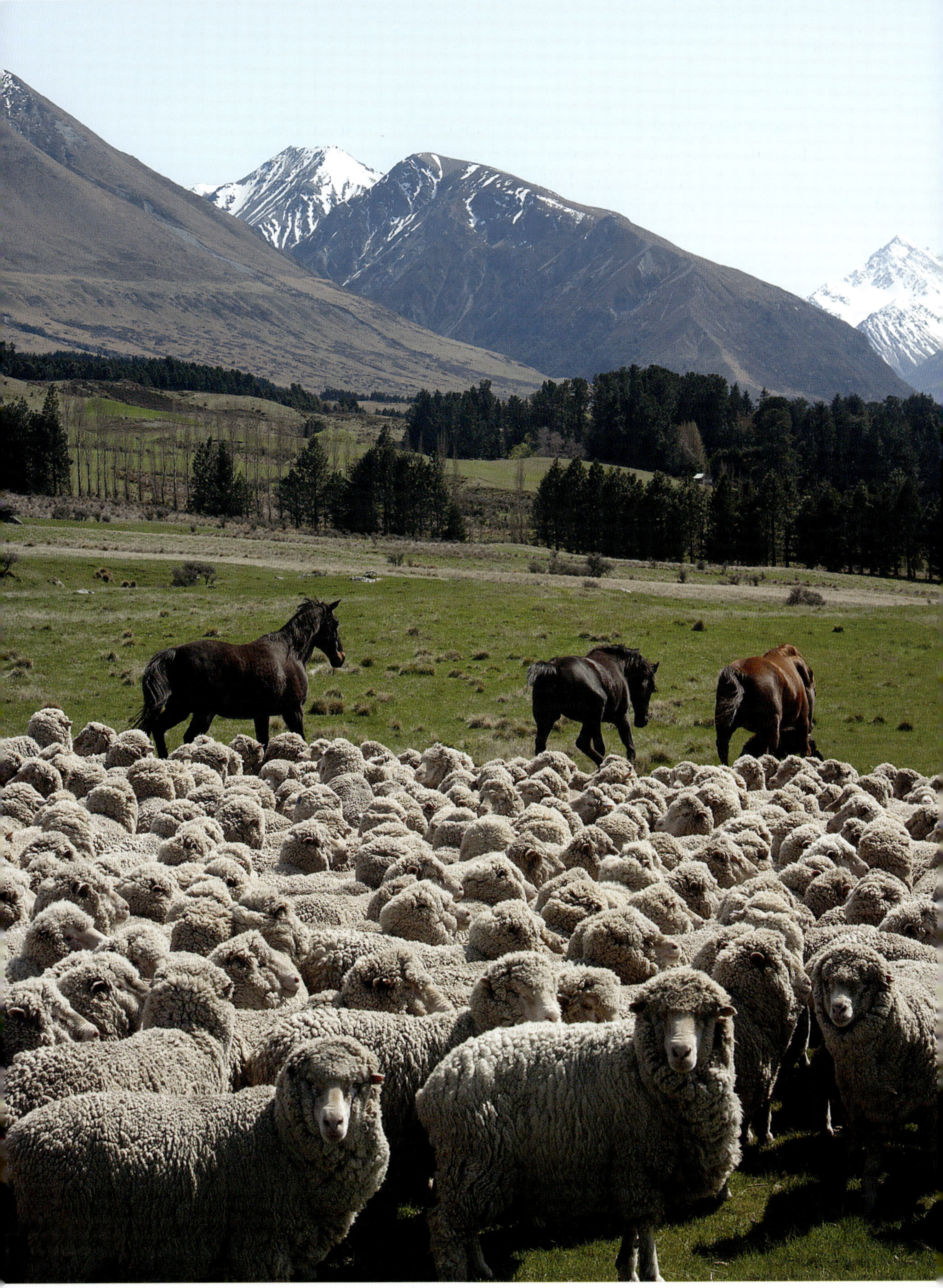

We get into the sheep paddock and work the mob and Malcolm's old .22 rifle lets off a shot or two to keep the dogs on their toes. 'My dog-scarer.' He hangs the ancient iron back in the cab then heads up to the deer paddocks to bring the stags in for velveting.

He likes his dogs but in the end they're as much tools as farm machinery. 'I had a dog once and it broke its leg. I take it to a vet in Christchurch. The vet has a look at the dog and says sorry, it's going to cost twenty-five hundred dollars to fix. I ask to see the X-rays. They show a complex fracture, bone running right through the meat of the dog's leg. I say it's not going to heal well, the dog's always going to be lame. Better put him down.

'The vet says okay, come back in an hour. I've lent my car to someone and I'm riding on the bus and I'm a bit surprised by this but I go back. Your dog's ready says the nurse. What? I say. He's dead isn't he? I'll get him for you, she says, and she comes back with the dog, all wrapped up in a parcel. Can't take him on the bus I say, but tell you what, can you get the collar off him? Okay, says the nurse, but her lip starts to tremble. Oh, I say, and the flea collar, it's only a month old.'

'Poor girl,' he says now. 'Another callous farmer.'

He drives into a deer paddock and manoeuvres behind the herd. Sue appears on her big white horse in her shorts and singlet with her blond hair blowing dramatically in the sharp nor'wester that has suddenly sprung up and looking a rare mix of the classical and the rustic, like Boadicea McSwannie. Sue likes working her deer on horseback. Her horse is fifteen-point-two hands and she is very proud of it. She bought it off TradeMe.

Jock the tricoloured dog decides it is time to prove Malcolm's theory. He gets in front of the deer and they bounce back as if on bungy cords. A young stag springs for the fence and twangs back with the sound of a breaking guitar string. But the rest begin to move quietly enough. They gather in front of the open gate in the way deer do, making up their minds whether to go through it or break. Then one turns its head towards the gate, and so do others, and one steps forward, then they all do, then they're belting through the gate and down the lane leading to the shed in a bunch. Sue climbs off her white horse and closes the gate. 'Young stags are like teenagers.' she says, 'They all run around like headless chickens until one of them gets an idea then they all go for it.'

Malcolm hangs back a little. Turns out he has been thinking about greenies. 'If they want to save the kiwi we should start eating them. No no, I'm serious. Give them to Mr Tegel. Tell him that for every ten thousand they breed they must release one thousand into the wild. Pretty soon we'd have kiwis everywhere. We'd have that many kiwis we'd be out night-shooting them. In ten years they'd be on the pest list.'

Jock cuts off his train of thought neatly as a skilled shunter. The dog gets in front of the stags and they break back, see two utes blocking their escape and go for the fence instead. One of the animals goes clear over the top of the two-metre wire. Another gets most of the way before a back leg gets tangled.

He hangs by a hoof, flapping around like some great fish caught in a net. He struggles, the wire twanging away like a banjo orchestra, dangling upside down until Malcolm seizes a wire-cutter and cuts him loose in a mighty final strum and the stag gets to its feet and bounds off down the hill with one of its expensive sticks of velvet broken and bloodied. That bloody Jock, roars Malcolm. Then another thought takes his fancy. Paul Henry has just quit his TV One breakfast-show job amid accusations of racist remarks. 'Paul Henry was a dick,' says Malcolm, 'but at least he was a redneck.'

SUE APPEARS IN the doorway of Hunters Cottage. 'Grab an apple,' she says. 'Laurie's coming by for you.' This could mean anything. What it means today, as it happens, is Laurie landing his Cessna at the airfield and cramming me into the luggage compartment alongside an engine. Peter Bush is in the front. A couple in the passenger seats watch with a bemused air. They're from Kerikeri, they say, as if explaining something.

We take off and fly up the valley. The woman says she and her husband had met Laurie and Anne once before, in Niue on holiday. Visiting the South Island they decided to drop in and say hello. Next thing they were in the aeroplane and, when Laurie discovered the man was an engineer, they were joined by various spare parts including the little engine beside me.

We head towards the Main Divide. They say nothing. We reach the head of the Rangitata River with Black Mountain high above us, Black Mountain Hut below.

This is *Lord of the Rings* country. Mesopotamia Station was the backdrop to scenes filmed around here. Mount Sunday on the other side of the river was Edoras, Black Mountain part of Helm's Deep. On the silver screen the hut has vanished but the trees around it are still there, and locals can work it out. Once Jackson had to stop filming for a day when someone on the Mesopotamia side lit a fire and smoke drifted into the scene.

Sue volunteered for the film as an extra. She was summoned for a battle scene but was too busy on the farm to go. Instead, she rode in Laurie's helicopter when horses used in the film escaped and he was called to round them up. She was able to wander around the set, agog. 'It was just incredible. It took them a long time to build. And when they left, all the tussocks, any plant or stone removed was plotted by GPS and later put back as they were. Incredible.'

The film crew has long gone, but the land remains magical. Ahead of us now the Havelock River runs into the Rangitata, its valley floor deep and dark as it turns towards the Southern Alps. Away to the left the oddly named Mount D'Archiac points its palisade of peaks up from a buttress of glaciers. The mountain was once the cornerstone of Mesopotamia Station, the boundary sliding up the South Forbes Glacier to the mountaintop in a sharp spike. Laurie climbed that mountain once. I could only look at it and shiver and wonder at the station's might.

Laurie is not looking up the mountain today. He is watching the riverbed below us where a trio of four-wheel-drive vehicles form a slowly moving caravan. 'Whenever there's a flood there are people caught up here,' he says, and I fancy Peter Bush blushes, for that is exactly the way he first came to the station. The nor'wester is getting up now and great balls of black cloud rolling over the tops threaten rain. 'Some of these guys have watched too many of those television ads and they think their four-wheel-drives can go anywhere.'

The Cessna glides down. Ahead is the Black Mountain Hut, a white box on the riverbank set by a small lake and surrounded by a few old pines and abandoned sheep yards. The riverbed is coming up fast and Laurie evidently intends landing there. The aircraft sinks towards what seems to be a solid bed of matagouri. At the last minute what looks like an animal track through the matagouri turns out to be a rough runway. Laurie lands smoothly, turns up a track and taxis to the hut.

It's a solid little building, three hours on horseback from the station homestead, built to withstand the fierce winds and heavy snow and a palace to those who seek refuge. For a musterers' hut it is even luxurious. The ceiling is lined with varnished ply, carpets cover the floor, the place nicely painted inside and out. Armchairs rest comfortably against the walls, padded chairs surround the formica table. A rough old wooden table knocked up by bush carpenters stands aside, a reminder of what once was.

Racks hold an eclectic collection of magazines for the storm-bound: *Fish and Game New Zealand, Next, Speedwheels, Country Life, New Idea*. A big gas stove stands beside shelves stacked with supplies: baked beans, nuts, toilet

> "It's a solid little building, three hours on horseback from the station homestead, built to withstand the fierce winds and heavy snow and a palace to those who seek refuge."

paper. Frying pans hang on hooks above the fireplace, near an old wooden larder with a door solid enough to keep out ravening armies either of rats or wayward hunters. A sign announces that during winter the water tap may freeze; best fill containers at night.

Air New Zealand staff have restored the hut, a token of appreciation for being allowed to use it. They did a thorough job. The door had been covered with a century's worth of musterers' names. One of the old musterers took his grandchildren up to the hut. 'I used this hut when I mustered these mountains,' he told them proudly, 'and here's my name on the door' (with a flourish). The names had gone. A newly painted white surface gave nothing away. The kids were sceptical. 'All gone,' says Laurie now. 'Oh well. Hard luck.'

He pulls the small engine out of the aeroplane's luggage compartment. It will replace the worn-out motor on a tank Laurie is using to spray broom in the constant fight to stop the weed choking the hillsides and river.

Already the broom is sparse here and as it disappeared it revealed something strange on a terrace above the hut: a wall, perhaps a hundred metres long, with the remains of side walls backing up to the bluff behind it. Two openings in the wall give access to the resulting enclosure.

Natural? Perhaps. But the wall is unnaturally straight, like a parapet, or a rampart. No one knows of anything else like it in the valley. It has a human touch, but constructing it out of the rocky ground would have taken a great deal of work.

European? An early homestead once sheltered beside the pines below. It might have been a reservoir, but one of New Zealand's biggest rivers runs alongside, and it doesn't run dry. Less than one hundred metres away lies a spring-fed lake, so clear that every detail of its pretty bottom can be seen. Nor were the Europeans who settled this valley given to massive earthworks. They built small wooden or stone cottages. They had too much else to do.

Maori? But why? Mesopotamia went about solving the riddle in the station's classic fashion.

An Englishman, Mark, came by. Mark was an archaeologist who needed a break from his work back home. He packed his bags and came to New Zealand. He and the Proutings shared a mutual friend and Mark bought two horses from the friend. He set off on a horseback journey around the South Island, riding from the top of the South Island down to Queenstown where he planned to sell his horses and go home. He rode over Erewhon to Mount Potts but his horses were tired and sore. He decided to cross the Rangitata River and ask Sue if he could rest at Mesopotamia for the day.

She looked at the state of his horses and realised that he would be there for much longer, several days at least. 'I told him he'd be put to work, which he was. I think he fixed a fence the first day and on it went. He had so much fun here he stayed six weeks.' When Mark said he was an archaeologist Malcolm's ears pricked up. Come and look at this he said, flew him up to Black Mountain Hut and showed him the wall.

Mark stayed up there five days. He excavated a small area of the ground behind the wall. He found, among other items, an old stone tool, probably a digging tool and almost certainly Maori. Sue: 'When he came back he was absolutely fascinated.'

He drew up a brief report, saying that the enclosure could have been built either by Europeans or Maori, European because it was built close to an old homestead built in 1850, Maori because it could have been on an unknown hunting or pounamu (greenstone) trail to and from the West Coast.

Early Ngai Tahu accounts tell of a pass at the head of the valley used to gather the precious pounamu. The Dennistoun Pass lies above the Rangitata catchment although it is a difficult path to the west. The historian W.A. Taylor wrote that it was 'extremely unlikely that the Maoris journeyed over the Dennistoun or other of the headwater saddles to Westland.' The Sealey Pass at the head of the Godley Glacier further south was a more likely route, he decided, as greenstone tools had been found at the head of that pass and early Europeans had made the trip: 'What Europeans could do, so could Maori explorers.'

Yet Mark the archaeologist concluded that on balance the structure was probably Maori and probably surrounded a kumara garden. Certainly Maori were familiar with the upper Rangitata, usually journeying up the Opihi River to Raincliff then up the Opuha, over a saddle, and down Forest Creek to the Rangitata River. And Te Wanahu Corner beside the road through Peel Forest marks a spot said to be the site of an ancient Maori battle. A band of North Island raiders searching for pounamu overcame Arowhenua iwi near Timaru. Survivors fled to Peel Forest and the Rangitata Gorge, but were overtaken by the North Islanders and their chief Te Wanahu was killed.

MORE TOOLS ARE needed to finish repairing the sprayer pump. We climb into the Cessna and Laurie taxis it back, past the hut to the runway. The Kerikeri couple are left on the job, and I fancy I see a flash of alarm in their eyes as they are abandoned far up the valley, surrounded by mountains, not knowing quite where they are, bereft of people or any means of support save an old musterers' hut, when all they had had in mind was a nice cup of tea with some people they'd once met on holiday.

EVERY DAY FROM now until well after Christmas will be spent making silage. Eleven thousand sheep, 500 cattle and 3000 deer demand whole warehouses full of winter feed, although here they call them silage pits. There are three pits, every one of them capable of sheltering an army. Even so, the station usually runs out by winter's end. The silage will be packed into the pits then covered and weighted with enough tyres to retread a boy-racer convention. The covers and tyres keep the air out, a measure necessary to make silage, but up here in the mountains the air often moves very quickly. Everything is doubled and trebled to survive the wind.

It is Sunday. Some people call it a day of rest, or a day off, or a penal-rates day. Here it's a working day like any other. The whole farm is working. A fleet of trucks has been unearthed from the sheds and they're being fitted with high sides for the silage they're going to start carting tomorrow. Malcolm is working on a huge steel gate with an arc welder. An engineer from down-country is fabricating, fitting, turning. A big auger is being checked over. One of the two tractors, the best one, has blown its radiator, which is being sent into Ashburton for repair. Always happens at the worst time, someone grumbles. They will have to get by without it for a couple of days.

On Monday morning a caravan is assembled at the machinery sheds: tractors, mowers, augers, rakes, trucks with their high sides up. But there's a last-minute hitch. Every able-bodied human being at the station has been pressed into service. Still they are a driver short. A tour bus driver turns up at the door of the smoko shed to say hello. He has the look of a man at one with the world, a man whose job is well in hand. His passengers have gone off up the valley on a long walk, and he can relax.

'So you'll be free for most of the day?' Malcolm asks.

'Yes,' says the driver, perhaps unwisely.

'How'd you feel about driving a truck?'

'Um, er, well, all right. Yeah, why not?'

They have their missing driver.

Engines are fired up. The caravan winds up the valley in the sullen heat of the morning, grey clouds boiling over the mountaintops. The line of vehicles turns up the Sugarloaf lane, climbs, enters a paddock where cut grass lies sweet-smelling on the ground. The long, long business of raking, filling the trucks, carting to the silage pits begins.

Christmas Day is a working day like every other in this frantic time. The festive season is the station's busy season, critical to the coming year. It won't wait for Christmas dinner. Christmas presents are exchanged briefly, then back to work. At Mesopotamia they celebrate Christmas at a better time, usually mid-June.

Ferg and Pieta have their Christmas money in the bank. They collected the bone buttons cast off by stags each year before they grow the new antlers, which are removed when they are soft, or velvet, so that all they have left to shed are the remnants of their antlers, or buttons. They have a big plastic bag full of them. 'Maybe twelve kilograms?' says Sue, hoisting the bag. They get between four and seven dollars a kilogram for the buttons and Ferg and Pieta collected $600 worth the previous year. It seems the ideal farm kids' occupation. Something created from hard work which would otherwise go to waste. Ferg and Pieta love their gardens. They have entered the school garden competition and their gardens are full of vegetables, sunflowers, sweet peas.

Sue got her Christmas present early. A hedge trimmer. The hedges needed doing. Malcolm unpacked it, set it up and was the first to use it. She hasn't touched it yet.

For New Year's Eve a dozen family and friends go up to the Felt Hut, the ancient musterers' hut lying beneath the famous pass into the Valley, Bullock Bow. They ride trail bikes over the pass, eat, sit around in the bush clearing and talk and in the dark mountain night usher in the new year. It is a truly high country celebration.

THIS IS ONE of those days when the torrid nor'wester lurks without striking. Its heat sears the still air although the sun is barely up, for it is only five in the morning. George, Sam, Nic and helpers have been on the job even earlier, filling the plunge dip, getting ready for the 7000 ewes and lambs, more than half the flock, which will swim a lap through toxic water to rid themselves of lice. Nic's cigarette never leaves his mouth.

A dozen men, women and one boy, Ferg, have been mustered to do the job. By five-thirty the first merinos are moving through the race. They don't like the idea of an early-morning swim. A dozen people and a dozen dogs are running, yelling, barking, flapping plastic pipes and plastic bags, hoisting reluctant sheep, and a great shouting and barking and baa-ing rises in the valley, the entire scene weirdly wrapped in dust shot through with shafts of early-morning sun. Clouds of little black flies and marauding sandflies hover over everyone. Malcolm dances around like a dervish, organising, barracking. 'When Malcolm shouts at you it's okay,' Rowie tells Jess, 'because he always shouts. But when *Sue* shouts you know you've really stuffed up.' Rowie grew up in the rabbiter's house down the road, Jess is a vet student.

The sheep are stubborn. George and Nic and anyone else who can lift fifty-to-sixty kilogram animals off their feet and throw them into the dip one after another try to keep them moving, but the merinos at first seem determined to resist to the last ewe, no wonder because this is more than a mere swim. The animals plunge into the dip and strike out for the far end but for the chemicals to work they have to be completely saturated. Both sides of the dip are lined with people holding dunking tools, a shallow steel letter S at right angles to a long handle. Each sheep is dunked at least twice and they come up gasping and spluttering and the lambs sobbing piteously.

At morning tea the question is why North Island cows lie down in their paddocks, while their South Island cousins stand. The debate is spirited, and not always complimentary to the north, but the consensus is that there's so much more feed in the north that the cows can take it easy.

Then there's the new Russian owner of Mount Potts Station on the other side of the river. He invited everyone in the valley to a big do, showing a nice appreciation of local customs: ladies a plate. He provided the booze, and is said to have got a shock: just about everyone in the valley turned up.

After tea and thick slabs of chocolate slice a new pen of sheep is chased into the race and the work goes on. If ever an animal was poorly designed for swimming it is a sheep, whose legs are knobbly and whose wool is made for comfort rather than speed, although it floats just fine and the dunkers have to lean hard on their poles to push them under, especially the woolly ones which are buoyant as beach balls. Jess's hands are blistered and raw from the previous day's dipping. She wraps them in rags and works on gamely. But pushing stubborn merinos through the race is harder work, and the dunkers aren't complaining. The occasional drowning sheep is fished out and resuscitated by palpitating ribcages with booted feet. The rest swim to the far end and climb out into holding pens, dripping gushers of brown water onto the concrete floors which pour it back into the dip in a filthy waterfall. Between pens the mixture in the dip is stirred with buckets attached to ropes, and a heavy steel plunger.

The last ewe swims its length five hours after the first was thrown in. The final mob is let out into a paddock and only the sceptical would deny they look relieved. Certainly everyone else is. Ferg has worked as hard as anyone.

The mixture, thick with mud and straw and sheep dags, is pumped out and everyone goes up to the homestead for a plunge into the swimming pool at the bottom of the garden. Nic's cigarette is still in his mouth when he gets out. Lunch is merino, of course. Sue has cut up sides of it and cooked it for five hours in orange juice, honey, garlic, soy sauce. Served with roast parsnip, salad and green vegetables, it is superb. The fourteen people around the lunch table eat with the kind of concentration that pays tribute to good food. That and a seven-hour slog down in the yards. Deep silence steals back into the valley.

THE AFTERNOON SUN is still warm and we're waiting by the stables, Peter Bush and myself, with dogs all around us. Heat radiates from the flattened oil drums of the building's cladding.

Soon enough the dogs realise that their bosses have gone elsewhere, and the only humans left are a couple of ingénues, easily managed. Most of them slip through the rails and vanish. They leave behind only a young black dog, still untrained, and Jock the tricoloured dog, who seems to be taking his disgrace seriously.

The three roosters strut into the stable yard, bright as posters, cocky as cocks. They begin scratching around in the dust as roosters do. We throw a bit of grass seed but they're not interested; the pitch of their combs suggests it's an insult after the toast they had for breakfast that morning outside our kitchen. They crow and cuss.

Suddenly the young black dog takes an interest. A chicken dinner takes shape and glows in his shadowy eyes. He bounds after one of the roosters, which shows a neat turn of speed, dodges and slips its tackle like an All Black winger. Jock watches with interest. Clearly he thinks this is a good idea, and there's no one around with anything like a gun. He decides to show the young feller how it's done. The rooster doesn't hang around. He knows trouble when he sees it. He slips under the bottom rail of the fence and scoots off up the hill like, well, a chicken with something even more dangerous than the Colonel after him.

The black dog blunders behind him, but Jock slinks through with a determined stalk that spells trouble for the cock. Still, we reason, the roosters didn't get where they are today without being able to handle a couple of sheepdogs. Evidently we're wrong.

'It can't handle two of them,' says Sue.

We slink off ourselves, although lacking Jock's panache; after all, it's really our fault. We should have called the dogs back.

The next morning dawns warm. Another nor'wester is poking its snout over the mountains, scarcely breathing as it limbers up for the day. The valley seems still as a grave, appropriately, for only two roosters turn up outside the kitchen window this morning. One of them is the bird last seen tearing off up the hill, all dignity gone, with two sheepdogs on its tail. Which will not happen again for a while, because now the cock has no tail. Where once feathers curved in a proud arch, there is nothing, not so much as a lonely bit of down. Instead, the rooster's rump shines through pinkly, showing signs of a doggy snack in a couple of raw patches. At least he's alive, I tell Sue. 'Yes, but where's the third one?' she says. Sue searches the bushes for feathers but the dogs have been smart. They've left no trace of their crime.

A MOUSE HAS made itself at home in the homestead's kitchen. It is a tricky little beast, expert in the geography. It knows its way through the maze of drawers and cupboards and bins that hold the huge quantities of cutlery, crockery, pots and pans and, of particular interest to the mouse, the food needed to keep a big sheep station up and running.

The mouse knows all about up and running. Sue opens a cupboard drawer and there it is, staring at her in the slightly indignant manner of a mouse interrupted in the course of its daily grind. Then it's off. 'Okay,' cries Sue, 'it has gone into that drawer, that's the only place it could have gone.' Speedy preparations are made for the mouse to depart this earth. But the mouse is speedier. The drawer is rodent-free. So is every other space within its reach. The mouse has vanished into thin air, not for the first time, because it is a proven escape artist.

Traps are set. The mouse neatly avoids them, although it sometimes nonchalantly pinches the bait. Clearly it considers itself a permanent member of the household. Pieta decides to even up the battle of wits. Beside a trap baited with cheese she sets her own. She tempts the mouse with a sultana covered in peanut butter.

Next morning, early, she nips into the kitchen. 'I've got good news,' she announces. 'I've Caught The Mouse.' Her smile engulfs her face. The mouse is spreadeagled in her trap, stone dead. Clearly its epicurean instinct led to its downfall. Pieta generously decides to share the glory. She studies the mouse and picks up her cat. 'I think Puddy pushed it in.'

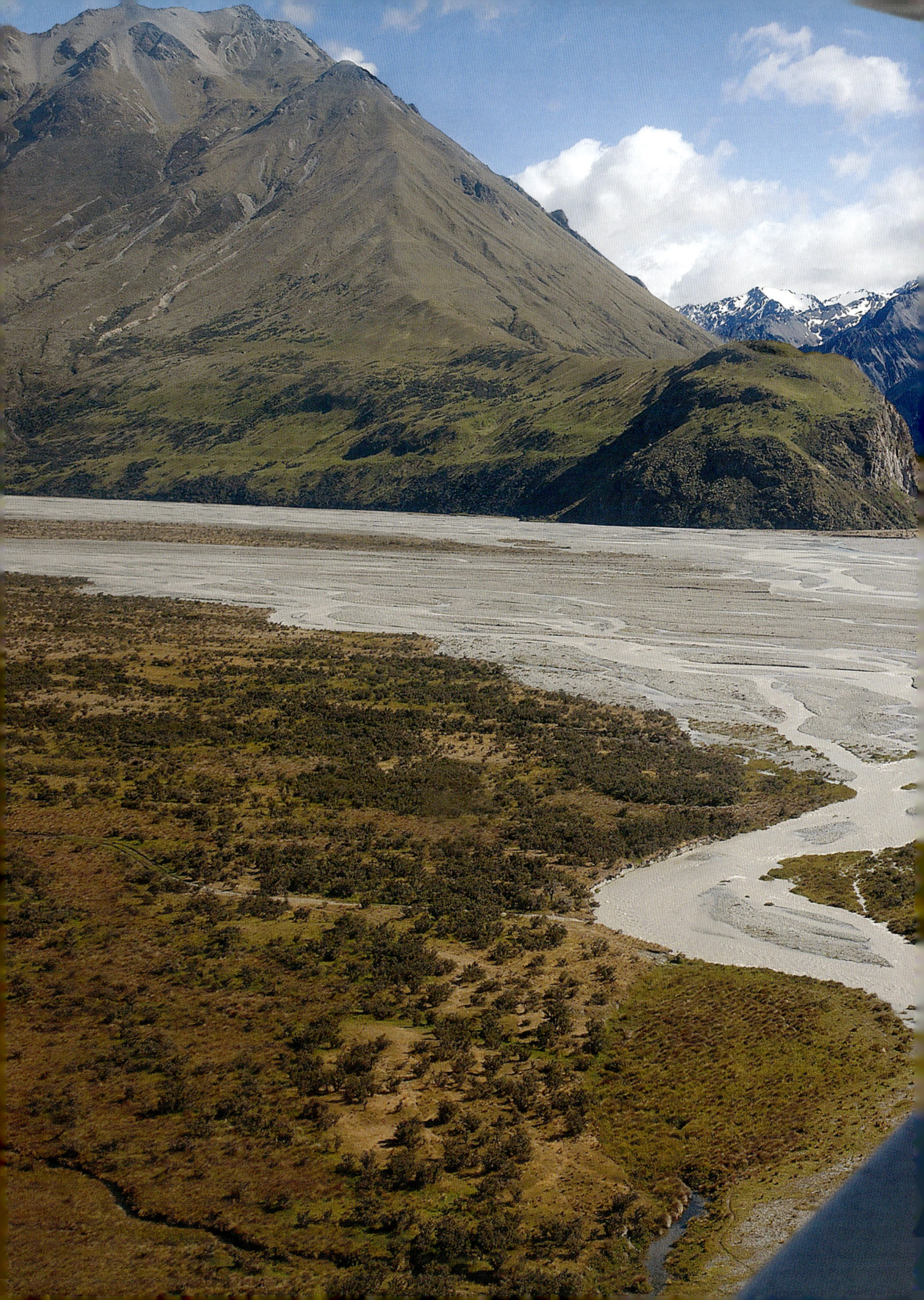

AUTUMN

ACHILLES • THE TWO THUMB RANGE • D'ARCHIAC • CROOKED SPUR • HOGGET • THE GROWLER • BRABAZON • NEUTRAL SPUR • CLYDE RIVER • ROCKY RIDGE • BLACK MOUNTAINS • LITTLE SPUR • FINLAYS • FORBES RIVER • BIG BUSH • BLACK BIRCH STREAM • TOP DOWNS • BULLOCK BOW SADDLE • BALACLAVA BASINS • EXETER PEAK • SINCLAIR RANGE • FOREST CREEK • INKERMAN • THE ROCKS • MOUNT SINCLAIR • SUGARLOAF • MOUNT HOPE

THIS MORNING IS so still, as if the air has emptied out of the valley leaving the mountains to preen themselves with only a wispy cloud fluttering around their balding peaks. We climb into a diesel four-wheel drive, open the big locked deer gate by the stream, drive past the curling rink now dry and cracked, and follow an intricate system of tracks up the terraces.

Sue has drawn a map, full of wobbly lines and gates and terraces leading us through the maze of tracks to the Bullock Bow at the top of the pass leading over to the Valley. The truck crawls along them, climbing steadily and passing through vast deer paddocks stretching all the way from the road into Mesopotamia to the foot of the Bullock Bow.

Even by truck the journey will take more than an hour. We drive slowly up the downs and terraces, weaving down gullies, fording creeks, threading through beech forest although there was never very much of it up here: even Samuel Butler found the Rangitata back country 'very bare of timber'.

The track is pinched between the sheer sides of the Ben McLeod Range on one side and the Sinclair Range on the other, the two angling towards each other and seeming sure to end in a thunderous clash of behemoths. The heavy steel and wire gates of the deer paddocks clank open and closed like doors in the halls of the mountain kings. They are chained, double-chained, locked. The mighty fence posts could have supported whole subdivisions of those 1970s pole houses. They are much heavier and stronger than usual; given the cost of building them in this hard, high country the station wants them to last. This is a giant enterprise. Everything is in scale with the country.

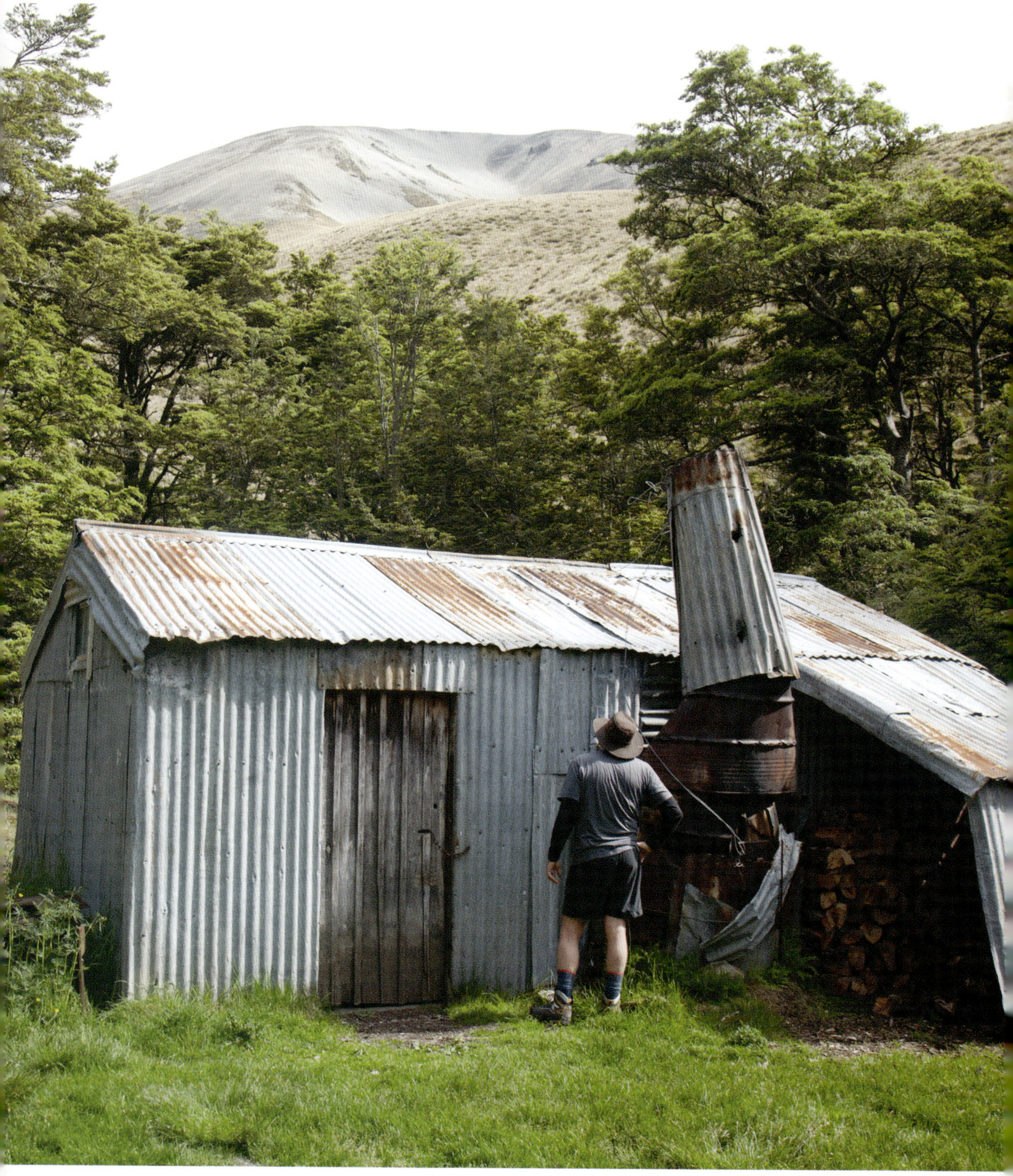

The mountains dwarf all known language; mighty, powerful, awe-inspiring, massive, indifferent. We crawl over the landscape, a moment in the timeless.

We are lucky. We have wheels and a track. Samuel Butler came up here on the horse he had not long learned to ride. He turned up Forest Creek and travelled not on the gentle terraces above the water, but along the creek bed, 'an ugly, barren-looking place enough'. He was right about that. The creek has slashed the country, a deep, dark cut running alongside the rock faces of the Ben McLeods.

He wrote, 'We went up a little gorge, as narrow as a street in Genoa, with huge black and dripping precipices overhanging it, so as almost to shut out the light of heaven. I never saw so curious a place in my life . . . A deep valley between two ranges, which are not entirely clear of snow for more than three or four months in the year.'

After hours of clambering over huge rocks and beating through matagouri thorns and the spiky spaniard he came to the site where he later built his first hut, 'all roof and no walls'. In fact it was on land owned by his neighbours, Acland and Tripp, but he built it anyway: he wanted to see whether the country was suitable for sheep before he built something more permanent, and intended spending a winter there. The hut was tiny, three paces wide and four long, and leaked, and had stones for seats, and should have been cold enough to freeze Butler's ambitions unto death, but despite his upbringing in the soft English countryside he lasted the winter in it, and in fact rather liked it with its beds of snowgrass and a cat to deal to the rats, cutting a hole for it in the thatch which could have been New Zealand's first cat-door.

Today a blind track leads off the main route and stops at the edge of the gully carved by Forest Creek. We look down on Butler's site, a little wedge of terrace where Butlers Creek forks into Forest Creek, guarded by the bluffs of Ben McLeod. It looks so gloomy we wonder that Butler did not catch the next boat home.

His hut disappeared long ago, of course; it was little more than a bivvy. But why this spot? Even in summer it looks dismal down there, hard to get into and just as bad to get out of. He must have wakened some nights with a Rangitata winter storm beating on the manuka thatch and the snow piling up outside and the creek rising and felt abandoned in an ungodly waste.

Once he left an old Irishman in here, on his own and without food for

← LEFT
The Felt Hut, an old musterers' hut nestling in bush below the famous Bullock Bow Saddle.

ten days. The man survived but I suspect that when Butler fired him not long afterwards he went straight down to the nearest pub, albeit a good day's journey away, to celebrate.

The track climbs onto the High Terrace, dips into a forested creek, slips through a patch of bush and forks. To the right it climbs onto Bullock Bow Saddle and down into the Valley hollowed out by Bush Stream and bounded by the looming bulk of Mount Sinclair on one side, the fearsome ridge of the Two Thumb Range on the other, with the mighty Mount Brabazon at the far end.

The two routes into the Valley are both hard. The rocky Bush Stream route at the far end leads through steep gorges and the Bullock Bow Saddle at the other is a deceptively gentle dip in the high Sinclair Range. It rises easily enough on the Rangitata River side to 1692 metres then drops quite steeply into the Valley. At the top is a piece of bent iron which once fitted under the neck of a bullock and through the wooden yoke on top: the Bullock Bow. Bullock Bow was to become part of the Mesopotamia legend, the funnel for the great musters of old. Here rivers of merinos mustered from all along the Valley poured over the saddle and down into the gentler front country of the station for the winter.

The musterers were more prosaic than Butler but just as awed by the country as they worked the bluffs and spurs of the Valley. They loved the rocks and the snow and the simple hard life. David McLeod, whose mustering days on the station are recorded in his book *Many a Glorious Morning*, wrote of a 'precipitous hell', the western face of Mount Sinclair dropping 'more than four thousand feet in a giant cascade of shingle slides and rugged bluffs of rotten rock into Bush Stream. All the western end of Mespotamia consists of great spurs springing like ribs from the backbone of the Two Thumb Range. Narrow and rock-crowned at their base, they leave great shingle basins at the head of each dividing creek, above which tower the rocky bastions of this magnificent ridge.'

Merinos could climb into inaccessible parts of this country and had to be winkled out by musterers and their dogs. It was dangerous work. McLeod once almost died. Charlie Gillman *did* die. Peter Newton recorded his death: Gillman's gang had mustered Camp Spur and the Balaclava Basins, where the land is squeezed so tightly it spikes up like clay from a fist. He'd been sent back to pick up some sheep stuck in the kind of bluffs which should not even

→ TOP RIGHT
Inside Felt Hut, rafters made of unpeeled beech from surrounding forest, furniture made of the same.

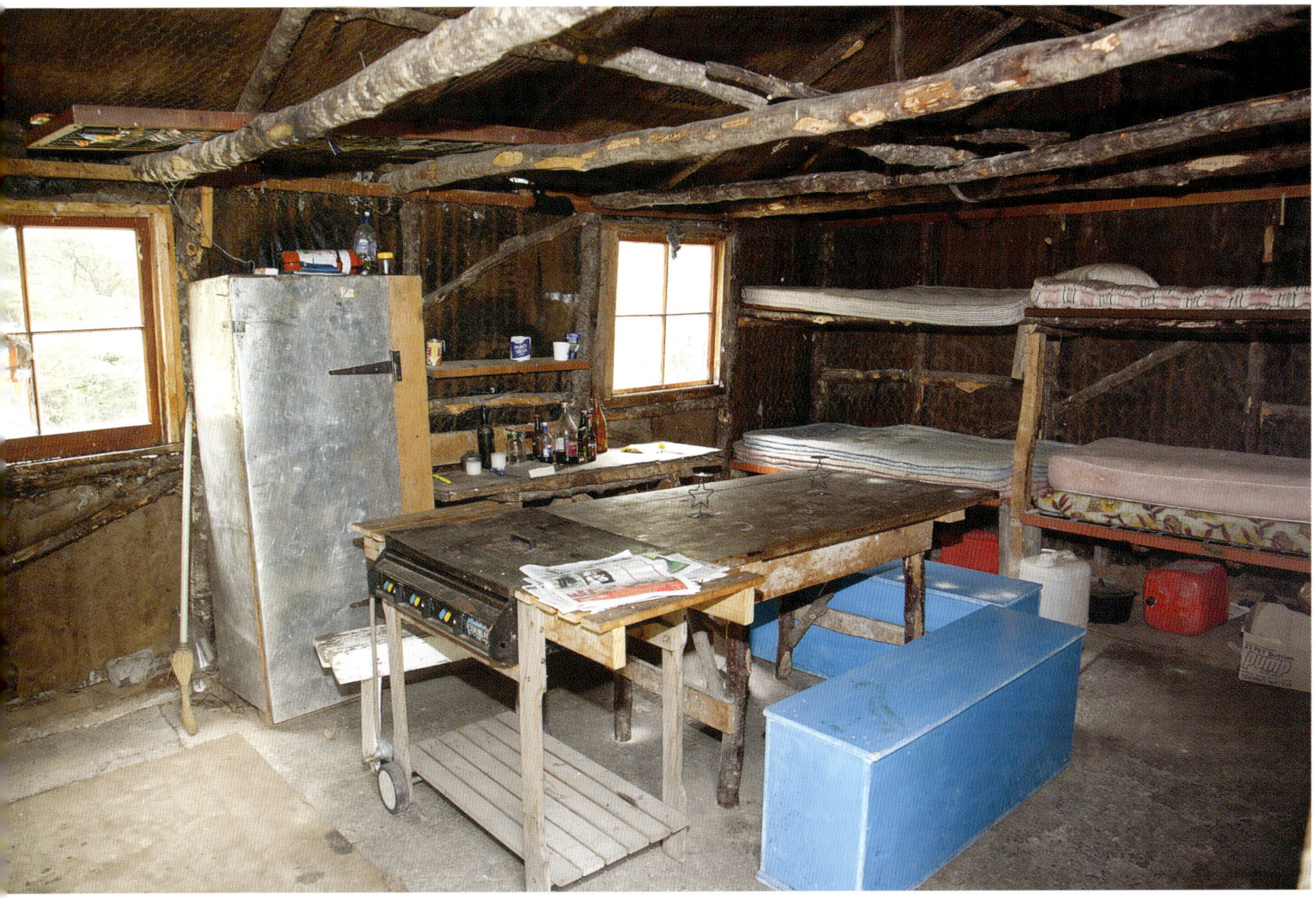

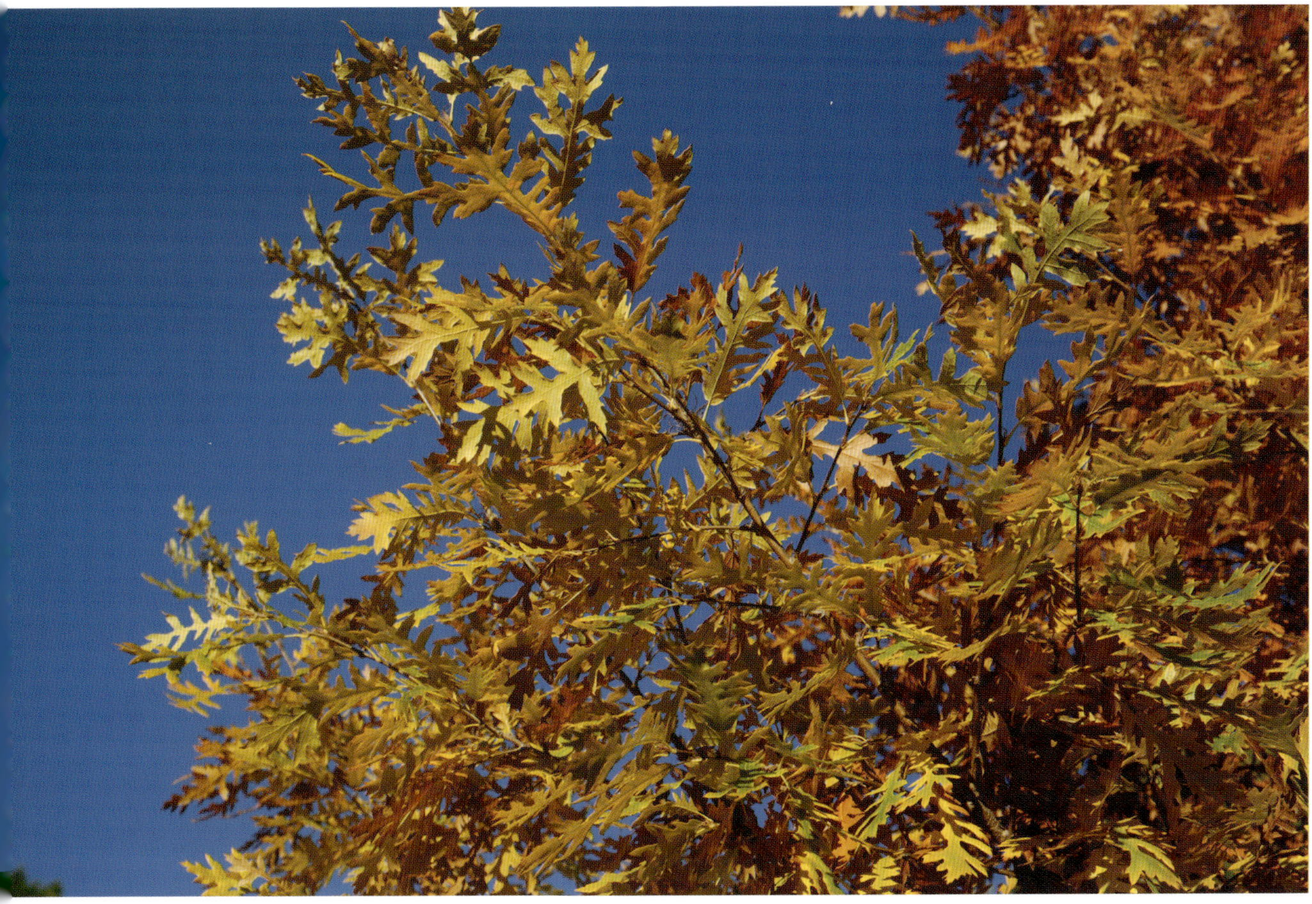

be viewed without crampons. He did not return. The gang searched for him and in the moonlight found his body at the bottom.

On a map of this terrain the contour lines are so close they are almost solid orange. This is overpowering country, and it makes intruders infinitesimal. Even now, though it is open to the public, only seasoned trampers and hunters make the journey.

To the musterers who worked the Valley, the Felt Hut nestling in bush below the saddle must have seemed as comfortable as the Savoy. They would light the fire below the old bath they'd filled from the stream and take their turn in the hot water and as the night wind blew and the snow lay around they must have wondered who would wish for anything finer, even if, as Malcolm often did, they took their turn at the tail end of the gang and lay in the residual swamp of half a dozen sweaty men.

Musterers no longer tread the Valley bringing down the merinos. The rich history and ambience of their huts is now available to anyone who wants to get a pamphlet from the Department of Conservation and make the trek though the mountains. The Felt Hut, though, is still Mesopotamia property. It stands in silent beech forest beside a stream flowing down to Forest Creek. The felt lining which gave the hut its name has gone but the hut is a tribute to musterers' huts everywhere, a niche in the national psyche, a monument to endurance and bush carpentry. It looks as ancient as the hills, although it is only a century or so old.

When the hut was rebuilt in 1947 it was transformed from a simple corrugated iron hut into one with slants and angles that would have an Auckland architect spouting new tracts on the New Zealand vernacular. Vertical sheets of corrugated iron are nailed to a framework of mountain beech saplings, which also provided legs for the two tables inside. The iron is inscribed with a roll of honour which has survived the elements for decades: the names of musterers going back more than sixty years.

Its chimney is made of forty-four gallon drums, halved. Its bunks are padded with one or two kapok mattresses depending on their age and thickness. Pillows measure their age in rings of spilled tea and drool, like old trees. Two bottles of beer and a flagon half-full of port grace a rough wooden shelf above a technical innovation: the pantry is clad in stainless steel armour against rats.

I remember Laurie saying, 'I've always appreciated an abode for what it is. One of the huts at Messie has got a dirt floor and you can't stand up in it. But when you're in there on a stormy night you think it's a palace. You think you're a lucky bastard for the shelter it gives.'

Prouting brothers Don, Frank and Laurie feature prominently in the corrugated iron record. A 1964 entry enshrines an annual hunting trip by Frank and Laurie: seventy-seven deer.

IN A PARTY of five I set off for the Crooked Spur Hut, the old first base for the great musters through the Bush Stream Valley. We cross and recross the stream, which is more like a river, its flow strengthening as we get closer to the gorge. We climb over a high knuckle of rock where the stream turns hard right on its way out of the Valley. Here Mount Sinclair drops to the stream bed in rock faces so abrupt it is hard to see how anything, dogs, sheep or musterers, could ever have found a hold. Beech trees cling impossibly.

The hut is a steep climb from the stream, its big holding yard on flat ground beside rusting oil drums cut in half longways and sunk into the ground as dog kennels. There's one luxury: a newly installed DOC lavatory gives a view all the way through the gorge to the Rangitata. Three kea herald the next morning, the early sun gilding a golden landscape.

The Valley is a land within a land, with its own peaks, spurs, ridges, valleys and streams running down to join Bush Stream at its bottom. It is a vast tawny wilderness between the grey solemnity of its mountain guardians, and despite my companions I've never felt so alone.

The Stone Hut, a day's tramp up the Valley, is now only partly stone. The rest is the ubiquitous corrugated iron, the old stone walls lying in heaps beside it. Its door is inscribed with memoirs of past musters. It has a picturesque fireplace but nothing in the treeless landscape to burn. The toilet seat is weighted with a cast-iron camp-oven lid that slams shut like a vault. A tahr stag watches from a neighbouring ridge.

In the morning we leave the Valley floor and start the long climb up the Bullock Bow. The morning is so silent we are startled by a pair of paradise ducks. The iron bow rattles loose in its little pile of rocks jutting from the bald saddle at the top. I imagine the relief musterers must have felt as they stood here looking down at the Rangitata, close to the end of their work. But I feel Ash's regret that those epic journeys have gone.

MIST COVERS THE mountaintops, fraying as it drips into the valley. The golden poplars are revelling in autumn, lighting the grey morning. The mist thins. Shades of blue tint its top, tantalise with a hint of sun, then it lowers once more in a determined, shroud-like manner suggesting we can expect no more frivolity this day.

The black Angus herd has come down from the mountains. The river was rising, a nor'wester was forecast, best get them downriver while the going was good, too bad if it was a few days early. If the cows made a break for the river it was too easy for calves to be swept away.

A new Wwoofer is working on the station, Jimmy, a Scot; a fellow with a steady eye who sees himself at a crossroads in his life, one that might be sorted out by a monastic spell in the mountains.

Mesopotamia is down a man. Malcolm the tractor driver has left. His going is a touchy subject. Malcolm the farmer doesn't say much about it except: 'They say you shouldn't speak ill of the dead, or blokes who work for you.'

Malcolm is up early today, flying Ash, the shepherd, up the valley in the family Cessna searching for stragglers. They see a few left on Mount Sunday, where once trod the herdsmen of Peter Jackson's Edoras, and some on the river flats. They decide to leave the Mount Sunday cows for another day. Ash goes after the main mob on his quad-bike. Ash's father is mustering somewhere in the mountains to the north.

Malcolm drives up the flats in his Land Cruiser, thick matagouri scraping the sides with the sweet smell of rosehips red on their bushes, bumping over the tawny tussock, Jimmy on the back spotting the cattle. 'There!' He shouts, bangs on the roof, points. He leaves nothing to chance. Malcolm has a sharp tongue for mistakes. Six black cattle, almost hidden in the matagouri.

Malcolm takes the dogs, works behind them, moves them down. The utes follow. Sue rides her beautiful white horse, which she calls a grey. When she stands in front of it, the horse nudges her, nuzzles. Mutual admiration. Ferg arrives on his little farm bike and moves out to one side, entirely confident. The cows join the rest of the bunch.

Malcolm explains how to move a beast with two vehicles, drawing diagrams in the dust of his ute door. One vehicle behind, one to the side, reversing positions if the animal breaks away. 'Like', he says, 'cops boxing in a suspect.' American television has a very long arm.

He skilfully breaks one cow away from the rest, backing, reversing, nudging as it tries to get back to the herd, edging it towards a gate. Planes, helicopters, bikes, utes may lack the romance of classic musters, but they work.

→ RIGHT
Differing tastes in farm transport: Malcolm in his ute, Sue on her horse.

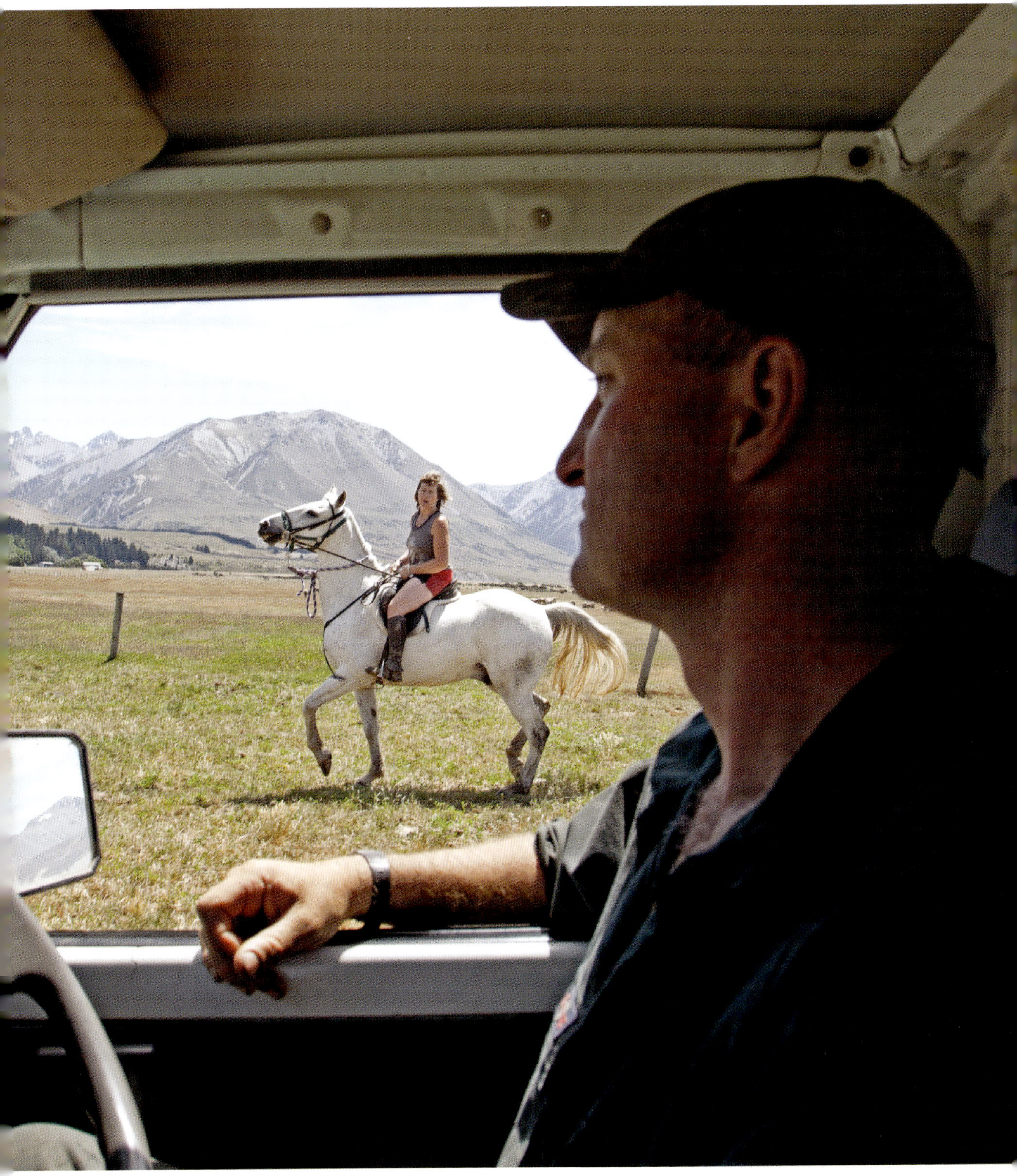

There is lolly cake for morning smoko and afterwards Malcolm calls Ash on the radios they carry.

Ash: 'I wasn't sure whether you wanted to carry on before lunch or what.'
Malcolm: 'Nah, come in for lunch, we'll do it after. Where are you now?'
Ash: 'At home, just drying my socks.'
Malcolm: 'Soft.'

Lunch is merino hogget, slow-roasted in rosemary and mint and sweet chilli sauce. It is tender and delicious, deep brown with little fat, with only a faint suggestion of the Sunday joint. Sue put it into the oven at seven thirty and it cooked for five hours tended by Wendy, a middle-aged Wwoofer from England's south coast who first came to work on Mesopotamia with her husband several years back and became a good friend. Since then her husband has died, but there's no such thing as a sentimental journey here. Wendy, now alone, has painted the old school white with green trim. It's a very different kind of holiday.

NEXT DAY DAWNS with a glimpse of the tops. Streaks of snow down the rock. A skiff of snow, Malcolm says. Just a skiff. It is beautiful, but he doesn't like it. In fact, he says, he hates snow. It is a part of life in the high country, of course, but it makes his life harder.

A skim of frost lies on the ground. The breeze flowing up the valley has a razor's edge. Mount Sinclair, benign all summer, has begun to frown, hinting at the violence to come. An amphitheatre of mountains now reaches into the clear sky, although the Two Thumbs remain hidden in cloud. Sun lays a benign hand on the land, turns the tussock to gold. Matagouri turns black in the cracks and crevices. Trees around the homestead light up. The way to Bullock Bow opens like a yellow road.

They move the bulls, cows and calves into the yards. Get in another bull from a far corner of a paddock. He is lame, and it makes him dangerous. Malcolm says, 'He could come at you quickly. An animal in pain . . .'

The cattle are run through the yards. The vet arrives to test the cows for tuberculosis. The calves are drafted off into the pens. A sea of black faces, and sometimes a white one, flows around the yards. The valley is one huge bewildered bellow.

Ash scales the yard rails as if he is walking on air. I'm sitting on a top rail talking to Jimmy. We get on to Malcolm. 'Are you going to say what a kindly tolerant man he is?' Jimmy asks.

I haven't met many high country farmers who have not stamped their personality on their farms. Given the huge country some of them live in, it can be quite a task. Hardly surprising that some are larger than life, matching their territory. When there is a job to be done, nothing else matters, or counts, or is allowed to intrude.

Roses do well here in the Rangitata. They are thorny and tough. It is no place for shrinking violets. Sometimes, says Jimmy, when Malcolm is yelling at him, he thinks he'll be out of here next week. Then he looks around at the country, or maybe he'll get a ride up the valley in Malcolm's helicopter, and he thinks well, perhaps he'll stay for a bit longer.

I know Malcolm thinks highly of Jimmy, and I tell Jimmy so. Jimmy is amazed. He looks at me as if I'm joking, sees I'm not, and is thinking it over when the Messie factor cuts in. Ash is tagging calves. They're bucking and bawling and Ash has his work cut out. 'What are you doing?' he yells at the unfortunate Jimmy. 'Get over here and do some work.' Jimmy flies off the top rail as if on wings. Doesn't pay to be idle here. Later it is revealed that we weren't paying attention. His name is John, not Jimmy, and he's not a Scot, he's English. He disappears not long afterwards. Apparently the monastic life in the mountains is not for him.

TODAY THERE ARE fourteen people around the lunch table with the station people, stock agents and helpers. Another Jimmy, son of a neighbouring farmer, has taken a week's holiday from the station where he works above the Rakaia Gorge. He's helping out because he likes the work. A busman's holiday.

Two young women are part of the Duke of Edinburgh's Hillary Award youth development programme, which requires entrants to complete sections involving service to other people, adventure, physical recreation, learning non-physical skills, and living and working for a week away from home with comparative strangers. Working at Mesopotamia seems to cover the entire field.

The main dish is venison from a fallow deer. Malcolm and Jimmy have butchered a carcass which had been hanging in the killing shed for a few days. Malcolm had sawn at a joint with his knife, muttering that his mother Anne could just lay her knife across a joint and it seemed to separate effortlessly. No matter how he tried, it would not work for Malcolm.

The fallow venison is delicious. It nods faintly in the direction of supermarket venison then strikes out on its own. Sue has roasted it in black treacle, black bean sauce, soy sauce and garlic. We agree it's a toss-up which is better, fallow or merino, but everyone is happy to be able to make the comparison. After lunch the transports arrive, huge bright red-and-blue truck and trailer combinations which back up to the loading race as easily as if they were Mini cars.

The calves run along the race, fill the top and bottom decks. Lots of noise, shouting, bellowing. The Duke of Edinburgh women go about their task with firm and determined step. The truckies estimate they'll take one and three-quarter hours on the run to the saleyards in Temuka, twenty minutes to unload. Next day, in a fast car, I take two hours over the journey and make a mental note not to meet any stock trucks on the narrow metal road when I'm going the other way.

Even before the last truck leaves the station, funereal-black cows are wandering away from the yards as if every one of them has made the decision at the same time: they've lost. The only calves left are replacements for the breeding cows. The valley fills with a great booming moan.

SALE DAY. It starts with a wild whoop as Malcolm comes down the stairs, and a cheer from Ferg.

The day dawns bright, a tiny lace of cloud at the valley's head, a crust of ice on

→ RIGHT
A long way from the boulevards of France, Sophie turns her horse behind a herd of Angus cows and calves.

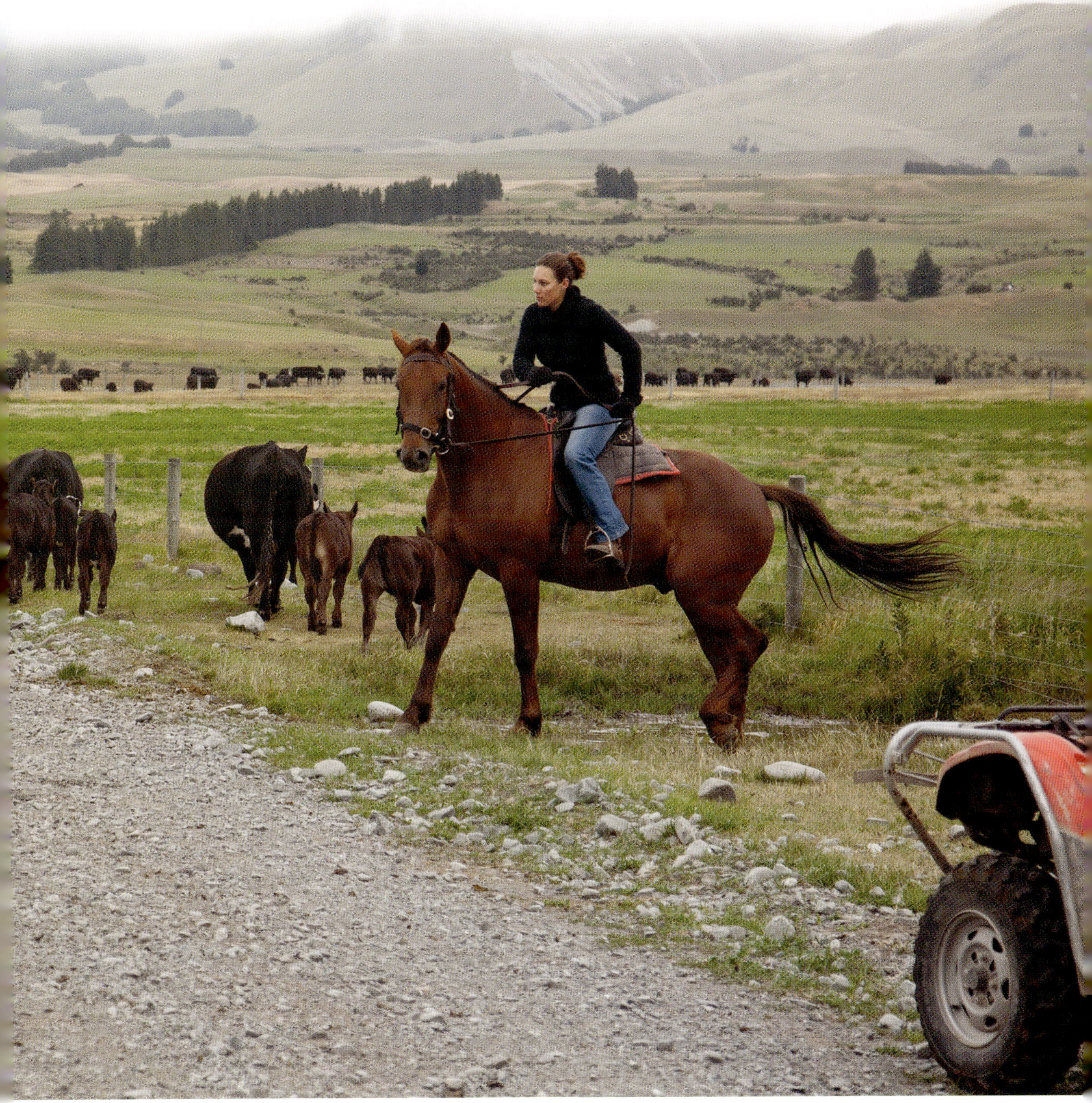

the water lying in the wheelbarrow outside and presaging the end for grass growth. Everyone piles into their cars and heads for Temuka. Today, the calves are being sold.

The perfect little South Canterbury town slumbers in the sun, its main street full of untouched old hotels, the Royal Hotel promising patrons the chance for a big-screen view of the royal wedding that week: 'You are invited,' says the poster. Three months later the hotel would be badly damaged by the June earthquake.

The saleyards spread over one side of town. The two-storeyed solid block building beside the stock agents' offices and cafeteria is built like an amphitheatre, which of course it is. Seats and a gallery running around three sides accommodate men in elastic-sided boots and floppy hats, women in their town clothes lending a festive air. Malcolm cruises around, talking to stock agents, catching up with farmers.

For this is one of the times when the work pays off, when all the stock management, worrying, feeding and tending comes to fruition, when farmers see how the animals they produce show up against their neighbours' with their report card in an absolutely clear and direct form: a cheque.

Below them, in the arena, the calves burst out of one door, mill and stamp. Yardmen in yellow jackets urge them on, rap on rails, tap rear ends with plastic tubing. The calves quieten. The auctioneer begins his chant. These calves, he cries, 'are from Mesopotamia, right at the top of the Rangitata Gorge.' They look good.

Already prices are up on the previous year's. 'Nice quiet animals,' says the auctioneer. The bidding starts, goes up in bounds, finishes in jerks, stops. Mesopotamia is just pipped at the post for top price of the sale, but from the smiles on the Proutings' faces anyone can see that's just a technicality.

Everyone goes off to a cheery restaurant in town and celebrates. It has been a good day. Wool is buoyant, venison is doing well. Mesopotamia's produce is fetching good prices. It is not the kind of boom that catapulted first Malcolm senior then Laurie into prosperity, but a hint of rose is creeping into the station's view of its prospects.

So the year goes around, but of course it is never the same. Ash has handed in his notice. The theory in the homestead is that Sophie wants somewhere livelier. I ask her later. Yes livelier, she says, and warmer. This separation from Mesopotamia is terminal.

The last time I saw him I told Ash that in a couple of weeks he'd be sitting on a boulevard somewhere in France twirling a glass of Pernod with Sophie beside him and wondering whether pushing a herd of Angus cattle through the autumn chill of the high country was just a dream. He looked disconcerted for a moment then shrugged, laughed.

When they returned to New Zealand they moved on to a station in the Canterbury foothills, quite close to Christchurch. Sophie applied for a visa, and asked her friends for supporting letters testifying that her relationship with Ash was genuine.

I wrote that she had worked long hours on Mesopotamia Station, the work was often hard and dirty, that their cottage was old and very cold in the harsh winters, and only someone deeply in love would put up with it. Others must have said the same, for a short while later Sophie wrote thank-you letters: 'They must have liked your letters at immigration!!! They allowed me to stay and work and they did it in two days.'

DOWN ON HER own farm Neroli has made a serious career change. The high country pioneer, the mountain queen, the born farmer, has become a beauty queen. Of sorts. She bought a beauty parlour in Ashburton and made such a success of it that now she owns two, and who knows?

'It has grown off its nut. Tell you what, there's going to be a franchise next.'

The long rides in the dark, the skinned knees, the time she was frozen to her saddle are far behind her. Now she clips the pride of Ashburton women instead of merinos, dips delicate heads into shampoo basins instead of ewes into the trough, climbs the business ladder rather than Wild Man's Hill. Her salons offer facials, massage, waxing, electrolysis, Botox, the full suite. 'Harley is doing a great job on the farm. I was getting knocked around. I wear make-up now. I wear a uniform with badges on it. I miss the farm. I don't know how long I'll do this. Maybe it's my mid-life crisis. But it's very profitable. And it's working.'

IN TEMUKA, BIG round cups of latte arrive on the wooden table. Tomorrow, back on the station, the station will hunker down for winter. The cycle will start again.

You are invited 2 the Royal Wedding Friday Night 7.30 at the Royal in Temuka

↖ WOOL SALE IN TEMUKA. CLOCKWISE FROM TOP LEFT
Sale day at Temuka: a Royal invitation.

The auctioneer plays to packed galleries.

A farmer gets some advice.

Sue and Ferg (middle row, second and third from right).

Stock in the yards awaiting sale.

Malcolm (second from left) catches up.

Malcolm Prouting (snr)
1917–1981

THE FIRST PROUTINGS TO OWN MESOPOTAMIA STATION

Thelma Prouting (née Gifkins)
1915–2004

→ Don

Frank

Laurie
1943–

Ray

Valmai

Allan

Jennifer

→ Peter

PROUTING
FAMILY TREE

Laurie
1943–

FIRST OWNED MOUNT ARROWSMITH STATION THEN, AFTER THE DEATH OF MALCOLM SENIOR, MESOPOTAMIA

Anne
(née Rasmussen)
1944–

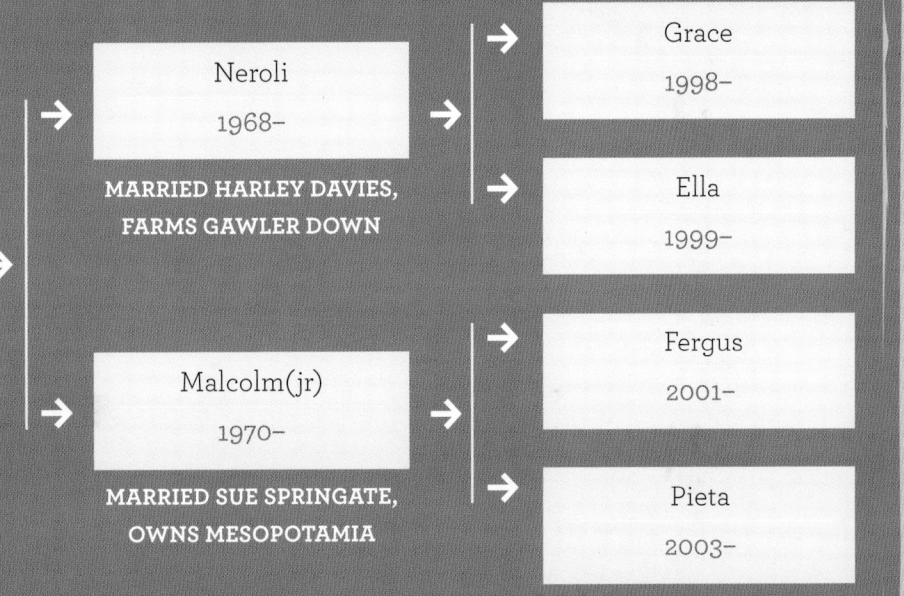

Neroli
1968–

MARRIED HARLEY DAVIES, FARMS GAWLER DOWN

Malcolm (jr)
1970–

MARRIED SUE SPRINGATE, OWNS MESOPOTAMIA

Grace
1998–

Ella
1999–

Fergus
2001–

Pieta
2003–

> The high country musterer has been part of New Zealand backcountry folklore for as long as the merinos have climbed above the snowline. Sadly they are fast becoming a vanishing breed. It is my special privilege to say a huge thanks for allowing me to share with them one of Messie's legendary annual musters.
>
> **PETER BUSH**
>
> We thank Creative New Zealand for their support of this project; and Barbara Larson, our editor, and Nicola Legat and Kate Barraclough for fitting it together and making it work.